Exploring the Second Language Mental Lexicon

THE CAMBRIDGE APPLIED LINGUISTICS SERIES

Series editors: Michael H. Long and Jack C. Richards

This series presents the findings of recent work in applied linguistics which are of direct relevance to language teaching and learning and of particular interest to applied linguists, researchers, language teachers, and teacher trainers:

In this series:

Interactive Approaches to Second Language Reading *edited by Patricia L. Carrel, Joanne Devine and David E. Eskey*

Second Language Classrooms – Research on teaching and learning *by Craig Chaudron*

Language Learning and Deafness *edited by Michael Strong*

The Learner-Centred Curriculum *by David Nunan*

Language Transfer – Cross-linguistic influence in language learning *by Terence Odlin*

Linguistic Perspectives on Second Language Acquisition *edited by Susan M. Gass and Jaquelyn Schachter*

Learning Strategies in Second Language Acquisition *by Michael O'Malley and Anna Uhl Chamot*

The Development of Second Language Proficiency *edited by Birgit Harley, Patrick Allen, Jim Cummins and Merrill Swain*

Second Language Writing – Research insights for the classroom *edited by Barbara Kroll*

Genre Analysis – English in academic and research settings *by John M. Swales*

Evaluating Second Language Education *edited by J. Charles Alderson and Alan Beretta*

Perspectives on Pedagogical Grammar *edited by Terence Odlin*

Academic Listening *edited by John Flowerdew*

Power and Inequality in Language Education *by James W. Tollefson*

Language Program Evaluation – Theory and practice *by Brian K. Lynch*

Sociolinguistics and Language Teaching *edited by Sandra Lee McKay and Nancy H. Hornberger*

Contrastive Rhetoric – Cross-cultural aspects of second language writing *by Ulla Conner*

Teacher Cognition in Language Teaching – Beliefs, decision-making, and classroom practice *by Devon Woods*

Second Language Vocabulary Acquisition – A rationale for pedagogy *edited by James Coady and Thomas Huckin*

Text, Role and Context – Developing academic literacies *by Ann M. Johns*

Immersion Education: International Perspectives *edited by Robert Keith Johnson and Merrill Swain*

Focus on Form in Classroom Second Language Acquisition *edited by Catherine Doughty and Jessica Williams*

Exploring the Second Language Mental Lexicon

David Singleton

Trinity College Dublin

PUBLISHED BY THE PRESS SYNDICATE OF THE UNIVERSITY OF CAMBRIDGE
The Pitt Building, Trumpington Street, Cambridge CB2 1RP, United Kingdom

CAMBRIDGE UNIVERSITY PRESS
The Edinburgh Building, Cambridge CB2 2RU, United Kingdom
40 West 20th Street, New York, NY 10011–4211, USA
10 Stamford Road, Oakleigh, Melbourne 3166, Australia

First published 1999

Typeset in Sabon 10.5/12pt CE

A catalogue record for this book is available from the British Library

Library of Congress Cataloguing in Publication applied for

Printed in the United Kingdom at the University Press, Cambridge

ISBN 0 521 554969 hardback
ISBN 0 521 555345 paperback

For Emer

Contents

Series editors' preface xi
Foreword xiii
Acknowledgements xvii

I INTRODUCTION AND PROLEGOMENA

Introduction 3

1 Lexis and the lexicon: some general considerations 8
Language seen as words 8
Defining the word 10
The domain of the lexicon 14
Concluding summary 38

II RESEARCH REVIEW

2 Lexical development: an overview 41
The lexical challenge 41
L1 lexical development: from first words to semantic hierarchies 52
L1 and L2 lexical development: a preliminary assessment of similarities and contrasts 79
Concluding summary 81

3 Modelling the lexicon 83
Some models of the mental lexicon 84
Modularity and the mental lexicon 111
Connectionism 121
Concluding summary 128

4 The L2 mental lexicon: a law unto itself? 130
Form and meaning in the L2 mental lexicon 130
Separation/integration between the L1 and the L2 mental lexicon 167
Concluding summary 189

III EVIDENCE FROM THE TRINITY COLLEGE DUBLIN MODERN LANGUAGES RESEARCH PROJECT

5 The Trinity College Dublin Modern Languages Research Project in broad outline 193
Subjects 194
Methodology 194
Computerization 216
L2 lexicon-related issues explored to date using MLRP findings 217
Concluding summary 219

6 Findings on form and meaning in the L2 mental lexicon 220
C-test results from the pilot phase of the project 220
C-test results from 1990 onwards 224
Word association test results 233
Concluding summary 236

7 Findings on the cross-linguistic factor in lexical processing and acquisition 238
C-test data from the pilot phase of the project 239
C-test data from 1990 onwards 242
Other data 246
Concluding summary 249

8 Findings on communication strategies 251
Communication strategy research within the MLRP 252
Strategic L2 lexical innovation: a case study 254
Cross-linguistic strategies and individual learner contrasts 257
Reflection and strategies in L2 learning 260
Concluding summary 264

IV CONCLUSION

A recapitulation, some inferences and some hopes for the future 269
The ground covered in this book 269
Some implications of the foregoing discussion 271
Exploring the L2 mental lexicon: some hopes of things to come 275

References 280
Index 328

Series editors' preface

Influenced by the dominant preoccupation in theoretical linguistics with phonology, morphology and syntax during the first two decades of its modern existence, SLA research, too, from 1960 to 1980 heavily emphasised morphosyntax, and to a lesser extent phonology. L2 vocabulary, like interlanguage pragmatics, was largely ignored by all but a handful of researchers, few of whom specialised in the lexicon. Things have changed somewhat in the past ten years, perhaps again in part because of the retreat by many linguists from theories which required a plethora of detailed syntactic rules to handle low-level grammatical phenomena in favour of syntactically less powerful ones, and of theories, such as LFG, which handle the same phenomena through lexically based or sensitive rules of various kinds. A similar move can be seen in child language acquisition research over the same period, as exemplified by the work of Pinker, P. Bloom, and others.

The past decade has witnessed a welcome and much needed change, of which *Exploring the second language mental lexicon* is the most recent example. David Singleton's contribution should serve language educators and applied linguists well in at least three ways. First, his book provides an extensive review of much of the recent first and second language work, in both developmental and experimental psycholinguistics. Second, the book contains the most comprehensive exposition available of the methodology and research findings on L2 vocabulary development from the longitudinal study Singleton and others conducted under the auspices of the Trinity College Dublin Modern Languages Research Project. Third, implications are drawn for theory building in this area, and for the kind of research needed next. Based on the literature survey and Project findings, moreover, there is useful, suitably modulated discussion of pedagogical options in L2 vocabulary instruction. With this interweaving of theory, research and practice, we believe David

Singleton's volume makes an appropriate and welcome addition to the Cambridge Applied Linguistics Series.

Michael H. Long
Jack C. Richards

Foreword

The beginnings of this book can be traced back to some remarks made by Paul Meara while he was external examiner for the M. Phil. course in Applied Linguistics run by the Centre for Language and Communication Studies, Trinity College, Dublin. He suggested that what the Centre needed in the area of applied linguistics was a research project to which both staff and students could contribute and which would generate a data-bank on which both staff and students could draw. It was our acting on this suggestion that gave rise to the Trinity College Dublin Modern Languages Research Project (TCD MLRP), out of which came first a renewal of my interest in lexis, and then, in the fullness of time, the idea for the present volume. It so happens that the project data have led me to criticize some of Paul's early conclusions concerning the L2 mental lexicon, and he may now wish that he had kept his counsel when he was in Dublin! However, for myself, I have every reason to be grateful to him for what he prompted me to undertake. This particular and personal debt of gratitude is, of course, additional to that owed to Paul by all of us who work in the area of L2 lexical acquisition and processing for the way in which he kept discussion of L2 lexical issues alive during a period when the L2 lexical harvest was being attended to by very few labourers indeed.

From one point of view, this has been a very good time to write a book about the L2 mental lexicon. After all, there certainly seems to be no longer any lack of inclination on the part of L2 researchers to work in the lexical field; quite the contrary! From other points of view, however, the task of giving a straightforward account of what research tells us about L2 lexical acquisition and processing is more difficult than ever. Not only has the recent vast increase in the amount and the range of L2 research focusing on lexical matters as traditionally defined rendered all hope of providing anything approaching an exhaustive survey of such research utterly vain, but the very conception of what is to be included under the heading of lexicon has expanded to the point where almost any L2 acquisition/processing research can be seen as relevant to the L2 mental lexicon.

What is the aspirant L2 lexical commentator to do in such circumstances? Give up? Carry on regardless? I have preferred a third option, namely, to carry on regard*ful*! That is to say, not to abandon the enterprise, but to approach it in the full awareness of the problems that surround it. Accordingly, I have not attempted to broach more than a select few of the lexical research avenues that it would have been possible to explore, since to have tried to do otherwise would have spread the discussion thin to the point of insubstantiality. Nor have I shrunk from admitting that, the way things are going, the entire lexical construct may be on the verge of collapse. My choices in respect of the research issues and directions to be treated in these pages will not meet with the approval of all my readers, but, on the other hand, given the current flood of publications on the L2 lexicon, there is absolutely no shortage of other constellations of choices available for consultation to those whose needs and predilections are not satisfied here.

As well as referring to research conducted by others, I have not scrupled to refer to research that my Dublin colleagues and I have carried out – in particular, the research which has proceeded under the auspices of the above-mentioned TCD MLRP. Since, as I have indicated, it was this project that was responsible for my recent return to the sphere of lexical research, and since my view of the L2 mental lexicon has been crucially shaped by what I have found on delving into the data which the project has yielded, it seemed only appropriate to give a sizeable place to the project research in the present publication.

A number of people have been especially supportive of my efforts to bring this volume to a happy conclusion. Chief among these is my wife, Emer, to whom the work is dedicated. Throughout the period of my researching and writing the book, a period marked by a succession of family illnesses and bereavements and by a variety of other difficulties, Emer was unstinting not only in the indispensable contributions she made to managing and analysing the MLRP data, but also in the encouragement and companionship she offered me in what I at times experienced as something resembling the punishment of Sisyphus! Hard as this may be for a 'lexicon person' to admit, I simply cannot find the words adequately to express my thanks to Emer for being by my side in all of this.

I also wish to thank my colleagues in the Centre for Language and Communication Studies. Some – David Little, Jennifer Ridley and Ema Ushioda – were active collaborators in the MLRP, enriching the project with perspectives and insights which without their input would simply have been absent; others – notably Ailbhe Ní Chasaide and John Saeed – had a different role, supplying useful advice, information and feedback on diverse topics on which they were infinitely more expert than I. A particular word of thanks is due to David Little. As Director of the Centre, he not only provided the MLRP with a departmental base but also supported the MLRP with some of the funds generated by the Centre's vacation teaching – effectively furnishing us with a modest research grant.

At a less local level I am indebted to literally scores of colleagues and graduate students around the world who were good enough to discuss their research with me and generous enough to send me working papers, articles and books reporting on the fruits of their endeavours. The 'lexical network' of the European Second Language Association (EUROSLA) was especially helpful in this connection, but I made further invaluable contacts through my work with the Association Internationale de Linguistique Appliquée (AILA) and through my membership of the Association for French Language Studies (AFLS) and the Association for Language Awareness (ALA). I count myself fortunate indeed to have been the beneficiary of such positive aspects of the 'global village'!

I should in addition like to record my deep appreciation of the superb quality of the guidance which I received at the hands of the anonymous CUP reviewers who read earlier drafts of the book and of the CUP Editors who were assigned to the project, Alison Sharpe and latterly Mickey Bonin. I owe a very great deal to Alison in particular; she made a major contribution to the shaping of the volume in its early stages and subsequently saw it through its most critical stages of development. Alison's surname becomes her well insofar as it evokes intellectual acuity, but not so well in terms of what it might suggest regarding her general manner, which is actually as far from being sharp as is imaginable – and undoubtedly the more efficacious for being so!

Finally I wish to express my gratitude to a number of institutional entities:

- to the Library of Institiúid Teangeolaíochta Éireann/the Linguistics Institute of Ireland for service well beyond the call of duty in assisting me in tracking down some of the less readily available publications referred to between these covers;
- to the Trinity College Dublin Departments of French, Germanic Studies, Italian, and Spanish (now Spanish and Portuguese) for the co-operative spirit they showed in the context of the MLRP;

- to the Trinity College Dublin Arts/ESS Benefactions Fund and Academic Development Fund for generous financial support in respect of the research on which this volume is based;
- and to the Board of Trinity College Dublin for granting me two six-month leaves of absence while I was preparing this book.

I am all too aware that, despite all the advice and assistance I have received from the above, the volume has many flaws. These flaws are, to coin a phrase, all my own work. But then, to err is human; indeed, according to a Chinese proverb, even the gods and fairies make mistakes!

David Singleton
Dublin, December 1997

Acknowledgements

The editors, authors, and publishers are grateful to the authors, publishers and others who have given permission for the use of copyright material identified in the text. It has not been possible to identify, or trace, sources of all the materials used and in such cases the publishers would welcome information from copyright owners.

Morton, J. 1964a. *A Preliminary Functional Model for Language Behaviour.* In *International Audiology 3* on p.85; Morton, J. 1979. *Word Recognition.* In *Psycholinguistics Series 2: Structures and Processes.* ELEK on p.87; Morton, J. and K. Patterson. 1980. *Deep Dyslexia.* M. Coltheart, K. Patterson and J. Marshall (Eds.). Routledge and Kegan Paul on p.89; Forster, K. 1976. *Accessing the Mental Lexicon.* In *New Approaches to Language Mechanisms.* R. Wales and E. Walker (Eds.). Amsterdam: North Holland on p.100; Levelt, W. 1989. *Speaking: from Intention to Articulation.* Cambridge MA: MIT Press on p.107; Meara, P. 1984. *The Study of Lexis in Interlanguage.* In *Interlanguage.* A. Davies, C. Criper and A.P.R. Howatt (Eds.). Edinburgh University Press on p.132; Hatch, E and C. Brown. 1995. *Vocabulary, Semantics and Language Education.* Cambridge University Press on p.133; O'Gorman, E. 1996. *An Investigation of the Mental Lexicon of Second Language Learners.* In *Teanga: The Irish Yearbook of Applied Linguistics 16.* Dublin: IRAAL on p.134; Singleton, D. and D. Little. 1991. *The Second Language Lexicon: Some Evidence from University-level Learners of French and German.* In *Second Language Research 7.* Arnold on pp.221, 222, 223, 224, 240 and 241; Little, D. and D. Singleton. 1992. *The C-Test as an Elicitation Instrument in Second Language Research.* In *Der C-Test. Theoretische Grundlagen und Praktische Anwendungen. Volume 1.* R. Grotjahn (Ed.). Bochum Brockmeyer on p.225; Singleton, D. and D. Little. 1992. *Le Lexique Mental de l'apprenant d'une Langue Étrangère: quelques aperçus apportés par TCD Modern Languages Research Project.* In *Acquisition et En-*

seignement/Apprentissage des Langues. R. Bouchard, J. Billiez, J.M. Colletta, V. de Nuchèze and A. Millet (Eds.). Grenoble: LIDILEM Stendhal University on p.226; Singleton, D. 1993a. *Modularity and Lexical Processing: an L2 Perspective. In Current Issues in European Second Language Research. B. Kettemann and W. Wieden (Eds.). Tübingen: Narr on pp.226-227; Singleton, D. 1993-94b. L'acquisition du Lexique d'une Langue Étrangère. Paris: ENCRAGES on pp.229 and 234; Singleton, D. 1994. Learning L2 Lexis: A Matter of Form? In The Dynamics of Language Processes: Essays in Honor of Hans W. Dechert. G. Bartelt (Ed.). Tübingen: Narr on pp.229 and 234; Singleton, D. 1996a. Formal Aspects of the L2 Lexicon: Some Evidence from University-level Learners of French. In Approaches to Second Language Acquisition. Jyväskylä Cross Language Studies Series 17. K. Sajavaara and C. Fairfeather (Eds.). Jyväskylä : University of Jyväskylä on pp.231 and 232; Ridley, J. and D. Singleton. 1995b. Contrastivity and Individual Learner Contrasts. In Fremdsprachen Lehren und Lernen 24. On pp.249 and 259; Ridley, J. and D. Singleton. 1995a. Strategic L2 Lexical Innovation: Case Study of a University Ab Initio Learner of German. In Second Language Research 11. Arnold on pp.255 and 256; Ridley, J. 1997. Reflection and Strategies in Foreign Language Learning. Frankfurt am Main: Peter Lang Verlag on pp.261 and 262.*

PART I

INTRODUCTION AND PROLEGOMENA

Introduction

Robert Galisson's volume *De la langue à la culture par les mots* (Galisson, 1991) begins with a discussion of the marginalization of the lexical dimension in L2 language teaching which resulted from the widespread adoption of audio-lingual methodology after the Second World War – a marginalization which has, according to Galisson, continued to a large extent under the more recent 'communicative' régime. Whether or not one accepts every detail of Galisson's rather grim portrayal of the place of vocabulary in L2 teaching over the last five decades, it is clear that he has a point. What is equally clear, however, is that he is not alone in wishing to redress the situation. Since the early 1980s there has been a positive explosion of publications on vocabulary aimed at L2 teachers, L2 teacher trainers and L2 course designers (see, e.g., Carter, 1987; Carter & McCarthy, 1988; Gairns & Redman, 1986; Hatch & Brown, 1995; M. Lewis, 1993, 1997; Nation, 1990; Schmitt & McCarthy, 1997; Tréville & Duquette, 1996; Wallace, 1982; Willis, 1990), and many of these publications have started from concerns very similar to Galisson's.

The re-valuation of the lexical dimension in the L2 teaching domain echoes, and to an extent reflects, a similar shift towards a greater preoccupation with the lexicon in linguistics in general. It is not that linguists have changed their basic view that the lexicon is that part of a linguistic model which deals with 'idiosyncratic information' (cf., e.g., Radford, 1981: 118ff.); it is rather that their researches have led them to the conclusion that very much more of the functioning of language than they had previously imagined *is* idiosyncratic. A dramatic illustration of the sort of finding that has brought about this change of perspective was presented by the computational linguist Maurice Gross at the Ninth World Congress of Applied Linguistics (AILA 1990), when, during the course of his paper (Gross, 1990), he had occasion to remark that, of 12,000 'simple' French verbs he had studied, no two had proved to have precisely the same syntactic profile. The response to such findings has

been, essentially, to 'slim down' the general syntactic elements in linguistic models and to assign more and more responsibility to the lexicon. Cook & Newson's remarks cited below specifically refer to the evolution of Chomskyan models in this regard, but can in fact be taken as fairly generally applicable:

> many aspects of language that earlier models dealt with as 'syntax' are now handled as idiosyncrasies of lexical items; the syntax itself is considerably simplified by the omission of many rules, at the cost of greatly increased lexical information. (Cook & Newson, 1996: 19)

What this implies in psycholinguistic terms is that the major challenge of learning and using a language – whether as L1 or L2 – lies not in the area of broad syntactic principles but in the 'nitty-gritty' of the lexicon:

> learners . . . need to acquire an immense amount of detail about how individual words are used. The comparative simplicity of syntax learning . . . is achieved by increasing the burden of vocabulary learning. (Cook, 1991: 118)

Given the importance thus ascribed to the lexicon in language acquisition and processing, one might expect there to be a wealth of research available and in progress on lexical acquisition and processing. As far as L1 research is concerned, there is indeed an abundance of material in print on the lexicon (for an introductory survey, see Aitchison, 1994), partly because lexis has always been a major focus of such research. Thus, L1 acquisition research has from its earliest origins been interested in first words, numbers of words at different stages of development, lexically based concept development, etc., etc. (see, e.g., Singleton, 1989: Chapters 1 & 2), and there is also a long research tradition relating to L1 verbal memory (see, e.g., Wingfield & Byrnes, 1981). More recent developments in psycholinguistics – experimental, observational, theoretical and clinical – have also in no small measure had an L1 lexical focus, continuing and building on earlier traditions in acquisition and memory studies, and also probing the organization of lexical knowledge, particularly the interconnections between elements involved in the construction and functioning of the lexicon such as input and output, form and meaning, spoken and written representations, etc. (see, e.g., Garman, 1990: Chapter 5).

With regard to the investigation of the L2 mental lexicon (cf. Meara, 1983a, 1987, 1992), the situation is not quite so rosy, despite the fact that such research has a certain pedigree (see, e.g., Meara, 1996a) and despite the impression that may be given by the recent rash of publications in this area. In an article published in 1991, the complaint is voiced in respect of L2 lexical research that:

> the number of publications is out of all proportion to what has become known about vocabulary acquisition as a result of empirical research ... Good research appears to be scarce and is often focused on certain aspects, so that no clear overall picture emerges. (Mondria & Wit-de Boer, 1991: 250)

Similar thoughts have been repeatedly expressed since by one of the pioneers of L2 lexical research, Paul Meara (e.g., Meara, 1992, 1993a). The deficiencies to which such observations refer are especially regrettable in the light of the fact that lexical knowledge is now known to be an absolutely crucial factor across the whole spectrum of L2 activities (see, e.g., Kelly, 1991; Koda, 1989; Laufer, 1992; Laufer & Nation, 1995; Linnarud, 1986).

However, the news is not all bad on the L2 front. An increasing amount of effort is now being devoted to studying the L2 mental lexicon, as can be judged from, for example, the appearance in the last few years of a number of compilations of research papers relating to L2 lexical acquisition and processing (see, e.g., Anderman & Rogers, 1996; Coady & Huckin, 1997; Harley 1995a; Huckin, Haynes & Coady, 1993; Schreuder & Weltens, 1993; Singleton, 1993–94a). Moreover, this research is attracting an increasing amount of interest; it is surely significant in this connection, for instance, that four major symposia at the Eleventh World Congress of Applied Linguistics (AILA 1996) dealt with aspects of L2 lexical competence, and that these were among the best attended of the conference. My own view is that enough 'good' research has been published on the L2 mental lexicon in recent times to warrant a substantial review of the studies in question, and this is in part what the present volume seeks to provide.

Mention has already been made of the interest being shown by L1-oriented lexical research in the interaction between different aspects of lexical acquisition and processing components. Clearly, in research relating to the L2 mental lexicon, the same topics arise. Moreover, in the case of L2 research, there are further complicating questions deriving from the fact that knowledge of more than one language is present in the situation – questions which include, notably, on the one hand, the degree to which the L2 lexicon resembles the L1 lexicon in terms of the respective roles of form and meaning, and, on the other, the extent to which the L2 lexicon is separate from or integrated with the L1 lexicon. These latter issues constitute leitmotivs in the discussion that follows. However, the more general debates concerning the way in which lexical knowledge is internalized and organized are by no means ignored. On the contrary, a large part of the book is devoted to contextualizing the L2-focused discussion in a more general overview of lexical research, much of which is based on studies of the L1 mental lexicon. Indeed, the contextualization of L2 lexical issues goes further still. Given especially that, as has already been indicated, there has been a general shift in the way in which the lexicon is viewed by linguists, it seems only proper that any discussion of the mental lexicon should take some account of the recent insights of linguistics at large – some of which actually begin to call into question the whole concept of the lexicon as a distinct entity or construct.

One particular body of research findings that is dealt with here is that generated by the Trinity College Dublin (TCD) Modern Languages Research Project, which I have co-ordinated since its inception (see Singleton, 1990a). The project was initiated on a pilot basis in 1988 and became fully operational in October 1990. It was essentially a project of the TCD Centre for Language and Communication Studies, but it also had the co-operation of the TCD Departments of French, Germanic Studies, Italian, and Spanish and Portuguese. It was organized on two levels. At Level I, data about general education, language-learning experience and language use were sought via a questionnaire from all first-year undergraduate students of French, German, Italian and Spanish. At Level II, subsamples of students of French and German were observed more closely, L2 and related introspective data having been elicited from them at regular intervals. The project did not focus exclusively on the lexicon, but it yielded results which shed some useful light on lexical acquisition and processing in the older and/or more advanced L2 learner. Many of the results in question have been reported in articles published in diverse journals and edited collections in various corners of Europe, but the present volume has furnished an opportunity to summarize them and to take a more integrated look at what they appear to show.

To come finally to some detail about the content and structure of this book, the volume falls into four parts. Part I, 'Introduction and Prolegomena', is, as its title suggests, introductory in nature; Part II, 'Research review', deals with previous research relevant to the mental lexicon emanating from sources other than the TCD Modern Languages Research Project; Part III, 'Evidence from the Trinity College Dublin Modern Languages Research Project', is devoted to the methodology and the lexicon-related findings of this project; and Part IV, 'Conclusion', seeks to draw the various threads of the volume together. There follow some further indications of what is attempted in the different parts of the book.

- Part I is composed of the present introduction and Chapter 1, 'Lexis and the lexicon: some general considerations', which begins with some comments on the importance of words in both the popular and the specialist conception of language, goes on to outline and assess different approaches to defining the concept of word, and finally addresses the very thorny problem of delimiting the domain of the lexicon – including discussion of lexis and grammar, collocational aspects of the lexicon, lexis and phonology, lexis and orthography, and lexical semantics.
- Part II is made up of Chapters 2, 3 and 4. Chapter 2, 'Lexical development: an overview', offers some thoughts on the challenge posed by lexical acquisition in various sets of circumstances and reviews some of the evidence and controversies relating to L1 lexical acquisition – ending with a preliminary evaluation of the similarities and differences between L1 and L2 lexical development. Chapter 3, 'Modelling the lexicon', reviews some of the available models of lexical processing, assesses the plausibility and the relevance to the lexicon of the notion that the mind is organized in self-contained 'modules', and explores in a lexical perspective the 'connectionist' view of mental functioning. Chapter 4, 'The mental lexicon: a law unto itself?', looks at L2 lexical acquisition, organization and processing in the perspective of its two most controversial dimensions – on the one hand, the question of the respective roles of form and meaning in the L2 lexicon and, on the other, that of the degree of separation or integration between the L2 mental lexicon and the L1 mental lexicon.
- Part III covers Chapters 5, 6, 7 and 8. Chapter 5, 'The Trinity College Dublin Modern Languages Research Project in broad outline', reports on the general nature of the project and also outlines the L2 lexicon-related issues which have been explored to date using Modern Languages Research Project (MLRP) data. The content of Chapters 6, 7 and 8 is entirely apparent from their titles, which are, respectively, 'Findings on form and meaning in the L2 mental lexicon', 'Findings on the cross-linguistic factor in lexical processing and acquisition', and 'Findings on communication strategies'.
- Part IV consists of a brief concluding summary and a teasing out of some theoretical and practical implications of the discussion which precedes it.

1 *Lexis and the lexicon: some general considerations*

Before we can begin to discuss lexical acquisition and lexical processing, we need to address the difficult issue of what the lexicon actually is and how it relates to other aspects of language. This chapter begins by noting the importance of the word-concept in our perception of language and by exploring the problem of defining this concept, but then devotes its greater part to a discussion of the broader issue of the domain of the lexicon.

Language seen as words

If there were no other reason for being interested in the lexical dimension of language, such an interest would readily enough be justified by the fact that for most people language *is* largely a matter of words. As Stubbs (1986: 99) puts it, 'when people think of a language, they think almost invariably of words'. A sense of this perception can be had from some of the ways in which language and language use are referred to in everyday English:

I want a **word** with you.
That child never says a **word**.
I can't understand a **word** he says.
A **word** in the right ear will do the trick.
Her **words** are perfectly clear on this point.
There are some **words** on the back of the packet.
The **wording** is all wrong.
You'd better **re-word** that or you'll have a major dispute on your hands.

A similar pattern can be found in other languages. In French, for example, the term *parole*, which means 'word', also means 'speech'. The Italian and Spanish cognates of *parole* – *parola* and *palabra* respectively – share its dual meaning, and the same kind of ambiguity attaches to Modern Greek *logos*. In Swedish the expression *en ordets man* (lit. 'a man of the word') is applied to a man who is a skilled speaker (cf. Hiberno-English *good with the words*). In German one way of saying 'to refuse someone permission to speak' translates literally as 'to take away the word from someone' – *einem das Wort entziehen*. In Japanese[1] the term *kotoba* ('word', 'phrase', 'expression') is often abbreviated to *koto/goto* and used as a suffix in a number of expressions referring to speech – e.g., *hitokoto o iu* (lit. 'one-word say' = 'say a few words'), *hitorigoto o iu* (lit. 'by-oneself-word say' = 'talk to oneself'), *nakigoto o iu* (lit. 'cry-word say' = 'make complaints'), *negoto o iu* (lit. 'sleep-word say' = 'talk in one's sleep').

Nor is it surprising that words should have such a privileged status in the popular understanding of what language is. After all, they are vital to linguistic communication. A much-quoted statement in this connection is that of Wilkins:

> Without grammar very little can be conveyed, without vocabulary nothing can be conveyed. (Wilkins, 1972: 111)

Wilkins goes too far here, since there is some evidence that intonation alone can communicate at least the general direction of an intended speech act (see, e.g., A. Ellis & Beattie, 1986: 163ff.). However, in broad terms, the point he makes has considerable validity.

Awareness of words seems to develop early in the normal course of language acquisition – considerably earlier than awareness of syntax (see, e.g., Brami-Mouling, 1977; Brédart, 1980; Brédart & Rondal, 1982). Nor is lexical awareness confined to literate societies, as the following much-cited quotation from Sapir relative to his fieldwork with Native Americans makes clear:

> The naïve Indian, quite unaccustomed to the concept of the written word, has nevertheless no serious difficulty in dictating a text to a linguistic student word by word; he tends, of course, to run his words together as in actual speech, but if he is called to a halt and is made to understand what is desired, he can readily isolate the words as such, repeating them as units. (Sapir, 1921: 33–34)

Even the specialist study of language has been highly 'lexicocentric' in many of its aspects. In phonology, for instance, the test for phonemic distinctions using minimal pairs (*pin/bin*, *tip/top*, *wreath/wreathe*, etc.) clearly depends on the notion of lexical differentiation. On the grammatical plane, the very terms *syntax* (< Greek *syntaxis* – 'putting together in order') and *morphology* (< Greek *morphé* – 'form') bespeak a lexical starting-point. Thus, 'putting together' of

[1] I am grateful to Ema Ushioda for the Japanese examples included here.

what? Answer (at least traditionally): words.[2] And 'form' of what? Answer: words.[3]

Defining the word

Although the word is clearly central to both the non-specialist and the specialist understanding of language, one would look in vain for a simple definition of the word concept. As any introductory treatment of the topic will make clear (see, e.g., Ullmann, 1962: 36ff.; Lyons, 1968: 194ff.; 1981: 39ff.; 1995: 46ff.; Palmer, 1971: 41ff.; Picoche, 1977: 13ff.; Cruse, 1986: 35ff.; R. Carter, 1987: 3ff.; Jackson, 1988: 1ff.; Saeed, 1997: 55–56), what is meant by the term *word* will depend very much on the level of abstraction at which a given speaker/writer is operating, the linguistic 'level(s)' being discussed, and the extent to which semantic content is being treated as criterial.

With regard to level of abstraction, there are two points. On the one hand, words can be thought of in terms of types or tokens; the phrase *Tomorrow, and tomorrow, and tomorrow* will be thought of as containing five words (*tomorrow*, *and*, *tomorrow*, *and*, *tomorrow*) or two words (*tomorrow*, *and*) depending on whether one is viewing words as tokens (actual occurrences of any items) or types (items with different identities). Likewise, the phrase *Going, going, gone* will be considered to comprise three words (*going*, *going*, *gone*) on a count of tokens but only two words (*going*, *gone*) on a count of types. On the other hand, there is a usage of *word* according to which this last phrase would be judged to contain just one word – the verb *go*, represented by two of its various forms (*going* and *gone*). The abstract unit based on a collection of forms thus seen as constituting in some sense a single lexical entity is often referred to technically as a *lexeme* or a *word expression*, while its concrete 'representatives' are referred to as *word forms*. For practical purposes (dictionary entries, etc.), lexemes have conventional citation forms; an English noun lexeme will be cited by the use of a singular form (*woman*, *sea*, *wall*, etc.), a French verb lexeme will be cited by the use of an infinitive form (*aimer*, *finir*, *vendre*, etc.), a Latin adjective will be cited by the use of a nominative masculine singular form (*bonus*, *parvus*, *fortis*, etc.), and so on.

[2] Cf. Crystal's definition in his *First dictionary of linguistics and phonetics*: 'SYNTAX ... A traditional term for the study of the rules governing the ways words are combined to form sentences in a language' (Crystal, 1980: 346).

[3] Cf. Crystal's definition: '**morphology** ... The branch of grammar which studies the STRUCTURE OR FORMS OF WORDS' (Crystal, 1980: 232).

As far as words and linguistic 'levels' are concerned, a simple example will illustrate the various possibilities on this front. Consider the word *builds*. As an orthographic entity it is a series of letters – *b* + *u* + *i* + *l* + *d* + *s*; as a phonetic entity it is a continuous burst of noise with particular acoustic characteristics having to do with the modalities of its production; as a phonological entity it is a sequence of units which are functionally relevant in the sound structure of English – /b/ + /ɪ/ + /l/ + /d/ + /z/; at a morphosyntactic level it is the third person singular form of a verb; and at a semantic level it is (among other things) synonymous with *constructs*.

Mention of semantic characteristics brings us to the question of the role of meaning content in defining words. A distinction has since ancient times been drawn between content words (otherwise known as full words or lexical words) and grammatical words (otherwise known as empty words, form words or function words). Words described as content words are those which are considered to have substantial meaning even out of context, whereas words described as grammatical words are those considered to have little or no independent meaning and to have a largely grammatical role. Examples of the former would be *tree*, *chair*, *teacher*; and of the latter, *the*, *it*, *of*. This distinction is not, it has to be said, unproblematic, since many so-called grammatical words – e.g., prepositions such as *within* and *towards* and conjunctions such as *although* and *while* – are clearly far from devoid of semantic content. In any case, we need to treat the 'content' metaphor with some caution (cf., e.g., Lapaire, 1994; Moore & Carling, 1982: esp. Chapter 4). If we deploy it at all, we need to bear in mind that what linguistic units 'contain' is certainly not exhausted by the traditional notion of 'semantic substance' (Lapaire, 1994: 127). (Actually, if the distinction between content words and grammatical words is to be made, a more satisfactory way of making it is in terms of set membership: grammatical words belong to classes 'whose membership is virtually constant during the lifetime of an individual speaker' (Cruse, 1986: 3), whereas content words 'belong to classes which are subject to a relatively rapid turnover in membership, as new terms are coined and others fall into obsolescence' (*ibid.*)).

In the light of the foregoing, it is hardly surprising that attempts to provide a general characterization of the word are quite diverse in the criteria they propose. The majority of such attempts suffer from the deficiency of failing to offer any illumination of the differentiation between lexemes and word forms (see above), and there are other problems associated with most of them too.

One approach is to identify the word in orthographic terms – as a sequence of letters bounded on either side by a blank space. This works reasonably well up to a point for languages using writing systems such as the Roman or Cyrillic alphabet, but is not helpful when it comes to languages (such as Chinese and Japanese) whose writing systems do not consistently signal word boundaries or where one is dealing with languages or language varieties which are not customarily written (e.g., local varieties of Colloquial Arabic) or have never been written (e.g., many of the indigenous languages of the Americas). Also, it seems odd to adopt literate criteria given that, as we have seen, the word is in no sense a *product* of literacy, and that literacy is, in terms of both the history of human language and the development of the individual, a relatively late bloom.[4]

Phonetic characterizations of the word are difficult because individual words rarely stand out as discernible units in physical terms in the ordinary flow of speech. As Ullmann (1962: 40–41) points out, such lack of phonetic independence 'may have permanent effects on the form of a word', leading to various kinds of reshaping. Thus, some words in English have lost their initial /n/ because this was felt to belong to the indefinite article (e.g., *auger* < Old English *nafu-gar*; *apron* < Old French *naperon*), while others have 'stolen' the /n/ from the indefinite article (e.g., *an ewt* > *a newt*; *an eke-name* > *a nickname*). One possible approach on this plane mentioned by Lyons (1968: 199–200) is to define the word as 'any segment of a sentence bounded by successive points *at which pausing is possible*'. However, as Lyons comments (*ibid.*: 199), since speakers do not normally pause between words, the 'potential pause' criterion is best seen merely as 'a procedural help to the linguist working with informants', and does not qualify as a 'theoretical definition'.

The possibilities for characterizing the word in phonological terms seem more promising at first sight. For example, in certain languages (e.g., English) words tend to have only one stressed syllable (e.g., *póle*, *pólar*, *polárity*, etc.). Another instance of a word-related phonological phenomenon is the case of vowel harmony in the Finno-Ugric languages (cf. Ullmann, 1962: 43), where the nature of the vowel in the stem of a given word determines the choice of vowels in all its suffixes – thus, in Hungarian: *kegy-etlen-ség-ük-ben* (lit. 'pity-less-ness-their-in' = 'in their cruelty') versus *gond-atlan-ság-uk-ban* (lit. 'care-less-ness-their-in' = 'in their carelessness'). Thirdly, there is the fact that in a particular language a specific phoneme or cluster of phonemes may be found only seldom or not at all in a given position

[4] This is not to imply that writing systems are always or necessarily parasitic on spoken language (cf. Calvet, 1996).

in the word; for instance, in English /z/ is relatively rare at the beginning of words and the '*ng* sound' (/ŋ/) does not occur at all in this position. One problem with phonologically based characterizations of the word is that they tend to be highly language-specific or at best language-type-specific; vowel harmony, for example, is restricted to a very limited number of languages. Further, such characterizations often have to be seen as descriptions of broad tendencies rather than as foolproof 'discovery procedures'; thus, with regard to stress in English, many units that are recognized as words in that language typically do not actually take stress in ordinary speech – e.g., *and*, *but*, *by*.

To the non-specialist, a semantic definition of the word in terms such as 'the minimum meaningful unit of language' (Carter, 1987: 5) may look attractive, and, moreover, unlike all other approaches, a semantic approach would seem to have the advantage of including the means for distinguishing between different lexemes. However, as Carter makes clear, the relationship between single words and particular meanings is far from simple:

> For example, there are single units of meaning which are conveyed by more than one word: *bus conductor*, *train driver*, *school teacher*, *model railway*. And if they are compound words do they count as one word or two?
> (Carter, 1987: 5)

Carter goes on to evoke the case of grammatical words (see above), whose role in the transmission of meaning is open to question. A further obvious point to be made about the idea of words being minimum units of meaning is that there are actually units *below* the level of the word which function as semantic units. The reference here, of course, is to bound morphemes such as inflections of plurality (e.g., the *s* in *cats*) and tense (e.g., the *ed* in *wanted*), and affixes such as *pre* (as in *predetermine*) and *ish* (as in *brownish*).

The characterization of the word that seems to be least problematic is a grammatical definition. This is particularly interesting in the light of current discussion relating to the interpenetration of lexicon and grammar – of which, more later. The grammatical approach uses the criteria of 'positional mobility' and 'internal stability' – which essentially goes back to Bloomfield's (1933) definition of the word as a 'minimal free form'. Words are 'positionally mobile' in the sense that they are not fixed to particular points in a sentence. Thus, for example, the order of words in *the boys noisily drained their teacups* is variously permutable – e.g., *the boys drained their teacups noisily*, *noisily the boys drained their teacups*, *their teacups the boys drained noisily*. 'Internal stability' refers to the fact that within words, morphemes are consistently sequenced relative to one another; thus the morphemic constituents of, respectively, *boys*, *noisily*, *drained* and *teacups* are not permutable – so that **sboy*, **ilynois*, **lyinois*, **lynoisi*, **noislyi*, **yilnois*, **eddrain*, **cupstea*, **scuptea*, **steacup*, **teascup* and **cupteas* are not possible versions of the words in question. Lyons (1968: 203–204) points out that 'positional mobility' and 'internal coherence' are independent of each other, so that in principle there might be a language where word order was fixed but where word-internal morpheme order was variable. In fact, no such language has yet been discovered. However, the converse case – of words which are 'internally stable' but not 'positionally mobile' – is attested even in English:

> The criterion of positional mobility would fail to define the 'definite article', *the*, as a word: it cannot be moved from one place in the sentence to another independently of the noun it 'modifies'. (Lyons, 1968: 204)

Lyons remarks that the fact that the one criterion but not the other applies in such instances can be taken to indicate that the items in question are not as 'fully' words as items to which both criteria apply. This clearly casts further light on the above-discussed distinction between content words and grammatical words, since items to which the criterion of positional mobility fails to apply seem to fall consistently into the latter category.

The grammatical characterization of the word is not only the least problematic but also the least language-specific. Phonetic and semantic perspectives, though offering little in strictly definitional terms, may suggest useful practical procedures to the field linguist working with informants. As far as orthographic and phonological criteria are concerned, they apply in different ways and different degrees to different languages – to the extent that 'what we call "words" in one language may be units of a different kind from the "words" of another language' (Lyons, 1968: 206). This does not, however, mean that the use of the term *word* may not be applied other than arbitrarily across languages, since, to quote Lyons yet again, 'the relevant features whereby words are established for different languages all tend to support their identification as structural units' (*ibid.*).

The domain of the lexicon

In any case, the notion of lexicon does not depend on the precise way in which we characterize the word for any given language. The crucial point about the lexicon as it is typically understood by linguists is that it constitutes that component of a language or knowledge of a language which has to do with what one might call 'local' phenomena – the meanings of particular elements of a given language, the phonological and orthographic forms of these elements, and the specific ways in which they collocate and colligate. In what follows, we shall look at these various dimensions of the lexicon in reverse order, beginning with colligation and collocation, moving on to phonological and orthographic dimensions, and ending with a discussion of lexical semantics.

Colligation: grammar and the lexicon

Colligation is the term which has in some quarters been used for many years to refer to the phenomenon of words being 'tied together' by, as it were, grammatical necessity. In the past it has largely been applied to a rather restricted range of relationships – e.g., the relationship between a verb and the form of complement it takes (*forbid to* X, *prohibit from* X*ing*, etc.), the relationship between an adjective and its prepositional accoutrements (*invulnerable to* X, *exempt from* X, etc.) (cf., e.g., Carter, 1987: 55ff.). However, the recent trend in linguistics has been towards a much wider conception of the interaction between lexicon and grammar, to the point where the separability of the two domains has been increasingly called into question.

Let us begin our discussion of the lexico-grammatical interface by thinking about the normal contents of dictionaries, which, after all, provide the usual metaphor for the lexical component of linguistic knowledge. Dictionaries – even quite basic dictionaries – contain a good deal more information than just the citation forms and the meanings of individual words. Here is an example of an entry (chosen at random) from *The Concise Oxford Dictionary* (Allen, 1990):

> **succumb** /sə'kʌm/ *v.intr.* (usu. foll. by *to*) **1** be forced to give way; be overcome (*succumbed to temptation*). **2** be overcome by death (*succumbed to his injuries*). [ME f. OF *succomber* or L. *succumbere* (as SUB-, *cumbere* lie)]

One notes that as well as the orthographic and phonological forms of *succumb* and its most frequent senses, the entry provides information about its grammatical categorization and subcategorization (*v.intr.* = 'intransitive verb'), its usual complement (noun phrase introduced by *to*) and two of its frequent collocates (*temptation*, *injuries*), as well as some etymological details.

The only element in this information which is superfluous to the person whose purpose in consulting the dictionary is to find out how to deploy and/or to interpret the word in question is the etymological material. The role of the grammatical component of the entry is to enable the dictionary-user to employ the item concerned in combination with other words or to construe combinations of words in which it occurs. Thus, the dictionary-user will learn from the above entry that *succumb* must be used in syntactic environments like the first rather than the second of the sentences below.

He succumbed to his injuries.
*He succumbed his injuries.

He/she will also learn from this entry that, in the sentence that follows, *Nero* refers to the person who was overcome and *temptations* refers to what overcame him.

To the temptations of power Nero finally succumbed.

Lexicographers constantly find themselves up against the problem of how best to display and integrate such grammatical information in dictionary entries (see, e.g., Cowie, 1983; Carter, 1987: 128ff.; Herbst, 1987; Sinclair, 1987a; Aarts, 1991; Lemmens & Wekker, 1991), which of itself already says a great deal about the difficulty of separating lexis and grammar. After all, if the endeavours of people as word-oriented as dictionary-makers oblige them also to confront morphosyntax, this surely constitutes evidence that partitioning off lexis from grammar is less than straightforward.

Such evidence is particularly persuasive when it emanates from the researches of computational lexicographers such as Gross (see, e.g., Gross, 1991). Gross and his colleagues at the Laboratoire d'Automatique Documentaire et Linguistique (LADL) are working on a system of electronic lexicons of French designed for use by computer programs performing analytical and synthetic operations on texts within the context of data-bank manipulation and machine translation. Such systems have heavy demands of coherence and explicitness placed upon them, since they have to be capable of recognizing, decoding, selecting and combining words without the online intervention of 'native-speaker intuitions'. They thus confront linguistic reality in a very concrete and dynamic manner, which renders the kinds of problems they throw up particularly worthy of note. And it turns out that the principal theoretical problems which emerge from the construction of such electronic lexicons are 'essentiellement ceux de la séparation entre lexique et grammaire' ('essentially those having to do with the separation of lexis and grammar') (Gross, 1991: 107).

Gross points out (*ibid.*: 107ff.) that the reading of sentence meaning has to have recourse to lexical information, since a given syntactic structure does not yield a single distribution of syntactico-semantic functions. The examples he uses (which work in English as well as in French) are:

Luc a avoué ce vol à Guy. ('Luc confessed this theft to Guy.')	(The *prima facie* interpretation is that Luc is the agent of the theft.)
Luc a attribué ce vol à Guy. ('Luc attributed this theft to Guy.')	(The *prima facie* interpretation is that Guy is – or at least may be – the agent of the theft.)
Luc a décrit ce vol à Guy. ('Luc described this theft to Guy.')	(The *prima facie* interpretation is that neither Luc nor Guy is the agent of the theft.)

Gross's collaborator, Lamiroy (Lamiroy, 1991), makes a similar point, namely that sentences which are identical in structure and which may be very close in meaning are not necessarily susceptible to the same kinds of syntactic transformations, the applicability of these latter being dependent on the particular words deployed in the structures in question. Among the examples she uses (which again also work in English) are the following:

Cette question concerne Pierre. ('This question concerns Pierre.')	(May be passivized to *Pierre est concerné par cette question.* ('Pierre is concerned by this question.'))
Cette question regarde Pierre. ('This question regards Pierre.')	(May not be passivized to **Pierre est regardé par cette question.* ('*Pierre is regarded by this question.'))
Pierre est ravi de partir. ('Pierre is delighted to leave.')	(May be embedded in apposition in a structure such as *Pierre, ravi de partir, a embrassé tout le monde.* 'Pierre, delighted to leave, kissed everybody.')
Pierre est grossier de partir. ('Pierre is rude to leave.')	(May not be embedded in apposition in a structure such as **Pierre, grossier de partir, a embrassé tout le monde.* ('*Pierre, rude to leave, kissed everybody.'))

Few linguists these days would wish to differ from the general thrust of what Gross and Lamiroy have to say on these matters. In virtually every area and school of linguistics there is now explicit recognition of the vital interplay between lexis and grammar. Even in the most traditional recesses of the field the same kinds of claims about lexico-grammatical interpenetration are being made. Within the philological tradition, for example, Sandoz (1992) has been able to show that *-mentum* words in Latin tend to occur in a particular sentence position, namely in the predicate – a tendency he relates to the abstract quality of the meaning of such words.

As far as developments in theoretical linguistics are concerned, these have predominantly been in the direction of representing more and more grammar as lexically governed. Thus, for instance, in the Chomskyan model, passivization, which in the earliest work in transformational-generative grammar (e.g., Chomsky, 1957) was treated as a purely syntactic transformation, was later dealt with through the proposal of 'restructuring rules' postulated as operating within the lexicon (see, e.g., Radford, 1981: 136ff.). Indeed, a central principle of the 'Government and Binding' (GB) version of the Chomskyan model was the so-called 'Projection Principle', which stated that 'the properties of lexical entries project onto the syntax of the sentence'. Cook comments on this principle thus:

> The lexicon is not a separate issue, a list of words and meanings; it plays a dynamic and necessary part in the syntax. The knowledge of how the Verb *like* behaves is inseparable from the knowledge of syntax. . . . GB does not segregate syntactic and lexical phenomena. Consequently, many aspects of language that earlier models dealt with as 'syntax' are now handled as idiosyncrasies of lexical items; the syntax itself is considerably simplified by the omission of many rules, at the cost of greatly increased lexical information. (Cook, 1988: 11)

More recently, recognition of the grammatical role of the lexicon in linguistic theory has evolved still further. Recent hypotheses coming out of the Chomskyan tradition 'take the view that syntax is invariant; languages differ in their lexicons' (Cook, 1995: 63), and that 'language acquisition is in essence a matter of determining lexical idiosyncrasies' (Chomsky, 1989: 44). This lexicalizing tendency reaches its logical conclusion in Chomsky's 'Minimalist Programme':

> The process [of forming structures] must start from the lexicon as lexical elements will, on the whole, determine the content of any legitimate expression in a language. Chomsky . . . supposes that we start by selecting a set of lexical items from which the structural description . . . is to be built. (Cook & Newson, 1996: 319 – referring to Chomsky 1995)

The intermingling of lexical and grammatical knowledge is also recognized by psycholinguists. Cieslicka-Ratajczak (1994) adduces in this connection evidence from slips of the tongue, from tip-of-the-tongue phenomena, from word-association experiments and from aphasia studies. In relation to slips of the tongue, Cieslicka-Ratajczak quotes examples from Garman (1990) showing that 'word selection errors tend to preserve the word class of the target' (Cieslicka-Ratajczak, 1994: 107) – examples such as:

because I've got an **apartment** (appointment)
they have been **married** (measured)
(cited in Cieslicka-Ratajczak, 1994: 113)

Similar sorts of instances are cited from tip-of-the-tongue guesses – this time as collected by R. Brown & McNeill (1966) – in which, again, 'the syntactic category is mostly retained' (Cieslicka-Ratajczak, 1994: 107):

sympathy (symphony)
sarong, Siam, sympoon (sampan)
(cited in Cieslicka-Ratajczak, 1994: 113)

With regard to word-association evidence, Cieslicka-Ratajczak points out (1994: 107) that in word-association experiments 'the commonest adult response is a word from the same class'. Finally, concerning, data from aphasia studies, Cieslicka-Ratajczak notes (1994: 107) that such studies 'evidencing separation of words belonging to different categories, corroborate the view about strong links between words of the same class'. She quotes in this connection work by A. Ellis (1985, 2: 107–142), and she cites data from Allport & Funnell (1981) suggesting that in particular instances one particular grammatical category (in this case nouns) may be virtually all that remains available to the aphasic:

Water ... man, no woman ... child ... no, man ... and girl ... oh dear ... cupboard ... man, falling ... jar ... cakes ... head ... face ... window ... tap ... (cited in Cieslicka-Ratajczak, 1994: 113)

L2 lexical research is fully consonant with the above-discussed trend towards blurring the distinction between lexicon and grammar. One might point in this context to the investigations of researchers such as the following:

- Arnaud (e.g., 1989, 1992), whose work in the area of L2 testing has, according to his own account, signally failed to demonstrate that 'grammar tests' and 'vocabulary tests' tap fundamentally

distinct aspects of linguistic knowledge (see also, e.g., Corrigan & Upshur, 1982);
- Robinson (e.g., 1989), who, on the basis of his research into the role of 'core' vocabulary in L2 learning, argues that 'Learning about "grammar" . . . takes place through, not before, learning about lexis' (Robinson, 1989: 543);
- Laufer (e.g., 1990a, 1993–94), whose research into learnability in relation to L2 lexis leads her to characterize knowledge of a word as including knowledge of morphological structure and syntactic behaviour;
- Wilkins (e.g., 1994), who is currently attempting to integrate insights relative to the lexis–grammar interface coming from general linguistics into a theoretically adequate programme of L2 acquisition research;
- Little (e.g., 1994), who advocates 'a lexical approach to pedagogical grammar' adducing arguments from theoretical linguistics, psycholinguistics and classroom experience with L2 learners in favour of the position 'that the largest part of language learning is the learning of words and their properties, and therefore that pedagogical grammar should be inseparable from vocabulary learning/teaching' (Little, 1994: 114; see also, e.g., M. Lewis, 1993, 1997; Schanen 1995);
- Martohardjono & Flynn (e.g., 1995), who in their work on the age factor in L2 acquisition assimilate lexical learning to the learning of language-particular L2 grammar, categorizing them together as 'inductive processes', which, they argue, may – unlike 'biologically endowed' aspects of L2 proficiency – be susceptible to age-related effects.

Collocational aspects

If, on the basis of the above considerations, the lexicon must be held to cover at least a substantial portion of what we normally call grammar, it must also *a fortiori* include the collocational aspects of usage, that is to say the ways in which words 'keep company' with each other. We are all aware of the existence of compound words, and of the fact that they are not consistently interpretable in terms of their constituent parts; we know, for example, that *blackbird* is not straightforwardly equatable to *black bird*, nor *greenhouse* to *green house*, *whiteboard* to *white board*, *bluebottle* to *blue bottle*, etc., etc. What is perhaps less often recognized is that this kind of phenomenon extends to combinations of lexical elements that are not normally thought of as compound words. Palmer (1971: 45, 54) illustrates the point with some amusing examples: *heavy smoker* is not typically interpreted as 'nicotine-user with a weight problem', nor *criminal lawyer* as 'miscreant member of the legal profession', nor *artificial florist* as 'flower-seller of unnatural origin'!

These latter examples are all, as it happens, instances of adjectives which, when used attributively, have meanings that may differ from meanings associated with them in predicative position. Further examples are: *the late duke* versus *the duke who is late*; *the right person* versus *the person who is right*; *my old pal* versus *my pal who is old*. This grammatical dimension to the problem immediately leads us back, of course, to our earlier discussion of the interpenetration of lexis and grammar, but the effects in question are not explicable simply in terms of adjectival positioning. After all, *a heavy jockey* does denote 'a jockey who is heavy', just as *a criminal dictator* denotes 'a dictator who is criminal', and *an artificial tree* denotes 'a tree which is artificial'. The less transparent meanings borne by *heavy smoker*, *criminal lawyer* and *artificial florist* are specifically bound up with the juxtaposition of the particular words in question and with the relationship of the collocations which result to other collocations, notably *smoke heavily*, *criminal law*, *artificial flower*.

Whether or not the meaning generated by the combination of two or more particular lexical items is straightforwardly derivable from the individual meanings of the words concerned, it is clear that the collocations into which a given word may enter and the meanings that attach to its various partnerships need to be seen as vital elements in that item's lexical profile. Earlier we saw that lexicographers, despite the fact that their primary interest is in vocabulary, are obliged to confront grammatical issues, and it was argued that this fact constituted evidence in favour of a high degree of lexico-grammatical integration. As far as collocations are concerned, lexicographers have always recognized these as lying at the very heart of their concerns. The following entries from some quite recently published monolingual and bilingual dictionaries continue a centuries-old tradition of treating not only the individual word but also the items with which it frequently co-occurs:

cauliflower /ˈkɒlɪˌflaʊ(r)/ *n.* **1** a variety of cabbage with a large immature flower-head of small usu. creamy-white flower-buds. **2** the flower-head eaten as a vegetable. **cauliflower cheese** a savoury dish of cauliflower in a cheese sauce. **cauliflower ear** an ear thickened by repeated blows esp. in boxing. . . . (*The Concise Oxford Dictionary* – Allen, 1990)

FRITE [fʀit]. *n. f.* (1858; pour *pomme de terre frite*, de *frire*). *Généralement au plur.* Petit morceau de pomme de terre que l'on mange frit et chaud. V.

Chips. '*Il déjeuna d'un cornet de frites*' (DUHAM). *Bifteck frites:* accompagné de frites. . . . (*Le petit Robert* – Rey & Rey-Debove, 1979)

Karren ['karən]. *m.* -s/- **1.** cart; (*Handk.*) barrow; *Rail:* **elektrischer K.**, electric trolley; *Fig:* **den K. laufen lassen**, to let things take their course. **2.** *Pej: F:* (*Auto*) jalopy; **alter K.**, old rattletrap. (*Harrap's Concise German and English Dictionary* – Sawers, 1982)

luonto nature; *kävellä luonnossa* walk in the countryside; *luonnon tuhoaminen* destruction of the environment; *maksaa luonnossa* pay in kind . . . (*English–Finnish–English General Dictionary* – Särkkä, 1992)

It was in fact suggested some four decades ago that the entire lexicographical enterprise needed to be based on the collection and analysis of 'exhaustive collocations of the selected words' (Firth, 1957: 26). Such a suggestion is of a piece with Firth's view that the meaning of a word essentially *is* the sum of its linguistic environments. This is an extreme view and is undoubtedly wrong; near-synonyms at opposite ends of a scale of formality, such as *trip* and *peregrination*, would otherwise have identical or near-identical associated collocational patterns – which they most definitely do not (whoever heard of a *day-peregrination to Blackpool*?).

That is not to say, however, that collocational patterns are not highly informative about lexical meaning and usage; very much the reverse has been impressively demonstrated by the COBUILD project (see, e.g., Sinclair, 1987b, 1991). This project is in the process of computationally concordancing a vast and still-growing corpus of naturally occurring English data, with a view to the production of dictionaries and other reference materials which base their definitions and illustrations on the combinatorial patterns discernible in authentic discourse. The following is a typical COBUILD entry (cited in Krishnamurthy, 1987: 85), the meaning it assigns reflecting an exhaustive analysis of the collocations in which the word in question has been found to occur in the corpus (cf. Krishnamurthy, 1987: 81–84):

veritable /veritəbəˈl/ is used to emphasize a description of something and used to suggest that, although the description might seem exaggerated, it is really accurate. eg *The water descended like a veritable Niagara . . . I'm sure the audience has a veritable host of questions . . . . . . a veritable passion for the cinema.*

Sinclair and the COBUILD project represent a continuation of Firthian 'London School' linguistics and applied linguistics, which, while abandoning the strong version of Firth's stance on meaning, have maintained a consistent interest in collocational issues (see, e.g., Halliday, 1961, 1966; Sinclair & Jones, 1974; Hasan, 1987). This tradition – particularly in its Hallidayan manifestation – treats lexical collocation as analogous to and overlapping with morphosyntactic structure. The Hallidayan perspective would see the lexical distinction between, for example, *boy* and *girl* as comparable to the morphological distinction between *car* and *hovercraft* and the syntactic distinction between *car* and *shiny*, the argument running roughly as follows: just as *car* and *shiny* are unlikely to occur in precisely the same environments (thus, ✓*a big shiny car* but **a big shiny shiny*, **a big car car*), and just as *car* and *hovercraft* diverge with respect to their co-occurrence with the plural inflection *-s* (thus, ✓*cars* but **hovercrafts*), so *boy* and *girl* differ as far as their probability of collocation with a word such as *pregnant* is concerned.[5]

Also broadly within the London School tradition is Carter's work on collocations (see, e.g., Carter, 1987: Chapter 4 and *passim*). Carter notes that words may be more or less restricted in their collocability. Thus, a word such as *have* can enter into partnership with a vast range of other words, whereas a word such as *rancid* is likely to be found juxtaposed with only a limited set of items (*fat*, *butter*, *oil*, etc.). Carter shows also that combinations of lexical items may be more or less flexible in syntactic terms and more or less transparent semantically. In extreme cases, fixed expressions function as if they were single words. Thus, in the sentence *It's raining cats and dogs*, for example, the phrase *cats and dogs* operates as a 'chunk' which is to all intents and purposes unanalysable; it is syntactically immutable, and its meaning – 'hard', 'heavily' – is quite unrelated to the meanings of the individual words out of which it is composed.

There has been much emphasis in recent years on what Chomsky calls the 'creative' dimension of language use – on the fact that mastery of a language enables one to 'understand an indefinite number of expressions that are new to one's experience ... and ... to produce such expressions' (Chomsky, 1972: 100). Whilst it is clear that language has the potential at all times to be innovative and

5 Sampson (1980: 233) is dismissive of the Hallidayan conception of lexical collocation as a 'more delicate' level of grammar, claiming that the improbability of a sentence such as *This boy is pregnant* is explicable simply in terms of human physiology. He has a point. On the other hand, it would no doubt also be possible to find plausible explanations for some of the ways in which syntax works (and indeed some of the ways in which it does not work) in the extralinguistic *rerum natura* (physical constraints on possible types of action and relationships, category types and processes imposed by the structure of mind, perceptual limitations, memory factors, etc.). Moreover, recent empirical and theoretical developments across a range of schools of linguistics have, as we have seen, tended to increase rather than diminish the credibility of the notion of lexical and (at least a substantial proportion of) morphosyntactic phenomena being continuous with each other.

open-ended in the way Chomsky claims, it would be wrong to imagine that language use is always 'creative' in this sense. Many of the combinations of words that we deploy in our speech and writing are prefabricated – ranging from fixed idiomatic expressions such as the above-mentioned *cats and dogs* to 'semi-fixed' combinations such as *know one's onions/stuff* and *know/be up to all the tricks*. Cowie (1988) reports that an analysis of authentic data in preparation for the *Oxford Dictionary of Current Idiomatic English* (Cowie, Mackin & McCaig, 1975/1983) yielded literally thousands of such stable multi-word units. On the basis of such findings and on the basis of psycholinguistic evidence that fixed expressions and formulas have an important economizing role in speech production (see, e.g., Peters, 1983), Cowie concludes that there is a strong case 'for regarding stability of various kinds as an omnipresent feature of normal vocabulary use' (Cowie, 1988: 136).

Sinclair takes this notion a stage further in enunciating – on the basis of his experience with COBUILD – what he calls the 'idiom principle', which assigns to the deployment of formulaic combinations in language use a very salient role indeed:

> The principle of idiom is that a language user has available to him or her a large number of semi-preconstructed phrases that constitute single choices, even though they might appear to be analysable into segments. To some extent, this may reflect the recurrence of similar situations in human affairs; it may illustrate a natural tendency to economy of effort; or it may be motivated in part by the exigencies of real-time conversation. (Sinclair, 1991: 110)

Indeed, Sinclair is in the end inclined to conclude that lexical and grammatical choice are so tightly interconnected that it may no longer be sensible to treat them as distinct:

> While grammars and dictionaries continue to report the structure of language as if it could be neatly divided, many of those people who are professionally engaged in handling language have known in their bones that the division into grammar and vocabulary obscures a very central area of meaningful organization. In fact, it may well be argued on the basis of the work in this book that when we have thoroughly pursued the patterns of co-occurrence of lexical choices there will be little or no need for a separate residual grammar or lexicon. (Sinclair, 1991: 137)

Clearly, such a suggestion strongly reinforces what emerged from the earlier discussion of colligation. Even if one does not wish to draw quite such an extreme conclusion, enough has been said here to establish that the ranges of collocations into which words enter and

the semantic effects of the various combinations to which they contribute constitute a major feature of the lexical landscape.

Lexis and phonology

So far in this section we have been considering phenomena situated at what Martinet (e.g., 1949, 1957) calls the secondary level of articulation, the level at which smaller meaningful units (morphemes, words, etc.) combine into larger meaningful units (phrases, sentences, etc.). We have seen that a very great deal of what happens at this level is dependent on choice of a lexical kind. A natural assumption would be that things are very different at the primary level of articulation – the level at which meaning*less* units (in speech, minimal units of sound) combine to form meaning*ful* units (inflections, affixes, words, etc.).

Such an assumption would be correct in quantitative terms but not in qualitative terms. That is to say, it seems to be the case that lexical choice has vastly less impact on phonological operations than in the morphosyntactic realm, but, on the other hand, there is enough evidence of lexico-phonological interaction to rule out any idea that lexical and phonological phenomena exist in hermetically sealed isolation from each other. Of course, there is a trivial sense in which lexis and phonology interact: choice of lexical item determines the particular sound shape, the particular combination of phonological units – phonemes, stressed and unstressed syllables, and (in languages such as Chinese) tones – that is deployed. What we are concerned with here, though, is the proposition that individual lexical items or groups of items may have particular sounds probabilistically or even exclusively associated with them.

One very clear demonstration of the veracity of this proposition is the case of /ŋ/ in Modern Standard French. This sound, which has for generation upon generation been the normal word-final nasal in words such as *vin* and *pain* in many southern varieties of French, is an innovation in the more prestigious 'metropolitan' varieties of the language. It was brought into these varieties via loanwords from English – especially words ending in the morpheme *-ing* (see Singleton, 1992a: 49–50).[6] When such words first entered Standard

[6] Other recent English loanwords in Modern French whose *ng* is pronounced in the English fashion include *bingo* and *swing*. There were a few earlier-borrowed words from English and other languages which those educated speakers who knew the languages in question might well have pronounced with an /ŋ/ sound even at the time of these words' entry into French (e.g., the nineteenth-century borrowings *ring* and *junker*). However, the point about the *-ing* morpheme is that it has become a naturalized, productive suffix

French their *-ing* ending was pronounced in diverse ways, but, at least as far as the community at large was concerned, using phonemes from the Standard French repertoire – thus /ɛ̃/, /in/, /iɲ/. In recent years, however, *-ing* words like *parking*, *smoking*, *lifting*, etc. have increasingly been pronounced using an /ŋ/ sound. Now the point about this particular sound is that, although it is phonemic (e.g., it distinguishes *shopping* ('shopping') from *chopine* ('bottle [of wine]), it occurs in a very limited set of words which defy any kind of rigorous categorization. Spelling is no guide, since in most French words orthographic *-ng* simply signals the presence of a nasal vowel (*coing* = /kwɛ̃/, *poing* = /pwɛ̃/, *rang* = /rɑ̃/, *sang* = /sɑ̃/, *shampooing* = /ʃɑ̃pwɛ̃/, etc.). Nor can one even say that the /ŋ/ phoneme is systematically associated with English loanwords ending in *-ing*; after all, the above-cited loanword *shampooing* is not pronounced with a final /ŋ/, and in any case many of the *-ing* words in French pronounced with final /ŋ/ are not so much loans as new coinages – *e.g., footing* meaning 'jogging', *lifting* in the sense of 'face lift'. To sum up, there is a phoneme in Modern Standard French which is exclusively associated with a small number of lexical items and whose occurrence is, therefore, entirely dependent on the selection of one of these words.

In the above case, the phenomenon described is the product of language contact, but lexically determined aspects of phonology are not necessarily connected to the borrowing of sounds. The process known as lexical diffusion (see, e.g., Hudson, 1980: 168ff.; Aitchison, 1981: 95; Romaine, 1982: 254ff.) may or may not involve cross-linguistic influence, but what it always involves is an association between specific sets of lexical items and particular phonic probabilities. The classic view of sound change since the neogrammarians (*Junggrammatiker*) and especially since the advent of Saussurean structuralism has been that such change operates not in an isolated fashion but systematically, i.e., simultaneously across whole phonological systems. Thus, the nineteenth-century neogrammarians Ostmann and Brugmann (cited in Robins, 1967: 182–183) declared that sound changes took place according to laws that admitted no exceptions (*ausnahmslose Lautgesetze*) within the same dialect, the same sound in the same environment always developing in the same way. Similarly, the Saussurean Grammont (cited in Benveniste, 1966: 93) confidently observed in 1933:

Il n'y a pas de changement phonétique isolé ... L'ensemble des articulations

in French (see Singleton, 1992a: 49–40) and has thus caused the /ŋ/ sound to be genuinely incorporated into the phonemic repertoire of Standard French speakers at large.

d'une langue constitue en effet un système où tout se tient, où tout est dans une étroite dépendance. Il en résulte que si une modification se produit dans une partie du système, il y a des chances pour que tout l'ensemble en soit atteint, car il est nécessaire qu'il reste cohérent.

('There is no isolated sound-change ... The total articulatory range of a language indeed constitutes a system in which everything is connected, in which everything is in a relationship of strict dependency. Consequently, if a modification occurs in one part of the system, the entire system is likely to be affected by it, for the system must remain coherent.')

It appears that this view of sound change is fundamentally mistaken. The current indications are that when a sound change gets under way it spreads gradually (i.e., word by word) through the lexicon, so that whether or not the new sound is likely to occur is dependent not on the general phonetic/phonological environment but on specific lexical selection (see, e.g., Wang, 1969; M. Chen & Wang, 1975). An excellent illustration of such lexical diffusion comes from data on Belfast English collected in the 1970s. From these data it emerges that a shift from [ʉ] to [ʌ] is in process in Belfast English, but that the [ʌ] innovation is affecting different lexical items to varying degrees (see Maclaran, 1976; Milroy, 1978). Thus, the word *pull*, for instance, was pronounced [pʌl] in the data in question in about three-quarters of its occurrences, whereas the word *look* attracted the pronunciation [lʌk] in only about a quarter of its occurrences. In other words, as in the case of French /ŋ/, the deployability of a specific sound in Belfast English is lexically influenced – though in the latter case the influence is probabilistic rather than determinant.

Lexis and orthography

As far as the relationship between the lexicon and orthography is concerned, this is most obvious in the case of logographic writing systems such as that associated with Chinese.[7] In such an instance, orthographic choice is very specifically tied up with lexical choice. Thus, for example, the word *ren* ('person') will be written with a character specific to it: 人. Likewise with the words *shan* ('mountain') – 山 – and the word *shui* ('water') – 水. The situation in Chinese is actually a little more complicated than what is implied by the above. It is not the case that an individual word is always represented by a single character. For instance, the character 木 used alone stands for

[7] I am grateful to Xiao Hong for providing me with the information about Chinese characters upon which this paragraph is based. See also Calvet (1996), Chapter 4.

mu ('tree'); doubled (林) it stands for *lin* ('wood', 'small forest'); and tripled (森) for *sen* ('large forest', 'numerous', 'dark'). Also, certain characters may be combined with others in order to indicate phonetic characteristics of the word represented. However, the interaction between orthography and lexicon is nevertheless very clearly demonstrated by the Chinese writing system and by other systems of a similar kind.

With regard to syllabaries and alphabetic systems, much the same kind of situation applies in relation to the lexis/orthography interface as has been described in respect of lexis and phonology. That is to say, on the one hand, at a trivial level, choice of word will obviously determine which syllable symbols or letters are used. On the other hand, and much more interestingly, it sometimes happens that certain aspects of a writing system are particularly, or even exclusively, associated with a specific set of lexical items.

A case in point is that of the letter *c* in German when it is used outside the clusters *ck* and *ch*. When it is used alone, *c* is exclusively associated with foreign borrowings:

> Mit c schreibt man Fremdwörter wie Café, Comics, Copyright, Comeback, comme il faut, Cornflakes, Crackers, Annonce, Service, die oft noch andere, dem Deutschen fremden Buchstabenverbindungen bewahrt haben und meist auch anders als Deutsche Wörter ausgesprochen werden. (Berger *et al.*, 1985: 160)
>
> ('C is used in the spelling of foreign words such as Café, Comics, Copyright, Comeback, comme il faut, Cornflakes, Crackers, Annonce, Service, which have often retained other orthographic combinations which are alien to German and are also mostly pronounced differently from German words.')

As such foreign words become increasingly integrated into the German language, both their spelling and their phonology are Germanized, *c* being written as *k* or *z*, depending on its original pronunciation. Thus what was originally written as *Copie* is now written as *Kopie*, and what was originally written as *Penicillin* is now written as *Penizillin*. Other examples are: *Spectrum* > *Spektrum*, *Centrum* > *Zentrum*, *Accusativ* > *Akkusativ* (cf. Drosdowski *et al.*, 1991: 29). Where *c* is retained or reverted to in the spelling of such words, this is often a deliberate act on the part of advertisers and businesspeople, who thus seek to give a product or an event foreign chic or exotic connotations. So it is, for example, that cigarette advertisements sometimes contain the spelling *Cigaretten* rather than *Zigaretten*, and circus posters frequently prefer *Circus* to *Zirkus*. Of course, the fact that such an advertising ploy is possible strongly confirms the association of *c* with a particular type of lexical item – namely, foreign words.

A further point worth noting in this connection is the way in which grapheme-phoneme correspondences are, at least in some languages, highly dependent on the particular lexical item in which the letter combinations occur. The classic example of this phenomenon is the case of the combination *ough* in English, which corresponds to /ɒf/ in *cough*, /ʌf/ in *rough*, /aʊ/ in *bough*, /əʊ/ in *though*, and /ɔː/ in *ought*. Another oft-cited instance is that of final *s* in French which is usually not pronounced except before a following vowel, when (depending on the circumstances) it may come out as /z/, but which is always realized as /s/ in a specific set of words, including *as* ('ace'), *fils*, ('son'), *vis* ('screw').

Lexis and meaning

Finally in this discussion of the domain of the lexicon, we come to the question of meaning. There is, of course, no doubt that lexical choice and meaning are intimately linked. The most cursory glance at the following sentences – identical but for their final word – will convince anyone who needs convincing on this point. Each makes an entirely different statement about Nigel's tastes.

Nigel likes **oranges.**
Nigel likes **orang-utans.**
Nigel likes **oratorios.**
Nigel likes **orchids.**
Nigel likes **organdie.**
Nigel likes **orgies.**

However, it may not be without interest in the context of the present chapter briefly to explore some of the different ways in which lexical meaning has been approached by linguists and to draw such implications for the concept of lexicon as might emerge from such an exploration.

Traditionally, language has been seen as communicating meanings through the medium of concepts. On this view, each lexical item is associated with a concept, and each concept is the psychic representation of a referent in the 'real world'. Ogden & Richards (1936: 11) express this notion diagrammatically by means of their 'basic triangle', a simplified version of which is given in Figure 1.1.

One objection to this kind of proposal is that it implies that a unique lexical form is associated with a corresponding unique concept and thus fails to take account of cases of synonymy, where

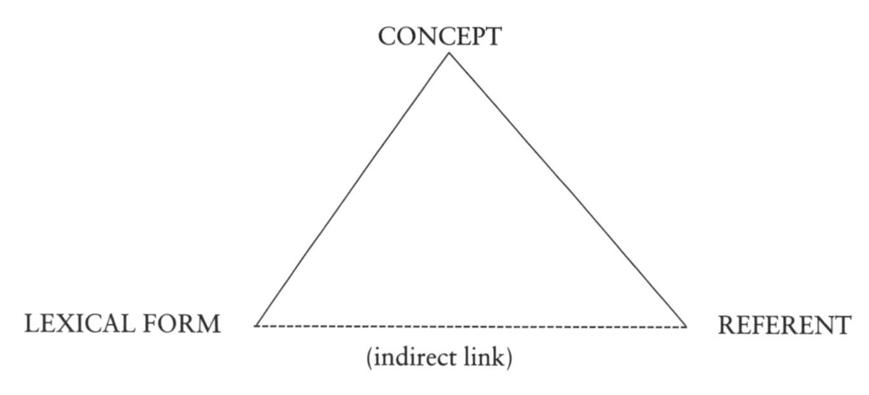

Figure 1.1 A simplified version of Ogden & Richards (1936) 'basic triangle'

more than one form is associated with a single meaning, and polysemy, where a single form is associated with a multiplicity of meanings. This difficulty might perhaps be overcome by complicating the proposed scheme in appropriate ways. However, there remains the problem that this whole approach is likely to lead to an 'atomistic view of language in which each word would be regarded as an isolated and self-contained unit' (Ullmann, 1962: 63).

The structuralist approach, on the other hand, gives atomism very short shrift. Structuralism, the foundation of virtually the entire edifice of modern linguistics, is generally taken to date from Saussure's *Cours de linguistique générale* (first published 1916; critical edition 1973), although some other linguists of the same period were certainly thinking along similar lines (see, e.g., Meyer, 1910). Its central thesis is summarized by Lyons as follows:

> every language is cut to a unique pattern and . . . the units which we identify . . . in the analysis of utterances . . . can be identified only in terms of their relationships with other units in the same language. . . . Linguistic units derive both their existence and their essence from their interrelations. (Lyons, 1973: 6)

Structuralism does not deny the relationship between words and their referents, but insists that this relationship is only part of the story. Saussure's much-cited analogy with monetary systems (in Chapter 5 of the Second Part of the *Cours*) is illuminating. Just as the value of a given coin (e.g., 5 francs) is a function both of the goods it will buy and of its relationship with other coins (e.g., 1 franc), so, says Saussure, the 'value' of a word derives both from the concepts for which it may be 'exchanged' and from its relationship with other words.

The structuralist semantics which was engendered by Saussure's ideas initially took the form of semantic field theory, or, as it is known in Germany, where it was initially most vigorously developed, 'lexical field theory' (*Wortfeldtheorie*). Lexical field theory posits that it is possible to identify within the vocabulary of a language particular lexical areas, 'sections of the vocabulary in which a particular sphere is divided up, classified and organized in such a way that each element helps to delimit its neighbours and is delimited by them' (Ullmann, 1962: 245). Trier, one of the early exponents of lexical field theory, had this to say about the relationship between the lexical field and meaning:

> Wir werfen ein Wortnetz über das nur dunkel und komplexhaft Geahnte, um es gliedernd zu fangen und in abgegrenzten Begriffen zu haben. (Trier, 1931: 2)
>
> ('We throw a net of words over that of which we have only a dark and complex inkling, in order to capture and organize it and to have it in demarcated concepts.')

Such emphasis on concepts was, however, far too mentalistic for other heirs of the Saussurean tradition, namely the American structuralists who looked to the work of Bloomfield for their inspiration. Bloomfield was concerned to enhance and protect the scientific status of linguistics. For him a scientific semantics had to deal in scientifically accurate definitions, and he claimed that, because of the limits of human knowledge, such definitions were hard to come by:

> We can define the names of minerals ... in terms of chemistry and mineralogy ... but we have no precise way of defining words such as *love* or *hate*, which concern situations that have not been accurately classified – and these latter are in the great majority. (Bloomfield, 1933: 139)

What is striking about this approach to linguistic meaning is not only its *naïveté* but also its disconnection from the Saussurean notion of the importance of system-internal relationships (see above), a notion that the Bloomfieldians were perfectly happy to apply in other areas – notably phonology and morphology. Its effect, moreover, was to turn mainstream American linguistics away from any interest in semantics for about three decades.

This was the situation when Lyons published his *Structural semantics* in 1963, in which he tried to find a way forward for semantics which was both comprehensive and operationally adequate. In this and subsequent works (e.g., 1968, 1977, 1981, 1995), he recognizes that aspect of meaning which derives from an expression's relationship with an entity or entities beyond itself. In his earlier works

(1963, 1968), he talks in a rather general way about the application of an expression, but he later distinguishes between reference – the picking out of a particular entity / particular entities by a particular expression in a particular utterance on a particular occasion – and denotation – the relationship between an expression and an entire class of entities. He also, however, places himself firmly in the Saussurean tradition and in the tradition of the lexical field theorists in emphasizing the network of meaning relations between expressions on which the meaning of an individual item partly depends. This aspect of meaning Lyons (from 1968 onwards) labels sense.

Among sense-relations Lyons distinguishes between paradigmatic (or substititional) and syntagmatic (or combinatorial) links. The former are those which hold 'between intersubstitutable members of the same grammatical category' (Lyons, 1995: 124), and the latter are those which hold 'typically, though not necessarily, between expressions of different grammatical categories (e.g., between nouns and adjectives, between verbs and adverbs, etc.), which can be put together in grammatically well-formed combinations (or constructions)' (*ibid.*). Syntagmatic sense-relations, about which Lyons says relatively little, constitute one aspect of the colligational and collocational dimension of the lexicon, which has already been discussed. As far as paradigmatic relations are concerned, Lyons focuses principally on synonymy, hyponymy and incompatibility, which he operationalizes in terms of entailment relations or meaning postulates (cf. Carnap, 1956).

Synonymy is defined by Lyons in terms of reciprocal entailment. Thus, if two sentences entail each other and differ by only one lexical expression, then the expressions in question are held to be synonymous: *Philip is very* ***rich*** entails and is entailed by *Philip is very* ***wealthy***; therefore rich and wealthy are synonyms. Similarly, hyponymy, the relation between more specific (hyponymous) and less specific (superordinate) terms such as *tulip* and *flower* is defined in terms of unilateral entailment: *I picked a* ***tulip*** entails *I picked a* ***flower***, but not vice versa. With regard to incompatibility, this can be defined in general terms, and also more specifically for particular types of incompatibility: complementarity, polar antonymy and converseness. Incompatibility is in general defined in terms of negative entailment: *William's scarf is* ***blue*** entails *William's scarf is not* ***red***, and so *red* and *blue* can be taken to be incompatible. As far as particular subcategories of incompatibility are concerned, in the case of complementarity not only does the assertion of one lexical item in a complementary pair (such as *alive* and *dead*) imply the denial of the other but the denial of the one implies the assertion of the other: *King*

*Kong is **alive*** entails *King Kong is not **dead***, and *King Kong is **dead*** entails *King Kong is not **alive***. Polar antonymy differs from complementarity by virtue of the gradability of polar antonyms; the assertion of one of a pair of polar antonyms implies the denial of the other, but the denial of the one does not necessarily imply the assertion of the other: *Kevin is **big*** entails *Kevin is not **small***, whereas *Kevin is not **small*** does not entail *Kevin is **big***, since it is possible to think of an entity as somewhere between big and small (middle-sized) in relation to some explicit or implicit norm; *big* and *small* are therefore said to be polar antonyms with respect to each other. Finally, converseness is the relation that holds between expressions in sentences (differing only in respect of the expressions in question) which imply the denial of each other but which, after particular kinds of syntactic permutation have been effected, actually entail each other: *Peter **lent** the keys to Gabriel* entails the denial of *Peter **borrowed** the keys from Gabriel*, but *Peter **lent** the keys to Gabriel* entails and is entailed by *Gabriel **borrowed** the keys from Peter*, and so *lend* and *borrow* are taken to be converses of each other.

Two important additional points about sense-relations *à la* Lyons need to be emphasized in the light of earlier discussion and what will follow in this and later chapters. The first is that sense-relations are recognized as holding not just between individual words but also between words and multi-word units:

> One might well say, for example, that the phrase *female fox* and *male duck* are synonymous with the lexical items *vixen* and *drake*, respectively. (Lyons, 1968: 451)

Similarly, the superordinate of *chair*, *table*, *sofa*, etc. is *piece of furniture*, and an alternative to *dead* as complementary of *alive* is the (rather unpleasant) fixed expression *gone the way of all flesh*. Indeed, sense-relations may hold between two or more multi-word units; for example, in a cricketing context the expressions *dismissed for nought*, *out for nought*, *out for a duck*, *out for a duck-egg* are all synonymous according to the criteria outlined above.

Mention of context brings us to the second important addendum in connection with sense-relations, namely that these latter are highly context-sensitive:

> utterances identical in linguistic form are understood differently in different situational contexts, and not only in 'special practical situations' without difficulty and with no evidence of restraint of any kind; and the fact of their being understood must be attributed to the relevant situational factors. Situation must be given equal weight with linguistic form in semantic theory. (Lyons, 1963: 24)

For an example, let us return to the world of cricket. The noun *run* in this context denotes a unit of scoring, and the noun *extra* denotes a particular type of run – one scored other than by a hit from the bat. Thus in this context a hyponymous relation holds between *extra* and *run*. In a farming context, on the other hand, the noun *run* denotes a particular type of enclosure (for fowls – e.g., *chicken run*) and is hyponymous to the noun *enclosure*.

Some schools of linguistics have tried to take structural semantics a stage further by attempting to explicate sense-relations between words in terms of 'components' of meaning or 'semantic markers' in much the same way that some approaches to phonology have sought to explicate relations between phonemes in terms of distinctive features, whether articulatory (voice, aspiration, nasality, etc.) or acoustic (consonantality, diffuseness, acuteness, etc.). For example, in a componential analysis, the relations between *man*, *woman*, *boy* and *girl* might be accounted for in terms of plus or minus values attaching to the components HUMAN, MALE and ADULT. This type of analysis obviously has strong similarities to the traditional decompositional dictionary definition. It has long been used in anthropological linguistics, in, for example, studies of kinship terms (see, e.g., F. Wallace & Atkins, 1960) and has been associated with broadly Chomskyan perspectives (see, e.g., Katz & Fodor, 1963; Katz & Postal, 1964; Jackendoff, 1990), but has also been favoured by semanticists without any specific research task preoccupations or theoretical predispositions (see, e.g., Leech, 1981).

Componential analysis has come in for some fairly heavy criticism over the years (see, e.g., Bolinger, 1965; Lyons, 1968: 470ff.; 1995: 114ff.; Saeed, 1997: 259ff.). Perhaps most controversial has been the assumption of some componentialists that the basic components of meaning are universal. This assumption runs into large empirical problems; even a seemingly surefire candidate for universality such as MALE, for example, looks rather less surefire when one considers the diversity of perceptions of maleness across cultures and the extent to which gender is a socio-cultural artefact (see, e.g., Gilmore, 1990). There is also the question of the relationship between the labels used to identify components of meaning; are these merely 'a kind of garbled version of the English, French, etc. of the writer' (Saeed, 1997: 260)? Not only garbled, some might say, but also potentially sexist, ageist and many other ists besides! A further frequent criticism is that componential analysis cannot cope with contextual and metaphorical effects; for example, how does an analysis of *boy* as [+HUMAN, +MALE, –ADULT] sit with the unexceptionableness of a question such as *Are we going for a pint, boys?* as addressed by a middle-aged singer to fellow-members of a choir in a situation where no one under the age of 30 is present? These and other points have not gone without response from componentialists (see, e.g., Jackendoff, 1992: Chapter 2; Leech, 1981: Chapter 7); however, at least some componentialists are prepared to admit that 'componential analysis is not the whole story' (Leech, 1981: 121). On the other hand, non-componentialists such as Lyons are perfectly happy to recognize that, because it is based on structural notions of sense, componential analysis is, 'at least in principle, fully compatible with [other approaches to structural semantics]' (Lyons, 1995: 117).

A particular version of the componential approach which seems to be less vulnerable to criticism than classic componential analysis is that which starts from the notion of prototypical sense (otherwise labelled stereotypical, focal or nuclear) (cf. Labov, 1973; Lakoff, 1987; Pulman, 1983; Rosch, 1978; Coleman & Kay, 1981). The notion of prototype, which is especially associated with psycholinguistic perspectives on meaning, is in this context to be understood as 'ideal exemplar' (Aitchison, 1994: 55) of a given category with an ideal set of characteristics against which candidates for inclusion in the same category can be matched. However, the matching process is envisaged as flexible. There does not have to be a complete match, just a sufficiency of similarity:

> This is how unbirdy birds such as pelicans and penguins can still be regarded as birds. They are sufficiently like the prototype, even though they do not share all its characteristics. (Aitchison, 1994: 55)

Such a conception of lexical meaning clearly takes us away from what Lyons (1995: 99) calls a 'checklist theory of definition', which allows for absolutely no indeterminacy. Clearly, prototype theory can cope far better than classic 'checklist' componential analysis with situations where 'boys' may be adult, 'guys' may be female, and 'ratbags' may be human!

A further development in the prototype concept in semantics is the idea that not only individual entities but also entire events may have prototypical features. This notion has been developed within script theory, which posits that we interpret experience – including linguistic experience – via 'scripts', general prototypes or templates for particular types of activity (cf., e.g., Schank & Abelson, 1977; Schank & Kass, 1988). For example, the prototypical scenario for eating out will include making one's way to a restaurant, being seated, ordering a meal from a waiter, being served the meal by the waiter, eating the meal, asking for the bill, paying and leaving. According to script theory, such event templates allow us to fill in information gaps that may be left by a given text or interaction on the basis of what we know about the typical way in which things proceed. Related to and overlapping with the notion of script is the notion of 'frame'; frames are conceived of as 'remembered frameworks' (Minsky, 1975) or mental plans relating to specific domains of knowledge which assist us in dealing with relevant situations. A restaurant frame, for instance, would include tables set with cutlery (plus perhaps candles and/or flowers), menus, wine lists and waiters. Also connected with script theory and the frame concept are schema-theoretic models of comprehension which are based on the idea that 'Every act of comprehension involves one's knowledge of the world as well' (R. Anderson *et al.*, 1977: 369).

The relevance of scripts and frames for lexical semantics is twofold. On the one hand, they provide a plausible underpinning for at least some aspects of syntagmatic sense-relations; one recalls Sinclair's above-cited remark about the recurrence of particular combinations of items having to do with 'the recurrence of similar situations in human affairs' (Sinclair, 1991: 110). On the other hand, schemata also relate to paradigmatic aspects of meaning, constituting one of the likely sets of mechanisms whereby contextual information is brought to bear on paradigmatic relations (cf. Hatch & Brown, 1995: 152–153). For example, the noun *drink* is in some contexts synonymous with *alcoholic beverage*, *bevy*, *jar*, etc. and in other contexts not; it so happens that in the contexts where the above synonymous relationship is indicated, the prototypical scenarios (e.g., 'night out in the pub') include the consumption of alcohol, and in contexts where it is not indicated, the prototypical scenarios (e.g., 'children's birthday party') do not include such an element.

Having now concluded our whistle-stop tour of some of the principal points of interest in the development of lexical semantics, what are we left with concerning the nature and the domain of the lexicon? At least three thoughts spring to mind by way of response to this question. First, lexical meaning is no different from other aspects of language in being in part a function of the network of interrelationships between the relevant units. One clear implication of this is that one cannot hope to deal adequately with the meaning of a particular lexical expression (whether as a semanticist or as a language learner) without regard to the ways in which that expression relates semantically to other expressions. A second element of a response to the above question has to do with the scope of sense-relations. We have seen that such relations hold not only between words, but also between words and multi-word lexical expressions and within pairs and groups of multi-word expressions. This underlines the fact – already clear from the discussion of colligation and collocation – that the lexicon cannot be just an inventory of individual words but must also cover a large variety of combinations of words. Third, we can note that a consideration of context is necessary in the very definition of lexical sense-relations and that contextual influence on meaning is a major issue in the debate about how best to describe and represent semantic relationships between lexical expressions. It is difficult not to infer from this state of affairs that orientation to context is one of the lexicon's vital parts and that any attempt to address the meanings of individual lexical entries in isolation from context is doomed to failure.

Closing remarks regarding the domain of the lexicon

In the light of the foregoing, the question that probably poses itself at this point is: has the notion of lexicon now lost all definition? To put the problem facetiously, have we reached a stage where linguistics and lexicology are co-extensive? The answer to both these questions is probably no, but not a resounding no. The usual line of argument offered in favour of a distinct concept of lexicon is that, however many data may be accounted for partly or wholly in lexical terms, it is nevertheless still possible to identify linguistic phenomena which can be described without reference to lexical particularities: for example, general design features such as double articulation (see above) and universal grammatical principles such as structure dependency.[8]

It is true that, as has been noted earlier, a number of phenomena which were in former times seen as independent of lexical considerations are now widely acknowledged to be essentially lexical in nature, and it must also be admitted that further research may well cause similar shifts of perspective in the future. However, it still seems plausible to suppose that, whether or not one wishes to talk in Chomskyan terms about 'Universal Grammar', there may always remain aspects of language that will have to be recognized as standing outside the lexical specificities of individual languages.

Precisely which aspects of language or any specific language are to be allocated to the lexicon and which are to be treated as lexicon-independent is not an issue that the present volume will attempt to resolve. It is in this connection always possible to 'play safe' and to

[8] Structure dependency is the principle 'common to the syntax of all languages' according to which 'operations on sentences such as movement require a knowledge of structural relationships of the words rather than their linear sequence' (Cook, 1988: 6).

treat as lexical those areas which are most self-evidently language-particular – forms and meanings of individual items, collocational patterns, 'local' colligation (e.g., complementation of verbs), etc. On the other hand, even if one takes the line (as the present work does) that in our present state of knowledge it still makes sense thus to demarcate (provisionally) an area of language under the heading of lexicon, it would be unwise to assume that the lexical construct will in the end prove to be either theoretically or empirically dissociable from all other linguistic or psycholinguistic domains.

Concluding summary

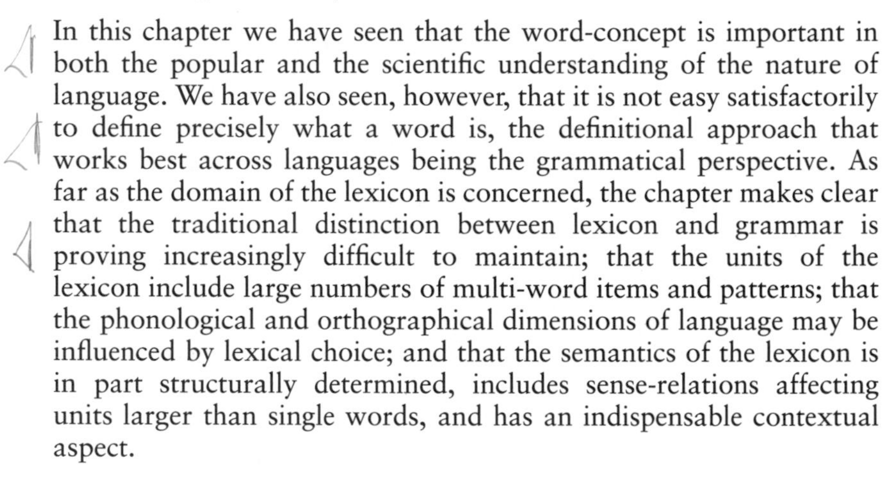

In this chapter we have seen that the word-concept is important in both the popular and the scientific understanding of the nature of language. We have also seen, however, that it is not easy satisfactorily to define precisely what a word is, the definitional approach that works best across languages being the grammatical perspective. As far as the domain of the lexicon is concerned, the chapter makes clear that the traditional distinction between lexicon and grammar is proving increasingly difficult to maintain; that the units of the lexicon include large numbers of multi-word items and patterns; that the phonological and orthographical dimensions of language may be influenced by lexical choice; and that the semantics of the lexicon is in part structurally determined, includes sense-relations affecting units larger than single words, and has an indispensable contextual aspect.

PART II

RESEARCH REVIEW

2 *Lexical development: an overview*

L2 lexical development does not happen in a vacuum. By definition, it takes place against the background of lexical development in at least one other language. The present chapter begins with some thoughts on the nature of the challenge posed by L1 and L2 lexical development in different circumstances. Thereafter, it attempts to summarize current perspectives on L1 lexical development, touching on some of the theoretical issues that arise in this context. The chapter then concludes with a few preliminary words on the question of the degree of similarity/difference between L1 and L2 lexical development.

The lexical challenge

Clearly, the lexicon develops and expands in a variety of circumstances under the impetus of a variety of stimuli – for example, in infancy and early childhood, during schooling as L1 literacy skills are established, in the course of the 'naturalistic' acquisition of an L2, and in the framework of formal L2 instruction. This list is far from exhaustive; indeed, since language is so all-pervasive in human life, and since lexis is so all-pervasive in language, there must be few situations which do not offer opportunities for lexical development of one kind or another.

Certainly it would be entirely mistaken to believe that this process is confined to what happens 'at the mother's knee' or in the primary-school classroom – even as far as L1 lexical acquisition is concerned. Thus, for example, a number of researchers have written about the vast quantity of new slang expressions that are taken on board in the teenage years and which serve to define group membership (see, e.g., Britton, 1970; E. Nelson and Rosenbaum, 1968; Schwartz and Merten, 1967). One can also in this context refer to the work of Smedts (1988), who, in a study of first language word-formation proficiency in Dutch between ages 7 and 17 found that his 7-year-old subjects displayed a mastery of, on average, only 14% of a range of Dutch word-formation rules, that his 13-year-olds knew just 51% of the rules tested, and that even his 17-year-olds demonstrated a command of no more than 66% of these rules. In fact, L1 lexical development extends far beyond the teens. J. B. Carroll concludes (1971: 124) from his review of a number of lexical studies that L1 vocabulary tends to increase significantly up to at least the age of 40 or 50, while Diller (1971: 29) reports research which suggests that there is no point before death at which L1 vocabulary acquisition can be predicted to cease. It is true that among older adults the capacity to recall memorized lexical items in experimental conditions is in general somewhat lower than in younger adult subjects, particularly in respect of speed of response (see, e.g., Arenberg, 1983; Hussian, 1981: 6ff.), but the ability to learn new lexis remains in place, and indeed the evidence is that there are always elderly subjects whose performance does not fall below the levels set by younger adults. Bearing these facts in mind, it may nevertheless be worthwhile to focus on the four types of lexical development mentioned above as exemplars of the varieties of challenge involved, if only because they are probably more extensively researched than lexical development in other situations.

Lexical acquisition in infancy

Let us consider first the case of lexical acquisition in infancy. Much has been written about Chomsky's 'poverty of the stimulus' argument in relation to language acquisition (see, e.g., Chomsky, 1988: Chapter 1; Cook & Newson, 1996: 81ff.; M. Harris, 1992: 15ff.). Normally this argument is conducted in relation to syntactic phenomena, the claim being that the data available to a child could never provide sufficient evidence for the induction of the highly abstract syntactic foundations that need to be present in order for language to function. However, a similar argument can be and has been applied to the lexical dimension. Thus, Chomsky claims that the rate of lexical acquisition in the child is so rapid and precise that one has to conclude 'that the child somehow has the concepts available before experience with language and is basically learning labels for concepts that are already part of his or her [innate] conceptual apparatus' (Chomsky, 1988: 28).

Chomsky is not alone in suggesting that the child's lexicalization of his/her world is supported by innate structures. A variety of philosophers, psychologists and linguists have been led by a consideration of the challenge confronting the child in this connection to posit innate properties such as 'the desire for the detection and conquest of an objective world' (Cassirer, 1944: 133), 'the need of symbolization' (Langer, 1960: 41), 'semantic concepts that are linguistic universals' (Katz & Postal, 1964: 16), 'some special features of human action and human attention that permit language to be decoded by the uses to which it is put' (Bruner, 1975: 2), 'conceptual resources' (Fodor, 1979: 222; see also Fodor, 1975, 1981, 1987a), 'a constrained universal apparatus for representing ... meanings' (Pinker, 1994), etc. Nativist proposals have also been advanced in relation to the strictly formal aspects of early lexical development. For example, Cutler (1994) proposes an innate sensitivity to speech rhythm, which she sees as enabling young children to exploit the rhythmic structure of the language of their environment (whether 'stress-timed' or 'syllabus-timed') in order to isolate word units of that language. M. Kelly & Martin (1994) also take a nativist line, although in this particular case the capacity in question is seen as shared across a range of species and used in a variety of domains. The capacity they refer to is sensitivity to probabilistic patterns in the environment, which would seem to have high utility in a range of aspects of language acquisition – one such being the identification of likely word boundaries on the basis of the internalization of cue frequencies.

Whatever may be the truth of this suggestion of innate facilitating factors in respect of early lexical development, we can point to other ways in which the process may be helped along. One such may be the particular nature of child-directed speech:

> Adults talk to children more slowly, in shorter utterances, with repetition of key words, and in a higher pitch than they talk to other adults (Garnica, 1977). This makes it easier for children to identify the units (i.e. the words) that make up the utterance. (McShane, 1991: 140; see also, e.g., Snow, 1986)

There has been some fairly fierce debate about the effect of caregivers' input on children's language development (see, e.g., M. Harris, 1992: especially Chapters 2–5). This debate has essentially revolved around the effect of the presence, absence and/or frequency of particular features in adult speech on children's grammatical development. The proposition that the above types of input tuning assist the child in isolating lexical units is less often seriously questioned.

Cutler, however, claims (1994: 86–87) that the above-described features cannot be absolutely indispensable to isolating word-units, as there are cultures in which child-directed speech is not discernibly distinct from adult-directed speech. Such a claim would need to be looked at rather closely; as Snow (1986: 84ff.) has shown, what at first sight seems to be unmodified input, may actually turn out to be input which has been tuned in a different way. A further argument put by Cutler in favour of her view that the word-isolation enigma is not ultimately solved by reference to child-directed speech is that, whatever its degree of modification, such speech is typically connected: 'Even though phrases may be short, they are still phrases' (*ibid.*: 87). This argument does not, however, take account of the fact that one very widely used aspect of child-directed speech is ostensive definition – the definition of single words by pointing at their referents and naming them (see below) – in which word units are ready-isolated for the child by the caregiver. None of this is to suggest that the particularities of child-directed speech explain everything; on the other hand, it seems implausible to see them as having no role as aids to word isolation.

Extracting units from the undifferentiated speech stream is only one of the tasks the child needs to perform:

> There is for him also the endless stream of undifferentiated experience. This is something we can imagine only very imperfectly, for once in any language we have organized experience to form an objectified world we can never reverse the process.
>
> Perhaps it is here that the secret of the mystery lies – perhaps it is *the way these two tasks enmesh* that explains how a child is able to perform his astonishing feat of learning. (Britton, 1970: 37)

The expression 'endless stream of undifferentiated experience' in the above is almost certainly too strong, suggesting as it does that concept development is impossible in the absence of language – whereas we know that pre-linguistic/extralinguistic conceptualization (whether or not it is innately guided) is a feature of ontogeny both within our own species and beyond it (see below). The 'enmeshing' of the two tasks in question, however, is obviously mediated by the providers of linguistic input, namely the caregivers, and here again the manner in which caregivers proceed may be of some relevance. Thus, a feature of speech directed at very young children is that it tends to be focused on the 'here and now'. The results of a study of mother–child interaction by M. Harris *et al.* (1983), summarized below by M. Harris & Coltheart (1986), illustrates the point very well:

> Almost all maternal utterances concerned the child's immediate environment; 70% referred to an object on which the child was currently focusing attention and 40% related to actions that were actually being

carried out, or could be predicated from past experience of similar sequences. (M. Harris & Coltheart, 1986: 41)

One much-discussed aspect of caregivers' reference to objects of joint attention which has already been mentioned is ostensive definition. As Markman (1993) notes, this seems to be an important part of the process of giving early L1 acquirers access to lexical meaning:

Some variant of ostensive definition makes up a large part of the way very young children acquire new words because they do not yet know enough language for one to define a new term for them or contrast with other terms, and so on. (Markman, 1993: 156)

However, establishing lexis–meaning links via 'ostension' is by no means as straightforward as it might appear:

the person interpreting the 'definition' must know in advance the significance of the gesture of 'pointing' in this context (and must know that 'definition', rather than something else, is intended) and, more important, he must correctly identify the object that is pointed to. (Lyons, 1968: 409)

Markman herself concludes from such considerations – citing, among others, Carey (1978), Markman & Hutchinson (1984), Mervis (1987), and Quine (1960) – that children must approach word learning with certain innate assumptions (see also above) which guide their hypothesizing about what words can mean, namely the whole-word assumption (novel labels refer to whole objects), the taxonomic assumption (labels refer to objects of the same kind rather than thematically related objects), and the mutual exclusivity assumption (different labels applied to the same object do not refer to the same properties of that object).

Whatever assumptions its functioning depends on, however, ostension cannot serve as anything other than a heuristic device. Given (a) polysemy, (b) the context sensitivity of lexical meaning, and (c) the non-referring, non-denoting nature of so many words, ostensive associations between individual forms and individual referents will not actually take the early language acquirer all that far relative to where he/she needs to go in order to be able to make sense of and with the lexis of his/her language. Even in relation to form, the contribution of ostension is limited, since learning to recognize isolated lexical forms will, self-evidently, only begin to equip the language acquirer to cope with the challenge of identifying those same forms amidst the continuous phonetic flow that is normal speech.

L1 vocabulary development in the context of the acquisition of literacy skills

Let us move now to the matter of L1 vocabulary development in the context of the acquisition of literacy skills. One obvious aspect of this development is the addition of an orthographic dimension to the entries already present in the mental lexicon. To be noted, however, is the fact that the precise nature of this dimension varies considerably from writing system to writing system:

> Only Korean systematically represents phonemic *features* in its orthography: the place of articulation of a phoneme is indicated by the shape of the corresponding grapheme, and the manner of articulation ... is shown by the addition of diacritics ... In some orthographies the *syllable* is the central unit (e.g. Japanese *kana*), in others the *word* (Japanese *kanji*); but in those systems we call alphabetic the *phoneme* is the primary unit ... (P. Smith, 1986: 475–476)

Undoubtedly, different systems pose different kinds of challenge to the learner and rely on different kinds of ability. Thus, for example, the capacity to discriminate auditorily between minimal pairs such as /bʌn/ and /bɪn/ appears to be highly relevant to reading development in alphabetic systems (see, e.g., M. Clark, 1976), but would seem to be less crucial in logographic systems, where written forms appear to tap directly into stored meanings without reference to phonology (see, e.g., Tzeng & Wang, 1983).

There also seem to be writing-system-related differences in respect of what one might call the qualitative lexical effects of the acquisition of literacy skills. There is some evidence, for example, that the acquisition of literacy skills in an alphabetic system induces an ability to manipulate the individual phonemes out of which words are composed (see, e.g., Morais *et al.*, 1979), whereas the acquisition of such skills in a purely logographic system fails to bring about such segmental awareness. Hsia, for example (1994a, 1994b), found that Cantonese-speaking subjects who had learned to read only in Cantonese – without the benefit of phoneme-segmentation training – performed significantly less well on phoneme-segmentation tasks in both their L1 (Cantonese) and their L2 (English) than Cantonese-speaking subjects who were receiving some segmental training in the course of studying Mandarin (Putonghua).

With regard to the relationship between literacy skills and vocabulary size, it is certainly not the case that in order to read a given text one first has to acquire a detailed knowledge of every single lexical item which it contains (cf. the misleading observations of the

Plowden Report on this issue (HMSO, 1967: 197) and Britton's critique thereof (Britton, 1970: 163)). Dollerup *et al.* (1989) point out that, whether one is talking about L1 or L2 reading, stable word knowledge centring around the most frequent items in a language is only one of three lexical components which a reader exploits when reading, the other two being (a) an arsenal of decoding strategies that may be brought to bear on unfamiliar words and (b) the text which is actually being read and which provides the context within which 'word knowledge and strategies can interplay' (Dollerup *et al.*, 1989: 30).

Looking at that literacy skills–vocabulary size connection from the opposite point of view, it is obvious that accession to literacy brings with it an increased range of opportunities for learning word meanings – both via ostensive or quasi-ostensive routes and by use of context. With regard to ostension or quasi-ostension, this is provided by word–picture juxtapositions (on the blackboard, in picture-dictionary-type books, on wall-charts, etc.), and by all the written definitions of words in terms of other words that teachers and textbooks provide from the earliest stages of schooling. As for use of context, the extent to which this plays a role in reading has been a matter of some debate. The present evidence is that expert readers do not routinely proceed in a manner consonant with Goodman's (1967) notion of a 'psycholinguistic guessing game' (see, e.g., Stanovich, 1980) – presumably because they do not usually need to. Pre-readers and beginning readers, on the other hand, do rely heavily on context (see, e.g., Biemiller, 1970), and experienced readers certainly fall back on context-related strategies when unfamiliar words are encountered (West & Stanovich, 1978; Stanovich *et al.*, 1981). The general assumption is that the process of decoding unfamiliar words in context – in reading as in the handling of spoken language – leads to lexical acquisition. Britton puts it thus:

> it is from successive experiences of words in use – words used for some actual profit or pleasure – that a child builds up his resources . . . (Britton, 1970: 163)

Worth noting in this connection is the finding of R. Cohen *et al.*, (1992) that children with early reading experience have a better grasp of basic concepts than children without such experience, which suggests that accession to literacy accelerates lexical development and the fine-tuning of concepts that goes with it.

Lexical development in the context of naturalistic L2 acquisition

With regard to lexical development in the context of naturalistic L2 acquisition, the problem faced by the learner here resembles that which confronts the infant – to the extent that in relation to speech, again, the challenge is to isolate lexical units in the speech stream and to make connections between such units and the meanings they are intended to communicate. There is, of course, a major difference between the L1 and the L2 situation in this latter regard: the learner already has experience of making relevant connections between lexical forms and meanings in his/her L1. Also, however great the distance in typological terms between the L1 and the L2, there will always be, as Lyons pointed out many years ago, some degree of cultural overlap between them, which means that at least some of the concepts which have been lexicalized during L1 acquisition will have the capacity to facilitate entry into the classification of reality offered by the L2:

> We cannot say in advance in what area of culture this will be, although anthropology, sociology and psychology may suggest some general features that may be assumed to be present in the 'Weltbild' of all societies . . . it is *via* this cultural overlap that entry is made into the semantic system of another language . . . We identify certain features of the cultures as common and learn the lexical items which are applied to them. It is such lexemes and expressions whose use we learn quickly and without difficulty. (Lyons, 1963: 40–41)

Naturalistic L2 learners appear to receive much the same kind of help – including at least some measure of ostensive definitional help – from their interlocutors as do infants acquiring their L1. Speech directed by native speakers at non-native speakers – termed foreigner talk or foreigner register – has been observed in a number of studies (see, e.g., Arthur *et al.*, 1980; Ferguson, 1975; Freed, 1981; Hatch *et al.*, 1978) to be slower, composed of shorter sentences, grammatically more correct, and lexically more restricted than speech between native speakers. One needs to treat with caution the notion that such adjustments are straightforward 'simplifications' (see, e.g., Maclaran & Singleton, 1984a, 1984b; Meisel, 1977), but there is little doubt that they are intended to facilitate comprehension, and it is plausible to suppose that, in the early stages of L2 learning at least, they assist the process of lexical development.

Mention has already been made of the fact that previous experience of dealing with meaning in the L1 can facilitate lexical development in the L2. There is a good deal more to be said about cross-linguistic influence – both its positive and its potentially negative aspects. Such issues are discussed at length elsewhere in the book (see Chapters 4 and 7), but it is worth pointing out immediately perhaps that the effects of cross-linguistic influence on L2 lexical development may be quite dramatic. For example, an English-speaking learner of French will quickly realize that most English words ending in *-ation*(/eɪʃən/) have French counterparts ending in *-ation*(/asjõ/) (cf., e.g., Kellerman, 1977, 1979). This realization, when it dawns, can have the effect of causing to be instantly 'acquired for French' the entire stock of English *-ation* words, which obviously represents a considerable developmental leap at relatively little cost. On the other hand, it will lead to a faulty internalization of those words which constitute exceptions to the general trend – *combinaison* rather than *combination, inclinaison* rather than *inclination* (where the mathematical sense is intended), *oraison* rather than *oration*, etc.

A further dimension of cross-linguistic influence in naturalistic L2 lexical acquisition concerns the role of reading. It may seem odd to mention literacy skills in the context of naturalistic acquisition. However, given knowledge of a language or languages which is/are related to the target language and which shares/share with it a common or similar writing system, it is perfectly possible to make sense of written text in an L2 without any prior formal instruction in reading that particular language. Thus, for example, anyone with a knowledge of German and English will readily be able to access the gist of the following snippets from a Dutch hotel brochure – without, indeed, any previous exposure to Dutch whatsoever, naturalistic or otherwise (cf. Singleton & Little, 1984b), never mind formal instruction in the reading of Dutch:

Prachtig gelegen … aan de rand van het vriendelijke dorpje Groesbeek.
sauna en watersport in de directe omgeving …
Meerdaagse 'all in' arrangementen …
drie sterren hotelaccommodatie …
groot zonneterras …
De gezellige kleine bar voor een aperitief …
(Brochure for the Hotel-Restaurant De Wolfsberg, Groesbeek. n.d.)

Moreover, anyone with a knowledge of German and English having these extracts in front of them will experience no difficulty in identifying the Dutch words for individual meanings such as 'edge' (*rand*, cf. German *Rand*), 'environs' (*omgeving* – cf. German

Umgebung), 'accommodation' (*accommodatie*, cf. English *accommodation*), etc. One can therefore take it that L2 lexical acquisition from written text is in principle possible even (given conditions such as those illustrated above) when literacy skills have not been formally learned in respect of the language in question. It is, of course, also possible in this fashion to acquire pronunciations or senses of L2 words which do not conform to the norms of the L2. Thus, for example, Dutch *prachtig* ('splendid') has a final /x/ rather than the final /ç/ of its German cognate *prächtig*, a distinction that might well fail to be made if *prachtig* were initially acquired from written sources.

L2 lexical acquisition in a formal instructional setting

Moving on now to the question of L2 lexical acquisition in a formal instructional setting, what has been said in relation to the role of previous acquisitional experience and of cross-linguistic influence in naturalistic L2 lexical acquisition also applies in the case of formal L2 lexical acquisition. Moreover, formal L2 lexical acquirers, like naturalistic L2 lexical acquirers and L1 lexical acquirers, also seem to benefit from input tuning on the part of teachers when the latter are using the target language – the phenomenon labelled 'teacher talk' in the literature (see, e.g., Krashen, 1981: 128 ff.; R. Ellis, 1985: 145–146). Studies by Henzl (1973, 1975) and by Gaies (1977, 1979) suggest that L2 speech addressed by teachers to pupils is likely to be characterized by more standard-like pronunciation, more frequent occurrence of lexical items with general meanings, less idiomaticity, and greater syntactic simplicity, relative to inter-native-speaker discourse.

Particularly to the fore in most L2 classrooms as compared with naturalistic interactions between native speakers and non-native speakers is the ostensive/quasi-ostensive dimension of input tuning. Traditional approaches to L2 teaching have, in their lexical dimension no less than in other spheres, been radically atomistic or 'synthetic' in the sense in which Wilkins applies the term:

> A synthetic language teaching strategy is one in which the different parts of language are taught separately and step-by-step so that acquisition is a process of gradual accumulation of the parts until the whole structure of the language has been built up. In planning the syllabus for such teaching the global language has been broken down probably into an inventory of grammatical structures and into a limited list of lexical items. (Wilkins, 1976: 2)

Thus, the time-honoured way of dealing with vocabulary in L2 teaching is to instruct one's pupils simply to learn off lists of L2 words together with their L1 translation equivalents. In such circumstances the problem facing the learner is hardly one of isolating individual units from the speech stream in order to process them. One notes that atomistic techniques for teaching L2 vocabulary are advocated even in very recent writing on language education. For example, Grenfell (1995) writes approvingly of 'oral presentation ... through flashcard-generated repetition' of a lexical item such as *dog* followed by a sequencing of questions offering diminishing degrees of 'scaffolding' – thus:

1 This is a dog yes or no?
2 This is a dog or a cat?
3 What is this? (Grenfell, 1995: 145)

Another atomistic technique much discussed in the literature is the so-called 'keyword' technique. Nation exemplifies this by reference to the case of an Indonesian learner of English trying to learn the English word *parrot*:

> First, the learner thinks of an Indonesian word that sounds like *parrot* or like a part of *parrot* – for example, the Indonesian word *parit*, which means 'a ditch'. This is the keyword. Second the learner imagines a parrot lying in a ditch! The more striking and unusual the image, the more effective it is. (Nation, 1990: 166)

Formal L2 instruction is likely, then, to give the learner a great deal more help in getting to grips with individual lexical items than the naturalistic acquisition environment. The atomistic techniques mentioned can no doubt be helpful in the early stages of an L2 programme in giving learners a foothold in the L2 lexical system. On the other hand, as every language teacher knows, and for reasons already discussed, mastery of individual forms and meanings in isolation is absolutely no guarantee of a capacity to recognize or appropriately deploy the words in question in context. Accordingly, an exclusive or even a very heavy reliance on atomistic techniques is unlikely to be a recipe for unqualified success.

Another point of difference between the formal and the informal setting is that the former is almost certain to foreground reading and writing to a far greater extent than the latter. There was, of course, a time when – in the wake of the audio-lingual 'revolution' (see, e.g., Singleton, 1982) – the teaching of reading and writing were long delayed in the L2 classroom. However, for various reasons, this policy has been largely abandoned, the present tendency being for classroom L2 learners to be introduced to written texts – often 'authentic' texts at that – from quite an early stage. The simple process of reading such texts for meaning undoubtedly promotes some measure of vocabulary acquisition, but, in addition, a whole range of exercises and tasks have been developed to exploit written text to the maximum in a vocabulary-learning perspective. These include not only diverse types of reading-comprehension exercises, but also tasks involving the extraction and grouping of words from the same lexical subsystem, the analysis of contextual meanings of words into denotational and/or connotational components, the gathering from texts of evidence about the collocational possibilities of particular words, and so on (for examples and discussion see, e.g., Little *et al.*, 1989). Such text-based approaches have the virtue of starting from language in real use and of dealing with lexical meaning as ultimately a function of context – in keeping with the way in which meaning is mediated in normal natural-language communication.

The one great disadvantage attending vocabulary learning in a formal L2 classroom is that, as compared with all the other sets of circumstances outlined above, it provides such a tiny amount of input for the learner to work on. There are, admittedly, circumstances where L2 formal instruction is embedded in a situation of naturalistic exposure (typically in a country where the L2 is in everyday use in the community at large), and there are also instances of somewhat larger amounts of input being provided in class via immersion programmes. However, where the L2 course is the only source of input, the gap in input amounts is massive; I have estimated elsewhere (Singleton, 1989: 236) that more than eighteen years of classroom L2 exposure would be needed to supply the same amount of L2 input as just one year of naturalistic exposure. The case of L1 formal instruction is different, of course, in that it *typically* takes place against a background of naturalistic exposure in the community and/or in the home.

L1 lexical development: from first words to semantic hierarchies

We turn now to a more detailed exploration of L1 lexical development. Given that detailed case studies of child language acquisition go back at least as far as the end of the eighteenth century (e.g., Tiedemann, 1787) and have been undertaken by such eminences as Charles Darwin (1877) and Hippolyte Taine (1877), it is hardly surprising that we know so much about early lexical development. What *is* surprising is that we do not know more, and that some of the patently fundamental questions about the emergence of the lexicon have still not been satisfactorily answered. Some of these questions will be touched on in the following exploration of research relating to (1) the relationship between the first meaningful words produced by the child around the age of twelve months and everything that precedes this milestone and (2) lexical development during the period following the onset of word production.

The relationship between the first words and what precedes them

Phenomena that have been discussed in this connection and which warrant examination in the present context are speech-sound discrimination in infants, concept development before the onset of word production, and the characteristics of late babbling.

Speech-sound discrimination in infants

With regard to speech-sound discrimination, the results of some widely cited experiments conducted by Eimas *et al.* (1971) appear to show that newborn infants are sensitive to critical voice onset time (VOT) differences. VOT refers to the point at which the vocal cords begin to vibrate relative to the release of a closure effected to produce a voiced plosive such as [b] or a voiceless unaspirated plosive such as [p] or a voiceless aspirated plosive such as [pʰ]:

> In a fully voiced plosive, for example, the vocal cords vibrate throughout; in a voiceless unaspirated plosive, there is a delay before the voicing starts; in a voiceless aspirated plosive, the delay is much longer, depending on the amount of aspiration. (Crystal, 1980: 378)

In Eimas *et al.*'s experiments, sensitivity was investigated via a sucking habituation/dishabituation technique. When the same sound was played continually to an infant sucking on a 'blind nipple' his/her rate of sucking gradually decreased. If then an adjustment to the sound stimulus triggered a renewed increase in the rate of sucking, this was taken to indicate that the change had been perceived and the habituation affect thus disrupted. Eimas *et al.* found that infants of just one month in age showed evidence of discriminating between synthetically produced sounds which in terms of their VOT values would be categorized as voiced and voiceless plosives respectively, and that these same infants failed to distinguish between sounds which diverged by the same VOT difference but whose differences failed to cross the voiced/voiceless boundary.

Results such as these (see Eimas, 1985, for an overview of studies yielding similar findings) could be interpreted as indicating the presence of a specialized linguistic mechanism – part of an innate, species-particular language faculty (see, e.g., Martohardjono & Flynn, 1995). On this view, lexical development would be assisted from the very beginning by a phonetic endowment specifically tailored to the demands of the task of acquiring human language. Unfortunately for this position, the capacity to perceive categorical distinctions of the kind described above is not peculiar to humans. It has been shown, for example, that chinchillas (Kuhl & Miller, 1975, 1978), rhesus monkeys (Morse & Snowdon, 1975) and macaque monkeys (Kuhl & Padden, 1982, 1983) also manifest categorical discrimination in relation to the voiced/voiceless opposition.

Another dimension of the categorical perception issue is the notion that 'early perceptual abilities will be refined and altered by experience with a particular language' (Goodluck, 1991: 17) within the first few months of exposure to input from a particular language. A number of studies looking at infants during this very early period have produced results which have been interpreted along precisely these lines:

> Typically, . . . infants from two linguistic communities were presented with the task of discriminating two pairs of contrasts: a contrast phonemic to one language and a contrast phonemic to the other language (e.g., Eilers *et al.*, 1979; Lasky *et al.*, 1975; Streeter, 1976). If infants discriminated the contrast used phonemically by speakers of the language to be learned, and infants from the other language group – where the contrast was not used phonemically – did not show evidence of discrimination, the difference was attributed to the former group's previous exposure to the particular contrast in question. (MacKain, 1988: 54)

MacKain (e.g., 1982, 1988) questions the logical validity of this interpretation. She argues that language-particular phonemic contrasts are discriminated perceptually only from the point at which sound–meaning correspondences begin to be fully recognized around the end of the first year, and she cites in support of this view a longitudinal study by Werker & Tees (1984) of six infants' discrimination of two non-native contrasts:

> Infants were tested when they were about 8, 10, and 12 months of age. The results were striking; while all six of the infants tested discriminated both nonnative contrasts at 8 and 10 months of age, none of the six infants discriminated either nonnative contrast by 12 months of age. (MacKain, 1988: 55)

In short, the picture is not a clear one. It is probably legitimate to conclude with, for example, Moreau & Richelle (1981: 48) that the general discriminatory capacity of neonates, while unlikely to represent a specifically linguistic mechanism, nevertheless constitutes an ability which language-particular development exploits. However, we also have to concur with Goodluck (1991: 18), McShane (1991: 84) and others that the development of language-particular perceptual boundaries is not something about which it is possible to come to very firm conclusions at the present time. If, on the other hand, it in the end turns out that the onset of the discrimination of language-particular phonemic contrasts coincides, as MacKain suggests, with the beginnings of meaningful lexical development, this will surely say something about the pivotal role of lexical development within the broader process of language development.

Concept development prior to the onset of word production

With regard to concept development in the child before he/she starts producing words, the state of the debate is not dissimilar to that pertaining to the issue of categorical perception. That is to say, there is no real doubt about the existence of concepts in the child's mind before productive language makes its appearance, but it is less easy to answer satisfactorily the question of where such concepts come from and that of precisely how early conceptualization relates to later lexical development. Some powerful evidence in favour of the existence of prelinguistic concepts comes from experiments using habituation/dishabituation techniques. For example, an experiment conducted by Bomba & Siqueland (1983) built on the well-known fact that infants who have been familiarized with a particular visual stimulus and who are then offered a choice between the familiar stimulus and a new stimulus will usually look longer at the novel stimulus. Bomba & Siqueland familiarized 3–4–month-old infants with distorted versions of a simple geometrical shape (square, triangle or diamond, and then presented them with an undistorted version of the relevant shape together with an undistorted version of a shape that had not previously been shown. The result of this experiment was that the infants preferred to look at the novel shape. From this Bomba & Siqueland conclude that their subjects had successfully constructed prototypical concepts of the shapes to which they had been exposed despite the fact that the instances of the shape of which they had experience were imperfect (see also, e.g., Younger & Cohen, 1983).

Further evidence of conceptualization prior to word production is provided by the work of Bruner and his colleagues. For example,

Scaife & Bruner (1975) show that by around 8–9 months infants reliably follow their caregiver's line of regard, a phenomenon which Scaife & Bruner interpret as 'shared reference', that is to say, purposive behaviour which has as its goal the seeking out of the referent of the caregiver's gaze. In this connection, Bruner (1980) cites Butterworth's (1979) observation that if the caregiver was looking at a blank space rather than a particular object, the infant turned back to check the mother's face. Such behaviour can be taken to indicate not only some understanding on the infant's part of the referentiality of attention but also a general conception of the range of likely referents for the caregiver's gaze. Intentionality of communication is also suggested by Butterworth's findings. This last inference is supported by the use of pointing gestures by children in the months before they utter their first word (see, e.g., Bates *et al.*, 1975; Bruner, 1975).

As we saw in the first part of this chapter, it has been suggested by some that concepts are innate. Campbell (1986) considers two possibilities in this regard. First, he examines the notion that an innate primitive concept framework might be quite fulsome:

> Fodor's notion is that it must indeed be very rich – in which case there is an obvious objection, namely that an ontogenetic mystery has been dispelled by postulating a phylogenetic one! (Campbell, 1986: 44)

Second, he looks at the idea that an innate conceptual framework might be comprised of a rather small set of rather general concepts. He cites (*ibid.*) against this proposition evidence from R. Brown (1958a), K. Nelson (1973a) and Ninio & Bruner (1978) that the first lexicalized concepts are in fact 'of *moderate* generality' and that the earliest words denote 'objects (attribute-clusters) rather than properties':

> So evidence from early lexical development suggests that the earliest kind [of] concepts mastered define functionally significant categories of object rather than the elementary universal attributes needed to 'bootstrap' concept development. (Campbell, *ibid.*)

Neither of these objections, of course, constitutes a final argument against the innateness of concepts, but both demonstrate that this solution is not an unproblematic one. Nor can it be plausibly claimed that the presence of concepts in the minds of non-language-using infants sets human beings apart from other species. From the cognitive and representational capacities of the higher apes (see, for instance, Premack & Premack, 1983; Savage-Rumbaugh & Lewin, 1994), down to the 'dance' performed by the humble honey bee to indicate the location and likely yield of food sources (see, e.g., Von

Frisch, 1967), nature everywhere bears testimony to the fact that conceptualization is not uniquely human, which is no doubt why Chomskyans tend to focus more on stimulus independence, syntactic principles, neurological architecture and ease of acquisition than on the conceptual dimension when they put the case for the species specificity of language (see., e.g., Chomsky, 1979a: 449ff.; 1980a: 239–240; N. Smith & Wilson, 1979: 30–31).

There are other possible approaches to what is inborn as far as concepts are concerned. Piaget, for example, sees concepts as the result of, on the one hand, the nature of the biological 'hardware' with which the infant comes equipped into the world (e.g., the particular characteristics of the human sensory system), and on the other the operation of an innate mode of intellectual functioning 'a specific manner in which we transact business with the environment' (Flavell, 1963: 43; see, e.g., Piaget, 1952, 1979; Piaget & Inhelder, 1969). The intellectual functioning in question is conceived of as having two main characteristics: (1) adaptation to the environment, assimilating it to the organism on the one hand and accommodating the system to what it is trying to assimilate on the other, and (2) organization, interrelating, co-ordinating and structuring the procedures involved in adaptation. For Piaget it is through the interaction between this basic mode of intellectual functioning and the environment that all cognitive structures are created. The first phase of this interaction, according to Piaget, is the 'sensori-motor stage', when the child establishes relations between sensory activity and motor actions:

> Emerging concepts about objects are closely linked to the child's growing understanding of space, spatial relations and the notion of objects and people being located in a common space. By exploring the world in terms of actions and their effects, young children come to realize that objects can be acted upon in different ways and that actions often result in objects changing their location . . . (J. Harris, 1990: 82)

There is a good deal of intuitive appeal about Piaget's account. However, its status as an object of empirical investigation is unclear, a widespread criticism of Piaget's entire theoretical edifice being that it is 'so vague as to be virtually unfalsifiable' (Boden, 1979: 153).

Not dissimilar to Piaget's idea of an innate intellectual *modus operandi* is the notion that the child brings to the task of concept development 'innate similarity standards' (Quine, 1975: 69ff.), in other words a capacity to group objects together on the basis of properties shared with each other and/or with some prototypical member of the group. The above-cited evidence from Bomba &

Siqueland's (1983) experiment would seem to favour this view, as would evidence from a variety of experiments showing that children from 9 months onwards are quite adept at sorting tasks involving different kinds of object – the consistent finding from such studies being that children sequentially touch objects in one category after another (K. Nelson, 1973b; Ricciuti, 1965; Starkey, 1981; Sugarman, 1981). On the other hand, young children seem not to be very successful at using a single elementary fixed attribute as a basis for sorting or matching (see, e.g., Inhelder & Piaget, 1964; Kemler & Smith, 1979; Vygotsky, 1962).

Yet another possibility regarding the role of innate factors in concept development is that there may be 'some special features of human action and human attention' (Bruner, 1975: 2) which are inborn and which facilitate various kinds of communicative decoding. According to Bruner, thanks to this capacity to decode communicative behaviour, the child acquires a number of primitive categories – 'ACTIONS as carried out by AGENTS and having EFFECTS of particular KINDS in particular PLACES' (*ibid.*: 5) – categories which 'case grammarians' such as Fillmore (e.g., 1968) have referred to as 'deep case notions' and which in recent Chomskyan linguistics have been referred to as theta roles (see, e.g., Cook & Newson, 1996: 49ff., 159ff.):

> the infant first learns pre-linguistically to make the conceptual distinctions embodied in case grammar and, having mastered privileges of occurrence in action sequences in which these distinctions are present, begins to insert non-standard signals that mark the distinctions. (Bruner, 1975: 6)

This is an interesting and plausible idea, but it remains speculative. It is worth noting that the line taken by Fillmore in his earliest pronouncements on 'case grammar' was that the 'deep cases' *themselves* were universal, innate concepts, and that for Chomskyans too theta theory is part of innate Universal Grammar.

With regard to the relationship between early concept development and later vocabulary development, according to Piaget, the specialized developments in assimilation that occur during the sensorimotor stage result in the acquisition of the 'symbolic function'. One aspect of accommodation identified by Piaget is imitation – the replication by the child of an external phenomenon. Piaget sees this imitative aspect of accommodation as supplying the infant with his/her first signifiers capable of representing absent significates. Eventually, says Piaget, the child develops the capacity to create internal as well as overt representations, in other words to evoke mentally imitations – i.e., images – that were previously made through movement or gesture. Representations are initially more or less private, non-codified signifiers ('symbols', in Piaget's terminology) which bear some similarity to their significates, but subsequently the child begins to deploy 'signs' whose meanings are socially shared but in an entirely arbitrary relationship with the relevant forms. Piagetians have attempted to justify their postulation of a continuity between general cognitive development and language development by reference to a variety of research findings which, however, tend to be in the nature of demonstrations of broad parallelisms rather than detailed diachronic correlations. Inhelder, for example, cites (1979: 203) a correspondence between early difficulties with the passive and difficulties with ordering operations generally, both sets of difficulties being resolved around age seven. She also refers to the child's initial attribution of a purely aspectual function to verbal tense markers:

> Toute la question est de savoir pourquoi l'enfant opte d'abord pour la signification aspectuelle. D'une façon générale, au cours du développement cognitif, il centre, comme on le sait, son attention initiale sur les états et les résultats d'actions avant de pouvoir rendre compte de leurs transformations. De nombreuses recherches concordantes nous portent à croire que les lois de la raison tendraient à expliquer en partie l'évolution des marques de nature sémantique. (Inhelder, 1979: 203–204)

> (The whole question is to know why the child first chooses aspectual meaning. In general during the period of cognitive development he centers his initial attention, as we know, on the conditions and results of actions before he can account for their transformations. Many researchers concur in leading us to believe that the laws of reason would tend to explain in part the evolution of the markers of a semantic nature.) (Piattelli-Palmarini, 1980: 136)

R. Brown's (1973) exploration of the cognitive underpinnings of the appearance of functors in the speech of children acquiring English as a first language also relies on the positing of what the child can be expected to have conceptualized at particular points and the observed order of acquisition. He notes that in the earliest stages just two prepositions were used by his subjects with sufficient frequency for the data to be meaningfully analysable. The prepositions in question are *in* and *on*, which are exponents of relatively simple topological notions. The following is Cromer's summary of the essentials of the evidence and argument in this connection:

> The nouns used with *in* were objects that could contain other objects, i.e. they were objects having cavities or containing internal spaces, such as bag, box, briefcase. The nouns used with *on* were all objects which had flat surfaces which could support other objects, such as floor, shelf and table. . . .

> Although there is not a careful study of the spatial relations children use at their first stages in speech, it is clear that they are able to express the spatial concepts encoded by *in* and *on* before they acquire any prepositions. In particular situational contexts, phrases like 'put box' can be reliably interpreted by adult observers as encoding *in*; and 'pot stove' uttered while pointing to a pot on the stove will be interpreted as encoding *on*. (Cromer, 1991: 25)

Bruner's approach to this problem is somewhat different. He and those who follow him claim that joint attention between caregiver and child constitutes the matrix out of which both concept development and, subsequently, naming are born (see, e.g., Bruner, 1975, 1974–75, 1983; Ninio & Bruner, 1978). Evidence of the prevalence of joint attention in caregiver–child interaction – from a study conducted by M. Harris *et al.* (1983) – was cited in the previous section. A later study conducted by M. Harris and her colleagues (M. Harris *et al.*, 1986) lends further weight to the joint-attention perspective. In this study the early language experience of three relatively slow language developers was compared with that of children developing at a normal rate. It emerged that, as compared with the mothers of the normal developers, the mothers of the slower developers were more likely to initiate new discourse episodes without an accompanying related action and less likely to make reference in their speech to objects of the child's current focus of attention.

As we saw earlier, 'ostension' may play a role in turning joint attention to good effect in terms of giving pre-established concepts linguistic expression. On the other hand, as we also saw, 'ostensive definition' is not the straightforward process that it is often imagined to be. In any case, such 'special teaching' is almost certainly less important than the mapping from concept to form occasioned by meaningful interaction in situations that the child has already charted in conceptual terms – speculatively sketched by K. Nelson (1981) as follows:

> the child may have a primitive concept of car already, one involving his experiences with the family car, toy cars, cars seen on the street. At some point and for as yet unfathomable reasons, he may hear his father say, Do you want to go in the car?, and conclude that 'car' is the word that refers to his concept, even though he has not been taught the word specifically. (K. Nelson, 1981: 150)

Nelson goes on to refer to the argument that the numbers of words acquired in early to middle childhood (about 20 per day) simply could *not* be acquired if 'special teaching' were required in each instance (*ibid.*).

It may be worth adding as a coda to the foregoing discussion of various kinds of evidence relating to concepts and lexical development that, whilst such discussion typically focuses exclusively on the productive aspect of lexical development, there is a fair amount of evidence that children begin to recognize and respond to some of the words they hear well before the onset of word production. Thus, for example, Griffiths (1986: 284) cites Leopold's (1939, 1947) report of his daughter Hildegard turning her head in response to her name during her seventh month and Valentine's (1942) report of a child of $5\frac{1}{2}$ months evincing 'faint signs of recognition' of his name *Baba* and producing a smile every time he heard the word one month later. More recent studies (Gunzi, unpublished; M. Harris *et al.*, 1991) are cited by M. Harris (1992). According to her, these studies show that 'some children can respond appropriately to words or phrases, independently of their wider non-verbal context, when they are as young as 7 months' (M. Harris, 1992: 69). If it is the case that words are beginning to be recognized this early as in some sense significant, then we may wish to speculate that language could have some role in shaping concept development rather sooner than is popularly assumed, although the notion that language development builds on concepts that (somehow or other) are already available to the child is not fundamentally challenged thereby.

To summarize, there seems to be enough evidence around to make a persuasive case for what Cromer calls the 'weak form' of the 'cognitive hypothesis':

> we are able to understand and productively to use particular linguistic structures only when our cognitive abilities enable us to do so. Our cognitive abilities at different stages of development make certain meanings *available* for expression. (Cromer, 1991: 54)

Whether there are, in addition, as Vygotsky (e.g., 1962) and later Chomsky (e.g., 1979b, 1986) have claimed, components of language development in general and the development of the lexicon in particular which arise from mechanisms which are specific to the linguistic domain remains an open question.

The characteristics of late babbling

Babbling is the second of the four early developmental milestones which are most consistently referred to in the child-language literature. These are: (1) cooing, which begins between the ages of one and four months and which is characterized by vocalizations with a vowel-like quality, (2) babbling, which has its onset between four and eight months and which is characterized by combinations of vowel-like and consonant-like sounds (including reduplications such as *baba*, *mama*), (3) the one-word utterance stage, commencing around the end of the first year, when the child begins to produce meaningful one-word utterances, and (4) the two-word utterance stage, starting between eighteen and twenty-four months, when the child begins to put words together within the same tone group (for further discussion see, e.g., Singleton, 1989: 9ff.). The babbling stage is thus that which immediately precedes the first productive evidence of what is sometimes called 'true speech' in the shape of meaningful one-word utterances. A question that fairly obviously arises, therefore, is whether the babbling stage and the one-word utterance stage are continuous with each other or entirely separate developments.

Those who espouse a nativist view of language acquisition tend to cast rather a cold eye on the notion that early vocalizations may be continuous with 'true speech'. Thus, for example, Goodluck disparages the babbling shift (otherwise known as babbling drift) idea as follows:

> An early hypothesis was that there was a shift during babbling towards the sounds of the language to which the child was exposed (R. Brown, 1958b). There now seems little to support this idea. (Goodluck, 1991: 21)

The roots of the nativist approach to the babbling-drift question lie in Chomsky's attack on the behaviourist perspective on language acquisition (see, e.g., Chomsky, 1959), which conceived of language acquisition as a process whereby unconditioned vocalizations were gradually shaped into communicative 'verbal behaviour' through the 'selective reinforcement' of responses that were appropriate to particular stimuli (see, e.g., Skinner, 1957).

Against babbling drift Goodluck cites evidence (Locke, 1983: 13ff.) that adults 'do not find it easier to identify the language background of older babblers than younger babblers' (Goodluck, 1991: 21). She fails to mention a whole range of other evidence which runs in a contrary direction. First, there is the experimental evidence (Rheingold *et al.*, 1959; Todd *et al.*, 1968; Weisberg, 1963), noted by D. Stern *et al.* (1975) that 'infant vocalizations can be conditioned, using the human voice or other social stimuli as reinforcers'. One can also refer in this connection to Bateson's (1975) finding that even very early in the babbling phase an alternating pattern of vocalization between child and caregiver is often created or shaped by the latter. We do not need to accept a full-blown behaviourist interpretation of such evidence in order to see it as indicating that babbling can be changed by the influence of ambient stimuli.

Second, there is the evidence that while there are certainly (physiologically and possibly neurologically triggered) discontinuities in the process of phonological development, there is absolutely no question of any sharp break in developmental progression. Stark (1986), discussing segmental development, puts it this way:

> Vocal behaviours that are characteristic of one stage ... may persist into succeeding stages and new landmark behaviours may have their antecedents in preceding stages. Thus discontinuities, though the most salient aspect of vocal development, do not describe that development completely. (Stark, 1986: 172)

Crystal (1986) has similar things to say about prosodic development; he identifies five stages in this development, but it is perfectly clear from his account that he sees these different stages as in important ways continuous with each other.

Third, there is the evidence that the vocalizations of children in the later babbling phase are beginning to shift in the direction of the phonology of the language of their environment. Thus, Weir (1966), on studying children in the babbling phase from American, Arab, Chinese and Russian backgrounds, discovered that, from about age six months, the intonational variation produced by the Chinese children (Chinese being a language in which tone is phonemic) was markedly greater than that produced by the other groups (the background languages of which do not deploy intonation phonemically). Similarly, De Boysson-Bardies *et al.* (1984) found that their adult subjects were able to distinguish French, Arab and Chinese children of eight months on the basis of the intonation of their babbles (see also Hallé *et al.*, 1991; Whalen *et al.*, 1991).

It is interesting that the more persuasive evidence concerning cross-linguistically related phonological variation in the period prior to the onset of word production comes from studies of prosody. For evidence of such variation at the segmental level we have to go to studies of children in their second year and who have thus passed the one-word utterance milestone. For example, Moreau & Richelle (1981: 50) cite in this connection a study by De Boysson-Bardies *et al.* (1981) of a child between 1;6 and 1;8 being raised in a Francophone environment in which they found that nasal vowels were more frequent in the speech of their subject than in the speech of children of the same age range with an Anglophone background – as reported by Oller *et al.* (1976). One possibility is that, as Locke (1988: 15ff.) suggests apropos of other issues, properties that are amenable to holistic processing – intonation, rhythm, etc. – are acquired earlier than properties that require analysis, for reasons

having to do with the maturation of the brain. Locke cites a wide range of studies showing that infants are aware of and can produce prosodic variation from a very early age (Eilers, *et al.*, 1984; Kuhl & Miller, 1982; Leopold, 1947; Morse, 1972; Spring & Dale, 1977; Tuacharoen, 1979), and he also refers to evidence that the right hemisphere operates as 'a holistic, parallel, Gestalt processor' (Moscovitch, 1977: 198), that it develops in advance of the left hemisphere (Geschwind & Galaburda, 1985), and that it plays a greater role in children's processing of language than in adults' (Witelson, 1977). With regard to sound segments, the signs are that the dominant determinants of segmental sound patterns right into the phase of early lexical acquisition are 'low-level properties of the speech-production system' (B. Smith, 1988: 99) and, as we have seen, that phonemic contrasts may be discriminated perceptually only from the beginning of the one-word utterance stage (MacKain, 1988). It could well be that, in terms of formal development, babbling drift affects only prosody during the period prior to word production, that segmental patterns begin to undergo systemic change only after the onset of word production, and that, even then, the earliest lexical items produced are auditory–vocal shapes acquired formulaically via the workings of the right hemisphere. This latter idea is proposed by Locke, who expresses the view that 'the transition ... to phonemic codes occurs, typically, only after the child has achieved a working vocabulary approaching or exceeding 50 words' (Locke, 1988: 17).

The notion of a formal continuity between babbling and 'true speech' is broadly supported by the foregoing, even if one has to accept that the shift towards the phonology of the background language specifically at segmental level happens only after the one-word stage has been entered. The continuity hypothesis receives further support from evidence which brings the semantico-pragmatic dimension into the picture. Such evidence has been variously interpreted, but it is difficult not to see it as in general favouring a gradualist model of development towards the referential use of speech.

From an early stage, particular types of babbling may be associated with particular activities. Stark calls this a 'recognitory' function:

> It is ... possible that the vocal behaviours of babbling have a higher level 'recognitory' function with respect to objects towards which the infant's gaze is directed. In normal infants the alternating opening/closing movements of tongue and jaw in reduplicated babbling may be strongly associated with visual inspection and/or manipulation and mouthing of objects (Stark, 1980), activities with which infants in these vocal developmental periods are intensely preoccupied. (Stark, 1986: 170)

Babbling is also put at the service of the expression of wants and of causing them to be met. Dromi (1987) notes the general acceptance of the proposition that infants are involved in effective intentional communication long before they begin to talk (see also Bretherton, 1988: 226ff.). (As we have already seen, such communication may be mediated by an act as simple as the turning of the head.) Citing evidence from the work of Bates *et al.* (1979) and of Dore (1974, 1978), Dromi goes on to say that from a particular point onwards speech sounds are brought into play:

> During the last months of the pre-linguistic period, infants utilize both gesture and speech sounds to gain adults' attention and/or to carry out basic pragmatic acts such as imperatives, declaratives and volitions . . . (Dromi, 1987: 14)

This has been a recurrent theme in the literature for decades. Thus, Vihman & Miller (1988) quote M. M. Lewis's (1936) citation of Lorimer's (1928) observation that children use their own 'bits of babble' for communicative purposes. Examples to be found in the literature of the phenomenon concerned include a signal of wanting something out of reach [e e e] reported by Lewis (1936), a vehement protest sequence ([nə nə nə nə nə]) reported by Bloom (1973: 90), a 'general want expresser' ([ə:] or [ə̃:]) reported by A. Carter (1974: 86, 1979: 75–76), and an indicator of pleasure at seeing something come into view [i i i] reported by Moreau & Richelle (1981: 54).

When adult-like forms begin to be used, they also seem to have – in the main – situational, general pragmatic rather than labelling functions. Such forms seem often to start as imitations in specific contexts. For example, Vihman & Miller (1988: 158) report their subject Molly imitating her mother saying 'Uh oh, where'd it go?' as she dropped rings into a jar; later in the same session Molly was observed spontaneously to utter a version of *uh-oh* ([ʔaʔaʔo]) when she dropped a comb, and to perform a version of *where'd it go* ([hʌtikʌ]) when her mother dropped a brush and said 'Uh-oh'. Particular forms then appear to become attached in a quasi-ritual manner to particular actions or action sequences. An oft-cited example of this is Barrett's (1983, 1986) description of his twelve-month-old subject Adam's use of the utterance *dut* ('duck'), which he produced excitedly as he knocked a toy duck off the edge of the bath but which he never said when the duck was actually floating in the water. As Aitchison (1994) comments, *dut* for Adam appeared to be a 'ritualized accompaniment to a whole scenario, and could perhaps be best translated as "Whoopee" or "Here goes"' (Aitchison, 1994: 171). Other similar instances that crop up in the literature are the use of the word *hello* only in the context of holding a telephone receiver (M. Harris *et al.*, 1991) and the use of the word *bye* only in the context of replacing a telephone receiver (Bates *et al.*, 1979).

It is worth qualifying the above with the statement that not *all* early uses of adult-like forms are context-bound, although these latter do seem to dominate the scene at this stage. Thus, M. Harris (1992: 77ff.), reporting a study of the ten words of each of four children, notes that of the total of 40 words, 22 were expressions that were bound to one particular context in the sense set out in the previous paragraph (e.g., *choo-choo* accompanying the activity of pushing a toy train along the floor). Of the rest, 4 were non-nominals (e.g., *more*) occurring in two or more contexts that to some extent resembled each other (in the case of *more*, for example, contexts where the child was reaching out for something), and 14 were nominals that referred context-flexibly to a particular object or class of objects (e.g. *shoes* uttered by the child while looking at a picture of shoes, pointing at his/her own shoes or holding the shoes of a doll).

As for the relationship between the child's earliest pragmatic, situation-bound signifiers and later lexical development, for some commentators (e.g., Dore, 1978; Dore *et al.*, 1976; Lock, 1980; McShane, 1979, 1980, 1991: 143ff.; K. Nelson, 1973b), the transition from context-determined communicatively deployed babble and early versions of adult lexis to genuine word production is abrupt, triggered by a sudden 'naming insight'. Thus McShane suggests (1991: 146) 'that a major representational change occurs that initially leads to the development of naming and subsequently to the beginnings of two-word utterances', and he argues 'that change can be characterized as an insight'. For others (e.g., Barrett, 1986; Bates *et al.*, 1979; A. Carter, 1978a, 1978b, 1979), referential meaning develops gradually through the repeated recurrence of the same items in different contexts, and there is no single moment when performative structures become propositional (cf. Bates *et al.*, 1975). Dromi (1987: 15) cites in this connection a study by Gillis & DeSchutter (1984) of a Dutch-acquiring subject who extended the transitional period from pre-verbal communication to early speech 'for a number of months during which he acquired no new words but rather used a small number of old words in different repeated contexts'. Gillis & DeSchutter's hypothesis is that this 'plateau' stage is a period during which the child develops conceptual skills that are the indispensable underpinning for the referential use of words. Bretherton (1988), in similar vein, refers to a study by Volterra *et al.* (1979) which investigated the early use of words in 25 American and Italian children aged 9–12 months and which seemed to indicate developmental progression rather than sudden turning points:

> For example, one child in the study merely imitated the *mama* sound at 9 months, but said *mama* to make requests when she saw her mother at 10 months. By 12 months she used *mama* when looking for her mother or any other person. (Bretherton, 1988: 232)

A possible compromise solution between the sudden-insight view and the continuity view would be that in the first few words acquired by the child the referential dimension emerges gradually, but that once the trick is learned, as it were, the process prior to referentiality is passed through increasingly rapidly and finally becomes superfluous. In any case, we should be under no illusions about the difficulty of settling this matter – not least because of the problems researchers face in attempting to sort out what are words and what are not in the late babbling stage. The forms taken by a child's first lexical adventures are often extremely idiosyncratic and unstable. Indeed, even well into the 'true speech' phase, radically different versions of words can be produced within a few seconds of each other. For example, Moreau & Richelle (1981) report the following of a child (Alain) aged 2;2:

> à quelques secondes d'intervalle, Alain, parlant d'une framboise, produit les séquences /ʒôbwaz/, /ʃâbwas/, /lôbrwazœ/ et /ʒâbwazœ/. (Moreau & Richelle, 1981: 55)

> (speaking about a raspberry [French *framboise*], Alain produced the following sequences within a few seconds of each other: /ʒôbwaz/, /ʃâbwas/, /lôbrwazœ/ and /ʒâbwazœ/.)

There is also the fact, noted by Vihman & Miller (1988: 159ff.) that imitated adult-like forms are frequently embedded in 'jargon' (i.e., 'long strings of variegated babble which are sentencelike in their intonation patterns' (Vihman & Miller, 1988: 159)). One might almost speak in this connection of adult forms being recycled as babble. Conversely, as we have seen, babble sequences are regularly recycled as primitive signifiers. More complicatedly still, there are cases of sequences of babble (*mama* is one such) which – across languages and cultures – have been recycled by caregivers as 'baby talk' and are fed back to the child as meaningful words, which the child then may imitate, incorporate into 'jargon', etc. and eventually deploy communicatively. Defining what counts as a lexical (or pre-lexical) item amidst this tangle is no easy matter, and this in turn means that tracing the development from pre-verbal situation-bound utterances to referential words is no easy matter either.

Lexical development following the onset of word production

M. Harris (1992: 69ff.), following a number of other researchers (e.g., Barrett, 1986; K. Nelson, 1988; K. Nelson & Lucariello, 1985), identifies three stages of early lexical development: (1) a phase during which the child is endeavouring to discover what words are, how they can be used to refer, and what category or categories of entities particular words can be applied to; (2) a 'vocabulary explosion' phase – after about 30 or more words have been learned – characterized by a very marked increase in the rate of lexical development; (3) a phase beginning around age 3–4 which is marked by the revision, reorganization and consolidation of lexical knowledge.

Phase 1

Perhaps the first comment that needs to be made about the phase of lexical development up to the point where about 30 words have been acquired is that early progress tends to be rather sluggish. M. Harris (1992: 70 – referring to M. Harris *et al.*, 1988, and to M. Harris *et al.*, 1991) notes that 'up to 5–6 months may elapse between the production of the first word and the production of the tenth'. The slowness of vocabulary expansion in this period is also well illustrated by findings from some of the 'classic' studies of lexical development such as those cited below.

M. Smith's (1926) investigation of vocabulary size in young children of different ages yielded the following averages:

at 10 months – 1 word	(N = 17)
at 12 months – 3 words	(N = 52)
at 15 months – 19 words	(N = 19)
at 18 months – 22 words	(N = 14)

Castner's (1940) survey of a sample of 40 18-month-olds discovered the following distribution of vocabulary sizes:

1–5 words	22%
6–10 words	30%
11–15 words	27%
16–20 words	10%
21–25 words	0%
26–30 words	3%
'Innumerable'	8%

The relatively slow rate of progress indicated by such findings is undoubtedly linked to the nature of the challenge of working out – with or without the assistance of relevant innate mechanisms – how to communicate with words, of linking particular forms in the adult input to particular communicative possibilities and of replicating the forms in question (see discussion in the previous subsection and in the earlier section on the 'lexical challenge'; see also K. Nelson, 1988).

Of interest also in the above figures from Castner's study is what they reveal about variation in rate of progress from child to child. To quote Harris again:

> Some children produce very few words before the age of 18 months; others begin to use words when they are under 1 year of age and can produce 30 different words by the time they are 15 months old. (M. Harris, 1992: 70)

M. Harris (*ibid.*) dates such variation back to the very outset of children's coming to grips with lexis, citing evidence of variability in the time-lag between initial indications of word comprehension and the first beginnings of word production, and of variability in the numbers of words that are understood by individual children before they begin to produce words (Bates *et al.*, 1988; M. Harris *et al.*, 1991; Gunzi, unpublished).

A factor that has been identified as relevant to variation in somewhat later vocabulary development is variation from child to child in the degree of efficiency of phonological working memory in creating accurate memory codes for lexical forms encountered. For example, S. Gathercole & Baddeley (1989) found, with reference to the L1 vocabulary development of young children, that a phonological memory score based on a pseudoword repetition test correlated significantly with a vocabulary score at age 4 and with subsequent vocabulary acquisition. Similarly, the findings of another S. Gathercole & Baddeley study (1990) suggest that phonological short-term memory is a greater factor than either non-verbal intelligence or age in certain L1 language disorders in children. It seems reasonable to assume that phonological memory variation is also a contributory factor in relation to individual differences in respect of the very early stages of lexical acquisition. Another factor is presumably variation in the amount and quality of input that children receive. This notion is supported by the results of a study reported in M. Harris (1992: 77ff.) of the first ten words of four first-born children and of the input conditions which underpinned the acquisition of the items concerned. The results in question favour 'the view that the early stage of lexical development is firmly rooted in the child's experience of hearing particular words frequently being used in the same contexts'. They also suggest that 'words that are salient to the child in this early stage are those in which the context of use actively involves the child' (M. Harris, 1992: 92; see also the above discussion of the Brunerian approach to pre-verbal concept development).

Turning now to how the child applies his/her first words, we can note that four (not incompatible) kinds of statement relative to early word meanings are to be found in the literature – (1) such meanings are vague and fluid, (2) they are over-extended relative to the meanings of the words in question as used by adults, and (3) that they are under-extended relative to the meanings of the words in question as used by adults (4) that they reflect a 'basic' level of categorization. Concerning (1), we can cite Guillaume's observations on his son's use of a form *blablab*:

> «*blablab*» ... désigne l'acte de faire vibrer les lèvres avec le doigt, puis la bouche, surtout celle d'un portrait d'enfant, puis tout portrait, tout dessin, les cartes illustrées ... toute feuille manuscrite ou imprimé, un journal, un livre, mais exprime aussi l'acte de «lire» ou le désir de lire. (Guillaume, 1927: 8)
>
> ('*blablab*' ... refers to the act of making the lips vibrate with the finger, then the mouth, especially that of a child's in a picture, then any picture of a person, any drawing, illustrated cards ..., any piece of paper with writing or printing on it, a newspaper, a book, but also expresses the act of 'reading' or the desire to read.)

Similarly, Bowerman (1978) reports that her daughter first used the word *kick* in the context of propelling a ball forward with her foot, but that subsequent uses of the word were associated with kicking an immovable floor fan, pushing her stomach against a mirror or a sink, moving a ball with the wheel of her tricycle, watching a moth fluttering on a table, and with the sight of cartoon tortoises kicking their legs in the air.

In cases such as these it is not too difficult to see pathways and commonalities between the various uses of the words in question. However, as Bowerman herself observes, it is not at all straightforward to isolate similarities between the relevant features and/or to come to any very clear conclusions about which feature or features is or are critical. It might also be speculated that some of the divergent uses to which early forms are put may be explicable in terms of homophony or form-based association. Thus, for example, Vihman & Miller's (1988) subject Molly associated a set of phonetically similar forms ([baba], [papa], [bəbaɪ]) with both dolls (*baby*) and waving good-bye (*bye-bye*) (p. 163).

With regard to over-extension, E. Clark, whose name is most

closely linked to research into this aspect of early lexical meaning, distinguishes two main categories:

> over-inclusions, where children extend a term to other categories from the same taxonomy, e.g., *dada* used for both the father and mother, *baby* used for self-reference and all children, *apple* used for apples and for oranges; and analogical extensions where children use a term for objects from other taxonomies on the basis of perceptual similarity, e.g., *cotty-bars* (= bars of a cot) extended to an abacus on the wall and to a picture of a building with a columned façade, or *comb* extended to designate a centipede. (E. Clark, 1993: 34)

Two of the most widely quoted examples of over-extension are the application of the word *moon* to a grapefruit half, lemon slices and a hangnail (Bowerman, 1976), and the use of the word *clock* to refer to real clocks, meters, dials, timers, a buzzing radio, a telephone and a medallion (Rescorla, 1980).

Clark's early (1973) view of over-extension was that it pointed to an initial assignment of meaning on the basis of salient perceptual characteristics – shape, sound, taste, touch, etc., and that this meaning was then gradually brought into line with adult usage by a narrowing down of its scope through the successive addition of further features. Clark's Semantic Feature Theory, as it was called, swiftly ran into difficulty. One focus of attack was the nature of the features involved; K. Nelson (1974) suggested that these might be function- or (inter)action-based rather than perceptual. More damaging than a criticism of this kind, however, was the evidence that over-extension is not necessarily the typical starting-point for lexical semantic development that it was once thought to be, over-extended words accounting for no more than a third (Rescorla, 1980) and in some data sets less than a fifth (Barrett, 1978, 1986; Gruendel, 1977; K. Nelson, 1982) of lexical production. In fact, it is beginning to look as if under-extension rather than over-extension may be the usual point of departure. Other lines of criticism include the claim that there is no single basis for over-extension (Barrett, 1986; K. Nelson, 1988) and the arguments that Clark's account ignores the possibility that young children may engage in metaphorical extension of meanings (see, e.g., Elliot, 1981: 85ff.; H. Gardner *et al.*, 1975) or that they may sometimes represent compensatory communication strategies (McShane & Dockrell, 1983) – approximations deployed to cover lexical gaps. A further possibility is that some apparent over-extensions may actually be consequences of form-based confusion or association (Vihman & Miller, 1988) of the type mentioned above in relation to the fluidity of early lexical meanings.

More recently, Clark (1983, 1987, 1993) has emphasized the role of contrast and of conventionality in her treatment of over-extension data:

> [Children] take the adult language as their target in memory and in production; they repair their own forms to approximate adult ones; and they give priority to adult forms over others. In assuming contrast, they assign different meanings to different forms. This leads them on occasion to reject terms as potentially synonymous ... (Clark, 1993: 100)

Her present view is that an early word will be over-extended until a different word in the same semantic domain is encountered, at which point over-extension into the semantic range of the new word will cease; further words acquired in the domain in question will place more limits on over-extension, and so it continues. This model of lexical acquisition is reminiscent of semantic field theory of the first few decades of the twentieth century (see, e.g., Trier, 1931), sharing with it a very narrow, exclusively contrast-based conception of lexical relations. Lyons' (e.g., 1963, 1968, 1977) approach to structuralist semantics (see above, Chapter 1) broadened this conception as far as semantic field theory was concerned, but, as McShane (1991: 154) points out, this theoretical advance is not taken account of in Clark's Contrastive Hypothesis. McShane also cites (*ibid.*: 154–155) V. Gathercole's (1987) argument that evidence of overlapping extensions in children's use of object words (Merriman, 1986a, 1986b) runs counter to Clark's notion that when a new word is acquired it will be pre-empted from overlapping semantically with already established items. Furthermore, to the extent that the Contrastive Hypothesis rests on the idea that over-extension is the beginning-point of lexical semantic development, it is as vulnerable as Semantic Feature Theory to alternative perspectives on over-extension (see above).

In relation to under-extension, this may take the form of situational under-extension of the associational, quasi-ritual kind described earlier – the use of the form *dut* only as an accompaniment to knocking a toy duck off the edge of the bathtub, etc. There is, however, a second variety of under-extension which is not context-bound and which has to do with the restriction of the range of referents to which a word is applied. For example, M. Harris reports 'early uses of "clock" to refer only to wall clocks, "music" to refer only to a hi-fi system in the child's home, and "light" to refer only to ceiling lights with a conventional shade' (M. Harris, 1992: 71). Three further examples are culled by Dromi from the literature:

> Lewis (1959) notes that his son initially applied the word *fafa* (flower) only to pictures of flowers and not to real flowers ... Similarly, Bloom (1973)

> observed that her daughter restricted the word *car* to cars moving on the street ... Reich describes in detail the development of the meaning of *shoe* for his son between eight and sixteen months, and also concludes that initially the meaning of the word was very narrow. (Dromi, 1987: 40)

Under-extension has been the object of rather less research attention than over-extension. However, Griffiths (1986: 300) reads the relatively low numbers of over-extensions in the very early stages of lexical development as indicating that 'the characteristic early path is for nominals to be '*under-extended first and only later to apply to a wider range of entities* (perhaps then going as far as "over-extension"'. Such a pattern would certainly be easier to relate to the evidence we have suggesting that the majority of first words produced are situational under-extensions. A path which leads from context-bound under-extension to context-flexible under-extension to input-driven broadening of extension and over-extension and subsequent refinement of extension is a good deal easier to make sense of than one which leads straight from context-bound under-extension to over-extension.

Concerning the notion of a 'basic' level of categorization, Rosch *et al.* (1976) suggests that there is a universal principle of category formation in accordance with which the process of category formation starts from a point where the categories are 'maximally differentiable from each other', this process being guided partly by the 'correlational structure of the environment' and partly by 'selective ignorance and exaggeration' on the part of the categorizers:

> This is accomplished by categories which have maximum cue validity – i.e., categories that have the most attributes common to members of the category and the least attributes shared by members of other categories. ... Segmentation of experience occurs to form basic levels which maximize the differentiability of categories. ... basic objects are the most general classes at which attributes are predictable, objects of the class are used in the same way, objects can be readily identified by shape, and at which classes can be imaged. ... basic object categories should be the basic classifications made during perception, the first learned and first named by children, and the most codable, most coded and most necessary in the language of any people. (Rosch *et al.*, 1976: 435)

Waxman (1994: 234), evaluating the claims made by Rosch *et al.*, notes that some researchers (Mandler, 1988; Mandler & Bauer, 1988; Mandler *et al.*, 1991) have argued that infants' first conceptualizations are at a more abstract level than that posited by Rosch and her colleagues. However, she goes on to cite a range of studies (Anglin, 1977; R. Brown, 1958b; Mervis, 1987; Mervis & Crisafi, 1982) in support of the view that 'the weight of evidence overwhelmingly favors the developmental primacy of the basic level' (*ibid.*), showing as they do that pre-school children consistently 'succeed in classifying and labeling objects at the basic level long before they do so at other hierarchical levels' (*ibid.*.). Campbell (1986: 44), as we have seen, also finds in the literature plenty of evidence (Brown, 1958a; Nelson, 1973a; Ninio & Bruner, 1978) that the first lexicalized concepts are 'of *moderate* generality'.

Phase 2

The particular characteristic of the stage beginning from the point where the child has acquired upwards of 30 words is what is sometimes called a vocabulary explosion – that is to say, a significant increase in the rate of lexical expansion. This 'explosion' is often attributed to the arrival by the child at a particular developmental landmark, the insight that the world is composed of things that have names. The debate which has revolved around this postulation of the appearance of a 'naming insight' was outlined earlier during the course of the discussion of the transition from late babbling to 'true speech'. It is clear, however, that, for whatever reason, lexical development accelerates dramatically in Phase 2. Two concomitants of this acceleration are, on the one hand, a sort of naming obsession and, on the other, a capacity to learn new words after minimal exposure. In this phase 'children start to ask for the names of objects and they go around labelling everything for which they do know the name' (M. Harris, 1992: 72). There is also evidence (e.g., Carey & Bartlett, 1978; K. Nelson & Bonvillian, 1978) of very 'fast mapping', with children at this stage demonstrating a capacity to acquire a new item – at least as far as objects and colours are concerned – after exposure to just one occasion of use.

With reference to the above, it is interesting to note that the expansion of referential vocabulary in general seems to surge ahead especially swiftly during this phase, while expressions such as *bye-bye* and *no*, which do not have a representative function, are acquired at a rather more sedate pace (K. Nelson, 1973b). This is seen by advocates of the 'naming insight' perspective as grist to their mill. They are also inclined to claim that there is a qualitative difference between the use of the very first words produced – when 'the child does not appear freely to control his or her words to refer or to communicate' (McShane, 1991: 145) and what one observes after the vocabulary spurt – which is that the child 'will readily name objects on request and will use an object's name spontaneously to refer to that object' (*ibid.*). This latter view does not seem to be strongly supported by M. Harris's (1992) findings, which, as we saw above in the discussion of late babbling, suggest that some measure of context-flexible referentiality is present even amongst the first ten words produced. On the other hand, one could argue, as McShane (1991: 146) does, that words used in the presence of objects may be associative responses to those objects – however context-flexible – rather than genuine symbolizations.

Whether or not Phase 2 is in fact characterized by a qualitative shift in the direction of genuine referentiality, the child continues for a considerable period to be limited in his/her understanding of the relationship between words and concepts. K. Nelson (1988) observes that for the child at this stage of development the relationship is one-to-one. In some instances this hypothesis works reasonably well but in other cases it seems to act as an impediment to acquisition. An oft-cited example of the kind of problem that can arise concerns the mastering of the full semantic range of the word *same*, to which Karmiloff-Smith drew attention some years ago (1979). *Same* has two rather different meanings; it can mean 'having precisely the same identity', as in *Shall we watch the same video again, or do you want a different one?*, or it can mean 'having very similar attributes', as in *These sweets all taste the same*. Karmiloff-Smith found that before the age of 5 years children would treat *same* as having a single application, the 'same attributes' one, and that the 'one and the same' application began to figure only from about age 5 onwards.

Phase 3

M. Harris characterizes the third phase of lexical development in childhood – that which follows the initial 'vocabulary explosion' – as 'a period of revision, reorganisation and consolidation of knowledge' (M. Harris, 1992: 73). It seems to have its onset in the pre-school period, but it is clear that some of the reorganizing processes that begin at this point continue through the years of primary schooling and, indeed, according to Anglin (1970: 99), at least until college entry age. The rate of vocabulary expansion in the pre-school years tends to be extremely rapid (up to 10–20 words per day), and at the same time the lexicon begins to be reorganized in two ways:

> One is the reorganisation of lexical items into domains of related words, which allows the child to represent information about relationships between individual words. The other is the development of a more complex mapping between words and word domains on the one hand and concepts on the other. (M. Harris, 1992: 74)

Anglin's (1970) widely cited account of the growth and restructuring of word meaning, based on a wide-ranging trawl through the literature as well as the results of a series of experiments of his own, makes reference to three aspects of the process: (1) a shift from syntagmatic to paradigmatic associations between word meanings in the mental lexicon, (2) a progression towards a more abstract approach to relationships between words, and (3) the development of a lexico-semantic classification of the world in terms of superordinateness and hyponymy.

Anglin (1970: 13) reads the evidence (R. Brown & Berko, 1960; Entwisle *et al.*, 1964; Ervin, 1961; Woodworth, 1938) as indicating that the syntagmatic–paradigmatic shift occurs between five and ten years. He describes it in terms of 'the reliable finding that the responses of young children in free association are of a different part of speech than the stimulus words (syntagmatic), whereas the responses provided by older subjects are predominantly of the same part of speech (paradigmatic)' (Anglin, 1970: 13). He cites from Woodworth (1938) the examples of the stimulus *table*, which most commonly elicits the response *eat* from children but *chair* from adults, and the stimulus *dark*, which most commonly elicits the response *night* from children but *light* from adults. He also concurs with the classic interpretation of such results – i.e., that they show lexical development to involve, as R. Carter (1987: 150) puts it, 'an increasing perception of syntactic, semantic and conceptual *relations* between words':

> The increase in paradigmatic responses can be viewed as reflecting the accretion of semantic markers (McNeill, 1968) and the developing organization of vocabulary into syntactic classes (Brown & Berko, 1960) . . . (Anglin, 1970: 14)

Anglin's own experiments showed that children were less likely than adults to sort words according to syntactic class (*ibid.*: 29ff.) and that words freely recalled by adults were more likely to cluster paradigmatically than words freely recalled by children (*ibid.*: 54ff.); however, the results of a free-association experiment he conducted with this issue in mind were inconclusive (*ibid.*: 64ff.).

Anglin interprets the above results as supporting his proposals regarding the development of a more abstract treatment of word meaning in older children and adults. He sees abstraction as related to what was earlier discussed under the heading of over-extension, and he draws a distinction between (over-)generalization which happens before children have arrived at the point of discriminating perceptually between given entities (e.g., dogs and horses) and that which occurs subsequent to discrimination. He refers in this connection to Brown (1958b), who talks about 'abstraction before differentiation' and 'abstraction after differentiation', and he cites what Brown has to say about the child's application of a word such as *bow-wow* to all quadrupeds:

> He generalizes from failure to distinguish dogs from cats from cows from horses. The adult classifies all of these as quadrupeds even though he sees their species and even their individual differences. The adult abstracts from many perceived differences to find a common quality in a single exemplar and generalizes where he has not differentiated. ... While high abstractions may be a primitive process when they are accomplished in the absence of differentiation, they may be an advanced process after differentiation.
> (R. Brown, 1958b: 286)

Anglin goes on to cite a number of empirical studies the results of which are consistent with the postulation of just such a trend towards generalization/abstraction as the lexicon develops: for example, Woodrow & Lowell's (1916 – cited in Meara, 1996a) finding that children produce fewer superordinate responses in word-association tests than adults, and the finding by Bruner and his colleagues (Bruner & Olver, 1963; Bruner *et al.*, 1966) that the ability to generate 'equivalence relations' (i.e., superordinate points of similarity) was correlated with age. Anglin's own empirical work focusing on equivalence relations yielded similar results:

> A child does almost as well as an adult at generating predicates for words bound by a concrete relation; a child does not do nearly so well as an adult when the relation is abstract. (Anglin, 1970: 93)

Differing degrees of semantic abstractness, as Anglin notes, are also manifested in younger and older subjects' different levels of acceptance of collocations of different kinds and of metaphorical usages. In this connection R. Carter (1987: 151) refers to Asch & Nerlove's (1969) finding that 3-year-olds will categorically deny that adjectives such as *bright*, *hard*, etc. can be applied to people, whereas by age 12 a great deal more flexibility in the use of such terms can be seen to have developed.

Progress in the direction of abstraction/generalization further relates to the development of hierarchical relations among word meanings:

> the child first appreciates the similarity among small groups of words and only later sees the similarity among increasingly broad classes. At first he might see that *roses* and *tulips* are *flowers*, that *oaks* and *elms* are *trees* ... Somewhat later he might realize that the objects he had classed as *flowers*

are similar to the objects he had classed as *trees*, in that both are *plants*. (Anglin, 1970: 14)

The above evidence of a syntagmatic–paradigmatic shift and of concrete–abstract progression is relevant to this suggestion, as is Anglin's finding (1970: 73ff.) that adults' recall of groups of words is facilitated by the spatial organization of such material to conform to hierarchical relations among words, whereas this kind of spatial organization of items has noticeably less effect on children's recall performance. McShane (1991: 148–149) suggests that the precursor of the development of taxonomies based on superordinate-hyponym relations is the earlier conceptualization of collection relations. He cites the finding by Callanan & Markman (1982) that 2-year-olds admit, for example, the collective appellation *toys* applied to a disparate group of playthings, but do not necessarily accept that each individual item (a ball, a doll, etc.) can be called a *toy*. McShane also refers to Markman's (1985, 1989) suggestion that the acquisition of mass nouns may assist children to come to grips with notions of superordinateness, and her observation that many superordinate expressions in English and other languages are mass nouns (*furniture*, *money*, etc.).

Finally, with regard to the second dimension of lexico-semantic reorganization mentioned in the earlier quotation from M. Harris (1992) – that which leads to the abandonment of an assumption of one-to-one relations between words and meanings – one can refer to the research of Karmiloff-Smith (e.g., 1979, 1986), from whose work the example of the development of two functions for the word *same* was cited at the end of the previous subsection. Another lexical (at least in the broad sense – cf. Chapter 1) area focused on by Karmiloff-Smith is the development of functions of the definite article in French, which, she claims, proceeds in three phases: (1) a phase between roughly the ages of 3 and 5½ during which the functions of the definite article are extremely narrow, the plural definite article being used principally to mark pluralization and the singular definite article being used essentially deictically; (2) a phase up to about age 8 during which different functions of the definite article are beginning to develop, but are redundantly marked by the addition of separate morphemes:

Thus, whereas smaller children used *les X* . . . to convey pluralization, children of the second level added *tous* in the same situation (*tous les X*) in order to convey totalization also.[1] (Karmiloff-Smith, 1986: 464)

[1] *Les* is the plural form of the French definite article. *Tous* is the masculine plural form of the French word for 'all'.

and (3) a phase between about 8 and 12 where the plurifunctionality of the definite article is gradually internalized and the over-marking of functions typical of the previous phase wanes and disappears. In relation to the last phase, Karmiloff-Smith cites examples of self-correction which point in the direction of precisely the process she postulates, examples such as the following from an 8-year-old:

Tu as caché toutes les voitures rouges ... enfin, les voitures rouges (Karmiloff-Smith, 1986: 465)

('You've hidden all the red cars ... I mean the red cars')

This kind of development would appear to be related to what Anglin has to say about the development of more abstract relations in the lexicon generally, apropos of which a number of the examples cited above in connection with Anglin's proposals can also be seen in a developing plurifunctionality perspective – e.g., the older child's application of *bright* to persons as well as to things, of *toy/toys* to individual items as well as to collections, etc.

L1 and L2 lexical development: a preliminary assessment of similarities and contrasts

On the basis of the exploration of the various topics raised in this chapter, it is already possible to make some preliminary remarks concerning the degree to which L1 and L2 lexical development parallel each other and diverge. We have seen that the challenge faced by L1 and L2 acquirers is to an extent comparable. Thus, the difficulties faced by the L1 learner in extracting lexical units from the speech stream continuum and relating them to concepts and intentions are shared by the L2 learner – certainly the naturalistic L2 learner. We have also seen, however, that similar kinds of help are made available to both categories of learner in terms of the tuning of input, 'ostensive' definitions, etc. The acquisition of literacy skills would appear to have a similar impact in both cases also. It may well be that both categories of learner are in addition assisted by innate mechanisms of one kind or another, although it has to be said that among those who espouse a Universal Grammar view of language acquisition there are many who are inclined to believe that innate mechanisms cease to operate beyond a particular maturational point and are thus unavailable to older L2 learners (see, e.g., Bley-Vroman, 1989, 1994).

The two major differences between the L1 and the L2 learner are that the latter, on the one hand, is at a more advanced stage of development in both physical and cognitive terms and, on the other, by definition, has already been through the process of acquiring a language. There is no question, then, of L2 learners having to re-traverse the various 'milestones' that are associated with the L1 development. L2 learners do not coo or babble, and when they utter in their target languages their utterances are from the outset mostly comprised of combinations of meaningful elements. Moreover, the ways in which words relate to extralinguistic reality and the ways in which they may relate to each other are already known (at least tacitly) by the L2 learner. Accordingly, most of the above discussion of the relationship between pre-verbal development and 'true speech' and much of what was said on the topic of L1 lexical development after the onset of word production is irrelevant to L2 acquisition. However, even in these areas there are at least points of contact between the L1 and the L2 experience.

In the phonetic domain, just as pre-verbal L1 learners have to struggle to replicate the sound shapes of the language of their environment from a starting-point – babbling – which is not necessarily very helpful phonetically, so L2 learners have to come to grips with sounds of the L2 that may bear little resemblance to those of their L1. Also, while L2 learners have (tacitly) internalized the principle of phonemic distinctions and its role in keeping lexical items distinct, they, like L1 learners, still have to work out which phonetic differences are phonemic and which are not; indeed, the fact of having one phonological system already in place can be a source of hindrance as much as of help in this matter – as every piece of evidence concerning phonological interference not to mention millennia of *flied lice*-type jokes amply testify. It is also interesting to note that the relative efficiency of phonological working memory is as important in determining the rate of L2 lexical development as it is in determining the rate of L1 lexical development (see, e.g., Baddeley *et al.*, 1988; Papagno *et al.*, 1991; and see below, Chapter 4).

In the conceptual/semantic domain, too, there are parallels between L1 and L2 lexical development. Of course, L2 learners – even if their exposure to the L2 begins in childhood – start from further down the road of concept development than infants confronting the task of L1 acquisition. Indeed, many of the meanings and meaning hierarchies that are lexicalized in a given L1 and have already been internalized by the L2 learner will be recyclable with only minimal adjustment in the L2. On the other hand, however close the 'cultural overlap' between two language communities, there will always be areas and items of meaning which do not correspond. In some instances the L2 learner is faced with totally new concepts. More often – and perhaps more problematically – the meanings of the L2, reflecting the cultural specificities of its particular language community, are differently structured and distributed as compared with those of the L1. Thus, Lado (1957: 116), writing of the differences between (Anglo-)American and Hispanic culture in respect of perceptions of and attitudes towards animals, points out that whereas in English both humans and animals have *legs*, *backs* and *necks*, Spanish distinguishes between the human leg (*pierna*) and the animal legs (*pata*), between the human back (*espalda*) and the animal back (*lomo*) and between the human neck (*cuello*) and animal necks (*pescuezo*). He also observes that the concepts of animals *getting nervous* and of animal *hospitals* and *cemeteries* do not exist in Hispanic culture. It is hardly surprising, in such circumstances, if lexical fluidity, over-extension, under-extension and associative shifts occur in L2 development just as they do in L1 acquisition. The existence of L1 knowledge can admittedly be seen, from one point of view, as setting the L2 versions of these phenomena apart in some sense, but, on the other hand, in both the L1 and the L2 case the process of apprehending the semantic range of newly encountered words is constrained and shaped by the particularities of the experience the learner has had of the word itself, of related words and of the relevant concept or concepts. The fact that, in the L2 case, experience of related words and relevant concepts includes experience of such words and concepts in a different language and culture might, from another point of view, then, be seen as a mere detail.

Concluding summary

In this chapter we began by looking at the challenge posed by the task of acquiring a lexicon in a given language – notably in respect of isolating lexical units in the speech signal and connecting them with appropriate semantico-pragmatic content and in respect of using written input as a basis for adding to one's lexical stock. It emerged from this discussion that there is considerable similarity between the L1 situation and the L2 situation in terms of the nature of the challenge faced by the learner.

We went on to explore:

1 the relationship between the first meaningful words produced by the child around the age of twelve months and everything that precedes this milestone;
2 lexical development during the period following the onset of word production.

With regard to (1), the key question addressed was that of whether lexical development is continuous or discontinuous with earlier development. While no absolutely definitive answer to this question is forthcoming, the balance of evidence does appear to argue for continuity. Continuity is not, however, to be equated with gradualism in this context, since there may be instances where particular semantico-pragmatic milestones need to be attained before certain other developments (including formal developments) can occur. With regard to (2) it is clear that, whereas formal factors are certainly not absent during the period in question, the principal operative processes are semantico-pragmatic in nature – from learning to refer in the early stages to constructing abstract semantic hierarchies of categorizations as development proceeds.

Finally, we returned to the question of the relationship between L1 and L2 development. It was recognized that L2 lexical development differs markedly from L1 lexical development insofar as it lacks a pre-speech dimension and insofar as it takes place in the presence, as it were, of an already acquired lexicon. However, it was also noted that L2 learners have a number of difficulties in common with L1 learners in their struggle to isolate meaningful units and connect them with aspects of reality, to internalize and replicate the formal characteristics of these units, and to puzzle out and store their precise meanings.

3 *Modelling the lexicon*

In Chapter 2 we looked at the question of how lexis is acquired. In the present chapter we turn our attention to the equally fascinating issue of how the lexis that is acquired is managed; in other words, we shall be considering the structure of the lexical storage system and the ways in which that system is accessed under different conditions. We shall also be looking at lexical processing within two broader theoretical frames of reference – respectively, the modularity hypothesis and connectionism.

The present chapter concerns itself mostly with research which does not have a specifically L2 or bilingual focus. However, in research relating to the L2 mental lexicon the same kinds of organizational and operational issues arise as in L1-focused research, the difference being that in the L2 case they are further complicated by questions having to do with precisely the fact that more than one language comes into the picture. These latter questions – (1) the degree to which the L2 lexicon resembles the L1 lexicon and (2) the degree to which and ways in which the L2 lexicon interacts with the L1 lexicon – will be addressed in Chapter 4. With regard to (1), we have already seen in Chapter 2 that there are some similarities between the challenges posed by, respectively, L1 lexical acquisition and L2 lexical acquisition; and we shall see in Chapter 4 that such similarities extend into the operational sphere. We can therefore take it that most of what is said in the present chapter in respect of L1 lexical processing is also relevant to L2.

The chapter begins with a review of some of the available models of lexical processing and of the research evidence that they seek to account for. It then assesses the plausibility and the relevance to the lexicon of the notion that the mind is modularly organized. Finally, it explores connectionism in a lexical perspective.

Some models of the mental lexicon

A distinction is made by Garman in his (1990: 260ff.) discussion of lexical modelling between direct and indirect models. He compares the processes posited by the indirect type of model to those required to negotiate a dictionary or a library, each of which is internally organized in such a way as to facilitate two-stage access via a search procedure and then a retrieval procedure. Direct models, on the other hand, are predicated on one-stage access, the metaphor used by Garman in this case being that of a word-processing package which allows items stored by name to be accessed simply by the typing in of as many letters as are sufficient to identify the relevant name from among all the names available. We shall begin in this section by looking at two oft-cited and influential representatives of the direct kind of model – Morton's logogen model (see, e.g., Morton, 1964a, 1968, 1969, 1970, 1978, 1979; Morton & Patterson, 1980) and Marslen-Wilson's cohort model (see, e.g., Marslen-Wilson, 1980, 1987, 1989a, 1990, 1993; Marslen-Wilson & Tyler, 1980; Marslen-Wilson & Welsh, 1978) – before examining the best-known exemplar of the indirect type of model, Forster's (1976, 1979, 1981, 1989) search model of lexical access. We shall then conclude our brief trawl through lexical models by considering Levelt's (1989) 'blueprint for the speaker', which is actually not, or rather not solely, a model of lexical processing, but which ascribes a central mediating role to the lexicon and has accordingly been widely referred to in the context of discussion of the mental lexicon (see, e.g., Bierwisch & Schreuder, 1992; De Bot, 1992; De Bot & Schreuder, 1993; Gass & Selinker, 1994).

Morton's logogen model

The logogen model began as an attempt to account for Morton's (1961, 1964b) finding that there was a relationship between the distribution of lexical responses in sentence-completion tasks – involving items such as *He asked the way to the* _________ – ('transitional probability') and the time taken to recognize certain items in sentence contexts ('visual duration threshold'). This relationship is summarized by Morton as follows:

> any context which increases the probability of words in a generation situation would be expected to lower their threshold of recognition. (Morton, 1964a; reprint: Oldfield and Marshall, 1968: 152)

It is modelled as shown in Figure 3.1.

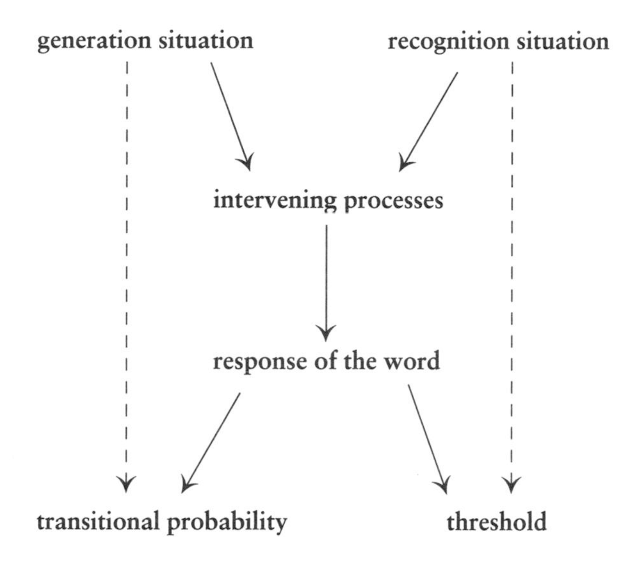

Figure 3.1. Morton's first attempt to model the relationship between transitional probability and visual duration threshold (after Morton, 1964a, Figure 1)

Morton postulates that when a lexical response becomes available there is an 'event' in 'a part of the nervous system' which he initially labels simply as 'neural unit' and to which he in his later writings applies the technical term 'logogen'. He attributes the following properties (P1–P4) to these neural units:

P1 When a unit fires, a particular word is available as a response.
P2 Each unit has a basic, relatively stable, level of activation.
P3 The level of activation can be increased by noise or by outside events.
P4 Each unit has a threshold; when the level of activation exceeds the threshold, the unit fires. (Morton, 1964a, reprint: 148)

Property 3 above refers broadly to context effects, which will be something of a leitmotiv in this chapter. The notion that a prior processing event can facilitate a subsequent processing event is a very familiar one in psycholinguistics and is the basis of the experimental technique of priming, defined by Aitchison as follows:

> A technique used in experimental studies, in which a person is prepared for a subsequent word or utterance. For example, the word *winter* might 'prime' the word *snow*, in that after hearing *winter* a person would be likely to recognize *snow* more quickly in a **lexical decision task** (deciding whether a sequence of sounds or letters is a word or not). (Aitchison, 1992: 72)

Clearly the closest relationship between two items is absolute identity, and, indeed, words prime themselves very effectively. That is to say, if a word is re-presented after an initial presentation, it will be recognized significantly more quickly than if the initial presentation had not taken place.

Morton's model evolved in various ways over subsequent years as more and more experimental and observational evidence was taken account of. In the version current in the late 1960s and early 1970s, there were just three components (see Figure 3.2):

- the logogen system, i.e., a collection of mechanisms – one for each word in a given individual's lexicon – specialized for collecting acoustic evidence (contributed by auditory word analysis), visual evidence (contributed by visual word analysis) and semantic evidence (from the cognitive system) concerning the presence of words to which the logogens correspond;
- the cognitive system, i.e., a collection of semantic information of various kinds, directly connected via a two-way link to the logogen system;
- the response buffer, – i.e. a component responsible for generating spoken or written word production, directly connected to the logogen system via a unidirectional link (logogen system → response buffer).

A basic principle of operation of the model is that any input will be likely to supply evidence to more than one logogen. For example, in the case of the processing of the printed word *cat*, 'the output from the visual analysis might include the attributes <three letter word>, <tall letter at the end>, <initial *c*>, <final *t*>, and so on' (Morton, 1970: 206). Such information is relevant not only to *cat* but to other words too. Accordingly, the attribute <three-letter word>, for example, will be expected to excite not only the logogen for *cat* but the logogens for all three-letter words. Hence the need for the model to incorporate thresholds. Among the fairly widespread excitation of logogens that is set off by a given input, it is necessary that one logogen – on the basis of all the available data – should reach such a level of excitation that it 'fires', in order that the appropriate word should be selected. In fact, Morton's (1970) conception was that there were two such thresholds, one controlling access to the cognitive system and the other controlling access to the response buffer.

One of the frequently observed phenomena addressed by the double-threshold idea and by the proposed architecture of connectivity between the components of the early logogen model was the

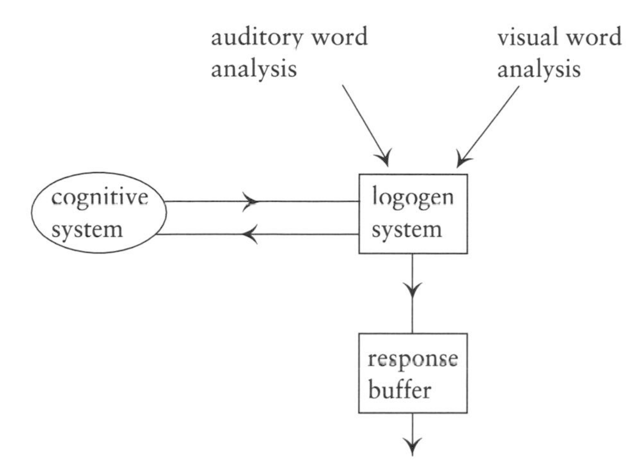

Figure 3.2 The essential components of the early version of the logogen model (based on Morton, 1979: 113, Figure 1, 138, Figure 5)

anticipatory nature of many deviations in reading aloud. When people read aloud they often produce errors that appear to be induced by contextual material which lies ahead of the point they have reached in their vocalizing of the text. The logogen model can explain this in terms of the possibility of words passing the cognitive system threshold before gaining access to the response buffer, the point being that such words can then be fed by the cognitive system directly back into the logogen system to influence (via the direct line between the logogen system and the response buffer) the (mis)reading of items in the response buffer.

Another point arising from the early logogen model has to do with the rate of decay of activation. Morton assumed that once a logogen had 'fired', activation relative to the word in question would have to diminish very rapidly; otherwise there would presumably be interference with the identification of subsequent items. Morton's (1968) suggestion was, in fact, that logogen activation levels after 'firing' returned to something like their original value in about one second. However, there is a further issue to be taken into consideration, namely the above-mentioned question of priming. Where priming effects manifest themselves in very short-term experiments involving lapses of no more than a second or so between initial presentation and re-presentation, they can readily be explained by reference to Morton's hypothesized time-scale for activation decay. But what of the longer-term priming effects which some of Morton's own experiments turned up and which other researchers have found to last for many hours (see, e.g., Scarborough *et al.*, 1977)? Morton's answer to this point is summarized by M. Harris & Coltheart (1986) as follows:

> It is assumed ... that each time a logogen reaches its threshold, the value of that threshold is lowered; and this value then slowly drifts up towards what it had been, but never quite reaches the previous level. ... long-term priming effects are explained ... by assuming that after threshold has been reached activation dies down rapidly at first ... but does not quite reach the normal resting period: there follows a long period during which there is a slow decay of residual activation – a period measured in hours or even days. (M. Harris & Coltheart, 1986: 140–141)

Morton's original assumption was that the detectability of a given word would be enhanced across the board by any prior encounter with any related stimulus – identical, similar or connected, mental, spoken, written or pictorial. As Garman puts it:

> In Morton's model, evidence about the occurrence of a particular word comes potentially from all modalities, and these inputs are in a 'conspiratorial' relationship with one another ... and they all combine to lower what Morton calls the recognition threshold of the relevant stored forms. (Garman, 1990: 278)

Unfortunately for this view, some experimental evidence casts doubt on the notion of cross-modal priming. Thus, for example, findings from a study by Winnick & Daniel (1970) suggested that whereas reading a printed word aloud facilitated its later recognition in printed form, no such facilitation in this specific respect was brought about by naming a picture of the word's referent or by producing the word in response to a definition. Indeed, some of Morton's own work confirmed the absence of a cross-modal priming effect; for example, Morton's 1978 study failed to demonstrate facilitation of visual word identification by prior exposure to auditory versions of the words in question (cf. also Clarke & Morton, 1983). Accordingly, Morton was led to revise his model in such a way as to allow for separate, independent logogen systems for different types of input. The essential features of the revised version are presented diagrammatically in Figure 3.3.

Another respect in which the revised model altered the earlier conception relates to input-output connectivity. Whereas in the earlier model the connection between input and output was presented as an indirect one – via the logogen system – in the later version direct pathways are envisaged between both the input analysis processes (both auditory and visual) and the response buffer. This is to account for the ability to pronounce visually or auditorily

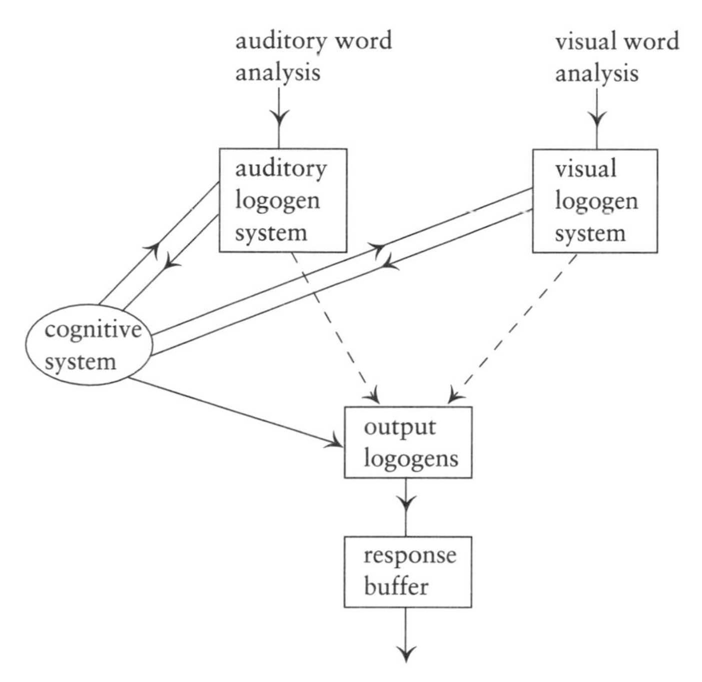

Figure 3.3 The essential components of the revised version of the logogen model (based on Morton & Patterson, 1980: 95, Figure 4.2b)

presented non-words on the basis, in the former case, of knowledge of graphological-phonological correspondences which transcends knowledge of individual words (cf. Campbell, 1983; Gough, 1972), and, in the latter case, of the replicating capacities of phonological working memory (see above, Chapter 2). Non-words clearly cannot trigger the firing of logogens since these latter have to correspond to real lexical items in storage and so, logically, there must be some way in which such non-words can be processed without reference to the logogen system. Moreover, it is also probably the case that in certain circumstances even real words are read aloud or pronounced without being processed at a level other than the purely formal level; who, for example, has not had the occasional experience of mechanically repeating or reading aloud a passage of a language they know without the least scintilla of interest in or comprehension of content being involved?

One should note that, as Morton has been perfectly ready to acknowledge (e.g., 1978), the above representation is still deficient in at least two respects On the one hand, it ought to incorporate a separate pathway for picture recognition and naming, including an input 'pictogen' system (cf. Seymour, 1973). On the other, the output system is under-differentiated. To be fully complete, the model ought to be equipped with three separate output pathways – one for spoken output, one for written/printed output and one for graphic output (to capture the capacity to draw the referent(s) of lexical input).

Mention of separate output pathways brings us back to the whole question of the componentiality of Morton's model and of the degree of independence of certain of the components. We have seen that Morton's reading of the available experimental evidence persuaded him in revising the model to posit wholly unconnected auditory and visual systems. This particular aspect of the model has attracted criticism from some quarters, on the basis that, whilst the postulation of distinct auditory and visual systems seems sensible, to represent the two systems as entirely independent of each other goes beyond the evidence. For example, Garman (1990) raises the question of lexical-decision responses to items presented visually. He notes that correct *yes* responses can be seen as mediated via the visual system, but that correct *no* responses pose a problem for the model. He sketches a possible solution in terms of an 'access clock' which would, as it were, bring down a guillotine and signal *no* if no visual logogen were triggered within a given time, but again the evidence is awkward:

> . . . this suggests that all such responses should be equivalently slow; it is therefore difficult to reconcile with the observed effect [i.e., the effect of slowing down lexical decision-making of homophone non-words (e.g., *sist*, resembling *cyst*)]. Such findings would seem to argue for a link between visual–auditory analysis . . . but this is explicitly rejected in the model. (Garman, 1990: 285)

Emmorey & Fromkin (1988: 132), also, cite some psycholinguistic findings which appear to run counter to Morton's later view on the question of the unconnectedness of auditory and visual lexical processing:

- the facilitation of visual (real) word recognition when the word (e.g., *pale*) is preceded by a homophone prime (e.g., *pail*) (Humphreys, Evett & Taylor, 1982);
- faster identification of spoken words (from a list) rhyming with a cue word when the cue word and the rhyming word were orthographically similar (e.g., *glue*, *clue* versus *grew, clue*) (Seidenberg & Tanenhaus, 1979; Donnenworth-Nolan *et al.*, 1981).

On the other hand, they also cite evidence from a surface dyslexic, Kram (cf. Fromkin, 1985; Newcombe & Marshall, 1985), which supports the notion of the separation of orthographic and phonological representations (with interconnections). Following a brain injury, the patient in question seems to have substantially lost access to orthography. Thus, he pronounces *cape* as /sæpi/ and writes *kap* on hearing the word; he can define the word when he hears it but not when he sees it in print:

> If the orthographic representation is not listed separately from the phonological representation one would have to posit either impairment to orthographic representation of each lexical item, or a complex impairment of the multitude of connections to these representations leaving the pathways to the phonology intact. By positing separate sub-lexicons with interconnecting addresses ... the impairment is more simply explained.
> (Emmorey & Fromkin, 1988: 133)

The simpler explanation referred to is, of course, that the brain injury has resulted in the disruption of the connection which normally links the phonological sub-lexicon to the orthographic sub-lexicon. On the basis of this kind of evidence, Fromkin (1985) retains componentiality in her own model of the lexicon – which includes a phonological lexicon, an orthographic lexicon and a semantic lexicon – but posits a grapheme–phoneme conversion subsystem as well as a bi-directional link between the phonological and the orthographic components.

Marslen-Wilson's cohort model

A criticism of the logogen model which has not so far been mentioned is Forster's (1976) observation that it is difficult to see how this model can prevent the more frequent item *bright* being more available than the low-frequency target item *blight* in response to the input /blaɪt/, given that higher frequency implies higher levels of activation for the relevant logogen. As Garman (1990: 280, 286) points out, this problem is essentially about the difficulty of making precise statements about notions such as 'threshold' and 'activation level'. Marslen-Wilson's cohort model offers a possible answer to this problem, since it aspires to state exactly for each word where the critical activation level occurs.

The cohort model postulates a set of auditory word detectors which are activated by input from a spoken word and which go into operation as soon as the uttering of the word commences. As soon as the first sounds of the incoming item are processed, all the detectors for words beginning with that acoustic sequence – otherwise known as the relevant word-initial cohort – are fully activated. Each member of this cohort of word candidates then continues to monitor subsequent input, mismatches removing themselves progressively from the running, until a single word candidate finally tallies with the input:

> Unlike logogens, these elements are assumed to have the ability to respond actively to mismatches in the input signal. Namely, at such point as the input diverges sufficiently from the internal specification for an element then that element will remove itself from the pool of word-candidates ... eventually only a single candidate remains. At this point we may say that the word is recognized. (Marslen-Wilson & Welsh, 1978: 56–57)

What this means is that, in contradistinction to the varying degrees of activation posited by the logogen model, the classic cohort model allows for just two states of activation for a particular item: on (for as long as it forms part of a cohort of word-candidates) or off (when it fails to be selected for the word-initial cohort or is eliminated from the cohort). One should perhaps add, however, that this very simple binary approach to activation levels has been complexified slightly in a more recent version of the model (Marslen-Wilson, 1987), which envisages that, instead of immediately eliminating themselves, non-matching members of a cohort will go into an activation decline in the absence of further bottom-up support.

The cohort model also in principle identifies the precise point – its 'uniqueness point' – at which a word is recognized. This can be illustrated by reference to the word *elephant* (/'elɪfənt/). The word-initial cohort for /'elɪ/ would include words such as *elevate* and *element* (though presumably not *elephantine* or *elephantiasis* because of the absence of primary stress on the first syllable in these words). However, at the point where the /f/ sound occurs the cohort will have only *elephant* and its inflectional variants (*elephants*, *elephant's*, *elephants'*) left, since no other word in English begins with the sequence /'elɪf/. This then is the uniqueness point for *elephant*. The system seems to have the advantage of maximal efficiency; thus, for *elephant* to be identified prior to the occurrence of /f/ would run the risk of occasioning cases of mistaken identity, whilst to wait for more phonemes to be uttered beyond that point would be inefficient insofar as it would increase recognition time to no purpose in terms of gains in accuracy levels. The system also makes possible the definition of a point at which non-words are recognized as such. This is the point at which the sequence of phonemes uttered fails to correspond to any word in the language in question. Thus, for English, the non-word recognition point in *bnoil* will be the occurrence of /n/, since no English word begins with the sequence /bn/, while in the case of *relationshif*, the critical point will coincide with the very last sound /f/, since until this is uttered the possibility of a match still exists.

The experimental evidence in favour of Marslen-Wilson's proposals is quite strong (see, e.g., Marslen-Wilson, 1978, 1984, 1987; Marslen-Wilson & Tyler, 1980; Tyler & Wessels, 1983). For example, it has been shown that the time taken to recognize non-words will be shorter where recognition points come early in words and longer where recognition points come late, even though the decision time is identical if measured from the point at which the critical phoneme is uttered (Marslen-Wilson, 1978). It has also been shown (*ibid.*) that in phoneme-monitoring tasks, where subjects have to check spoken words for the presence of a particular sound and press a button when they hear it, the reaction time from the point at which the target phoneme appears will be shorter when the phoneme occurs late in a word than when it occurs early. Marslen-Wilson's explanation of this latter result proposes that, instead of focusing on listening for the target sound, his subjects were primarily concerned to identify the incoming words and were then searching their phonological representations of the identified words for the presence of the phoneme in question. Accordingly, the time taken to detect the presence of the target phoneme was dependent on the time taken to identify a given word, which in turn depended on the position in the word of its uniqueness/recognition point:

> When a target occurs *late* in a word, it is likely to occur *after* the recognition point. Consequently, the word will often have been identified before the target has even occurred, and so reaction times will be short. In contrast, when a target occurs *early* in a word, it is likely to occur *before* the recognition point. Consequently, such a word can be identified only after the subject has heard phonemes occurring later than the target phoneme, and so reaction times will be long. (M. Harris & Coltheart, 1986: 161–162)

It will be recalled that the original (and abiding) inspiration of the logogen model was Morton's interest in context effects. This interest is very much shared by Marslen-Wilson and his collaborators. The bottom-up aspects of the cohort model which have been discussed so far constitute only one dimension of its representation of lexical processing, the other being everything that might go under the heading of contextual contributions. It is clear that in normal language use we are not usually called upon to process words *in vacuo*; individual lexical items are typically embedded in syntactico-semantico-pragmatically coherent concatenations of other lexical items. The cohort model, like the logogen model, assumes that available contextual information has a facilitatory impact on lexical processing. However, whereas the logogen model seems to suggest that context effects are mediated by a semantic component (the 'cognitive system') separate from, though connected to, the logogen systems, the cohort model posits that each and every entry in the mental lexicon is equipped with inferential procedures:

> each word would have built into its mental representation not simply a listing of syntactic and semantic properties but rather sets of procedures for determining which, if any, of the senses of the word were mappable onto the representation of the utterance up to that point. (Marslen-Wilson & Tyler, 1980: 31)

The way in which semantico-pragmatic information is seen as being used in the cohort model is essentially an 'on-line' view of things. That is to say, the notion that contextual factors pre-select words is rejected (Marslen-Wilson & Tyler, 1980) on the basis that context-driven pre-selection would in fact be a highly inefficient manner of proceeding, given the open-endedness and unpredictability of even normal everyday language use. Reflecting on this point, we might consider the following exchange:

A: Shall we go for a drink down at the Hat and Feathers?
B: No. I feel like seeing a play. Let's go to the Theodore Hotel. The Linthorpe Players are putting on a really hilarious Tom Stoppard play there in the function room. It should be a good laugh.
A: Tom Stoppard at the Theodore, eh? OK. I feel like a lager. They have a really great selection of lagers at the Theodore.

In this exchange, plumping immediately for what might have seemed the contextually most likely word would probably have led A into thinking that B was suggesting a visit to the theatre and would have led B into thinking that A was desirous of a laugh. In the light of this kind of consideration, Marslen-Wilson & Tyler propose that contextual information has no impact on the selection of the word-initial cohort, but that, once the cohort has been established, word candidates which are inconsistent with the context can begin to be deactivated. Thus, the cohort activated on the basis of the /lɑː/ of *lager* (/ˈlɑgə/ – assuming the interlocutors were speakers of Standard British English) would have included not only *laugh* (/lɑːf/), but also items such as *lamé* (/ˈlɑmeɪ/), *larva* (/ˈlɑːvə/) and *lath* (/lɑːθ/). According to Marslen-Wilson & Tyler's proposals, the contextually implausible *lamé*, *larva* and *lath* would have immediately begun to be deactivated, whereas the onset of the deactivation of *laugh*, a contextually highly plausible item, would have had to await the occurrence of /f/ in the input and the recognition of the divergence between this phoneme and the /g/ of the input sequence.

The evidence cited by Marslen-Wilson and his colleagues (e.g., Marslen-Wilson & Welsh, 1978) in favour of a role for context in lexical processing comes not only from their well-known speech-shadowing experiments but also from word-monitoring and rhyme-monitoring studies. In speech-shadowing tasks, participants are required to listen over headphones to a passage of text read aloud and are asked to reproduce it faithfully with as short a time-lag as possible. In some of the studies, words in the original passage were deliberately mispronounced. For example, *tragedy* would be pronounced as *travedy*. Very often subjects replaced such deviant items with the correct versions of the words in question, and in about 50 per cent of cases the corrections effected were in the nature of fluent restorations, that is to say, the substitution of the correct versions of the mispronounced words was not associated with any faltering or hesitation in the flow of the repetition. Fluent restoration is taken to be an indication that a decision regarding the target word has been reached on contextual grounds prior to and irrespective of its formal recognition point. In support of this interpretation one can cite Marslen-Wilson's (1975) finding that fluent restorations were offered markedly more frequently in contexts of normal coherent and cohesive prose than where there was any kind of syntactic or semantic dissonance between the mispronounced item and its linguistic environment. One can also cite Marslen-Wilson & Welsh's (1978) finding that fluent restorations occurred far more often when a word was highly predictable from context than when it was only moderately predictable. Such results are interpreted as follows in terms of the model: the more contextually predictable a word is, the shorter the sequence of sounds required to reduce the cohort to a sole candidate – with the attendant higher probability that the mispronunciation will occur in an unanalysed portion of the word and so will remain undetected.

With regard to word monitoring, this task requires subjects to monitor linguistic material for the presence of a particular target word, pressing a button as soon as they perceive the word in question. Marslen Wilson & Welsh's (1978) subjects were presented auditorily with sentences of two types: (1) normal coherent prose and (2) syntactically licit but semantically anomalous prose. In a third condition, (3), subjects were asked to monitor randomly ordered strings of words. The mean reaction times for the three conditions were as follows:

1	normal coherent prose	273 milliseconds
2	syntactically licit but semantically anomalous prose	331 milliseconds
3	randomly ordered strings of words	358 milliseconds

What is interesting about these results is not only that the decreasing support offered by context in the three conditions corresponds linearly to increasing reaction times but also that the time taken to recognize words in normal prose contexts (273 milliseconds) is nearly 100 milliseconds less than the average time taken to utter the words in the passage in question (369 milliseconds). This clearly demonstrates that in context, words are recognized on the basis of much less than their full form. Moreover, Marslen-Wilson & Welsh estimate that about 75 milliseconds of the 273 constitute the normal, unavoidable, lapse of time between the identification of the target and the pressing of the button, leaving about 200 milliseconds of actual processing time. Now, it turns out that there is evidence to suggest that in the processing of words in isolation, an average of 29 words are still present in the cohort after 200 milliseconds' worth of processing. When one compares this with the single item arrived at after 200 milliseconds' processing in a coherent, meaningful context, one cannot but acknowledge the plausibility of the notion of on-line contextual influence.

The rhyme-monitoring results (Marslen-Wilson, 1980) tend in the same direction. In this case subjects were asked to press a button on hearing a word that rhymed with a particular stimulus word. Again, the material to which subjects were required to attend was presented in three conditions: (1) normal coherent prose and (2) syntactically licit but semantically anomalous prose, (3) randomly ordered strings of words. It was found that reaction times in rhyme monitoring were approximately 140 milliseconds longer than reaction times in word monitoring. This was interpreted as suggesting that subjects identified words first and only then decided about their rhyming possibilities, this latter decision accounting for the additional 140 milliseconds. The results also showed that with normal prose the later the target rhyme cropped up in the context the more speedily it was identified; in the case of semantically anomalous prose, the same effect was discernible but to a much lesser extent, and in the randomly ordered strings condition, the effect was absent. These findings were read as further evidence in favour of a role for contextual constraints, the point being that in normal prose the greater the amount of material preceding the target, the greater the specificity of semantico-pragmatic and syntactic constraints on word choice and the greater the number of word candidates that can be deactivated in the light of these constraints. In the case of the syntactically licit but semantically anomalous prose, meaning-related constraints did not operate but syntactic constraints still did. In the case of the randomly ordered strings of words, there were absolutely no contextual constraints to accelerate cohort reduction.

The question of context effects will recur later in the chapter. To return for the present to the form-based aspects of the cohort model, these have come under critical scrutiny from a number of quarters. Garman (1990) calls into question what others (Matthei & Roeper, 1983: 39ff.) have called the 'beads on a string' view of speech perception that Marslen-Wilson's proposals appear to incorporate:

> the notion of segmental elements ... arriving at the ear over time is certainly oversimplified ... since any 'time slice' through the acoustic signal shows evidence of preceding and succeeding elements. The auditory perception of this signal is therefore not susceptible of discrete judgments of a very precise nature concerning the point at which particular elements 'arrive'. (Garman, 1990: 288)

However, nothing very crucial seems to hang on this objection, which, as Garman acknowledges, 'tends in the direction of recognition points that might actually be in advance of the segmentally defined uniqueness point – by some very small factor (*ibid.*).

Garman goes on (*ibid.*: 288–289) to cite Marcus & Frauenfelder's (1985) suggestion, which they support with numerous references to empirical studies, that speech-sound processing is probabilistic:

> it seems unlikely that such categorical decisions can be made with the noisy and ambiguous signal which is speech. ... Incoming phonetic information cannot always be categorically recognized solely on the basis of the acoustic signal. ... recent data ... supports the idea that phonetic information is evaluated probabilistically rather than categorically during the process of word recognition ... (Marcus & Frauenfelder, 1985: 164)

Marcus & Frauenfelder therefore do not see word recognition as wholly dependent on or exactly contemporaneous with the point at which the item in question diverges by one phoneme from all other items. Rather they claim that subsequent deviation between the target item and other items in the cohort also has to be referred to in arriving at a definitive recognition. They show that, on average – at least in English – over the six phoneme positions following the uniqueness point, deviation between the target item and other candidates increases more or less linearly at a rate of about 0.5 phonemes per position. This means that, if their proposals are correct, the statistical properties of the (English) lexicon would in any case allow words to be recognized very quickly after the strictly defined uniqueness point, which is broadly consistent with the evidence supporting the notion that recognition occurs around the same time as the occurrence of the uniqueness point (e.g., Marslen-Wilson, 1984; Tyler & Wessels, 1983). This criticism differs from Garman's in positing a recognition point slightly later than instead of slightly earlier than the uniqueness point, but, again, it does no real damage to the model, especially since Marslen-Wilson now takes a fairly flexible line regarding the organization of his model (e.g., 1987, 1989a, 1990, 1993) and, in particular, accepts that input continues to be monitored beyond uniqueness points and that the deactivation of word candidates is reversible.

Finally, there have been some questions raised about the importance attributed to the beginnings of words in the cohort model. Emmorey & Fromkin (1988), while acknowledging that there is a fair amount of evidence in favour of phonological organization by initial segment, also point to some evidence suggesting that ends of words also have some importance in phonological processing. On a somewhat different but related tack, Aitchison notes (1994: 218) that the earliest version of the cohort model 'required undistorted acoustic signals at the beginning of the word' and could not cope with a situation of uncertainty in this position: 'if a wrong decision was made, the wrong cohort would be activated'.

Emmorey & Fromkin (1988) cite the following evidence indicating that words are most easily accessed via their beginnings:

- the fact that subjects in a 'tip of the tongue' state can often access the initial sound or syllable of the word they are looking for even when all else deserts them (R. Brown & McNeill, 1966);
- the fact that patients suffering from anomia (i.e., word-finding problems) are often able to access the word they need if they are given the relevant first segment or syllable (Benson, 1979);
- that fact that in a timed test, subjects have been able to come up with many more words sharing initial segments than having any other portion in common (Baker, 1974).

As for arguments cited in support of a role for final parts of words, these include:

- the greater frequency of misperceptions on ends of words than on medial portions (Browman, 1978);
- the lesser frequency of speech errors on ends of words than on medial portions (Cutler & Fay, 1982);
- the greater accessibility in 'tip of the tongue' states of final compared with medial segments (Brown & McNeill, 1966);
- the greater difficulty of producing words sharing medial vowels than of listing rhyming words (Baker, 1974).

Emmorey & Fromkin are cautious in their interpretation of such findings:

> It may be the case that words are listed by final rhyme structure or final (stressed) syllable ... But these facts can be accounted for by processing strategies separate from the order of listing, or by 'recency effects' found in many memory experiments, i.e. the end of a word is heard more recently and thus might be more easily remembered. (Emmorey & Fromkin, 1988: 128–129)

The implications for the cohort model of the facts regarding the greater memorability/accessibility of ends of words relative to middles of words are, as Emmorey & Fromkin suggest, rather unclear. As for Aitchison's point, she herself recognizes (1994: 218) that it does not hold for the more recent versions of the model, which have become more fluid in their organization.

Forster's search model

We come now to an example of an indirect model, in which access is represented as a serial process involving first a search for a matching element in the relevant mode and then a guided retrieval of the full word. As has already been indicated, it is possible to compare this two-stage process to what happens when we look up a word in a dictionary or look for a book in a library. The first stage of consulting a dictionary (of a language in an alphabetic writing system) is the scanning of head-word forms listed in bold type on the left-hand side of each column until we find the one that matches our target item. We can then go on to check the full entry for pronunciation details, meaning(s), morphosyntactic specifications, stylistic information, etc. In a library we go first to whichever catalogue has a point of departure which coincides with the information we already possess about the book we require (author, title, subject, etc.). Having located the relevant reference in the appropriate catalogue, we can then use the shelf-mark associated with the item to guide us to the actual book on the library shelves.

Of these two analogies, the latter may be the more apposite (see, e.g., Matthei & Roeper, 1983: 188–189), given that we come to the task of lexical access from different starting points (phonological, orthographic, semantic) on different occasions just as we approach the task of finding books in libraries with different kinds of information available to us at different times. In Forster's model, the initial search is carried out with the help of a number of peripheral access files, one organized along phonological lines, one organized according to orthographic properties, one organized on a

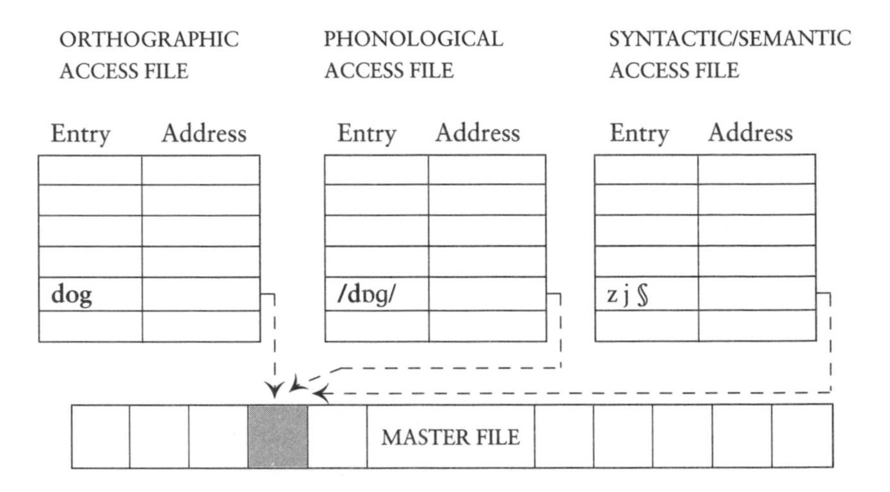

Figure 3.4 The essential components of Forster's search model (based on Forster, 1976: 268, Figure 4)

syntactico-semantic basis, etc. These correspond to the different library catalogues. These peripheral files contain listings of entries in the respective modes and also pointers (corresponding to shelf-marks) to the location of each entry in its complete form in the unitary master file (corresponding to the library shelves). The broad lines of the model are set out diagrammatically in Figure 3.4.

Thus, if one is processing spoken language receptively, one goes first, on this view, to the phonological access file; if one is processing written language receptively, one goes first to the orthographic access file; and if one is producing language on the basis of particular meaning intentions, one goes first to the syntactic/semantic access file. Once the unitary master file has been accessed, it can facilitate any kind of further operations on the word in question – whether these be in the realm of speaking, writing or understanding. It should be noted, however, that the peripheral access files are seen as absolutely autonomous in the sense that the information they contain is represented as strictly limited to the specific modality with which they are respectively concerned and that no connectivity is envisaged between the different access files. In general the model has the advantage of accounting for the intuition 'that an adequate lexicon must permit diversity of access but unity of storage' (Garman, 1990: 267). In other words, it seems to capture the fact that, while we are aware of coming to a given word, say *rain*, via a variety of routes – hearing it, reading it, processing its meaning – we do not usually consider /reɪn/ (phonological form), *rain* (orthographic form), and 'rain' (meaning) to be three different words but rather think of them as different aspects of or indicators of the same word – which seems to be precisely captured by Forster's representation of lexical relationships. On the other hand, as we have already seen during the course of discussion of the logogen model, to posit total autonomy for phonological and orthographic access respectively goes further in the direction of the separation of processing components than appears to be warranted by the evidence.

The access operation is represented as proceeding as follows. The properties of the stimulus form or meaning cause the search to be concentrated in a particular area or 'bin' of the relevant peripheral access file, but within that 'bin' items are checked serially in order of frequency until a match is found for the specifications of the stimulus. There is some vagueness in relation to the nature of the properties that are critical in the initial guiding of the search and, correspondingly, in relation to the bases on which the different 'bins' are constituted. With regard to phonological access, for example, presumably account needs to be taken (for reasons mentioned earlier) of initial segments, but (again for reasons discussed above) final segments may also play a role, as well, perhaps, as elements such as stress patterns and syllable structure. As for the suggestion that once the appropriate 'bin' has been targeted, subsequent search processes follow a frequency order, this has some intuitive appeal and seems to accord with the available evidence, but, as we shall see a little later, it is not without its problematic aspects. With regard to second-stage operations within the master file, it is envisaged that cross-referencing may occur at this level between words which are closely associated.

Before pursuing the questions raised by the proposals regarding the master file, however, let us return to the issues that have been raised in respect of the access files, namely those of autonomy and the role of frequency. Concerning the lack of provision in the model for connectivity between the peripheral access files, this lack fails to account in full for the evidence in respect of non-words. The fact that on lexical decision tasks it takes longer to reject a phonotactically licit non-word than it does to accept a real word (see, e.g., Gough & Cosky, 1977) can be explained in terms of the real word having an entry in the various files, and thus a *terminus ad quem* for the search processes, as opposed to the absence from the system of entries for non-words, with all that this implies for the necessity of a totally exhaustive (and futile) search. The fact that phonotactically illicit non-words are rejected more rapidly than phonotactically licit words and indeed more rapidly than real words are identified (see *ibid.*) is also explicable in terms of the model: whereas the last two categories of item cause a search to begin in a particular 'bin' of the phonological access file, the phonotactic illegality of the first category means that no 'bin' is found to correspond to the general properties of the stimulus, which in turn means that no search of entries can actually take place. However, the model provides no explanation for the fact that we are able to read non-words aloud and to attempt orthographic transcriptions of non-words we hear. These possibilities indicate the necessity for at least some system of grapheme–phoneme conversion. In addition, the fact that we are able to replicate pronunciations of non-words argues for a direct non-lexical link between auditory input and articulatory output, since a link via the file system is excluded by the absence of entries in the files corresponding to the non-words in question. Moreover, as we saw in connection with Morton's proposals for complete separation of phonological and orthographic access processes, there are various kinds of evidence which suggest that connections between phonological and orthographic processing exist at a lexical level too.

As regards the role of frequency, we need to ask whether what is being referred to is frequency of occurrence in the input generally, frequency of occurrence in the input attended to or frequency of output. We also need to be aware that frequency is modality-specific, that 'the frequency of the written form of a word may be different from the frequency of its spoken form' (Matthei & Roeper, 1983: 189). A further consideration in this context (cf. Matthei & Roeper, 1983: 184–185) is that word frequency broadly correlates with recency of occurrence in the input and output and that a frequent word is also likely to have been acquired early. How are we to know therefore whether the critical factor determining speed of access is relative frequency of occurrence as such (as not only Forster but also Morton – e.g., 1970 – would claim) or relative recency of occurrence (cf., e.g. J. R. Anderson, 1976; Scarborough, Cortese & Scarborough, 1977)?

So much for the characteristics of the peripheral access files; what now of the master file? This collection of individual (fully specified) lexical items is seen by Forster as having to contain some provision for connections between the items in question. One argument in favour of allowing for such inter-relationships is furnished by the earlier-discussed phenomenon of priming. The priming study cited in the context of Forster's proposals is that of Meyer & Schvaneveldt (1971). This was an experiment based on a lexical decision task in which items were visually presented in pairs. The results revealed that reaction times for the second member of the pair were shorter if this was semantically related to the first item. For example, the word *nurse* was more rapidly reacted to when preceded by *doctor* than when preceded by *table*. Forster's model tries to account for 'semantic priming' of this kind by positing cross-references in the master file between words that are related in meaning. With regard to the above example, the idea is that the retrieval of the fully specified item *doctor* will cause the item *nurse* to be processed via a direct search path within the master file without the necessity for a return to the relevant peripheral access file in order for this latter item to be dealt with 'from scratch'.

An alternative possibility suggested by Matthei & Roeper (1983: 189–190) and by Emmorey & Fromkin (1988: 143) within the general framework of Forster's model is that there might be two levels of semantic processing, a linguistic or lexical level and a non-linguistic, encyclopedic level:

> Another possibility would be to assume that the master file does not contain very much information about the meanings of words, just a sort of bare-bones specification of meaning. The entries would then be assumed to be linked in some way to another big file of information about the world, how it is structured and how it works. (Matthei & Roeper, 1983: 189–190)

Semantic cross-referencing according to this view would proceed via the general knowledge store. Thus, the master file item *doctor* would trigger reference to a constellation of information about doctors, including the information that they often work in hospitals alongside nurses, which would in turn trigger reference back to the master-file item *nurse*.

Unfortunately, neither Forster's explanation of semantic priming nor the general knowledge store perspective is very satisfactory. To take the latter first, this depends on the possibility of making a distinction between linguistic and non-linguistic or 'pragmatic' meaning. Emmorey & Fromkin are inclined to see this as unproblematic:

> That such a distinction exists seems to be unquestionable, as can be seen by the simple example of the difference between knowing the meaning of the word 'water' and knowing that its chemical structure is H_2O. Obviously one can know the first without knowing the second. (Emmorey & Fromkin, 1988: 143)

Are things really that simple? Let us look more closely at the example given by Emmorey & Fromkin. It is surely possible to see knowing the chemical composition of water in terms merely of having fuller access to the 'lexical' meaning of the word *water*. Such knowledge allows one, for example, to accept as semantically non-anomalous sentences such as 1 and 2 below in much the same way as one accepts 3 and 4 (whose acceptability would tend to be seen as linguistically based by semanticists of the Emmorey & Fromkin school):

1 Today we shall consider water and other hydrogen compounds.
2 Fish breathe water, just as we breathe air.
3 This is water, and here are some other liquids.
4 We drank some water.

Compare:

1a * Today we shall consider table-salt and other hydrogen compounds.
2a * Fish milk water, just as we milk cows.
3a * This is water, and here are some other solids.
4a * We ate some water.

From another – not incompatible – point of view, it is entirely possible to regard the 'everyday' or 'basic' meaning of *water* as simply a distillation into unconscious automaticity of what one knows 'pragmatically' from one's most frequent experiences with the substance to which the term most often relates.

Because of the relative frequency of uses of *water* which do not allude to the chemistry of its denotatum, one is, of course, able to understand and appropriately use the term in most contexts without any chemical knowledge, but is this qualitatively different from being able to deal with a polysemous word in many contexts without knowing more than one of its meanings? To stay with the example of *water*, unless one knows that this item can in certain contexts be applied to brine, perfumed alcohol, and amniotic fluid, one will make little sense of the following:

5 Water, water, everywhere,/ Nor any drop to drink.
6 He reeked of Cologne water.
7 When her waters broke, she knew the time had come to make a phone call.

However, not having these meanings of *water* at one's disposal will not prevent one from getting by without difficulty in the majority of situations where the word crops up.

Emmorey & Fromkin's statement that the distinction between linguistic meaning and pragmatic meaning is an obvious one is also undermined by the fact that it is a matter about which theoretical linguists have doubts and differences (cf. Maclaran, 1983). Within the Chomskyan school, for example, whereas some followers of Chomsky have taken essentially the Emmorey and Fromkin line (see, e.g., N. Smith & Wilson, 1979), Chomsky himself has consistently expressed worries over the possibility of making the distinction in question:

It is not clear at all that it is possible to distinguish sharply between the contribution of grammar to the determination of meaning, and the contribution of so-called 'pragmatic considerations', questions of fact and belief and context of utterance. (Chomsky, 1972: 111)

Do the 'semantic rules' of natural language that are alleged to give the meanings of words belong to the language faculty strictly speaking, or should they be regarded perhaps as centrally-embedded parts of a conceptual or belief system, or do they subdivide in some way? (Chomsky, 1980a: 62)

With regard to Forster's notion of direct cross-referencing within the master file, this has been called into question by some of Forster's own findings. Forster reports (1976) the results of an experiment involving pairs of words of different levels of frequency. The pairs in question were composed of two high-frequency words, two low-frequency words, one high-frequency word and one low-frequency word (so ordered), or one low-frequency word and one high-frequency word (so ordered). Forster's hypothesis was that in the mixed pairs, where the two items were semantically related, the frequency of the first item would determine speed of access. That is to say, he hypothesized that a high frequency first member of a pair would swiftly find a match in the relevant area of the relevant access file and trigger the retrieval of the fully specified item in the master file, and that direct cross-referencing within the master file would mean that the related low-frequency second member of the pair item would also be rapidly found despite its low frequency, because reference would not need to be made back to the access files where frequency was a factor. In the case of mixed pairs beginning with low-frequency items, the processing of both items would be slow because of the initial slowness of the search through the access file. Alas for this elegant hypothesis, the results of Forster's experiment show low-frequency items slowing down processing wherever they occur. It is by no means clear how such results are to be interpreted in the terms of the model.

Commenting on these and other similarly unclear results, Garman raises some fundamental questions about the soundness of the concept of cross-references in the master file:

do they effectively provide a separate search mechanism, and, if so, does this wastefully duplicate the function of the semantic access file? If there is no duplication, then what are the conditions under which one or the other search will be carried out? Are there sound-structure cross-references in the master file, and how far might these duplicate the operation of the phonological access file? (Garman, 1990: 270–271)

Such questions in turn lead Garman to put under close scrutiny the whole idea of a distinction between access files and master file and thus the very notion of two-stage lexical processing.

Levelt's 'blueprint'

So far we have been looking at models which are explicitly focused on the lexicon. Levelt's model, which is the subject of the present section, falls into a rather different category insofar as it seeks to address all aspects of language processing. However, as has already been indicated, its lexical dimension is particularly highlighted by its creator, who has continued to evince a special interest in lexical processing (see, e.g., Levelt, 1993a, 1993b). The work in which the model is elaborated (Levelt, 1989) bears the title *Speaking: from intention to articulation*, and, true to this title, the primary perspective of the model is a productive one, although receptive aspects of processing are not entirely ignored.

The model is represented diagrammatically as shown in Figure 3.5. There are in Levelt's conception two categories of component, declarative and procedural. The former – represented in the diagram by the curvilinear elements – deal in 'knowledge that', knowledge as facts – whereas the latter – represented in the diagram by the rectilinear elements – deal in 'knowledge how', knowledge of the steps to be taken in order to achieve particular goals (cf. J. R. Anderson, 1983; Ryle, 1949). Declarative knowledge required for language processing, according to Levelt, includes general information about the world (encyclopedia), information about the specifics of particular situations (situational knowledge), and information about stylistic appropriacy relative to specific sets of circumstances (discourse model). Also located under the rubric of declarative knowledge is lexical knowledge, both semantico-grammatical (lemmas) and morphophonological (forms). As far as the procedural components are concerned, these include:

- the Conceptualizer, responsible for message generation, microplanning and monitoring;
- the Formulator, responsible for giving the pre-verbal message a surface syntactic and phonological shape;
- the Articulator, responsible for executing as overt speech the phonetic plan emerging from the Formulator;

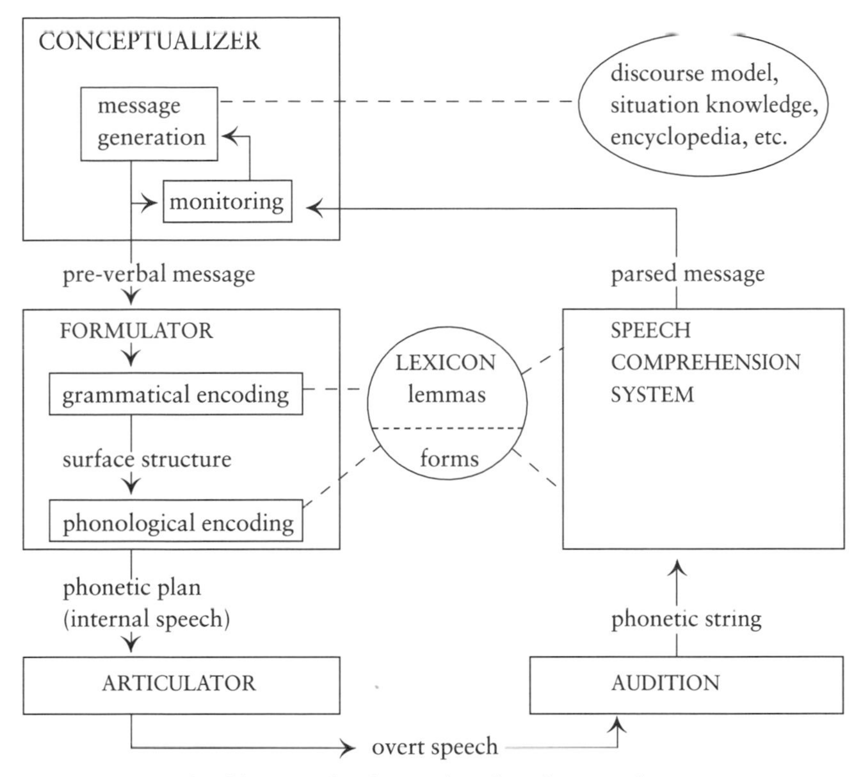

Figure 3.5 Levelt's blueprint for the speaker (based on Levelt, 1989: 9)

- the Audition component, responsible for analysing the speech signal into sound segments;
- the Speech Comprehension System, responsible for making semantico-grammatical sense of phonetic strings received.

To return to the lexical component, this, as has been mentioned, contains on the one hand lemmas and on the other hand forms (alternatively labelled lexemes in Levelt's terminology). A word's lemma is that which specifies its basic meaning, its syntactic category, its conceptual argument structure, its grammatical profile (e.g., in the case of a verb, whether or not it takes a direct object and whether or not it can take a dependent clause (relations to COMP), and its 'diacritic parameters' of variation (tense, aspect, mood, etc.)). The lemma also includes a 'lexical pointer' to the precise place in the lexicon where morphological and phonological information about the word in question is located. The following is Levelt's (1989: 191) outline of the lemma for *give*:

give: conceptual specification:
CAUSE (X, (GOposs (Y, (FROM/TO (X,Z))))) [i.e., X cause Y to pass from X's possession to Z's possession]
conceptual arguments: (X, Y, Z)
syntactic category: V
grammatical functions: (SUBJ [subject], DO [direct object], IO [indirect object]) relations to COMP: none [i.e., does not introduce dependent clauses beginning with complementizers such as *that*, *whether*, *if*, etc.]
lexical pointer: 713 [an 'address' chosen at random and arbitrarily coded]
diacritic parameters: tense
aspect
mood
person
number
pitch accent

As far as the lexical forms are concerned, these specify the precise morphological information that is necessary in order for phonological encoding to be able to take place – prior to the operation of the Articulator.

The part played by the lexicon in speech production is seen by Levelt as absolutely central; for him the whole set of formulation processes is lexically driven:

> This means that grammatical and phonological encodings are mediated by lexical entries. The preverbal message triggers lexical items into activity. The syntactic, morphological, and phonological properties of an activated lexical item trigger, in turn, the grammatical, morphological and phonological encoding procedures underlying the generation of an utterance. (Levelt, 1989: 181)

He refers to his assumption that the lexicon is the mediator between conceptualization and grammatical and phonological formulation as the lexical hypothesis:

> The lexical hypothesis entails, in particular, that nothing in the speaker's message will *by itself* trigger a syntactic form, such as a passive or a dative construction. There must be mediating lexical items, triggered by the message, which by their grammatical properties and their order of activation cause the Grammatical Encoder to generate a particular syntactic structure. (*ibid.*)

This view of the lexicon as mediator sits well with the evidence discussed in Chapter 1 of the interpenetration between lexis and grammar. On the other hand, the separation in the model of lexical meaning from encyclopedic knowledge is, as we have seen in the context of the discussion of Forster's model, rather more problematic.

A further question arises in relation to the representation of lexical knowledge as purely declarative. It is, after all, a commonplace among linguists that the lexicon contains word-formation or lexical-redundancy rules (see, e.g., Radford, 1981, Chapter 4; Cruse, 1986: 50), which make possible the generation of a potentially infinite number of new lexical forms. Since lexical creativity based on such possibilities involves a process and a goal, the psychological correlates of lexical-redundancy rules must surely be classed as procedural knowledge. Equally, from a receptive point of view, the attempt any reader or hearer will typically make to assign meaning and function to novel word forms cannot be a matter of the Speech Comprehension System accessing static lexical facts, but must, one would have thought, involve lexicon-internal consultation and cross-referencing processes – which again implies procedural knowledge. Indeed, the whole range of evidence discussed in earlier sections on context effects and priming seems to point in the direction of the lexicon being a dynamic rather than a static entity.

A further issue concerning the lexical dimension of Levelt's model is raised by Bierwisch & Schreuder (1992) and De Bot & Schreuder (1993), who see the necessity for an intermediary module ('Vbl') between the Conceptualizer and the Formulator. Their reasoning in favour of their proposal is that 'the conceptual structure presents the Formulator with fragments that exceed the size of one lemma's semantic representation', and that therefore there has to be a unit 'responsible for cutting up the fragment in chunks that can be matched with the semantic information associated with the different lemmas in the mental lexicon' (De Bot & Schreuder, 1993: 193). A further consideration they raise in this connection has to do with the fact that an individual may have more than one language and therefore more than one lexicon at his/her disposal and that different languages lexicalize the world differently. If, therefore, they argue, we assume (as Levelt does) that the pre-verbal message is language-neutral, 'then we are forced to assume that the Vbl function is sensitive to different lexicalization patterns and somehow "knows" which lexicalization pattern to choose' (*ibid.*: 195).

The relationship between the Conceptualizer and the Formulator is interesting from another point of view – namely that of the question of the degree of autonomy attributed to the various components of the model. Towell & Hawkins summarize the situation in this regard as follows:

> The production process is thought of as composed of relatively autonomous stages as specified by the boxes in the diagram. Processing has to be both

incremental and parallel to allow for the speed at which it must take place. Together this means that different parts of the message may be being processed at the same time (parallel), different parts of the message may be at different stages of the production process (incremental) and that these will not interfere with one another. In order to ensure that the message can nonetheless be delivered in the right order despite this flexibility there are buffer areas between the units which can delay delivery until the order is correct. (Towell & Hawkins, 1994: 168)

According to Levelt, the Conceptualizer learns what kinds of message can be coped with by the forms of a given language during the language acquisition process, so that during acquisition there has to be feedback between the Formulator and the Conceptualizer. Once the relevant ground-rules relative to the presentation of information to the Formulator have been established, however, such feedback is no longer required:

it is no longer necessary for the Conceptualizer to ask the Formulator at each occasion what it likes as input. In short, the systems have become autonomous. (Levelt, 1989: 105)

Such a view is reminiscent of Bever's (1981) suggestion that the 'psychogrammar' develops in interaction with perception and production processes but that once it has been established it becomes 'decoupled' from such processes and thus unavailable for further development. One objection to this kind of approach is that it is difficult to isolate a precise point at which the 'decoupling' can plausibly take place:

Most evidence suggests that ... the acquisition of pragmatic rules and lexis continues well into adulthood – being bounded perhaps only by death – and that even morphosyntactic and phonological development may persist well beyond puberty. This implies that communication between the processing systems and the psychogrammar has to remain open throughout an individual's life ... (Singleton, 1989: 220–221)

The same kind of argument can – *mutatis mutandis* – be applied to Levelt's notion that the Conceptualizer becomes 'decoupled' from the Formulator. If one accepts the view that first language acquisition continues into and through adulthood, and if one takes into account the fact that individuals also learn other languages at various stages in their life, the logical conclusion in Levelt's terms is that the autonomy of the Conceptualizer and the Formulator with respect to each other is not absolute even as far as the mature native speaker is concerned.

Levelt's model has in common with the earlier models discussed the fact that it is not only concerned with what the mental lexicon can plausibly be held to contain, but also with how the various postulated elements are to be seen as relating to each other. Perhaps the principal general point to emerge from the discussion of these models is that one should not be too quick to equate distinctiveness with unconnectedness. We have seen in a number of cases that a decision to represent particular components of the lexicon as operating in complete isolation from each other has been vulnerable to the criticism of being too strong in the light of empirical evidence. This particular cautionary message is of relevance not only to discussion in the remaining sections of this chapter, but also to discussion in later chapters of the relationship between the L1 mental lexicon and the L2 mental lexicon.

Modularity and the mental lexicon

We turn now to a view of mind which takes the notion of disconnectedness of different components of mentation very far indeed. In the present section we shall consider the view that the entire language faculty is a fully autonomous module, its operations impermeable to information from other sources, and we shall explore how this view relates to the lexical dimension of language processing both theoretically and empirically (for further discussion see Singleton, 1993a, 1998).

The tradition which recent approaches to modular processing claim as their pedigree is that of 'faculty psychology', whose origins are customarily traced back to the work of Franz Josef Gall (1758–1828), a German anatomist who developed the view that each intellectual and behavioural attribute was controlled by a particular location in the brain. He opposed this 'vertical' account of the nature of mind, in which the character of mentation was seen as dependent on the subject matter involved, to the prevailing 'horizontal' account of the mind, which represented mental operations as transcending content domains.

The current version of the modularity hypothesis is summarized by Garfield as follows:

> The mind is not a seamless, unitary whole whose functions merge continuously into one another; rather, it comprises – perhaps in addition to some relatively seamless, general-purpose structures – a number of distinct, specialized, structurally idiosyncratic modules that communicate with other cognitive structures in only very limited ways. (Garfield, 1987b: 1)

The kinds of systems that are hypothesized to be modular within this perspective include input systems such as certain components of the perceptual and the language-reception systems, and output systems such as aspects of motor control and language production. This view of the mind has two influential advocates in the persons of Noam Chomsky and Jerry Fodor, between whom, however, some differences exist: whereas Chomsky discusses modularity essentially in relation to language acquisition (see, e.g. Chomsky, 1980a, 1980b, 1988), Fodor's concerns are largely processing-oriented (see, e.g., Fodor, 1983, 1989).

The content of the language module: differing views

An important question that immediately arises is that of the actual content of the language faculty or module. Chomsky takes its central component to be 'grammatical competence', but does not come to any very firm conclusions about the precise boundaries of such competence. He questions, for example, whether the organization of sound belongs properly to the system of language rather than to other systems (1980a: 61), and, as we saw in the previous section, has long professed agnosticism about whether one can distinguish linguistic meaning from non-linguistic meaning. Fodor, for his part, seems to entertain no doubts about the intramodularity of phonetic/phonological processing. With regard to semantic processing, he takes a similar line to Chomsky's, although this does not prevent him from seeing the 'shallower' aspects of lexical processing as intramodular (see, e.g., Fodor, 1983: 64ff.; 1987a: 55ff.; 1989: 5ff.; Carston, 1988: 51ff.). Other modularists who have insisted that 'linguistic' meaning is clearly separable from other varieties of meaning (see, e.g., Emmorey & Fromkin, 1988; N. Smith & Wilson, 1979) have been content to regard the former as being represented and processed within the language module.

Neither Chomsky nor Fodor claims that the language module has absolutely no connection with other cognitive operations, nor that every aspect of cognition is modularly organized. (Fodor dismisses this latter notion as 'modularity theory gone mad' (Fodor, 1987b: 27).) It is obvious that the normal use of language requires an interface between language and other aspects of cognition, and Fodor and Chomsky both hold that this interface is provided by some kind of 'central', that is, general, non-modular, system which interconnects the modules and enriches their output with a range of experience accumulated from the previous operation of the various modules. The modularist position posits only, in relation to language, that there is a dimension of language-related cognition which is subserved solely by the language module, and that what happens within this particular dimension is impervious to 'central' knowledge and processes. On this view, the contribution of 'central' elements is a stage or level of language-related cognition which is separate from the strictly linguistic responsibilities of the language module.

It should be noted too that both Chomsky (e.g., 1981: 33) and Fodor (e.g., 1989: 11) admit to some reservations about the general empirical foundations of the modularity hypothesis. Both are obliged by the current state of the evidence to regard the question of whether or not language is subserved by a separate faculty as an empirical one. A very useful contribution to the debate in this connection from the modularist viewpoint would have been some neurolinguistic indications of a specific physiological correlate of an autonomous language module. However, such indications as are forthcoming in this area are not generally seen as offering unambiguous support for the modularity hypothesis (see, e.g., Jacobs & Schumann, 1992; see also Singleton's 1998 discussion of Linebarger, 1989).

Language processing in a Fodorian perspective

Despite such empirical uncertainties, the modular perspective on language and mind remains a powerful paradigm in linguistics and psycholinguistics. As has been indicated, the processing aspect of modularity has been the main focus of Fodor's writings on the topic, and it is also true to say that Fodor's version of the modularity hypothesis has been more influential than any other among psycholinguists working on processing issues. Accordingly, it is appropriate in the present context to pay particular attention to what Fodor has to say on the question of modularity in relation to language processing.

The main features of Fodor's characterization of the language module are as follows:

- Domain specificity: the notion that the language module is uniquely dedicated to a unique subject matter.
- Mandatory processing: the idea that we cannot hear utterances in a language we know without hearing such utterances as sentences.
- Inaccessibility to consciousness: the claim that most genuinely linguistic processes lie in the realm of the unconscious.
- Speed: the assumption that language processing is an inherently rapid process as compared with problem-solving activities such as chess.
- Informational encapsulation: the view that language-processing mechanisms are, as it were, blinkered with regard to data other

than the specifically linguistic data on which they are designed to operate – a view that for Fodor is the very cornerstone of his entire modular edifice, as well as the most controversial of his claims.
- Shallowness of intramodular processing: the suggestion that intra-modular language processing is an essentially formal matter, with no semantic analysis taking place 'inside' the items being processed.
- Neural hardwiring: the claim that the language module has its own particular neural architecture.
- Particular breakdown patterns: the interpretation of agnosias and aphasias as 'patterned failures of functioning' which cannot be explained in terms of 'decrements in global, horizontal capacities like memory, attention or problem-solving' (Fodor, 1983: 99).
- Specific developmental features: the reading of the research evidence on ontogenetic sequencing of language acquisition as indicating that much of language development is 'endogenously determined' (*ibid.*: 100).

As has been noted above, the most controversial aspect of the Fodorian conception of modularity is the notion that modules are 'informationally encapsulated' – the notion that, with regard to language processing, for example, general knowledge, contextual information, etc. have no role in intramodular linguistic 'computations'. In arguing for the informational encapsulation of modules, Fodor often refers to what he calls the 'teleological argument', claiming that modules are informationally encapsulated because they need to be in order to operate as efficiently as they do. One of the examples from visual perception he uses (1989: 11) is the case of someone spotting a 'yellow stripey thing' in New York and having to come to a rapid conclusion about whether it is a tiger. He argues that in such circumstances a perceptual system that was permeable to contextual expectations would not function rapidly enough to avoid disaster and that therefore modular processing needs to be 'as much like a reflex as possible' (*ibid.*).

Against this line of reasoning one can cite instances of people not believing and therefore not reacting appropriately to the evidence of their senses. Thus, in relation to language, one can point to what typically happens in situations where, for one reason or another, the expectation is that language *x* is being spoken but where, in fact, language *y* is being used. In such circumstances, comprehension tends to be blocked, even where both languages are familiar to the individual in question. For example, the following experiences were recently retailed to me by a native speaker of Finnish:

My sister, while studying in France, was once addressed on the street in Finnish. Only after several attempts by the speaker did she understand her own native language, the point being that she was expecting French. I have had a very similar experience trying to make Finnish out of something that was easy enough to understand when I realized it was English. (Service: personal communication)

Another body of evidence which seems to run counter to Fodor's point of view is that which emerges from the observation of the effects of deep hypnosis. With appropriate suggestion, a hypnotized subject may perceive and interact with objects and persons which are not present – or even totally fictitious – and may fail to perceive objects and persons which are present (see, e.g., Orne & Hammer, 1974: 136). Phenomena of this kind surely suggest that all perceptual systems are penetrable by higher-level information. Even reflexive responses may, apparently, be affected by hypnosis. Chertok, for instance, reports (1989: 63–64) cases where hypnosis sufficed to anaesthetize patients undergoing surgical operations, and even to arrest salivation and bleeding. If it is true that something as fast and as automatic as a physiological reflex can be influenced by externally implanted information or pseudo-information, then one surely has to question the credibility of the notion of informational encapsulation in language processing.

In any case, as Fodor acknowledges, such a notion appears to conflict with a large number of psycholinguistic findings, notably the findings of experiments involving reduced-redundancy procedures such as cloze.[1] It is a well-established fact that in cloze tasks the more predictable the target items in relation to the blanks (the higher their 'cloze value'), the better the performance of subjects attempting to fill the blanks will be. This looks like strong evidence of 'cognitive penetration' – evidence of the mechanisms involved in such tasks having access to subjects' expectations. To attempt to deal with evidence of this kind, Fodor (1983) deploys two lines of argument. His first is to question whether the mechanisms involved in the 'highly attentional' process of reconstructing degraded linguistic stimuli are the same as those which mediate 'automatic and fluent' processes. He cites in this connection Fischler & Bloom's (1980) finding that the recognition of test items where no degradation of the stimuli was involved was only marginally affected by

[1] 'In the cloze procedure words are deleted from a text after allowing a few sentences of introduction. The deletion rate is mechanically set, usually between every 5th and 11th word. Candidates have to fill each gap by supplying the word they think has been deleted.' (C. Weir, 1988: 49)

cloze value – and not at all affected by cloze value at high rates of presentation.

Fodor's second line of attack is to suggest that mechanisms internal to the language module may 'mimic' effects of 'cognitive penetration'. In support of this suggestion he refers to an experiment of Swinney's (1979) in which subjects listened to stimulus sentences along the lines of 'Because he was afraid of electronic surveillance, the spy carefully searched the room for bugs' – each containing an ambiguous word such as *bug* – and at the same time made lexical decisions about letter strings presented visually immediately after the occurrence of the ambiguous items (i.e., decided whether the strings in question constituted words or non-words). Swinney found a facilitation effect in relation to lexical decisions on strings forming words with meanings related to the meanings of the ambiguous words determined by their sentential contexts. Thus, the presentation of *bug* in the above sentence would facilitate a decision as to whether or not *microphone* was a word. However, what Swinney also found was that decisions on strings with meanings related to meanings of the ambiguous items which were not suggested contextually were also facilitated. Thus, the presentation of *bug* in the above context would also facilitate a decision on *insect*. To Fodor this finding indicates that what looks like general contextual effects in language processing may in fact be a matter of interlexical excitation. He hypothesizes that the mental lexicon is a sort of connected graph, with lexical items at the nodes and with paths from each item to several others, and that accessing an item in the lexicon consists in exciting the corresponding node, which also occasions the excitation of pathways that lead from that node:

> when excitation spreads through a portion of the lexical network, response thresholds for the excited nodes are correspondingly lowered. Accessing a given lexical item will thus decrease the response times for items to which it is connected. (Fodor, 1983: 80)

Fodor's conception of intramodular excitation of connected lexical forms relates to what he has to say about the relative shallowness of intramodular language processing. Citing evidence from his own work (Fodor *et al.*, 1980) that the recovery of the semantic definition of lexical items is not a prerequisite for processing syntax, he posits that the language module's operations are confined to the processing of 'linguistic and maybe ... logical form' (*ibid.*: 90). This brings us directly to the question of the mental lexicon in relation to the modularity hypothesis.

Modularity and lexical processing

The advantage, from Fodor's point of view, of confining his conception of the language module to that of a non-semantic processor is that it does not confront him with the intractable problem, discussed above, of where to draw the line between linguistic and non-linguistic meaning. However, on the one hand, his postulation of task-induced non-standard processing is a two-edged sword, and, on the other, it is not clear that what he says about the excitation of lexical nodes succeeds in circumventing the semantic/pragmatic issue.

Regarding the non-standard processing argument, if it is legitimate for Fodor to invoke such an argument in relation to modularity-challenging results elicited by cloze procedures, it must be legitimate for others to invoke it to account for modularity-friendly findings from other experiments. Indeed, it seems odd that Fodor should wish to claim that the restoration of degraded linguistic stimuli – by no means unknown in the ordinary use of language – may trigger non-standard processing, whereas he accepts as self-evidently indicative of normal processing the results of Swinney's (1979) experiment. After all, this latter involved subjects in consciously deciding whether or not visually presented strings of letters constituted words while at the same time dealing with a series of unconnected sentences presented in a different mode – i.e., aurally. Swinney's procedure strikes one as far more artificial and form-focused than any cloze task, and thus far more likely than cloze to provoke non-standard processing.

As for the explanation of apparent 'cognitive penetration' in terms of the excitation of complexes of lexical nodes, this seems plausible enough as a non-semantic account of what looks like a semantically motivated phenomenon until one stops to consider the nature of the interconnections it presupposes. The evidence is that such interconnections do indeed exist, but that they are (in the proficient language-user) primarily based on semantic relatedness (see, e.g., Aitchison, 1994). Indeed, if the nodal excitation posited by Fodor were not assumed to proceed along pathways linking semantically related items, then the 'mimicking' of contextual-semantic effects of which he writes would remain unaccounted for. The non-semantic process that Fodor posits as an explanation of evidence of context effects turns out, therefore, to be entirely dependent on connections between lexical nodes which derive from the denotative and connotative associations of the lexical items concerned. There is surely some inconsistency, to say the least, between Fodor's non-semantic conception of the language module and his postulation of lexical activation via meaning-based pathways. Moreover, the meaning-based character of these pathways brings us right back to the question of the nature of meaning.

A third possible explanation of context effects which preserves Fodor's notion of informational encapsulation of intramodular processing is that the effects in question are genuinely contextually induced, but that they are 'postperceptual' – that is, brought about by operations which (in language reception) come into play after the completion of intramodular processing and which take as their input the output of the module. On this view – proposed by Carston (1988) – exhaustive module-internal lexical access would be followed by parallel mappings and context-related choices between accessed items.

Let us not ignore, however, the possibility that what look like online context effects may actually *be* online context effects. Fodor himself notes that Marslen-Wilson's (1973) subjects were not only able to repeat linguistic stimuli with a time-lag of just a quarter of a second but also able to understand the words they were repeating. This means that not only formal aspects but also 'cognitive' aspects of lexical processing must be extremely fast as far as the reception of speech is concerned. More recent experiments by Marslen-Wilson have shown that subjects take no longer to relate an incoming utterance to discoursal context – even where pragmatic inferencing is involved – than to process it 'shallowly' (Marslen-Wilson & Tyler, 1987). Also relevant is the way in which subjects involved in speech shadowing (see above) exhibit highly fluent restoration of mispronounced words, these fluent restorations occurring far more frequently during the shadowing of normal prose than when the mispronounced words were anomalous with respect to context (see, e.g., Marslen-Wilson, 1975; Marslen-Wilson & Welsh, 1978). Other experimental findings (see Marslen-Wilson & Tyler, 1980) – already referred to – have shown that in a normal spoken prose context, target words which took on average 369 milliseconds to say could be identified on average within 200 milliseconds – which must mean that contextual information was somehow causing alternative possibilities to be eliminated while the words in question were still being uttered.

Another piece of evidence in favour of taking context effects at face value emerges from an experiment conducted by Foss (1982) in which he examined the influence of two aurally presented priming words on the identification of a target phoneme in a third aurally presented word. Foss discovered substantial priming across intervening words and sentences when coherent, meaningful sentences were used. For example, the recognition of /f/ in fish was primed in the following kind of context: 'The entire group examined the gills and fins. Everyone agreed that this was unlike any other fish caught in recent years.' However, when the words were jumbled into random lists, the priming effect disappeared. The fact that coherent contexts resulted in priming, whereas lists of words did not, surely constitutes counter-evidence to Fodor's notion that context effects are 'mimicked' by the activation of lexical networks in the mind merely through the occurrence of individual lexical forms. Carston's alternative view – that context effects are real but postperceptual – also receives little comfort from Foss's finding that initial phonemes of words (e.g., the /f/ in fish) were primed by previous context, and still less from Marslen-Wilson & Tyler's above-reported (1980) finding that context information took effect before the uttering of target words was complete.

How then to explain Swinney's cross-modal lexical priming results? One possible explanation lies in their very cross-modality, and, in particular, in the fact that reading was involved. The general view among experimental psychologists seems to be that reading processes differ from listening processes in terms of the extent to which they use context. It is indeed a psychological commonplace that whereas in speech perception, context effects are 'readily obtainable', 'in skilled reading ... context effects seem elusive' (A. Ellis & Beattie, 1986: 222). Thus, Fischler & Bloom's (1980) finding – the absence of facilitatory context effects from normal-speed reading – which Fodor cites against the whole concept of 'cognitive penetration', is normally interpreted as an indication of the particularity of the processing of the written signal with regard to use of context. A. Ellis & Beattie (1986: 225–226), for example, suggest that the ready decipherability of the printed word as opposed to the relatively impoverished nature of the speech signal favours 'bottom-up' rather than 'top-down' processing. If it is true that printed stimuli give rise to a greater measure of 'bottom-up' processing, then the fact that Swinney's experiments involved the use of visually presented letter-strings may well have triggered an across-the-board concentration on the characteristics of individual lexical items, with the result that contextually irrelevant meanings as well as relevant meanings were activated. The same argument can be applied to other cross-modal studies whose findings have been cited as pro-modular (e.g., Seidenberg *et al.*, 1982; Tanenhaus & Donnenworth-Nolan, 1984; Tanenhaus *et al.*, 1979).[2]

[2] Experimental evidence cited against an on-line role for contextual information in lexical processing from studies other than those with a cross-modal design tends to be ambiguous. Even modularists accept that such evidence is amenable to non-modular as well as modular interpretations (see, e.g., Tanenhaus *et al.*, 1987: 100–101).

This is not to say that context effects are entirely absent from processing where printed stimuli are involved. Even Swinney found that the contextually predictable meanings of his ambiguous items were more strongly activated than other meanings (see above). As far as tasks involving only reading are concerned, Fischler & Bloom (1980), while failing to find facilitatory context effects, did find that responses to words which were anomalous in context were inhibited relative to responses to contextually predictable words. This result too has been linked to the specifics of the reading process as opposed to the listening process. Harris & Coltheart (1986) note that in auditory word recognition we hear the sounds of any given word sequentially, which allows for the possibility of interaction between contextual information and recognition processes after only a part of the word has been uttered, but that, in contrast, in visual word recognition we have access to the whole word simultaneously, which abolishes any advantage in having a system which uses context to identify words before their production is complete.

> However, there is an advantage in having a system which can check word identification to see if the word which we have identified is consistent with context, and it is this checking procedure which Fischler and Bloom claim is causing the inhibition effects which they have demonstrated. (Harris & Coltheart, 1986: 170)

The claim here, in other words, is that the use of context in normal reading is 'postperceptual' because of the nature of the signal involved.

If lexical processing in reading does differ from lexical processing in listening because of the ready decipherability and instant availability of the signal in the former, it ought to be the case that rendering the written or printed stimulus more difficult to decipher will cause on-line context effects resembling those found in auditory word recognition to become discernible. And, indeed, this is what has been found (see A. Ellis & Beattie, 1986: 224). This brings us back to Fodor's suggestion that context effects in cloze tasks may be the result of the operation of some kind of abnormal back-up system. On the basis of the foregoing, we can probably accept Fodor's claim, but in a completely contrary sense to the one he intended. It appears to be the case that degrading the written/printed signal causes the reader to activate word-recognition processes which are normally reserved for the perception of speech. In other words, presenting readers with a degraded written/printed stimulus seems to rob the instruction-derived skill of reading of its specific signal-related characteristics in respect of lexical processing and to bring it closer to the 'primary' skill of understanding speech in terms of the degree to which context is exploited and relied upon.

Connectionism

Our final port of call in this chapter is the approach to language processing – indeed to all kinds of mental processing – known as connectionism or parallel distributed processing. The term 'connectionism' relates to the fact that this approach takes its inspiration from what is known about neurophysiological activity in the brain:

> During any brain activity, numerous brain cells are active, sending out signals to other neurons. Some signals are 'excitatory' (causing arousal), others are 'inhibitory' (causing suppression). The result is a 'network' of interconnected units. Arousal of any units causes them to be reinforced, whereas inhibition leads to the gradual loss of a connection. Psychologists have recently tried to build computer models which simulate this connectionist viewpoint. (Aitchison, 1992: 31)

> The connectionist account adopts the analogy of brain-style neuronal interactions (i.e. the fact that we have brains which are made up of millions of interconnected neurones which can be viewed as 'on-off' switches) and proposes that our cognitive system works in a very similar way. (Forrester, 1996: 152)

The alternative label, 'parallel distributed processing', refers to the claim made by connectionists that different portions of information are processed independently of one another ('in parallel') on different levels ('distributed').

One way of thinking about the contribution of connectionism to the modelling of language in the mind is in terms of a change of metaphor. Psycholinguists interested in language processing have in recent decades often drawn analogies with the operations of computers, talking about the 'articulatory program', 'programming errors', etc. Connectionists for their part have seen themselves as wishing to 'replace the "computer metaphor" as a model of the mind with the "brain metaphor"' (Rumelhart *et al.*, 1986: 75).[3] This is not a trivial change, however. It moves psycholinguistics in the direction of taking into account 'constraints from studies of the nervous system' (Broeder & Plunkett, 1994: 433), of proposing models which are alignable with 'neurophysiological reality' in much the same way that certain developments in syntactic theory have been motivated by

[3] 'Indeed, computer scientists are now designing machines called *neural networks* that attempt to imitate the brain's vast grid of densely connected neurons (J. A. Anderson & Rosenfeld, 1988; Levine, 1990).' (Wade & Tavris, 1996: 341)

an aspiration to greater 'psychological reality' in the sense of a requirement that 'a grammar provides us with a description of the abstract structure of the linguistic knowledge domain' which 'corresponds to the speaker's *internal* description of that domain' (Bresnan & Kaplan, 1982: xxiii).

Connectionism, modularity and parallel versus serial processing

The connectionist view of mind is usually taken to be antipathetic to the modular view discussed in the previous section. Thus, for instance, Cook & Newson (1996: 31) contrast the theory which 'divides the mind into separate compartments, separate modules, each responsible for some aspect of mental life' with 'cognitive theories that assume the mind is a single system, for example connectionism'. This is not, however, a universal view. For instance, Tanenhaus *et al.* (1987) posit different networks of connections for the parallel but autonomous processing of different types of information, which they see as merely a connectionist translation of the modularity idea and as doing no violence to the essentials of Fodor's theory. How can two such radically divergent views of connectionism co-exist?

We should note in this context that connectionism belongs to a much broader parallel processing perspective which stands in opposition to the serial processing perspective. As Garman (1990: 175) points out, the issue here is not about simultaneity versus sequentiality. Sequences of operations are found within parallel models, where successively presented domains (processing items/problems) obviously have to be dealt with successively; and simultaneity of operations is found in serial models, where different levels of operation may be simultaneously active though working on different domains – e.g., the processing of item *x* may be beginning at one level while the processing of item *y* is nearing completion at another. The essential difference between the parallel perspective and the serial perspective is that the former promulgates the notion of the independence of the different processing operations which are triggered by particular events and stimuli, whereas the latter represents processing as serially organized, with each stage dependent on the output of the previous stage.

The notion of independence of different processing operations in parallel models such as the connectionist one is not, however, (*pace* Tanenhaus *et al.*, 1987) in any real sense comparable to the Fodorian idea of informational encapsulation. Independence of processing in parallel models refers to micro-operations, and is not to be identified with a barrier between, for example, 'higher-level' semantic processes and 'lower-level' formal computations. Parallel-processing models are usually interpreted, on the contrary, as making claims about a high degree of top-down/bottom-up interactivity:

> lower-level processes can influence higher ones within the parallel-processing model, whereas in the serial model all higher-level processing [in speech production] is complete, for a given domain of processing, prior to any lower-level activity. By virtue of this, parallel models may be said to allow for interactive, on-line, bottom-up influences during the time course of [productive] language processing. (Garman, 1990: 174–175)

The symbolic paradigm and the connectionist paradigm

There is a further respect in which connectionism has been seen to pose a challenge to the Chomskyan/Fodorian view of language and mind. The Chomskyan/Fodorian view (in common with many others) is based on what is sometimes called the symbolic paradigm, the idea that cognition involves the manipulation of symbols:

> These symbols could refer to external phenomena and so have a semantics. They were enduring entities which could be stored in and retrieved from memory and transformed according to rules. The rules that specified how symbols could be composed (syntax) and how they could be transformed were taken to govern cognitive performance. (Bechtel & Abrahamsen, 1991: 1)

The connectionist paradigm, on the other hand, is 'distinguished from the traditional paradigm by the fact that it does not construe cognition as involving symbol manipulation', but offers 'a radically different conception of the basic processing system of the mind-brain ... inspired by our knowledge of the nervous system' (*ibid.*: 2). It sees knowledge in terms of connection strength rather than rules or patterns:

> In these models, the patterns themselves are not stored. Rather, what is stored is the connection strengths between units that allow these patterns to be recreated. (McClelland, Rumelhart & Hinton, 1986: 31)

Strong anti-symbolist claims have been made on the basis of Rumelhart & McClelland's (1986) simulation of the learning of past-tense forms using a connectionist architecture. They showed that quite a simple network could be trained to supply appropriate past-tense inflections/mutations for 506 English verbs, including 98 irregular verbs, stabilizing at a 91 per cent level of accuracy after 200 cycles of training. Moreover, the errors the network in question made *en route* resembled those made by children acquiring English as their first language. Elman (1990a) obtained not dissimilar results in respect of the acquisition of phonological structure. On the basis of their findings, Rumelhart & McClelland claim that language can be learned and processed without any recourse whatsoever to rules:

> The child need not figure out what the rules are, nor even that there are rules. The child need not decide whether a verb is regular or irregular. There is no question as to whether the inflected form should be stored in the lexicon or derived from general principles. (Rummelhart & McClelland, 1986: 267; see also, e.g., Seidenberg, 1995[4])

Some fairly sharp reaction to this kind of claim has come from Chomskyans. For example, Pinker & Prince (1988) point up divergences of detail between the network's output and that of children acquiring the same verbs, calling into question 'whether it is an accurate model of children' (*ibid.*: 81); Fodor & Pylshyn (1988) choose to interpret the connectionist proposals as relating merely to implementational, low-level phenomena; and Cook & Newson (1996) dismiss the fact that Rumelhart & McClelland's network can learn the particularities of English verb forms as of strictly no consequence from a Chomskyan standpoint:

> As these forms are peripheral to UG [Universal Grammar], whether they are learnable or not by such means has no relevance to the claims of the UG model. (Cook & Newson, 1996: 71)

An interestingly different tack is taken by Stevick (1996), who suggests that, in describing linguistic phenomena in terms of statements of 'rules', we may become the dupes of our own metaphors:

> We conclude (or at least we let our figures of speech give the impression) that these statements, the work of our minds and our hands, must be the cause (or must stand for the cause) of what we have observed, and we express this conclusion by saying, 'Rules govern behaviour.' (Stevick, 1996: 71; cf. also Elman, 1990b)

Stevick suggests that the term 'rule' might be better confined to the statements and that the term 'regularity' be deployed to cover the phenomena being described. In sketching an answer to the question of what causes such regularities, he suggests a possible line of demarcation between the two paradigms which, though expressed in less brusque rhetoric, actually chimes rather well with Cook & Newson's view of things insofar as it allows for the possibility of

[4] I am most grateful to Mickey Bonin for supplying me with the Seidenberg reference as well as the Plaut & Shallice and Regier references cited below.

both biologically endowed '*kinds* of regularities', which are assimilable to core UG principles, and learned specificities, which can be compared to the 'periphery' in UG terms:

> The *kinds* of regularities reflect inborn characteristics of the physiological equipment we use for networking. Some of these characteristics are very subtle, as yet undiscovered, and absent from the mechanical and electronic equipment used in connectionist investigations.
>
> The *specifics* of regularities come from what has previously happened to our networks. (*ibid.*)

Taking a somewhat broader approach to the question and taking it beyond the confines of the question of the relationship between connectionism and UG-style nativism, McShane (1991) suggests that an earlier version of the connectionist model (McClelland & Rumelhart, 1981) may provide a pointer to a compromise between connectionist and symbolic principles. The model in question is focused on reading. Letter identification is via an interconnected network of feature units with inputs to letter units:

> The individual letters are represented as units (and therefore as symbols) one level higher in the processing hierarchy. This level also forms an interconnected network along connectionist principles, which activates word units at the next highest level in the hierarchy. (McShane, 1991: 341)

For McShane, this kind of hybrid model combines the advantage of capturing bottom-up activation by sensory data with that of capturing top-down control from higher levels.

Connectionism and spreading/interactive activation

As was indicated at the outset of this chapter, one of the principal elements in connectionism is the concept of spreading/interactive activation, the idea that in language processing a multiplicity of nodes are excited by the arousal of a node to which they are connected. This notion ante-dated connectionism and has an existence outside as well as within the strictly connectionist school. Thus, for example, Dell (1986) relates his 'spreading activation theory of retrieval' not only to connectionist proposals (e.g., Cottrell & Small, 1983; Feldman & Ballard, 1982; Grossberg & Stone, 1986) but also to pre-connectionist 'interactive activation' models (e.g., McClelland & Rumelhart, 1981; Rumelhart & McClelland, 1982) and to other spreading-activation theories (e.g., J. R. Anderson, 1983; Dosher, 1982; Rumelhart & Norman, 1982). However, these different approaches to some extent blur into each other, and, indeed, have at various times involved the same researchers. Rumelhart, for instance, who is now known as a connectionist, has also worn an interactive-activationist hat and a spreading-activationist hat (see references above and in previous paragraphs). All three approaches posit parallel processing; connectionism and interactive-activation models share the assumption that activation not only spreads outwards to more and more nodes – the spreading-activation view[5] – but also moves backwards and forwards between the activated nodes; connectionism differs from the other two approaches in, broadly speaking, making no use of symbols and in postulating not only excitatory but also inhibitory signals.

Aitchison gives the following account of the workings of activation in the interactive-activation conception of lexical retrieval:

> an initial impetus progressively fans out and activates more and more words as it spreads along the various connections . . . As the activated links are inspected, those that are relevant get more and more excited, while those that are unwanted fade away . . . Since the current is flowing to and fro, anything which is particularly strongly activated in the semantics will cause extra activation in the phonology, and vice versa. (Aitchison, 1994: 206)

The connectionist picture would differ from the above on the one hand in envisaging the 'turning off' rather than just the 'fading away' of certain elements under particular impulses and also in representing 'words' as collections of connections rather than as stable, enduring symbols.

Connectionism, the lexicon and the future

We have seen that connectionism is characterized by a particular configuration of features, some of which it shares with other models. The particular models of the lexicon dealt with in the first part of the chapter demonstrate this overlap admirably. Thus, for example, the Morton model, the Marslen-Wilson model and the Levelt model all posit parallel processing. Only the Forster model is wholly free, as it were, from all taint of connectionism. Moreover, no doubt because it provides the promise of such a ready interlocking with the neurophysiological dimension of language processing (see above), the

[5] This is a simplification. The relationship between terminology and model type is not always as neat as is suggested here. For example, Dell's (1986) version of 'spreading activation' allows for 'positive feedback from later to earlier levels', a feature which 'makes processing in the network highly interactive' (Dell, 1986: 288). Indeed, Green (1993: 269) goes so far as to describe Dell's proposals as a 'three-level connectionist network'.

connectionist optique is exercising a growing influence in the sphere of lexical modelling. For instance, Marslen-Wilson's cohort model, which was always a parallel-processing model, has recently moved very much in the direction of becoming an interactive-activation model too (Marslen-Wilson, 1987, 1990). There has also, let it be said, been some movement from the connectionist side, with more recent versions of connectionism moving beyond a strictly formal account and allowing for access to some level of semantic representation (see, e.g., MacWhinney & Leinbach, 1991; Plaut & Shallice, 1994; Regier, 1996).

Almost everywhere one turns in the recent literature on the mental lexicon one finds references to connectionism. Aitchison, for example, cites (1994: 233) an observation from Elman & McClelland (1984) to the effect that computer modelling of lexical processing of the kind engaged in during the 1970s and early 1980s had not been notably successful. Aitchison goes on to suggest that the new-style connectionist modelling 'may be on the right track' in taking the brain as its inspiration:

> The human brain is capable of massive parallel processing: an uncountable number of connections can be made simultaneously. It activates many more connections than are strictly needed for almost every brain process, then suppresses those which are not required. These properties are found in some of the new 'connectionist' computer models with their intricate networks. (*ibid.*)

In an L2/bilingual perspective, Green (1993: 260) notes that the effect of a delay in lexical comprehension owing to competition between plausible L1 and L2 candidates for recognition has been modelled in a single-language framework (i.e., where the competitors are from the same language) using connectionist frameworks; Gass & Selinker (1994: 276) evoke the relevance of connectionism to current theories of how L2 words relate to each other in the learner's mind (see next chapter); and R. Ellis (1994: 407) refers to Schmidt's (1988) contention that connectionism is well-adapted for dealing with variability and 'fuzzy concepts'.

Ellis also quotes Gasser's (1990) assessment of the future role of connectionism, which will serve well as a coda to the present section:

> It is now clear that some form of connectionism will figure in a general model of human linguistic behavior. The only question is whether the role will be a minor one, relegated to low-level pattern-matching tasks and the learning of exceptional behavior, or whether the connectionist account will supersede symbolic accounts, rendering them nothing more than approximations of the actual messy process. (Gasser, 1990: 186)

Concluding summary

In the first part of this chapter we examined the better-known models of lexical processing. We looked at two influential representatives of the direct, or one-stage, type of lexical model – Morton's logogen model and Marslen-Wilson's cohort model; we explored an oft-cited representative of the indirect, or two-stage, type of model – Forster's search model; and we also considered Levelt's 'blueprint for the speaker', which, though not solely a model of the lexicon, has a great deal to say about lexical operations. In the second part we considered the implications for lexical processing of the idea that the mind is modularly organized, focusing, in particular, on Fodor's proposals in this connection. In the third part we explored the lexical dimension of connectionist models of mind.

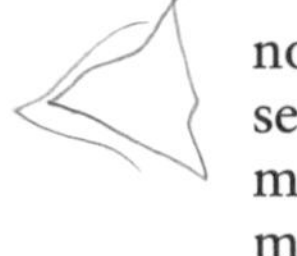

With regard to the logogen model, it was suggested that, while the notion of separate components for auditory and visual word analysis seems to be empirically supported, the notion that such components might be totally unconnected does not. With reference to the cohort model, some questions were raised about the strict linearity of its earlier versions, given the importance of ends of words in word recognition. It was recognized that the logogen model and the cohort model have in common the fact that one of their focal aims is the explication of context effects in lexical processing. Forster's model, for its part, was found to be wanting in relation to its proposals in respect of context effects, since the cross-referencing it posits to account for such effects requires either a strictly lexicon-internal solution based on the concept of a 'master file', which runs into empirical difficulties, or an appeal to a general knowledge store, which entails the making of a dubious distinction between linguistic and pragmatic meaning. As far as Levelt's 'blueprint' is concerned, it was seen as having the advantage, in envisaging the lexicon as mediator between conceptualization and grammatical and phonological encoding, of being in harmony with current views of the relationship between lexis and grammar; on the other hand, it was criticized for its suggestion that lexical knowledge is separable from encyclopedic knowledge, for its representation of lexical knowledge as static, declarative knowledge, for its incapacity, as it stands, to cope with multilingual processing, and for its postulation of a developmental point from which feedback between the formulation process and the conceptualization process simply ceases.

The modularity hypothesis was accorded its due place in the 'faculty psychology' tradition, and its relationship to Chomskyan thinking about the 'language faculty' was also noted. However, it was discussed principally in the perspective of Fodor's conception of the language module, and in particular in the perspective of the Fodorian notion of 'informational encapsulation' and the problem posed for this notion by evidence of lexical context effects. An outline was presented of a number of proposals to deal with apparent context effects in ways which leave the idea of informational encapsulation unscathed, but these proposals were found less persuasive than the simple expedient of taking on-line lexical context effects at face value, an approach which has strong empirical support.

Connectionism was presented as – on most interpretations – antipathetic to at least the Fodorian version of the modularity hypothesis and indeed to the entire 'symbolist' conception of linguistic knowledge in which it has its genesis. Some possible ways of reconciling symbolist and connectionist approaches were mentioned, and the relationship between connectionist models, spreading-activation models and interactive-activation models was briefly explored. Similarities between the connectionist representation of lexical processing and the models of Morton, Marslen-Wilson and Levelt were noted, and attention was drawn to the fact that, according to most commentators, the future evolution of models of the mental lexicon, and indeed of psycholinguistic models generally, will be heavily marked by the influence of connectionism.

4 *The L2 mental lexicon: a law unto itself?*

We come now specifically to the implications of the fact that an individual may have lexical knowledge relative not just to one language but to an indefinite number of languages. Reports often appear in the press about this or that individual claiming to speak dozens of languages. I myself had a teacher of French and German who – because of his peregrinatory upbringing – had, at least according to his own assessment, 7 languages to near-native level and a working knowledge of 13 more. While such impressive feats of polyglottism are relatively rare, most of us these days can perform – if only to the extent of understanding the signs in hypermarkets or ordering a meal – in at least one language other than our mother tongue, and research has demonstrated that lexical knowledge is an absolutely crucial factor across the whole spectrum of L2 activities (see, e.g., P. Kelly, 1991; Koda, 1989; Laufer, 1992; Laufer & Nation, 1995; Linnarud, 1986).

How then do we acquire, organize and process our lexical knowledge when more than one language is involved? Discussion of this issue in the present chapter will revolve around its two most controversial dimensions, both of which have to do essentially with the relationship between the L2 mental lexicon and the L1 mental lexicon. On the one hand, it addresses the view that the respective roles of form and meaning in the L2 lexicon are qualitatively different from their roles in the L1 mental lexicon. On the other hand, it examines the question of whether the L1 mental lexicon and the L2 mental lexicon develop and/or function separately or in an integrated manner.

Form and meaning in the L2 mental lexicon

As has been indicated, the question of the respective roles of form and meaning in the acquisition and processing of L2 lexis has been a prominent theme of recent debate. One claim has been that the basis of the operations of the L2 lexicon is phonological rather than semantic, that 'while in the native speaker's mental lexicon there are strong semantic links between the words, the connections between words in additional languages are primarily phonological' (Laufer, 1989: 17 – referring to Fromkin, 1971; Hatch, 1983; Soudek, 1982). This claim – though widely held – is not actually supported by the evidence that is available on the issue, and it has been specifically challenged in publications drawing on data from the Trinity College Dublin (TCD) Modern Languages Research Project (MRLP) (see Singleton, 1990a). The MLRP studies are discussed below in Chapter 6. The present section examines other relevant research findings, starting with the evidence from the Birkbeck Vocabulary Project – which is usually cited in favour of the 'phonological' view of the L2 mental lexicon – and going on to review evidence from research into intralingual and intralexical learnability factors, lexical memory research, research into context-based lexical guessing and acquisition, and research into the role of cross-linguistic influence.

The Birkbeck Vocabulary Project findings

The body of data which has been most frequently quoted in support of the 'phonological' view of L2 lexical operations – and which continues to be referred to in this connection (see, e.g., R. Carter, 1987: 159–160; Channell, 1988; Gass & Selinker, 1994: 276; Harley, 1995b: 7) – is that yielded by the Birkbeck Vocabulary Project word-association tests. Meara, who established and directed the Birkbeck Project, considered that the results of these tests revealed the L2 mental lexicon as 'quite different from that of the native speaker' (1984: 233–234; see also Meara, 1978, 1980). Some examples of the kinds of associates Meara's tests elicited are given in Table 4.1.

Meara's interpretation of his data can be criticized on the basis of a consideration of the nature of the Birkbeck tests and also on the basis of what is known about child/adult differences in performance on L1 word-association tests. Regarding the nature of the tests, one can note that, although Meara (1984: 231) presents his results as being founded on the use of 'very common' L2 items as stimuli, some of the examples he gives of the stimulus words used do not actually chime particularly well with this claim – comprising as they do quite rare items such as *caque* ('herring-barrel'),[1] *émail* ('enamel'), *toupie* ('spinning-top'), etc. In view of the rarity of such words, it seems

[1] On one occasion when discussing these data with a large class of students (100+), all of

Table 4.1. *Associations made by native English speakers to French stimulus words. All these associations illustrate some sort of phonological or orthographic confusion (Meara, 1984; 233, Table 2)*

Stimulus	Response	Source of confusion
béton	animal	bête
béton	stupide	bête
béton	conducteur	bâton
béton	orchestre	bâton
béton	téléphoner	jeton
béton	Normandie	breton
fendre	permettre	défendre
naguère	eau	nager
caque	poulet	cackle (?)
caque	rigoler	cackle
caque	gateaux [*sic*]	cake
semelle	dessert	semolina (?)
semelle	odeur	smell
traire	essayer	try
cruche	important	crucial
émail	lettre	mail
émail	chevalier	mail
dru	dessiner	drew
toupie	argent	2p (?)
toupie	cheveux	toupé
risible	lavable	rinsable (?)
risible	incre [*sic*]	rinsable (?)
jeter	hurler	hurl
mou	vache	!!!

likely that subjects' responses to them reflect less an L2 mental structure which is qualitatively different from that of their L1 lexicon than a simple state of ignorance which provokes a desperate casting about for lexical straws to clutch at. (This is all the more likely given Meara's implication that his subjects had relatively modest knowledge of the L2 when he talks about 'the small size of their vocabularies' (*ibid.*: 232).) The analogy may be drawn with L1 situations in which totally unfamiliar lexical items are encountered – situations that tend to provoke the making of wild guesses based on any clues to connections with known words which the sound or look of the

whom were native speakers of French, I asked if anyone present knew what *caque* meant. Not a single hand went up.

unfamiliar item may offer. Certain kinds of joke and television game show rely precisely upon this phenomenon.

Another possibility is that – again, especially given the relative rarity of certain of the stimuli – in some instances the items presented might simply have been mistaken for other words. Hatch & Brown (1995: 378–379) report some clear examples of such misidentification from an L2–L1 translation task where the L2 was English and the L1s were Spanish and Japanese:

English stimulus: *happened*	L1 translation: *felices* (Sp.)	'happy'
English stimulus: *worth*	L1 translation: *palabra* (Sp.)	'word'
English stimulus: *still*	L1 translation: *estilo* (Sp.)	'style'
English stimulus: *each*	L1 translation: *dono* (Jap.)	'which'
English stimulus: *incurred*	L1 translation: *fukumu* (Jap.)	'include'
English stimulus: *explosion*	L1 translation: *setsumei* (Jap.)	'explanation'

(extracted and adapted from Hatch & Brown, 1995: 379, Table 15.1)

Some further examples of this phenomenon are provided by Yongqi Gu (1996) from his study of the English vocabulary knowledge of 65 Hong Kong-based and 60 Beijing-based university students. Thus, for instance, 21 of his Hong Kong sample and 3 of his Beijing sample translated the word *precious* into their L1 as 'previous'. Meara acknowledges the possibility of such misidentification when he talks about 'orthographic or phonological confusions' (see Table 4.1 above). However, in so doing he undermines his own argument. If, for example, his subjects really did misperceive the stimulus *béton* as *bâton*, then the response *orchestre* is a perfectly straightforward case of a semantic associate.

Actually, relatively few of the responses reported by Meara are genuine 'clang' responses (responses related to stimuli in phonological terms only). Maréchal (1995), having re-analysed data obtained by Meara (1978) using a translation of the Kent-Rosanoff list (Kent & Rosanoff, 1910), concludes that clang responses are very much the exception:

> a closer look at his data reveals that among the 100 words [i.e. the 100 French stimuli used by Meara] 47 give rise exclusively to semantically related answers, and only 18 exclusively to phonologically related answers (in the 3 most common primary responses of the learners). These last are also the most difficult words of the list (e.g., rugueux, aigre, chou, tigre, amer). (Maréchal, 1995: 17)

We shall return to this matter of how 'phonological' the responses reported by Meara really are later in the discussion.

Table 4.2. *Analysis of English stimulus words and Cantonese speakers' most frequent responses (adapted from O'Gorman, 1996: 23, Table 1b)*

Where two responses are specified, this indicates that the items in question occurred equally frequently in the data.

Stimulus word	Most common response(s)
table	furniture
dark	night, black
man	woman
deep	dark
soft	hard
mountain	hill, high
black	colour
hand	finger
short	long
smooth	rough
command	order
woman	man, lady
cold	hot, winter
slow	fast
white	snow
needle	thread
girl	boy
health	wealth, body
moon	sun, night
king	queen

Further light is shed on this issue by a recent study by O'Gorman (1996) of the English L2 word-association test responses of 22 Cantonese speakers whose English was judged to be in the 'mid-proficiency range'. Although it is evident from the rhetoric of her report that O'Gorman was in this investigation expecting to find evidence favouring Meara's view, in fact her data tend – at least in relation to form and meaning – in quite the opposite direction, as Table 4.2 demonstrates.

The only clang associate among these subjects' most common responses is *wealth* (in response to *health*).[2] In all other cases the responses have clear semantic links with the relevant stimuli.

[2] Actually, even in this case one could argue that *wealth* has a syntagmatic relationship with *health*, given the number of times the two words and their derivatives crop up together in literature, prayer and popular sayings in English – in contexts in which the

With regard to child/adult differences in L1 word-association tests, Söderman (1989, 1993) places L2 data elicited by such tests in the context of L1 findings. Söderman recalls that 'clang' associates are very much in evidence in children's L1 responses to such tests. Referring to a number of studies conducted in the 1960s and 1970s (R. Brown & Berko, 1960; Ervin, 1961; Entwisle, 1966; McNeill, 1970; K. Nelson, 1977), Söderman points to the 'shift in response type' that has been found to occur when L1 word-association tests have been used with subjects of different ages. The strong implication of such findings is that the proportion of phonologically motivated responses produced reflects level of proficiency in a particular language rather than the status of the language in question in terms of nativeness or non-nativeness. Further evidence in support of this view is provided by Söderman's own work, which shows that a shift in response type is also discernible between less-proficient and more-proficient stages of L2 development. In fact, the shift in response type recorded goes beyond merely a reduction in 'clang' associates. Another attribute of child/adult L1 response differences is a lower proportion amongst adult responses of 'syntagmatic' associates and a higher proportion of 'paradigmatic' associates. 'Syntagmatic' associates are words which frequently collocate with the stimulus item (as in *sell~short*, *red~rose*, *steel~band*, etc.), whereas paradigmatic associates are words which could be substituted for the stimulus item (as in *sell~buy*, *red~green*, *steel~metal*, etc.). Söderman's results show that this shift occurs also in L2 lexical development.

Söderman's subjects were four groups of learners of English as a foreign language of different levels of proficiency. These four groups evinced a shift in response type in respect of the same English word-association test from proportionally more to proportionally fewer 'clang' associates and from proportionally more to proportionally fewer syntagmatic responses as L2 proficiency level increased. Similar findings emerged from a word-association test-based study of learners of Irish as a second language of differing levels of proficiency (Cunningham, 1990). This seems to point to what Ard & Gass (1987: 249) refer to as 'an increasing importance of semantically based factors in lexical organization as learners increase in proficiency'. Interestingly, though, Söderman does not interpret her

implication is that they are linked by more than mere rhyme. Thus, for example:

Say that health and wealth have missed me ... (Leigh Hunt, *Rondeau*)

... grant her in health and wealth long to live. (*Prayer for the Queen's Majesty*, *The Book of Common Prayer*)

Early to bed and early to rise
Makes a man healthy, wealthy and wise. (popular saying)

findings as indicating a simple causal relationship between increased *overall* linguistic proficiency and a *general* change in the way in which the lexis of that language is stored and processed. She notes (1989: 119) that even 'the word associations of the most proficient learners still contained a surprising amount of syntagmatic and clang responses', and that 'the least proficient group gave evidence of an impressive number of paradigmatic responses'. For her the changing distribution of response types is to be related to proficiency in respect of 'particular words': a specific lexical item will evoke different types of response at different stages of its incorporation into an individual's mental lexicon irrespective of the status (i.e., L1 or L2) of the language it belongs to and of the individual's global proficiency level in the language in question. This conclusion accords well with the above suggestion that some of the Birkbeck results were occasioned by the relative rarity of the stimulus items, and with what has been said about how native speakers cope with words in their language which are unfamiliar to them.

Actually, as Maréchal (1995: 18) points out, Meara himself (e.g., 1978) in some measure recognizes level of lexical knowledge as a factor in word-association response types. However, he fails to take account of this factor in the statements he makes (see above) regarding differences between the L2 and the L1 mental lexicon. Moreover, to the extent that he does bring it into the picture, he seems to see the organization of the L2 mental lexicon as evolving globally in a more L1-like direction with growing general proficiency, as opposed to Söderman's notion – supported by her data – that each lexical item has its own processing history, passing from a more 'phonological' to a more 'semantic' profile as it becomes more integrated into the internalized system.

Research into intralingual and intralexical factors in L2 vocabulary-learning difficulty

Research which looks at the L2 vocabulary-learning difficulties presented by L2-internal factors broadly supports the line taken in the foregoing discussion. A particularly interesting corroboration of the above analysis comes from research by Hulstijn & Tangelder (1991, 1993) which investigates the extent to which English word pairs similar in form and/or meaning were confused by learners of English of different levels of proficiency. Lexical confusions based on purely formal similarities have been extensively investigated by Laufer (e.g., 1988, 1990b, 1991a), to whose work we shall be returning below, but, as has been indicated, Hulstijn & Tangelder's studies are not concerned with only formally similar items, but specifically explore the relative roles of form and meaning in occasioning intralingual lexical interference.

Three experiments with this kind of exploration as their goal are reported by Hulstijn & Tangelder. Thirty-six English word pairs were used in these experiments, 12 involving similarity of form alone (F+M−) (e.g., *adulthood*, *adultery*), 12 involving similarity of meaning alone (F−M+) (e.g. *medium*, *moderate*), and 12 involving similarity of form and meaning (F+M+) (e.g, *historic*, *historical*). In the first experiment, a cued recall task, one member of the pair had to be written into a blank situated in a context (one or two sentences), the first letter of the word and its grammatical class being supplied. The format of the test is illustrated by the following pair of test items:

A Don't underestimate these small revolutionary groups. What we are talking about was a h .... (A [for adjective]) change and these people played a major part in it.
(important events with great influence over the years)

B At first people believed the newly discovered papers, allegedly written by Chaucer, false but later they proved to be autographs and manuscripts of h .... (A [for adjective]) interest.
(concerned with events of the past)

Four types of response were possible: (1) a correct response (e.g., *historic* in A); (2) an incorrect response involving the other item in the pair (e.g., *historical* in A); (3) an incorrect response with no connection to the correct response (e.g., *huge* in A); and (4) no response. This task was performed by two groups of advanced (university-level) learners of English and also by a group of English native speakers. For both the advanced learners and the native speakers the incidence of interference in the F+M− condition was at a significantly lower level than in the F+M+ condition, and interference in the F+M+ condition was at a significantly lower level than in the F−M+ condition.

The other two experiments deployed the same word pairs and test sentences as the first, but set recognition tasks where target words had to be selected from a number of alternatives. The second experiment, which was conducted with the same two groups of advanced learners as were involved in the first experiment, provided a choice of three possibilities for each test slot. One of these alternatives was the correct member of one of the 36 word pairs, the second was its 'counterpart' – the other member of the pair in question – and the third was related to the word pair concerned in different ways depending on the experimental condition: i.e., formally and semantically in the F+M+ condition, formally but not semantically in the F+M− condition, and semantically but not formally in the F−M+ condition. The test format for this second experiment is illustrated by the examples below:

A Don't underestimate these small revolutionary groups. What we are talking about was a .... change and these people played a major part in it.
A historiated
B historic
C historical

B At first people believed the newly discovered papers, allegedly written by Chaucer, false but later they proved to be autographs and manuscripts of h .... interest.
A historiated
B historic
C historical

The outcome of the experiment was that 'counterparts' were chosen significantly less frequently in the F+M− condition than in the F−M+ condition, and significantly less frequently in the F−M+ condition than in the F+M+ condition. These results coincide with the results of the first experiment insofar as purely phonological interference (F+M−) occurred least often in both, but there is a difference between the two experiments in respect of relative amounts of interference in the F−M+ and F−M+ conditions.

The design of the third experimental task differed from the second only to the extent that it (1) provided a choice of just two alternatives (the correct target word and the other member of its pair) and (2) required subjects to indicate how certain they were of their choice in each instance. Thus:

A Don't underestimate these small revolutionary groups. What we are talking about was a .... change and these people played a major part in it.
A historic
B historical
How certain are you about your choice?
A very certain
B reasonably certain
C not so certain
B At first people believed the newly discovered papers, allegedly

written by Chaucer, false but later they proved to be autographs and manuscripts of h .... interest.

A historic
B historical

How certain are you about your choice?

A very certain
B reasonably certain
C not so certain

In this case the test was administered to some intermediate learners (secondary-school pupils in their fifth year) as well as to advanced learners. A group of native speakers also took this version of the multiple-choice test. The results show a striking difference in error patterns across conditions between intermediate learners on the one hand and advanced learners and native speakers on the other. For the advanced learners and native speakers it was again the F+M− condition that generated the lowest level of interference, whilst for the intermediate learners all three conditions produced roughly similar amounts of confusion. There was also a difference in degrees of certainty across conditions: whereas advanced learners and native speakers felt 'not so certain' about their responses more often in the F+M+ condition than in the other two, the intermediate learners felt 'not so certain' in all conditions equally often. This latter difference was not, however, statistically significant

To summarize, Hulstijn & Tangelder found that meaning similarity caused more interference than form similarity for native speakers of English and for advanced learners of English as an L2 but not for intermediate learners of English as an L2. They argue that this difference can be explained in terms of the number of English words that had been integrated into the lexicons of the respective groups of learners and in terms of the extent of integration of particular items. Their view is that the task of acquiring the semantic characteristics of a word takes much longer than acquiring its formal characteristics; this, they say, accounts for the fact that native speakers and advanced L2 learners continue to be susceptible to semantic interference while being less prone to formal confusion. Hulstijn & Tangelder are, in other words, essentially at one with the view expressed above in seeing semantic integration as the more challenging component of the acquisition of any word in any language and in inferring that until semantic integration is properly under way the learner is bound to rely heavily on formal cues when dealing with the item in question.

As a footnote to Hulstijn & Tangelder's discussion, it may be worth saying that some of the examples given by Meara (1984: 233 – see above) of what he presents as phonologically or orthographically motivated responses by English speakers to French word-association test stimuli are in fact more appropriately seen as instances of intralingual interference based to a large degree on semantic considerations. For instance, the responses *animal* and *stupide* cited as elicited by the stimulus *béton* undoubtedly result, as Meara points out, from the assimilation of *béton* to another French word, *bête*. However, the process linking stimulus to response is far from purely formal in nature: the response *animal* is fairly obviously motivated by the meaning of *bête* in its substantival usage, namely, 'beast', 'animal', 'dumb creature', while the response *stupide* is based on the meaning of *bête* in its adjectival usage, to wit, 'stupid', 'foolish', 'unintelligent', 'idiotic'. Similar explanations can be applied to:

eau ('water') – elicited by *naguère* ('a short time ago') – cf. *nager* ('to swim');
permettre ('to permit') – elicited by *fendre* ('to split') – cf. *défendre* ('to forbid').

Laufer (1990a, 1991b, 1993–94, 1997) has reviewed a number of studies investigating a whole range of problems inherent in the nature of target words themselves. Her discussion of such 'intralexical' difficulties, as she terms them, ranges over both the formal realm and the area of meaning. Formal intralexical difficulty factors explored by Laufer include pronounceability, length, grammatical category and morphological complexity. The following is essentially a résumé of the points Laufer makes in her various publications under each of these headings.

In relation to pronounceability, Laufer points out that language learners are often observed to avoid words that they find difficult to pronounce (cf. Levenston, 1979), and she argues that such difficulty also affects comprehension. In support of this latter point she cites a series of experiments conducted by Gibson & Levin (1975) in which subjects of different language backgrounds were tested on their pronunciation and also their perception of a range of pseudo-words. The results of these experiments showed that those words which were easier to pronounce were also more accurately perceived. Such a result indicates that pronounceability is a facilitation factor for word perception in the absence of meaning. This in turn undoubtedly has implications in respect of the acquirability of the less pronounceable lexical items. Indeed, an early study by Rodgers (1969) of English-speaking learners of Russian demonstrated clearly that those Russian words which were easier for learners to pronounce (e.g., *haze*) were more likely to be retained than words which learners found more difficult to pronounce (e.g., *mgla*) (cf. the research on the link between phonological memory codes and vocabulary learning discussed below). One could argue that pronounceability is not strictly a quality intrinsic to a given L2 word, since it will depend to a very large extent on where the person attempting to pronounce the word in question is coming from in terms of his/her L1 sound system – as, indeed, Laufer herself suggests. On the other hand, pronounceability is also a factor in L1 lexical acquisition. Thus, Celce-Murcia (1978) found that her 2-year-old daughter Caroline, who was simultaneously acquiring English and French, avoided producing words in either language which she found difficult – preferring French *citron* /sitõ/ to English *lemon* and French *papillon* /papijõ/ to English *butterfly*, but preferring English *spoon* /pun/ to French *cuiller* and English *home* /om/ to French *maison*. The critical factor here would appear to be the state of phonological readiness for particular combinations (cf. Aitchison, 1994: 184ff.) rather than cross-linguistic inhibition.

With regard to word length, the evidence seems rather mixed. Rodgers (1969) did not find length to be a significant variable in his (above-cited) experiment. Stock (1976) found that English-speaking learners of Hebrew memorized one-syllable words more easily than two-syllable words, but, unsettlingly enough, also found that three-syllable words had a higher retention rate than one-syllable words. Phillips (1981) also identified length as a significant element in the learning of French words by English speakers, but found that it decreased as learners' proficiency increased. Coles (1982) discovered word length to have a strong effect on success rates in the recognition of the written forms of English words by non-native learners of English. In the light of these somewhat divergent findings, Laufer expresses some agnosticism about the possibility in any given case of straightforwardly attributing learning difficulty to word length. A more recent study by Hulme *et al.* (1991), not mentioned by Laufer, shows a clear word-length effect in verbal-memorization tasks in respect of not only L2 (Italian words) but also pseudo-words conforming to L1 (English) phonotactic constraints and real L1 (English) words. Two major methodological problems which may help to account for apparent contradictions in the evidence relating to word length are (1) word length can be variously calculated – in phonemes, graphemes, syllables or morphemes – and (2) it is difficult to disentangle length from other variables – notably morphological complexity. In any case, Hulme *et al.*'s results suggest that if there is a difficulty factor deriving from word length, it is not one which operates only in relation to L2 vocabulary learning.

The question of whether some L2 parts of speech are more difficult to learn than others is also not especially easy to answer in the light of the available evidence. Rodgers' (1969) subjects apparently found nouns and adjectives more readily learnable than verbs and adverbs. Phillips' (1981) subjects apparently had fewer problems learning nouns than learning verbs or adjectives, although this effect declined as they progressed in proficiency. Allen & Vallette (1972) suggest on the basis of observing L2 learners at different levels that adverbs and adverbial expressions pose particular problems. As Laufer points out, some of these findings can be accounted for in terms of the degree of morphological difficulty presented by verbs in a language such as Russian, and others can be explained by reference to the close similarity of certain adverbials in a language like French (compare *souvent* ('often') and *surtout* ('especially'), *tout de suite* ('immediately') and *tout d'un coup* ('suddenly'). On this basis, Laufer seems inclined not to see adherence to specific grammatical categories as a separate difficulty factor. A possibility not mentioned by Laufer but focused on by N. Ellis & Beaton (1995: 113 – citing Davelaar & Besner, 1988, and N. Ellis & Beaton, 1993) is that some parts of speech – notably nouns – are generally more imageable than some others and that this may account for the greater ease with which – at least according to some studies – they are learned. It may be worth recalling in this connection that in L1 acquisition, the phase of very rapid vocabulary expansion, the so-called 'vocabulary explosion' phase (see above, Chapter 2), 'is characterized by a rapid acquisition of one particular type of word: names for objects' (McShane, 1991: 146).

As far as morphological complexity is concerned, Laufer cites Stock's (1976) observation that among the most conspicuous problems of English-speaking learners of Hebrew are the inflexional paradigms of verbs, nouns and adjectives. She also refers to derivational complexity, noting, for example, indications from her own work (Benoussan & Laufer, 1984; Laufer & Benoussan, 1982) that L2 learners often misinterpret combinations of morphemes by virtue of assimilating them to what look to them like similar usages and combinations – equating *outline* with *out of line*, *falsities* with *falling cities*, etc. Much the same kind of remarks can be made about morphological complexity in this context as were made earlier about pronounceability. On the one hand, there is clearly a cross-linguistic dimension to the morphological problems posed by an L2; clearly, a major component of coming to grips with the morphology of an L2 is the processing of the similarities and differences between the target system and the L1 system. On the other hand, problems with morphology also characterize L1 acquisition. Braine (1971: 28–29), for example, refers to an unpublished study by Bar-Adon (1959) which shows that L1 acquirers of Hebrew do not master the morphophonemic alternations which characterize Hebrew verb conjugations until they are well into their teens. Similarly, in a large-scale study (already cited in Chapter 2) of the mastery of Dutch derivational morphology by L1 acquirers of Dutch between ages 7 and 17, Smedts (1988) found that the 7-year-olds were able to demonstrate knowledge of, on average, just 14% of the derivational relationships tested and that even the 17-year-olds knew, on average, no more than 66% of the derivational relationships in question.

Turning now to semantico-pragmatic intralexical difficulty factors, these, according to Laufer, include specificity of meaning, multiple meaning, metaphorical meaning, connotational and stylistic nuances, and synonymy. Concerning specificity, Blum and Levenston (1978) found that non-native learners of Hebrew tended to use superordinate, i.e., more general, terms where natives tended to use hyponyms, i.e., more specific terms – preferring to use, for example, the Hebrew equivalent of *put* instead of the equivalent of *impose*. One wonders, however, whether what is really in question here is intralexical problematicity as such. Laufer herself, after all, suggests that what is involved is a learning strategy aimed at maximizing the surrender value of lexical learning:

> Puisque l'hyperonyme couvre un domaine sémantique plus large et se prête à un plus grand nombre de contextes, l'apprenant qui le mémorise et l'emploie court moins de risques de faire une erreur que s'il apprenait l'hyponyme au domaine sémantique et aux possibilités d'emploi plus restreints. (Laufer, 1993–94: 106–107)
>
> ('Since the superordinate covers a larger area of meaning and is deployable in a larger number of contexts, the learner who memorizes it and uses it runs less risk of making an error than would be the case if he learned the hyponym with its more restricted area of meaning and possibilities of use.')

Multiple meaning as an impediment to L2 vocabulary learning was studied by Benoussan & Laufer (1984). Their subjects, Hebrew-speaking learners of English as an L2, failed to realize that the most frequent and familiar meanings of *since*, *while* and *abstract* did not fit the context of the passage in which the words occurred, where they had the force of, respectively, 'because', 'in spite of the fact that' and 'summary'. It was noted that in production these subjects preferred to express such concepts using the expressions *because*, *in spite of the fact that* and *summary* rather than to deploy polysemous words. The cross-linguistic factor obviously plays a role in such cases, L1–L2 differences in the range of meanings associated with individual items exacerbating any difficulties arising from polysemy itself.

Lexical difficulties arising from semantic opacity associated with certain idiomatic and metaphorical usages of words have been investigated by, among others, Dagut & Laufer (1985) and Kellerman (1978). Dagut & Laufer looked at Hebrew speakers' avoidance patterns in respect of phrasal verbs in English. They report that the most frequently avoided items were phrasal verbs characterized by metaphorical extension and by the semantic fusion of the individual components of the verb – *let down*, *show off*, *put up with*, etc. Kellerman, for his part, found that Dutch learners of English were disposed to translate literally and deploy in English translation equivalents of Dutch expressions which involved what they perceived as the core meanings of the participating lexis, but that they assumed this kind of direct transfer not to be possible (even though sometimes it was) where more peripheral, metaphorical meanings of the words were brought into play. Clearly, as Kellerman's work shows, there are complex cross-linguistic dimensions to problems in this area in addition to the problems inherent in the business of dealing with metaphorical meaning in any circumstances.

With regard to connotational and stylistic nuances, Laufer suggests, citing Dagut (1977), that the L2 learner is likely not to feel the connotational differences between pairs of words such as *skinny* and *slim* or *womanish* and *womanly*. She also notes the problems learners of English as L2 often experience in relation to register differences as they affect series of synonymous expressions such as *about*, *around*, *more or less*, *approximately* (cf. Halliday *et al.*, 1964: 88). Once again, as in the case of difficulties induced by polysemy and metaphor, the intrinsic difficulties posed by connotational and stylistic variation are reinforced by problems relating to cross-linguistic distributional differences – differences of the kind referred to by Lado four decades ago (see, e.g., Lado, 1957: 86–87).

Finally on the topic of semantico-pragmatic intralexical difficulty factors, we come to the question of synonymy. Linnarud (1983) and Laufer (1991c) provide indirect evidence that L2 learners have problems learning L2 synonyms. Both studies are concerned with lexical richness in L2 learners – Swedish and Israeli respectively – as revealed in these learners' essays, and both find a very marked difference between native and non-native writers of the same age in terms of lexical variation:

les dissertations des apprenants étrangers contiennent des répétitions, ils n'arrivent pas à décrire une même chose au moyen de mots différents. Si l'on retrouve partout les mêmes termes, cela implique que l'apprenant n'a pas une connaissance adéquate des synonymes. (Laufer, 1993–94: 109)

('the foreign learners' essays contain repetitions; they are unable to describe the same thing using different words. If the same words recur everywhere, this implies that the learner does not have an adequate knowledge of synonyms.')

Laufer infers that once an L2 learner has acquired one form to associate with a given concept, acquiring more labels for the same term seems like a waste of time and effort. If this is true, then the case of synonymy is comparable to that of specificity of meaning, in the sense that what appears to be involved is less a matter of an intralexical difficulty than of a learning strategy.

What emerges from the foregoing discussion of intralexical difficulty factors (based mostly on Laufer's treatment of the subject in various of her publications) is that such factors have very much to do with meaning as well as form. Moreover, the formal difficulties that seem to be reasonably well established exist in L1 as well as in L2. Accordingly, there is no evidence from this quarter that the L2 mental lexicon is an essentially form-driven entity. In the course of her exploration of L2 lexical difficulties Laufer herself acknowledges the particular challenge presented by the semantico-pragmatic aspects of L2 lexical acquisition:

La plupart des problèmes qui se posent dans l'apprentissage du vocabulaire ont rapport au sens. (Laufer, 1993–94: 102)

('Most of the problems in vocabulary learning pertain to meaning.')

The implication of this statement is that most of the work that the L2 mental lexicon is called upon to do in appropriating new vocabulary involves the processing of meaning rather than form. As Sonaiya (1991: 274) puts it, 'the primary task in vocabulary acquisition is seen as one involving continuous refining of meaning and readjustment of boundaries between lexical items that have already been acquired and subsequent items that are encountered'.

Some examples given by Hatch & Brown (1995) of lexical translation errors from intermediate to advanced Spanish-speaking and Japanese-speaking learners of English add further weight to the above, showing as they do that even fairly experienced learners dealing with relatively common words often manifest 'the need to refine meanings for words, to make finer distinctions' (Hatch & Brown, 1995: 383):

English stimulus: *windshield*	Meanings given: 'shutter', 'window', 'window frame'
English stimulus: *heavy*	Meanings given: 'strong', 'hard'
English stimulus: *path*	Meanings given: 'entrance', 'foot-bridge', 'road', 'street'
English stimulus: *rope*	Meanings given: 'string', 'ribbon', 'pipe'
English stimulus: *idol*	Meanings given: 'important thing', 'pretty thing'
English stimulus: *script*	Meanings given: 'handbook', 'scriptures', 'documents'

(extracted and adapted from Hatch & Brown, 1995: 384, Table 15.2)

Also relevant in this connection is Verhallen & Schoonen's (1993) study of lexical knowledge of monolingual and bilingual children in the Netherlands, focusing on six words (*neus* – 'nose', *roofdier* – 'predator', *wekker* – 'alarm clock', *geheim* – 'secret', *boek* – 'book', *haar* – 'hair'), which revealed that the bilingual children (of Turkish immigrant origins) 'produced fewer meaning aspects and the types of meaning aspects expressed are different from those expressed by the Dutch children' (Verhallen & Schoonen, 1993: 360).

Finally in this discussion of intralingual and intralexical difficulty, we return, as promised, to Laufer's (1990b) study of confusions between words of similar form – what she calls 'synforms', which attempts to address the question of whether there is a hierarchy of difficulty and a predictable sequence of acquisition in respect of lexical form. Her subjects were 321 adult learners of English as L2 and 207 adolescent school students of English as L1, and the pairs/groups of synforms on which her study was based were selected from a large, previously collected, corpus of lexical errors made by learners of English as L2. Her elicitation method comprised two multiple-choice instruments. One of these required subjects to choose appropriate words from among groups of English synforms for blank slots in sentences, and the other (administered second) required subjects to choose appropriate definitions for isolated English words from among groups of definitions for synforms.

The tasks in question demand, of course, a capacity to associate forms with meanings rather than just a knowledge of form. However, the hierarchy of difficulty that emerges from an analysis of the results of the study in terms of confusions between synforms seems to be definable in essentially formal terms. The four major categories of synform types on which this hierarchy of difficulty rests are: suffix synforms (e.g., *considerable*, *considerate*), prefix synforms (*super-*

ficial, *artificial*), vocalic synforms (e.g., *cute*, *acute*), and consonantal synforms (e.g., *addition*, *addiction*). In terms of these categories, the emergent hierarchy for both the learners of English as L2 and the native-speaker school pupils (on a scale of descending difficulty) is as follows: (1) suffix synforms (2) vocalic synforms, (3) prefix synforms (4) consonantal synforms (Laufer, 1990b: 289).

Laufer interprets this finding as indicative of a sequence of acquisition – common to L2 and L1 learners – relative to the development of the types of lexical/formal distinctions in question. In interpreting her results thus, she does, as she acknowledges, ignore certain criticisms of the 'accuracy order = acquisition order' principle, but she justifies her position in this regard by claiming that the criticisms in question have been amply responded to – by, e.g., Hatch & Farhady (1982), Borland (1984).

A slightly earlier study which is worth mentioning in this connection is that of Meara & Ingle (1986). This study analyses consonantal errors made by 40 Anglophone adolescent learners of French in 35 French words (sharing a Consonant–Vowel–Consonant–Vowel–Consonant phonological structure) which they had attempted to memorize. All the words had been orally presented in association with line drawings representing their meanings, and these same line drawings were subsequently used to elicit the items concerned. It emerges from the results of this experiment that the consonants at the beginnings of the words tested were significantly more resistant to error than consonants in other parts of the words. Meara & Ingle relate their findings to tip-of-the-tongue errors in L1, citing R. Brown & McNeill's (1966) finding that in such errors the initial consonant of the target word is often preserved. One can also, however, relate Meara & Ingle's results to Laufer's findings on synforms – to the extent that Laufer's subjects were less prone to confusion in respect of the beginnings of words (prefix synforms) than in respect of the ends of words (suffix synforms).

It does not seem entirely far-fetched to infer from the foregoing that beginnings of L2 lexical forms tend to be learned more easily, more quickly and therefore sooner than the middles or ends of words. There is evidence – such as that cited by Meara & Ingle – that something similar may be true of L1 lexical acquisition. However, there may be a distinction to be drawn here between lexical acquisition in adolescents and adults and lexical acquisition in young children. It appears, for example, that young L1 acquirers pay rather more attention to rhythmic patterns and stressed vowels than to initial consonants (see, e.g., Aitchison 1994).

Lexical memory research

To return to our main theme of the respective roles of form and meaning in the processing and acquisition of L2 vocabulary, the importance of meaning in dealing with L2 lexis is, paradoxically enough, underlined by recent work on the place of phonological short-term memory in L2 lexical acquisition (e.g., Baddeley *et al.*, 1988; Ellis & Beaton, 1995; Papagno *et al.*, 1991; Service, 1989, 1992, 1993, 1993–94; Service & Craik, 1993; Service & Kohonen, 1995). Let us preface our exploration of the implications of such research with first a brief look at the notion of short-term memory and then a summary of the findings of the studies in question.

A typical definition of short-term memory is the following:

> The capacity of the brain to hold information in a kind of immediate-access store for a short period after it has been presented. (Evans, 1978: 334)

Many psycholinguists and psychologists concerned with language use the term working memory or speech-processing memory to refer to the short-term phonological store in which 'raw speech' is held while the process of organizing its phonological representation into constituents and identifying their content and function is in train. Opinions about the precise capacity of working memory vary, but the tone group (which often coincides with the grammatical clause) is often cited as its likely operating unit. In any case, in McDonough's words,

> it is plain that there must be some kind of short-term storage for linguistic material and, since it is rather severely limited, the problem for both native and non-native speakers of the language is to extract the important information from it by calling up the necessary knowledge from long-term storage and applying interpretive processes as quickly as possible. (McDonough, 1981: 63–64)

Turning now to the findings of the studies referred to above, the subject of Baddeley *et al.*'s (1988) investigation was an Italian speaker (P.V.) with a deficit in short-term phonological memory. Attempts were made to teach P.V. pairs of meaningful words in her native language and in addition pairs of words each composed of an item in Italian and an item in an unfamiliar foreign language (Russian). Her performance in relation to the Italian word pairs was entirely normal, while her capacity to acquire new vocabulary in Russian was shown to be grossly impaired.

Papagno *et al.* (1991) looked at the effect of articulatory suppression on L2 vocabulary learning in children. They found that preventing subjects from subvocally rehearsing (i.e., silently repeating to themselves) the forms to be memorized failed to disrupt the learning of L1 paired associates but did disrupt the learning of L2 vocabulary – except in instances where subjects were able to make semantic associations between the L2 items and words in their L1.

Service (1989, 1992; Service & Kohonen, 1995) studied the acquisition of English as an L2 by Finnish children. She found that their capacity to repeat back and to copy English pseudo-words in tests administered before their English course began was a better predictor of their subsequent success at learning English than ability to match syntactic–semantic pairs in their L1 (Finnish). She concludes that the ability to represent phonological material in working memory underlies the acquisition of new items – particularly lexical items – in L2 learning. In a further study, Service (see Service, 1993, 1993–94; Service & Craik, 1993) investigated the relationship between working-memory phonological representations and L2 vocabulary learning in a group of English-speaking adults. Their ability to create working memory phonological representations was tested by asking them to repeat unfamiliar (Finnish) lexical forms presented to them aurally, and their L2 vocabulary-learning ability was tested via a task involving them in memorizing a list of English pseudo-words or Finnish words paired with English words. She found a positive correlation between repetition accuracy for foreign words and the memorization of novel items.

N. Ellis & Beaton's (1995) study involved English-speaking undergraduates of psychology with no previous knowledge of German in attempts to memorize German lexical items using various techniques. Ellis & Beaton found – among other things – 'significant correlations between the ease of pronunciation of FL [foreign language] words and their learnability' (N. Ellis & Beaton, 1995: 146), a finding which they interpret as providing support for the interpretation of earlier research such as the aforementioned:

> representation of the novel sound sequence of a new word in phonological short-term memory promotes its longer-term consolidation both for later articulation and as an entity with which meaning can be associated. The easier a word is in this respect . . . the easier it is to learn. (N. Ellis & Beaton, 1995: 147)

On the face of it, such evidence of the role of phonological representations in vocabulary learning appears to favour the suggestion that the L2 mental lexicon differs from the L1 mental lexicon in being essentially phonologically driven. Closer inspection of such evidence, however, leads to a rather different conclusion. To begin with, results of experiments carried out strictly with reference to L1 vocabulary learning also indicate an important role for short-term phonological store. Thus, for example, S. Gathercole & Baddeley (1989) found with reference to the L1 vocabulary development of young children, that a phonological memory score based on a pseudo-word repetition test correlated significantly with an L1 vocabulary score at age 4 and with subsequent L1 vocabulary acquisition. Similarly, the findings of another S. Gathercole & Baddeley study (1990) suggest that phonological short-term memory is a greater factor than either non-verbal intelligence or age in certain L1 language disorders in children. The indications are, therefore, that, whatever the precise extent or nature of the phonological memory factor in respect of vocabulary learning, it is a factor common to both L2 and L1.

Second, the L2 studies which have investigated the role of short-term phonological representations of L2 lexical items have dealt exclusively with novel, unfamiliar L2 lexis – items, in other words, which had not had any opportunity to become 'connected up' with subjects' internalized semantic schemas or networks. These are precisely the circumstances in which one would expect the efficient encoding of the actual shape of a word to be of prime importance; it is, after all, the only 'handle' the individual faced with the task of learning the item in question has on it. As far as L1 vocabulary acquisition is concerned, again, in the early stages of the integration of lexical items – in early childhood or in circumstances where one is getting to grips with previously unencountered items – a capacity to cope with the formal phonological aspect of the words in question is bound to assume a particular importance. It is interesting to note in this context that C. Brown & Payne's (1994) investigation via questionnaire of L2 vocabulary-learning strategies – summarized by Hatch & Brown (1995: 373) – yields a model of vocabulary learning based on five essential steps in which attention to form clearly precedes attention to meaning (the five steps being: (1) accessing sources of new words, (2) arriving at a clear auditory/visual image of the form of the new word, (3) learning the meaning of the new item, (4) making strong connections between form and meaning of the new word, and (5) using the new word).

Third, it emerges from certain of the above-cited studies that, novelty notwithstanding, the semantic factor is present even in the very early stages of learning L2 lexis. In one of the quoted studies, Service (1993, 1993–94; Service & Craik, 1993) found that her subjects' capacity to learn novel items significantly correlated not only with repetition accuracy for foreign words but also with performance on the task of learning pairs of familiar L1 words – a task taken to be largely semantically based. From this double correlation she infers that L2 vocabulary learning depends on the creation of both phonological and semantic representations in working memory, and on establishing connections between the representations in long-term memory. A further interesting finding in this connection comes from another of the above-mentioned studies. Papagno *et al.* (1991) discovered that whereas Italian subjects confronted with a Russian vocabulary-learning task and English subjects required to learn nonsense syllables and Finnish words appeared to need to rehearse the target items subvocally, this did not seem to be the case when the Anglophones were given the task of learning Russian lexis. During debriefing, these last reported having learned many of the Russian words by associating the items in question with English words, and a subsequently administered association test revealed that the Russian words concerned were vastly more association-rich for the English than for the Italian subjects. The implication appears to be that where subjects are prevented from constructing phonological codings they will, where possible, circumvent such disruption via semantic associations. This in turn suggests that, within constraints imposed by the experience of learners and the particularities of the items to be learned, semantic coding runs parallel to phonological coding in the processing of novel L2 lexis. Ellis & Beaton's study adds further grist to this particular mill, finding that, as well as pronounceability, imageability is a major facilitating factor in L2 word learning (see below).

In sum, the studies referred to tend to confirm rather than challenge the view that the operation of the L2 mental lexicon closely resembles that of the L1 mental lexicon and that the 'phonological factor' is not peculiar to L2 lexical processing, but is prominent in the early stages of dealing with particular lexical items in both L1 and L2 – not, though, as we have seen, to the exclusion of meaning-oriented operations. A study (mentioned earlier) by Hulme *et al.* (1991) into the contribution of long-term memory to short-term memory span provides further corroboration of the above reading of the evidence. Hulme *et al.* define the concept of long-term memory as 'a separate form of permanent memory representation that boosts recall in immediate memory tasks and that is not synonymous with short-term memory' (Hulme *et al.*, 1991: 688). Memory span is usually defined in something like the following terms:

> The maximum number of items that an individual can recall after they have been presented to him once. (Evans, 1978: 212)

In fact this definition does not quite fit the particularities of Hulme *et al.*'s study, in which memory span is calculated in terms of maximum list length at which accurate recall of the content of two lists occurred. However, the general sense of memory span in terms of amount of material memorizable for immediate recall purposes is retained in Hulme *et al.*'s approach.

Hulme *et al.*'s study was comprised of two experiments in verbal memorization conducted with native speakers of English. The results of the first showed that memory span was lower for English-like pseudo-words than for real English words. The second experiment showed memory span for Italian words to be lower than for English words, but also showed that providing the English translations for the Italian words in the learning task increased subjects' memory span for these words. Hulme *et al.* interpret their results as indicating a role for forms stored in long-term memory in short-term verbal memorization tasks. However, they concede that one connotation of long-term memory 'is as a system that relies on semantic rather than phonological information' (Hulme *et al.*, 1991: 688). Also, with specific regard to their results, they admit the possibility 'that semantic coding in long-term memory is also beneficial to performance in memory span tasks' (*ibid.*: 699). Given that the most obvious distinction between words and non-words, between L1 words in isolation and unfamiliar L2 words in isolation, and between L2 words with translations and L2 words in isolation is that of meaningfulness versus meaninglessness, they could hardly do otherwise!

N. Ellis (e.g., 1994a, 1994b, 1994c, 1995) has argued for a complete dissociation between the semantic and the formal aspects of vocabulary acquisition, claiming that the acquisition of semantic aspects of words necessarily involves conscious, explicit learning, whereas the acquisition of formal aspects of a word is essentially implicit and unconscious in nature. He cites in this connection evidence from studies of vocabulary and intelligence, priming studies, and studies of global amnesia (a condition resulting from damage to the hippocampus and limbic system in the middle brain). In relation to intelligence he notes that 'children with non-verbal IQs as low as 30 . . . can still complete the single word stage of language' (N. Ellis, 1994a: 41), but that the speech of severely mentally retarded children 'lacks content' (*ibid.*: 42) and that vocabulary size (which he links to 'the mapping between lexical, semantic and conceptual domains' – *ibid.*) strongly correlates with academic intelligence. The priming evidence he refers to 'comes from the interaction of depth of processing and the types of operation that we ask subjects to do with words' (N. Ellis, 1994c: 225). He quotes findings from both monolingual and bilingual studies suggesting that elaborative semantic processing of words has a positive effect on explicit memory of the items in question (as gauged by such tests as *yes/no* word recognition and free recall) but fails to affect implicit memory (as gauged by such tests as word identification and word completion), whereas mere exposure to lexical forms is associated with a precisely converse facilitation pattern. As far as the evidence from global amnesics is concerned, this strongly suggests a complete dissociation between implicit and explicit learning: amnesics 'show normal implicit learning yet . . . lose the ability to consciously recollect any events that occur after their brain damage' (N. Ellis, 1995: 108). With specific regard to amnesics' vocabulary learning:

> They show normal *implicit learning* of the perceptual aspects of novel word forms. . . . They show normal *implicit learning* of new motor habits and the motor aspects of novel word forms that are necessary for language production. . . . Yet amnesics are unable to learn the meaning of new words. They are severely deficient at developing new conceptual information and at making new semantic links. *Explicit learning* is involved in acquiring and processing word meanings. (*ibid.*: 108–109)

One has to tread carefully with the above evidence. In relation to IQ and language learning, for example, the fact that mentally retarded children may produce semantically anomalous utterances by no means implies that their speech is asemantic – 'lacks content'. (Transcripts I have seen of the speech of such individuals suggests quite the opposite to me – see Singleton, 1998.) Regarding the priming evidence, as N. Ellis himself admits (citing Balota *et al.*, 1991), the neat picture he paints is disrupted somewhat by a certain amount of contrary evidence. As for the evidence from amnesics, this does seem to show that learning the forms and learning the meanings of novel words need to be *initiated* by the operation of different items of neurological 'hardware'; what it does not show is that all aspects of the learning of form and meaning respectively are at all stages of a word's integration into the mental lexicon separately managed, nor that, if all systems are up and running, the different mechanisms do not 'talk to each other'. However, even if Ellis is correct in every detail of his interpretation of the research he cites, his thesis poses no problem for the claim that both form and meaning are involved in the processes of the L2 lexicon. On the contrary, it endorses this position. Indeed, given Ellis's view that the semantic aspects of a word are more demanding of intellectual capacity, his standpoint is entirely compatible with the earlier-sketched notion that the formal aspects of learning a new word may be to the fore in the early stages but that after an initial concentration on form, the longer-term and more challenging task for the learner is to come to grips with a word's meanings and use.

Further support for this notion of an increasing engagement with problems of meaning as the internalization of a word progresses comes from some earlier research into the operation of memory in an L2 context conducted by Henning (1973). In Henning's study, English tests of short-term memory, vocabulary recognition and language proficiency were administered to a group of native speakers of English and to students of English as an L2 from four different proficiency levels. Similar tests in Persian were administered to native speakers of that language and to students of Persian as L2. From an analysis of the errors produced by his subjects, Henning inferred that L2 learners at a low level of proficiency registered vocabulary more by phonological similarities than by semantic relatedness, whereas high-proficiency learners relied on associated meanings rather than sound similarities. A post-test revealed that – at least as far as the English data were concerned – the words which had generated 'acoustic' errors in the short-term memory test were generally known to the low-proficiency subjects. Presumably, the phonological orientation among such subjects had to do, therefore, with the fact that, whilst they might previously have encountered the words in question, their experience of the items concerned had been too limited for these to have become sufficiently integrated to activate relevant semantic associations with any degree of rapidity. In the case of the higher-proficiency learners, on the other hand, their semantically based errors seem to indicate that they had had sufficient exposure to the test items for networks of semantic associations to begin to be established around the words in question – though the process was, on the basis of the errors, clearly incomplete – to the point where such meaning-based connections were instantly available whenever the items in question cropped up.

Another dimension of the greater semantic orientation of more-proficient L2 learners in committing lexical items to memory is undoubtedly that they have a larger, more coherently structured stock of L2 vocabulary-based form–meaning associations into which to integrate new L2 items (cf. Laufer, 1990c, Section 3). This may be a further explanatory factor in relation to Henning's results, and it certainly helps to account for Cohen & Aphek's (1980) finding that of their subjects – all learners of Hebrew as an L2 – the more proficient ones tended to be more likely to generate associations for new L2 items in vocabulary-learning tasks. It is true that the associations concerned were often with words in the L1 (see below), and that not all the associations were semantic, but from the examples given it appears that a large number of them were target-language-internal. Thus, for instance, associative links are reported to have been made in the learning tasks between the new item *taxlit* ('objective') and *lehaxlit* ('to decide'), between the new item *koser* ('aptitude') and *kaseh* ('difficult'), between the new item *tipel* ('took care of') and *tipax* ('fostered'), etc. Clearly, it is impossible to exploit intralingual associations of this kind in lexical memorization unless the requisite associates are already in place and available.

Much recent discussion of semantic aspects of committing L2 words to memory has focused on image formation and imageability. Thus, for example, R. Ellis (1994: 554) refers to T. Brown & F. Perry's (1991) study of L2 vocabulary-memorizing strategies used by six upper-level classes of learners of English at the University of Cairo, in which a comparison was undertaken between (1) the keyword strategy (involving the formation of a visual image linking the target word and an acoustically similar word already known),[3] (2) the semantic strategy (involving an attempt to integrate the target word into existing meaning structures and (3) a combination of (1) and (2). The results of this comparison show the combination of keyword and semantic strategies to have been more effective – as measured by cued recall and multiple-choice tasks – than either strategy used alone in promoting retention. This seems to indicate that the greater the number of aspects of L2 word meaning attended to, the greater the likelihood of L2 target words being learned.

The above-mentioned keyword technique has been much discussed in the literature in the recent past and continues to arouse interest (see, e.g., Hulstijn, 1997). A. Cohen (1987a), reviewing studies focused on the keyword strategy, notes that a visually based strategy seems to be more effective with concrete than with abstract terms, which is unsurprising given the greater imageability of concrete items. He also notes that such a strategy seems to be less effective with young children, who appear not to be able to generate visual images so readily. A further point made by Cohen is that the keyword technique is less effective than verbal mnemonics with more fluent

[3] The keyword strategy has already been discussed and exemplified in Chapter 2. Two further examples are:

- An English learner of German, trying to remember the meaning of *Raupe* ('caterpillar'), could associate *Raupe* with the English word *rope* (sound familiarity), and construct a mental image representing a caterpillar stretched out in more than its fullest length (exaggeration helps!) on a rope.
- An English learner of French, trying to remember *paon* ('peacock'), might use the word *pawn* as mediator, imagining a chess-board on which all pawns look like peacocks. (Hulstijn, 1997: 205)

learners, who presumably have more material at their disposal on which to hang such mnemonics. N. Ellis & Beaton (1995: 114) refer to a range of verbal memory research which shows that 'the greater the imageability of a word – that is the degree to which it arouses a mental image – the more likely it is to be recalled' and that 'FL [foreign language] vocabulary items are learned in fewer trials and with fewer errors if non-verbal referents rather than native language words serve as stimuli'. With specific regard to keyword mediation, they refer to the results of numerous studies indicating the efficacy of the keyword method in both L2 and L1 vocabulary learning and in particular to a study by Atkinson & Raugh (1975) suggesting that, in order for the technique to work well, the keyword chosen has to be an effective reminder of the L2 word (and *vice versa*) and the keyword has to be easily incorporated into a memorable image link. Ellis & Beaton's own study confirms Atkinson & Raugh's findings and in addition demonstrates that 'keyword imageability is more important in translating from foreign to native language than from native to foreign language' (N. Ellis & Beaton, 1995: 152).

Taking the question of image formation and vocabulary learning beyond the particularities of the keyword approach, Tomlinson (1996) reports that visualization in the course of reading – whether in L1 or L2 – greatly enhances the impact of the text in question, not only in terms of comprehension but also in terms of the retention of specific content (including lexical content). Citing his own research and that of Padron & Waxman (1988), he notes that visualization among L2 readers appears to be less frequent among L2 readers than among L1 readers, but that those L2 readers who do visualize are those who do best in recalling the text:

> out of 19 students who were asked to read the poem *River Station Plaza* ... and then to reflect on the process of reading it only four reported visualising. What is most interesting is that these four students performed better than the others when asked after an interval to recall words from the poem and to write a summary of it. In fact in all my experiments the few students who reported visualising tended to achieve greater comprehension and recall than those who did not. (Tomlinson, 1996: 256)

Tomlinson interprets such results as indicating that visualization is a successful technique, which leads him to propose L2 teaching activities that encourage visualization. However, an obvious alternative (not incompatible) interpretation of the fact that visualization is more common among L1 readers than among L2 readers and the fact that it is more common among more-proficient L2 readers than among less-proficient ones is that this particular aspect of the semantic processing of words becomes more prominent as the words themselves become more familiar, which happens as lexical proficiency increases. Once again then we encounter evidence which fits the view that semantic processing increases as a function of degree of integration of words into the mental lexicon.

If we accept that there are semantico-pragmatic as well as formal dimensions to the entry of a new word into the learner's memory, we may still wish to pose questions about the precise nature of the form in which the word is encoded. Service (1992) suggests that even in the exercise of literacy skills the primary points of reference for accessing vocabulary are representations in memory of the sounds of the words in question rather than representations of their written form. Citing studies by Brady and others (Brady, 1986; Brady *et al.*, 1987; Brady *et al.*, 1986; Brady *et al.*, 1983; Snowling, 1981; H. Taylor *et al.*, 1989), she points out that in L1 studies, accuracy of pseudo-word repetition is a good predictor of performance in reading and spelling. In her own work with Finnish children, she found that both pseudo-word repetition accuracy and accuracy of the delayed written copying of pseudo-words were specifically related to foreign language learning success. The explanation she advances for this result is that not only accuracy of pronunciation but also accuracy in delayed written copying depend on the quality of traces in the phonological store. Her own results and those of other researchers also lead her to the view, as we have seen above, that the ability to create distinctive and durable phonological traces is a major factor in long-term L2 lexical learning. The logical conclusion that flows from this line of argumentation is that in the formal dimension of vocabulary learning, it is phonology which is critical.

Research into lexical guessing, incidental vocabulary acquisition and vocabulary acquisition through interaction

A fair amount of attention has been devoted in recent years to studying ways in which L2 learners use context in coming to grips with unfamiliar lexical items (see, e.g., Haastrup, 1991a; Huckin, Haynes & Coady, 1993; Nagy, 1997; Nagy & Herman 1985; Schouten-van Parreren, 1985). Nor is this a new preoccupation (see, e.g., Meara's 1996a discussion of Grinstead, 1915; Seibert, 1930). Some studies have been concerned to investigate simply the extent to which context aids the guessing of word meaning whereas others have attempted to gauge the impact on lexical acquisition of inferring word meaning in context. A typical example of the former is that conducted over a number of years by Ittzés (1991) with small groups of Hungarian learners of English. Her subjects were given two lexical guessing tasks, one involving unknown words in isolation and the other involving the same words in context (a passage from a textbook). Scores on the contextual task were consistently higher than those on the isolated words task. Interestingly, the same students did well and poorly on both tasks:

> On both tests, essentially the same students fell into the top or bottom group ... Those who were good at guessing the meanings of isolated words became even better at guessing in context ... Scores increased by 22% in the top group as opposed to only 7.8 % in the lowest group. (Ittzés, 1991: 362)

These results clearly indicate that the semantico-pragmatic clues furnished by a normal context facilitates the inferring of the meaning of individual lexical items, and they also indicate that learners exploit such help as is provided by context when dealing with unfamiliar L2 words.

A somewhat different kind of study in this area is that of Scholfield & Vougiouklis (1992). Again the language with reference to which the lexical guessing took place was English, but in this case the subjects were a mixture of native speakers of English and Greek learners of English of various levels of proficiency, and the unknown words were actually pseudo-words – non-existent combinations of elements (of Greek and Latin derivation) such as *consect*, *hemilyse*, *semiception*, plus some non-composites such as *malp*. With regard to the composite items, in all cases a plausible meaning could be assigned based on the regular meanings of the component parts in other combinations in English. Subjects were not told that the words did not exist in English. They were asked to give synonyms for the words in question in English or Greek or to paraphrase them in either language, and also to rate their confidence in their response on a five-point scale. The words were given either in context or in isolation, but the context condition was not monolithic; some contexts were quasi-defining ('convergent'), some were of no assistance with respect to the items being tested ('vague'), and some were misleading, essentially functioning in such a way as to simulate idiomatic usage ('divergent'). No doubt as a result of the contrivance of these various context types – two out of three of which were deliberately designed to be unhelpful – the results of the study do not show a clear overall advantage for contextually embedded words in terms either of guessing accuracy or of levels of confidence in the responses offered. On the other hand, an analysis of responses elicited by the different context conditions shows accuracy and confidence to be highest in the 'convergent' condition, somewhat less high in the 'vague' condition and lowest in the 'divergent' condition. What this suggests is that the subjects in question – both natives and non-natives – endeavoured to use contextual meaning in dealing with the unfamiliar items wherever context was available, but that they were unassisted or thrown off scent – and were conscious of such – where the contexts concerned had been expressly concocted to offer very scant clues or clues that were misleading.

Researchers interested in incidental vocabulary learning are concerned with the role of context not merely in lexical guessing but also in lexical acquisition. The general argument in favour of the notion that we must acquire L2 vocabulary without 'special teaching' is identical to that adduced by K. Nelson (1981) in relation to L1 vocabulary acquisition (see above, Chapter 2), namely that the amount of vocabulary that is assimilated far exceeds any reasonable assessment of the capacity of 'special teaching' (see, e.g., Hatch & Brown, 1995: 368–369; Nagy, 1997). An important reference point for discussion in this area is the work of Schouten-van Parreren (e.g., 1985, 1989, 1992), who emphasizes the role of inferring meaning from context in L2 reading, and who contends that such a process leads to better retention of vocabulary than having words and their meanings presented in an isolated manner – e.g., in lists. Other researchers whose view of vocabulary learning has a similar thrust include Bialystok (see, e.g., Bialystok, 1983), Nation (see, e.g., Nation, 1982, 1993; Nation & Coady, 1988) and Krashen[4] (see, e.g., Krashen, 1989; Dupuy & Krashen, 1993).

Schouten-van Parreren's basic assumption is that L2 words are more likely to be retained when their meaning is guessed from context, when, in other words, learners have expended mental effort in relating the unknown items to surrounding material and to already existing knowledge. The research she has conducted on the basis of this assumption has been of a qualitative nature and has been

[4] In some circles (notably North American circles) Krashen's name appears to be the first that comes to mind when the topic of incidental vocabulary acquisition is mentioned. It needs to be said that Krashen's conception of incidental vocabulary acquisition – in keeping with his general view of the role of input – ascribes little or no value to the kind of metacognitive strategizing recommended by some other researchers in this area It also needs to be said that the empirical basis for his particular pronouncements on this issue is open to question. Thus, his 1989 paper on incidental vocabulary acquisition was comprehensively and persuasively criticized on methodological grounds by Meara at the 1993 World Congress of Applied Linguistics (Meara, 1993a), and it is noteworthy that on that occasion Meara explicitly differentiated the work of Schouten-van Parreren and Hulstijn from that of Krashen in terms of the former not being vulnerable to the same kind of criticism as the latter.

directed towards discovering the various ways in which texts provide opportunities for embedding new words in meaning systems already stored in memory and towards establishing what the optimal conditions are for learning vocabulary from texts. Her research leads her to recommend a three-phase action sequence: 'guessing the meaning of the unknown word, verifying the guess (e.g., in a dictionary) and analysing the word form' (Schouten-van Parreren, 1989: 79).

Quantitative research carried out by Hulstijn (e.g., 1992, 1993–94) yields findings which broadly support the Schouten-van Parreren position (see also Dupuy & Krashen, 1993). His results from a series of experiments lead him to the following conclusions:

- The relevance of an unknown word in an L2 text to the informational needs of the reader is an important factor in determining the amount of attention given to that word.
- The phenomenon of acquiring L2 words incidentally, i.e., simply from engaging with L2 texts with a view to understanding them, is real but limited. That is to say, learners do pick up L2 vocabulary in this way, although the number of words per text which are learned in this way is modest.
- In a context of reading for comprehension, making an effort to derive the meaning of unknown words from the available contextual and formal clues improves such words' chances of being retained.

Both Hulstijn's and Schouten-van Parreren's findings imply a continual interaction between lexical item, contextual meaning and reading objectives, and they suggest that in incidental L2 vocabulary acquisition, as in other varieties of lexical acquisition, both formal processing and semantico-pragmatic processing have a contribution to make.

There has, admittedly, been some questioning of the approach taken by Hulstijn and by Schouten-van Parreren. For example, a study by Mondria & Wit-de Boer (1991) found that the 'guessability of words' from particularly 'pregnant' L2 contexts had no effect on their retention. However, as their own account recognizes, this finding was almost certainly connected with the fact that in their experiment the 'guessing stage' was followed by a 'learning stage' in which subjects were given the correct translations of the target items and were required to learn them. It is abundantly clear from Hulstijn's work that the 'effect of rehearsal and memorizing techniques completely washes out the differences between the processing of given and inferred meanings' (Hulstijn, 1992: 120).

A further sidelight on this question is cast by studies conducted by Paribakht & Wesche (1993, 1996, 1997). These looked at the differential effects on L2 vocabulary acquisition of (1) reading plus comprehension exercises plus further reading and (2) reading plus comprehension exercises plus further related exercises involving selective attention to words: word (form and meaning) recognition, morphosyntactic manipulation of words and word parts, interpretation of words in context, production of words in context. The same amount of time was taken up by either set of activities. The results of the studies indicate that, while both treatments resulted in considerable gains in vocabulary, the gains of the groups who did the further exercises were significantly greater than those of the groups who did not. Paribakht & Wesche's interpretation of these results is that contextualized instruction can improve on incidental learning and that vocabulary instruction based on reading texts appears to recommend itself as a pedagogical procedure. However, one notes that 'incidental' is here being used in a rather narrow sense. The contextualized instruction in question did not actually involve explicitly asking subjects to memorize specific items, and so it would be relatively easy to argue that any lexis acquired from the activities concerned was no less incidentally acquired than lexis acquired in the course of reading. After all, neither Schouten-van Parreren nor Hulstijn rule out the notion of deploying focused effort in incidental encounters with new words. Clearly, in order for the debate about incidental vocabulary learning to proceed with any degree of coherence in the future, a consensus will have to be reached about what is to be included and what is to be excluded under the term 'incidental'.

In any case, with regard to the form/meaning issue, it is clear that both in the Mondria & Wit-de Boer study and in the Paribakht & Wesche studies the learning activities added to the reading-for-understanding dimension had clear semantic as well as formal aspects. Accordingly, the basic conclusion drawn above in respect of incidental vocabulary-learning research – namely, that formal and semantic processing jointly contribute to L2 lexical acquisition – is in no way undermined by the findings of these studies.

As a footnote to the foregoing, it may be worth mentioning a study which appears to indicate that learners are quite aware of the way in which contextual meaning contributes towards the acquisition of new L2 lexical items. As part of a research project aimed at investigating the validity of the conscious use of lexical learning strategies, Cunha de Freitas (1992) asked 33 Brazilian basic-level learners of English about factors, circumstances and approaches that helped them to retain English vocabulary. At the very top of the list of items mentioned – significantly more frequently mentioned than any other item – were contextual associations; the subjects in the study reported that what helped them most in remembering and retrieving a given word was the range of connections and cues provided by the context in which they had encountered the word.

Our final topic in this brief discussion of contextual contributions to L2 vocabulary learning is that of the role of oral interaction. This line of research in relation to L2 lexical acquisition is a relatively recent development and has been particularly associated with the name of R. Ellis (R. Ellis, 1996; R. Ellis, Tanaka & Yamazaki, 1995). As R. Ellis points out, very few studies (he cites C. Brown, 1993, and Feitelson *et al.*, 1993) have focused on the acquisition of L2 vocabulary from oral input. (A major omission from Ellis's list is Duquette's (1993) study of context-based L2 vocabulary learning from audio and video input, which records significant gains from both input types.) Ellis claims not to have been able to find any investigations other than his own dealing with L2 lexical learning from oral interaction.

Both the above-cited papers by R. Ellis report on two studies, the 'Saitama study' and the 'Tokyo study', which involved substantial numbers of Japanese high-school students (79 and 127, respectively) in a listening task based on directions about where to place pictures of kitchen objects in a matrix picture of a kitchen. Different groups within the samples experienced different versions of the directions: 'baseline directions' (simple instructions derived from a recording of two native speakers performing the task), 'premodified directions' (more elaborate instructions derived from a recording of non-native speakers performing the task in interaction with a native speaker – in which clarifications requested and given in the interaction were incorporated as explanatory accompaniments to the directions), and 'interactionally modified directions' (baseline directions plus input elicited by requests for clarification addressed by subjects 'on line' to the native-speaker task administrator during their performance of the task). In subsequent testing of lexical comprehension, the 'modified' groups outperformed the 'baseline' group in each of the studies, and the 'modified' groups in the Tokyo study (the only one in which the relevant comparison was made) also outperformed the 'baseline' group in relation to retention. Regarding differences between the two 'modified' subsamples, at the level of comprehension, results were mixed. As far as vocabulary retention is concerned, in the Saitama study the 'interactionally modified' group outperformed the 'premodified' group in an immediate post-test (translation task 2 days after treatment) a second post-test (translation task 1 month after treatment) and a follow-up test (word–picture matching task 2 months after treatment). In the Tokyo study the 'interactionally modified' group demonstrated an advantage only in respect of the immediate post-test. However, from a re-analysis of the data from the Saitama study (reported in R. Ellis, 1996), it transpires that when an exposure-time factor is taken into account, a different picture emerges; thus, in terms of mean number of words acquired per minute of input, the 'premodified' group surpassed the 'interactionally modified' group.

Ellis draws from these findings the conclusion that while both of the above-described types of input modification seem in general to have advantages over 'baseline' input in terms of comprehensibility and the promotion of lexical acquisition, interaction may sometimes yield over-elaborate data which may hinder comprehension and retention. With regard to the main theme of the present section, the issue of form and meaning in the L2 mental lexicon, Ellis's results are clearly consistent with the notion that both formal processes and semantico-pragmatic processes are engaged in the learning of a new L2 item, since both kinds of input modification discussed in his studies involved, on the one hand, more repetition of the target items than in the 'baseline' input (and therefore more opportunities for subjects to hear and subvocally rehearse the relevant forms) and, on the other, the embedding of the target items in contexts which were – unlike the 'baseline' directions – constructed on the basis of requests for clarification (and therefore much more meaningful to subjects).

Research into the role of cross-linguistic influence

The time is past when it was necessary to make a general case for the existence of a cross-linguistic factor in L2 acquisition and use (cf. Singleton, 1981, 1987a). In relation to lexical aspects of L2 acquisition and use, cross-linguistic influence is particularly noticeable, clearly affecting both formal and semantic aspects of the words involved (see, e.g., Dechert & Raupach, 1989a, 1989b: *passim*; R. Ellis, 1994: esp. 316–317; Kellerman & Sharwood Smith, 1986: *passim*; Odlin, 1989: *passim*; Ringbom, 1987: *passim*, 1991; Swan, 1997). Nor is it the case that only L2 lexical operations are affected by it. L2 → L1 transfer – 'backlash interference' as Jakobovits picturesquely terms it – is widely experienced and has been widely attested in the literature for decades (see, e.g., Haugen, 1953; Jakobovits, 1969; James, 1971; Weinreich, 1953) and has been more recently studied particularly in respect of immigrant speech and L1 attrition (see, e.g., Backus, 1996; Boyd, 1993; Johanson, 1993; Olshtain,

1989; Romaine, 1989 – see discussion below in this subsection and in the second part of the chapter). Accordingly, there is absolutely no basis for the erection of any new L1/L2 dichotomy of the kind:

L2 mental lexicon = susceptible to cross-linguistic influence
L1 mental lexicon = not susceptible to cross-linguistic influence

Particularly relevant to the question of the relative contribution of formal and semantico-pragmatic dimensions of the L2 lexicon is the role of cognates, false cognates and imagined cognates. Laufer (e.g., 1990a, 1990c, 1993–94; Benoussan & Laufer, 1984) has explored this issue in some depth, and she has shown that learners constantly seek to make connections between new words they encounter in their target language and languages they already know, and that this happens, in some measure at least, even when the languages concerned are unrelated. Cohen & Aphek's (1980) study of learners' use of mnemonic devices (referred to above) in the context of L2 vocabulary learning also shows this to be the case. Two examples from their collection of associations attempted by English-speaking learners of Hebrew are:

Hebrew *mudaut* ('consciousness') – English *awareness* via *beware of the moody wolf*
Hebrew *hardama* ('anaesthesia') – French *dormir*

Where learners perceive a high degree of similarity between the target language and other languages at their disposal, they will be especially ready to forge such links, as the whole literature on psychotypology readily demonstrates (see, e.g., Kellerman, 1977, 1979, 1983; Ringbom, 1987).

This aspect of lexical acquisition – which has been studied for a considerable length of time (see, e.g., J. Anderson & Jordan, 1928, cited by Meara, 1996a) is interesting from a number of points of view. It has implications for the organization of the mental lexicon, specifically in respect of the relationship between L1 and L2 lexical knowledge (see below), and it is something which should certainly be considered in a pedagogical perspective (cf. Granger, 1993; Meara, 1993b). However, in the context of the present discussion, its principal interest is that it confirms that semantico-pragmatic processes are at work right from the outset of the learning of a new word, and that, as the earlier-cited results from Papagno *et al.* and Service also indicate, one of the ways by which these processes begin to connect up new words to internalized meaning systems is by assimilating them to words which are already known. One notes that formal similarity in such instances is merely the vehicle – the pretext, one might almost say – for semantic processes.

It was mentioned earlier that some of the examples given by Meara (1984: 233) of what he presents as formally motivated Anglophone responses to the Birkbeck French word-association tests are in fact more plausibly seen as instances of intralingual interference with a very substantial semantic component. Other items from among the examples in question constitute fairly clear instances of *inter*lingual semantic assimilation triggered by formal similarity. Thus, Meara is probably right in interpreting the response *rigoler* ('to laugh') to *caque* ('herring barrel') as motivated by assimilation of *caque* to the English form *cackle*, but the response in question is, just as or more importantly, motivated by the tacit positing of semantic links between the two words. Similarly with the following further examples from Meara's data:

odeur ('odour', 'smell') elicited by *semelle* ('sole [of shoe, foot]') – cf. English *smell*
essayer ('to try') elicited by *traire* ('to milk') – cf. English *try*
lettre ('letter') elicited by *émail* ('enamel') – cf. English *mail*

It appears that in the acquisition of new L2 lexical items, conflicts often arise between cross-linguistic semantic-associative processing and form-oriented processing aimed at constructing as close as possible a replica of the new word (cf. the discussion of memory-code research above). The learner then has the task of resolving this conflict by testing out the divergent hypotheses. A good example of this situation is provided by Giacobbe's (1993–94) Spanish-speaking female subject acquiring French naturalistically. In trying to deal with the French word *cuisine* ('kitchen'), this subject on the one hand associated it with the Spanish word for 'kitchen' – *cocina* – producing forms such as [kosin] and [kosi] and on the other hand endeavoured to replicate the French form faithfully, producing forms like [kusin] and [kwisin] (see also Giacobbe & Cammarota, 1986, and discussion below of Singleton's 1987b notion of 'assimilative encoding').

It also seems to be the case that inaccurate semantic associations made between forms in the languages at an individual's disposal may become fossilized. This can happen even where there is high proficiency in both languages. An example of such fossilization was recently provided by a research student of mine, a balanced bilingual in French and English, who in written reports in English on her project systematically used the word *apprenticeship* in contexts where *learning* was clearly the item required. She had obviously made an early connection between *apprenticeship* and French *apprentissage* ('learning') which continued to inform her use of the former. A similar much-cited instance is the way in which many Francophones use the English word *library* as if it meant the same as French *librairie* ('bookshop') – even at quite advanced stages of their learning of English (cf. Baetens Beardsmore, 1982: 47). An interesting variation on this theme is a phenomenon reported by Haugen (1953) and Weinreich (1953) (for further discussion see, e.g., Baetens Beardsmore, 1982: 37ff.; Romaine, 1989: 50ff.) whereby whole immigrant communities may assimilate a word from the language of the host community to a formally related word in their own language with a different meaning, *and then shift the meaning of the L1 word*:

> For example, Portuguese/English bilinguals in the United States have taken the Portuguese word *grossería* – 'rude remark' – and have extended it to refer to a 'grocery store' ... Weinreich (1953) says ... that the Italian American term *fattoría* originally meant 'farm', but then took on the meaning of 'factory'. (Romaine, 1989: 55–56; cf. discussion below of code-switching and code-copying)

Finally on this point, there is some evidence that awareness of lexical relatedness – including semantic relatedness – across languages is amenable to training. Thus, Tréville (1993a, 1993b) reports a study in which three groups of beginning learners of French as a second language and three groups of *faux-débutants* were, in the course of a 52–hour French language programme, given seven hours of instruction in recognizing, categorizing and interpreting French cognates of English words. A language-aptitude test based specifically on tasks revolving round cognates as well as French-language proficiency tests appropriate to the levels concerned were subsequently administered to these experimental groups and to two control groups which had received 52 hours of ordinary French classes. The language-aptitude test was a specially designed instrument – TARCE: Test d'Aptitude à la Récognition des Congénères Ecrits – which included grammatical-category identification, comprehension and cloze-type tasks in addition to recognition and formal derivation tasks. The experimental groups significantly outscored the control groups on TARCE, and they performed to the same standard as the control groups on the French language-proficiency tests.

Essentially, the cross-linguistic evidence reviewed above shows the interlingual facets of lexical operations to be semantic as well as formal and thus supports the view taken throughout this section that meaning is central to the functioning of the L2 mental lexicon. This evidence is entirely in keeping with what we have seen in earlier parts of the discussion, namely:

- that word-association test data – in what they indicate about both intra- and interlingual connections – fail to license a primarily 'phonological' conception of the L2 mental lexicon in contradistinction to a primarily 'semantic' conception of the L1 mental lexicon;
- that formal factors affecting L2 lexical acquisition also affect L1 lexical acquisition and that the principal challenge in both L2 and L1 is semantico-pragmatic rather than formal;
- that, in relation to the creation of L2 lexical memory codes, there is a meaning-focused dimension to even the earliest stages of this process;
- and that context-based L2 lexical processing and learning has both formal and semantico-pragmatic aspects.

Separation/integration between the L1 and the L2 mental lexicon

We move now to examine the question of whether the L2 mental lexicon is integrated with or separate from the L1 mental lexicon. This issue clearly relates to matters discussed earlier. For instance, one argument against the integration of L1 and L2 lexicons derives from the modularity hypothesis (see above, Chapter 3). As we have seen, there is some variation amongst modularists concerning which aspects of lexical operations are considered to fall within the domain of the language module. As we have also seen, however, at least some of those who have written on this topic seem to hold that a substantial part of the functioning of the L1 mental lexicon is intramodular (see, e.g. Emmorey & Fromkin, 1988; N. Smith & Wilson, 1979) and at least some hold that any L2 competence acquired beyond the childhood years is extramodular (see, e.g., Bley-Vroman, 1989). Taken together, these two positions imply that in the case of post-pubertal L2 learner, L1 and L2 lexical operations proceed in absolute isolation from each other.

Another 'separatist' line of argument[5] relates to the formal differences between languages, a topic touched on in Chapter 1. Thus, experimental research indicates that an individual faced with the task of working out the morphological structure of unfamiliar words will refer to the phonological composition of more familiar items and then analogize (see Bybee, 1988; Stemberger & MacWhinney, 1988). To take an example from French, someone encountering *brocanteur*

[5] I am grateful to one of my M.Phil. students, Stephen Van Vlack, for alerting me to this particular argument (Van Vlack, 1992).

('secondhand (furniture) dealer') for the first time would undoubtedly refer to the structure of words such as *vendeur* ('salesman'), *serveur* ('waiter') *assureur* ('insurance agent'), etc. in coming to the conclusion that *-eur* (/œʀ/) is the final morpheme of the item in question. Since the languages known to such an individual may have highly divergent phonological systems (e.g., /œʀ/ would not be a possible syllable in Chinese), the implication is that the search on which such analogizing tactics (or 'gang effects') depend runs through the lexicon of each language separately.

As far as arguments in favour of integration are concerned, these tend to come from the (obviously overlapping) areas of bilingualism research and research into cross-linguistic influence, both of which have also been touched on earlier – indeed in this very chapter. These arguments, and some balancing counter-arguments from the areas in question will be considered in some detail in the next two subsections. A further area of interest in this connection is research into communication strategies. This too will be dealt with below.

Bilingualism research[6]

Cook (1992, 1993) cites a wide range of evidence from bilingualism research conducted over the past 25 years which he sees as favourable to his view of 'holistic multicompetence'. Much of the evidence in question bears directly on the lexical dimension and specifically on the question of the separation/integration of mental lexicons. This evidence includes the following findings:

- reaction time to a word in one language is related to the frequency of its cognate in another known language (Caramazza & Brones, 1979);
- morphemic similarities between two known languages influence translation performance (Cristoffanini *et al.*, 1986);
- when processing an interlingual homograph (such as French/ English *coin*), bilinguals access its meanings in both their languages rather than just the meaning specific to the language being used (Beauvillain & Grainger, 1987);
- bilinguals consult the lexical stores associated with both their

[6] I am, of course, fully aware of the difficulties attaching to the definition of terms such as *bilingual*, *bilingualism*, etc. In the present context the reference is to research involving subjects with high levels of proficiency in more than one language – including (but not uniquely) subjects with two or more languages which they have acquired more or less simultaneously from infancy or very early childhood.

languages when taking vocabulary tests in one of their languages (Hamers & Lambert, 1972).

Further 'classic' evidence in favour of L1–L2 lexical integration includes, for example, Kirsner *et al.*'s (1984) finding that the presentation of a stimulus in one of a bilingual subject's languages primes his/her response to a corresponding stimulus in his/her other language and Green's (1986) finding that when a person has a reasonable command of two languages, lexical items are subconsciously activated in both languages, those in the language not required being subsequently suppressed.

Jessner (1996) refers approvingly to Cook's hypothesis and to the evidence he cites, and she goes on to adduce a number of more general arguments and evidence in favour of a holistic view of bilingualism/multilingualism, which, despite their generality, clearly have relevance to the present theme. Jessner points to:

- the impact of bilingualism/multilingualism in terms of positive developments in cognitive style and social competencies which transcend the use of any particular language (Peal & Lambert, 1962; Lambert, 1990);[7]
- the consequences of bilingualism/multilingualism in terms of increased metalinguistic and metacognitive awareness across the range of languages known to the bilingual/multilingual (Bialystok, 1991a; Malakoff, 1992; Malakoff & Hakuta, 1991; Mohanty, 1994);
- the association between bilingualism/multilingualism and creative, flexible, divergent thinking across an individual's linguistic spectrum (Ricciardelli, 1992);
- the tendency for bilinguals/multilinguals to be more sensitive than monolinguals in interpersonal communication – again in all their languages (Genesee *et al.*, 1975; Lambert, 1990).

To Jessner the above evidence suggests that bilingual/multilingual competence is an integrated entity 'consisting of dynamically interacting linguistic subsystems'.

As has been indicated, however, not all the evidence from bilingualism research straightforwardly favours the integrationist point of view. One obvious point is that (leaving aside the particular case of code-switching – see below) bilinguals use one language at a time. Precisely how bilinguals succeed in doing this is a matter of some

[7] The limiting condition for such positive effects is generally taken to be that both languages receive sufficient support (including attitudinal support) to sustain a high level of competence in both (see, e.g., Cummins, 1976; Skuttnabb-Kangas, 1976).

controversy, but the fact that they do it would seem to imply some degree of separation of the respective lexicons. Rather more dramatic evidence in favour of this point of view comes from studies of language loss occasioned by brain damage in bilinguals/multilinguals. In such instances of language loss, often all languages known to the individual are initially effaced and are then recovered one by one (the L1 not necessarily reappearing first). One example of this phenomenon reported by Grosjean (1982: 260) involved a native speaker of Swiss German who had received a serious head injury. The first language he recovered was French, a language he had learned as an adult and of which his knowledge was imperfect but which had pleasant associations for him. He subsequently recovered High German, but never recovered his L1, Swiss German. Whitaker (1978: 27) reports a not dissimilar case, that of an English classics scholar who recovered Greek, Latin, French and English (his L1) in that order.

With regard to the issue of how bilinguals manage to access the appropriate lexicon in their use of their languages, Grainger (1994; Grainger & Dijkstra 1992) discusses the question of the moment at which the information about the language affiliation of a given word is used by bilinguals in identifying an item. He notes the possibility that such information could be located at individual lexical entry level and also the possibility that the relevant information is represented at a higher level of lexical organization. In the first case, information about which language a word belonged to would be stored in the same way as phonological, semantic and syntactic information about that word:

> Ainsi, l'identification d'une forme lexicale spécifique donnerait accès à un ensemble d'informations concernant le sens, la prononciation, la fonction grammaticale, et la langue d'un mot. (Grainger 1994: 225)
>
> ('Thus, the identification of a specific lexical form would give access to a set of information concerning the sense, the pronunciation, the grammatical function and the language of the word in question.')

In the second case, information about language affiliation would be encoded in the actual structuring of the lexicon, 'les mots de chaque langue étant organisés dans deux réseaux distincts' ('the words of each language being organized in two distinct networks') (*ibid.*).

Grainger cites a great deal of evidence (Macnamara, 1967; Macnamara & Kushnir, 1971: 229; Kolers, 1966; Soares & Grosjean, 1984) in favour of the notion that context plays a role in accessing words in one language or another, and that bilinguals have more difficulty processing mixed sequences of words such as *Elle a vu des flowers dans le jardin* than with purely unilingual sequences (*She saw some flowers in the garden / Elle a vu des fleurs dans le jardin*). This appears to suggest that the opening word of the sentence 'switches on' the lexicon in one or other of the bilingual's languages, and that all lexical searching takes place initially in that particular lexicon. This is indeed the theoretical position taken up by the above authors, according to whom 'le bilingue peut fonctionner dans une langue sans qu'il y ait un contact quelconque avec les représentations lexicales de l'autre langue' ('the bilingual can function in one language without having any contact whatsoever with the lexical representations of the other language') (*ibid*.: 229). Further evidence which seems to favour this view comes from experimental work involving interlingual homographs (such as *four* (French 'oven', English '4')), the identification of which within lists of words from one or other of a bilingual's languages will depend on the frequency of that form in that particular language (Gerard & Scarborough, 1989).

Grainger is not, however, persuaded by this simple separatist line. He refers to a number of findings (some of which have already been mentioned) that clearly demonstrate 'on line' interaction between the word stores of bilinguals. For example, he notes Preston & Lambert's (1969) results from an experiment based on a bilingual version of the Stroop task, where subjects have to name the colour of the ink in which a stimulus word is written:

> les temps de dénomination augmentaient lorsque le mot écrit différait de la couleur à nommer (ex: BLEU écrit en rouge), et cela même lorsque la langue du mot différait de la langue dans laquelle le sujet devait nommer la couleur de l'encre . . . (Grainger 1994: 230)
>
> ('the naming times increased when the written word differed from the colour to be named (e.g., BLUE written in red), and this occurred even when the language of the written word differed from the language in which the subject had to name the colour of the ink . . .')

He also cites his own work with interlingual homographs (Beauvillain & Grainger, 1987 – see above), which indicates that an interlingual homograph primes target words in both of a bilingual's languages in lexical-decision tasks. That is to say *four* ('4' in English, 'oven' in French) was shown to prime *cuisine* ('kitchen', 'cooking' in French) even if it was situated in an English list and also to prime *five* even if it was presented amidst a sequence of French items.

He further cites the results (Grainger & Beauvillain, 1987) of presenting pairs of isolated words to subjects and noting the time taken to identify the second of the pair in same-language and different-language conditions. It turns out that the processing of a French word (e.g., *lire*, 'to read') is slower when preceded by an English word (e.g., *time*) than when preceded by a French word (*tort*, 'wrong') except where the words in question have distinctively French or English orthographic features (e.g., *voix*, 'voice', *show*). This seems to show that contextual information about language choice is used on a word-by-word basis rather than at a more general level and that it can be over-ridden by individual lexical traits of the target item. On the other hand, the inhibiting effects of changing language in the experiment were much stronger where the first word presented was in the bilingual's dominant language than where it was in his/her weaker language, which appears to indicate a basic level of activation for words in the dominant language which is higher than that for words in the weaker language.

Putting all these findings together, Grainger opts for a conception of receptive bilingual lexical processing in which, during an initial phase, lexical representations of items sharing formal properties with the stimulus item from both languages are activated – irrespective of the language context. Contextual information then comes into play at the phase of selection to reduce levels of activation of lexical representations in the inappropriate language and/or to raise levels of activation of lexical representations in the appropriate language. These effects are stronger where the contextual information derives from a dominant-language context. In other words, Grainger sees the evidence as running against the idea of bilingual lexical search as proceeding sequentially, language by language; rather he envisages the activation of all relevant lexical representations in both languages in response to a given stimulus, and a subsequent selection based on – *inter alia* – contextual information and the distinctiveness of the stimulus. On the other hand, the model presented by Grainger does clearly imply a level at which each language is separately represented, the lexicon of each language being more or less activated by the outcomes of lexical search and according to the degree of strength of each language.

De Groot (1993, 1995) also focuses on the processing implications of different lexical attributes. She reads the evidence she reviews as pointing not to a single representational system for a given individual with more than one language at his/her disposal but rather to a mixed representational system, where concrete words and words perceived as cognates across the two languages are stored in a 'compound' manner, whereas abstract words and non-cognates in the respective languages are stored in a 'co-ordinate' manner. The reference is to Weinreich's (1953) different categories of bilingualism

– subordinative, compound and co-ordinate. In subordinative bilingualism, according to Weinreich, L2 word forms are connected to L1 meanings via primary connections to L1 forms; in compound bilingualism the L1 and L2 forms are connected at the meaning level; and in co-ordinate bilingualism separate networks of form–meaning connections exist for each language. For Weinreich, these different types of bilingualism are associated with different kinds of learning experience: subordinative with learning an L2 through the L1; compound with school-based learning or with learning two languages in homes where the two languages are used interchangeably to refer to the same situations; and co-ordinate with the learning of two languages in entirely different contexts and/or in contexts where translation plays little or no role. However, as De Groot points out (1993: 33), Weinreich also recognizes (1953: 10) that a person's or a group's bilingualism need not be of a single type.

With regard to concrete words, De Groot refers to:

- word-association studies by Kolers (1963) and I. Taylor (1976) showing that responses were more often translations of stimuli in the case of concrete words than in the case of abstract words;
- Jin's (1990) lexical-decision study involving English/Korean bilinguals, in which a reliable semantic priming effect (facilitation based on meaning rather than form) was found across languages in respect of concrete words but not in respect of abstract words;
- her own research findings (De Groot, 1992; De Groot *et al.*, 1994) with Dutch/English bilinguals showing more rapid translation of concrete words than of abstract words.

In relation to the cognateness attribute, she cites:

- a large number of between-language repetition-priming experiments (Cristoffanini, Kirsner & Milech, 1986; Davis *et al.*, 1991; De Groot & Nas, 1991; Gerard & Scarborough, 1989; Kerkman, 1984; Kirsner *et al.*, 1984; Sánchez-Casas *et al.*, 1992; Scarborough *et al.*, 1984) the findings of which indicate that the cross-language priming effect 'is larger for cognates than for noncognates (in some studies), or that it occurs for cognates only (in other studies)' (De Groot, 1995: 173; cf. Woutersen's 1996a study, discussed below);
- some studies involving word-translation tasks (De Groot, 1992; De Groot *et al.*, 1994; Sánchez-Casas *et al.*, 1992) which show a cognateness effect:

  Cognates are translated faster, more often (fewer omissions),

> and more often correctly than noncognates. (De Groot, 1995: 173)

She concludes that concrete words and cognates are less segregated by language than abstract words and non-cognates.

Kirsner *et al.* (1993), looking at a similar range of evidence, also propose a mixed system of representations. They suggest that, as far as cognates are concerned, there may be integration at the formal level:

> morphology may be the critical feature for lexical organization, providing the pegs around which clusters of words are organized, regardless of language. . . . The proposition in the present case is that some fraction of the second language vocabulary is represented and stored as variants of the first language vocabulary. The size of this fraction is presumably determined by the extent to which the two vocabularies involve reference to a shared set of roots or stems. (Kirsner *et al.*, 1993: 228)

This is essentially a partially 'subordinative' solution. The suggestion seems to be that subordinative structure, which some research seems to indicate as characterizing lower levels of bilingual proficiency (see below), is a continuing feature of bilingual lexical organization in respect of cognate items at other levels of proficiency too. It should be clear, however, that what Kirsner *et al.* are *not* proposing is that the L2 lexicon is more 'morphologically' organized than the L2 lexicon. The reference in the above quotation is to a subpart of the L1 lexicon. The notion that formal aspects of words are important in the arrangement of their representations in both the L1 and the L2 lexicon is, of course, beyond dispute, as much of the discussion in the first part of this chapter shows.

A phenomenon which is highly relevant to the separation/integration issue is that of code-switching, which was mentioned earlier. The study of this phenomenon is fraught with terminological and methodological problems, especially at the lexical level. For example, there is a school of thought which places one-word switches in a different category from longer switches (see, e.g., Arnberg & Arnberg, 1985), and indeed some researchers are inclined to treat all one-word switches as loans in the first instance (see, e.g., Nortier & Schatz, 1992; Poplack, Sankoff & Miller, 1988; cf. discussion of immigrant communities' adoption of L2 semantics above and of code-copying below). However, the fact that bilinguals switch between languages – sometimes, apparently, without meaning to (see Shannon, 1991) – whether at a one-word level or over longer stretches, is highly relevant to the question of the separation/integration of lexicons. Indeed, even if one accepts that some of what looks like switching is in fact a kind of borrowing, this still implies a degree of what I have elsewhere called 'cross-lexical consultation' (Singleton, 1996c) and therefore seems to rule out absolute separation.

De Bot and Schreuder (1993) discuss code-switching data very much in a context of exploring the issue of language separation in bilinguals. They refer to the above-mentioned notion of a bilingual's languages being turned on and off, citing Obler & Albert's (1978) suggestion that the system needs to be more flexible than this notion implies, and they place in opposition in this context Paradis's (1981) idea of separately activated subsets and Green's (1986, 1993) proposals of varying levels of activation ('selected' – controlling the speech output; 'active' – playing a role in ongoing processing but with no access to the outgoing speech channel; and 'dormant' – stored in long-term memory but playing no role in ongoing processing). Some of the examples they give of code-switching from their data are:

(Dutch/MA [Moroccan Arabic])
asnu z-*zwakke punten*
'What the-*weak points*'
[What are the weak points?] (De Bot & Schreuder, 1978: 206)

(Dutch/English)
dat water dat liep direct *from* het dek in die grote regenbakken
'that water ran directly *from* the roof into those big water vessel[s]' (*ibid.*: 208)

(Dutch/French)
Tu es un *tof* copain
'You are a *nice* guy' (*ibid.*: 209)

Their conclusion on the basis of a close analysis of such examples is as follows:

> There are few empirical arguments for the assumption of qualitatively different storage mechanisms or processes. It appears rather that the activation metaphor can explain the degree of separation between languages. As noted, this is *not* an all or none [*sic*] mechanism and words from the non-intended language may always slip in. (De Bot & Schreuder, 1993: 212; cf. also De Bot & Bongaerts, 1996)

Finally in this subsection, let us consider the separation/integration issue in the light of the lexical development of bilinguals over time. According to one much-cited model of bilingual lexical development, that of Volterra & Taeschner (Taeschner, 1983; Volterra & Taeschner, 1978; see also E. Clark, 1987), bilingual children start out with a single lexical system which has just one entry (from one language or the other) for each meaning acquired. That is to say, according to Volterra & Taeschner, in the very early stages of bilingualism there are no translation equivalents across the languages being acquired. Their claim is that an ability to differentiate between languages – and thus a separation of the respective lexicons – begins to manifest itself only at or around age 2.

Quay (1995) adduces the following arguments against Volterra & Taeschner's model:

- researchers who have accepted it (she cites Döpke, 1992 and Saunders, 1988) have done so without any evidential basis for assuming its correctness;
- others (De Houwer, 1990; Lanza, 1990) have been quite frank about their failure to verify it from their data;
- evidence which has been cited in favour of the model (from Fantini, 1974, 1985) in fact relates to a case of the acquisition of two languages where the acquisition of the one got under way significantly before the acquisition of the other (rather than a case of simultaneous acquisition);
- Taeschner's own (1983) data from two Italian/German bilinguals (aged 1;11 and 1;6.15) respectively) in fact, on close inspection, yield quite considerable numbers of translation equivalents.

Quay's own study of an English/Spanish bilingual subject, Manuela, produces persuasive counter-evidence to Volterra & Taeschner's proposals: at age 1;5.15, 36% of Manuela's English vocabulary was matched by equivalents in her Spanish, and 40% of her Spanish vocabulary had equivalents in her English. Similar results were obtained by Zurer Pearson *et al.* (1995), who, in a study of the developing vocabularies of 27 bilingual children between ages 0;8 and 2;6, found translation equivalents in the speech of all but one of their subjects, such translation equivalents accounting for an average of 30% of all items coded in the two languages – both in the very early stages and later. In the light of such evidence, the two-stage model of bilingual lexical development proposed by Volterra & Taeschner looks distinctly implausible.

The fact that Volterra & Taeschner's hypothesis is unsupported does not mean, however, that the notion of a developmental dimension in bilingual lexical organization should be ruled out entirely. Woutersen (1996a, 1997) has suggested that Weinreich's (1953) different categories of bilingualism – subordinative, compound and co-ordinate (see above) – are at least in part associable with different stages or levels of bilingual development (cf. Potter *et al.*, 1984). While not denying the influence of context of acquisition as envisaged by Weinreich, she argues that at least as far as subordinative and compound bilingualism are concerned, there may also be a proficiency factor.

Woutersen bases her claim on findings obtained from lexical-decision experiments involving repetition priming conducted with three groups of Dutch learners of English of different levels of proficiency in English (secondary-school level, university level, and near-native level). The experiments required subjects to press a *yes* button or a *no* button according to their decision as to whether the phonetic string in either Dutch or English which they heard over headphones was or was not a real word. Woutersen's analysis of the results focused on the effect of the prior presentation of a synonym in the other language at her subjects' disposal. The results obtained showed an interlingual priming effect among the intermediate (secondary-school) learners for cognates but not for non-cognates, whereas among the high-proficiency and near-native learners there was an interlingual priming effect for both cognates and non-cognates. In other words, in the case of the less-proficient learners, only when there was interlingual overlap at the formal level did priming occur, whereas for the more proficient subjects, overlap at the semantic level was sufficient to trigger priming. Woutersen concludes that the less-proficient learners exhibit bilingualism of the subordinative type, whereas the highly proficient and near-native learners exhibit bilingualism of the compound type, the implication being that an individual's lexical organization moves from the former category to the latter as proficiency increases. Similar results were obtained in a subsequent study involving Dutch/Turkish, Dutch/English and Standard Dutch/Maastricht dialect bilinguals (Woutersen, 1996b; see also Woutersen, 1997).

One should perhaps be wary of taking this interpretation at face value. As in relation to the word-association test results discussed in the first part of this chapter, the concept of proficiency warrants close inspection in this context. As in the earlier case, it may be better to conceive of bilingual lexical organization on a word-by-word rather than a language-by-language basis. This is in line with much recent theoretical thinking on lexical processing and acquisition (e.g., Cook, 1996; De Bot & Bongaerts, 1996; N. Ellis & Schmidt, 1996; Meara, 1996b) and is also in keeping with recent suggestions regarding lexical organization by word type (see above). It is certainly plausible to assume, as Woutersen does, that certain of the effects she notes are related to different sorts and strengths of connection at different degrees of proficiency. However, whereas she seems to conceive of proficiency in global terms in respect of a given language, the deeper implication of her approach is that connections are established on a word-by-word basis and that, depending on the degree of integratedness of a particular word, the types and degrees of connections between form and meaning within the word itself and in relation to other items may differ markedly from those discernible in respect of other words, whether in the same language or in another known language. The reason for overall interlingual quantitative differences in this regard can then be explained simply in terms of the fact that the more proficient a person is in a given language, the greater will be the number of individual lexical items in that language which will have developed particular patterns of connections and particular levels of connection strength.

Other studies which have indicated a proficiency effect on bilingual lexical organization are reviewed by De Groot (1995). These include those by Kroll & Curley (1988) and H.-C. Chen & Leung (1989), both of which focused on adult bilinguals of different levels of proficiency and both of which used a methodology deployed in an earlier, less conclusive study (Potter *et al.*, 1984), namely picture-naming and word-translation tasks. In terms of the number of processing steps implied, a subordinative (or 'word-association') type of organization would be expected to be reflected in shorter response times for translating words from L1 to L2 (direct link) than for picture naming in the L2 (indirect link via 'picture memory', 'conceptual memory' and L1 word store), whereas a compound (or 'concept-mediation') type of organization would be expected to be reflected in equally long response times on both tasks (the processing routes being L1 → concept → L2, on the one hand, and picture → concept → L2, on the other). As it turned out, the results of both studies suggested a subordinative structure in low-proficiency adult bilinguals and a compound structure in high-proficiency adult bilinguals. Similar findings emerge from a number of studies using a bilingual version of the Stroop test (see above), with between-language interference typically being much greater at lower levels of L2 proficiency than at higher levels (Abunuwara, 1992; H.-C. Chen & Ho, 1986; Mägiste, 1984; Tzelgov *et al.*, 1990). Clearly, the same circumspection and deconstruction are required relative to the notion of proficiency in these cases as in respect of Woutersen's findings.

Research into the role of cross-linguistic influence

Some general remarks about the prevalence of cross-linguistic influence in lexical operations were made in the first part of the chapter, and some indications of specific ways in which such influence may manifest itself were discussed at that point in support of the view that the L2 mental lexicon is, like its L1 counterpart, characterized by a high degree of meaning orientation. Further research findings pointing to a cross-linguistic factor in lexical operations were explored in the above review of bilingualism research perspectives on L1/L2 separation/integration in lexical organization. It is obvious that such evidence of cross-linguistic influence at the lexical level fatally undermines any notion of a complete separation between the L2 lexicon and the L1 lexicon. In what follows, some additional examples of studies yielding information about cross-linguistic aspects of lexical acquisition and processing will be adduced from different research traditions, and a caveat will be entered regarding a possible overinterpretation of cross-linguistic data.

One research approach which has yielded a particularly rich harvest of evidence of cross-linguistic influence at work in the L2 lexicon is error analysis. Thus, for example, Grauberg's (1971) analysis of the written errors in German made by 23 first-year students of German at Nottingham University reveals that, of the 186 errors isolated, 102 were lexical, and that, of these lexical errors, 50% had a cross-linguistic dimension, 35 being based on a faulty perception of equivalence between English and German, and 16 consisting in the complete transfer of English expressions. An example of the former error category is the use of *entschließen* ('to make up one's mind') in a context where *beschließen* ('to resolve', 'to determine') was required, the faulty perception clearly being that *entschließen* corresponded to *to decide* in all circumstances. An example of the wholesale transfer of an English expression is the Germanizing of *I found my way to ...* (*ich fand meinen Weg zu ...*). In the first type of case, an L2 lexical form is associated with an L1 meaning; in the second type of case, known L2 forms are used to create L2 clones for L1 expressions in order to bridge lexical gaps (see discussion of communication strategies below). In both types of case it is evident that L2 learners are drawing on connections between L2 items and their L1 lexical stock, and, indeed, the second type of case shows learners experimenting with newly forged cross-lexical connections.

Similar findings emerge from my own study of English, Spanish, Irish and Latin influence on the semantico-grammatical aspects of the French interlanguage of an English-speaking learner of French (Philip) who had had three brief stays in France, who had studied Irish and Latin at school, and who had acquired Spanish during a three-year working visit to Spain (Singleton, 1983, 1987b). The transfer errors identified in this study are all lexical in a broad sense, and indeed the vast majority are lexical even in a narrow sense. The kinds of errors noted by Grauberg are discernible in these data too, the difference being that – probably because of psychotypological factors (see, e.g., Kellerman, 1977, 1979, 1983; Ringbom, 1987) – one of the L2s (Spanish) is actually slightly more prominent as a source of transfer than the L1 (English). Thus, individual L2 items are used with non-French meanings and whole expressions are imported from non-French sources. Examples are given below:

savoir ('to know (a fact)') used in the sense of 'to know (a person)' (*connaître*) – meaning of *savoir* identified with meaning of English *know*
champ ('field') used in the sense of 'countryside' – meaning of *champ* identified with meaning of Spanish *campo* (which covers both 'field' and 'countryside')
dans l'après-midi (used in the sense of point of time) – transfer of English expression *in the afternoon*
pour le matin (used in the sense of point of time) – transfer of Spanish expression *por la mañana* ('in the morning')
pour exemple – transfer of English expression *for example* / Spanish expression *por ejemplo*

In addition, Philip's data contain numerous examples of coinages based on English and/or Spanish lexical forms. For example:

[tipi'kal] for *typique* (cf. English *typical*)
[ab'rir] for *ouvrir* (cf. Spanish *abrir* – 'to open')
[kõserva'tif] for *conservateur* (cf. English *conservative* / Spanish *conservativo*)

One possible explanation for at least some kinds of productive transfer errors is that what is involved is 'assimilative encoding' (cf. discussion above of Giacobbe's 1993–94 data), that is, the identification of elements in the L2 input with elements already in store from other languages and the adjustment of the form or meaning of the new elements according to the model of the known elements:

> Take the case of [vɔ], which Philip substitutes for *voix* ... There is a reasonable chance that Philip had actually encountered *voix* in speech addressed to him ... If so, it seems quite likely that the presence of Spanish *voz* and Latin *vox* in his long-term memory facilitated his processing of this item at every level ... Now the point is that any facilitative influence from *voz* or *vox* would very likely have been registered as part of the coding for *voix*, so that this coding might have included information such as: sounds similar to *voz* and *vox* but lacks a final consonant; means roughly the same as *voz* and *vox*. Such a coding would inevitably have yielded something like [vɔ] when referred to for productive purposes. (Singleton, 1987b: 337)

Self-evidently, such an explanation rests on the assumption that the lexicons of languages other than that being used for communicative purposes are continuously available for consultation, even while communication is in process.

An alternative explanation for productive transfer errors uses the metaphor of 'borrowing' (cf., e.g., Corder, 1978, 1983; Kellerman, 1977, 1979, 1983; Krashen, 1981: 67) – the idea here being that the learner expands his/her resources in language *x* by dipping into his/her knowledge of language *y*, 'converting' forms from language *y* into items that sound or look plausible in language *x*, or extending meanings attached to forms in language *y* to known forms in language *x*. A likely example of this from Philip's data is his use of a form [sɑ̃'sil] in a context requiring the form *simple*. There is no form like [sɑ̃'sil] meaning 'simple' in French, and so this cannot be a case of assimilative encoding. There is, however, a form *sencillo* in Spanish meaning 'simple'. Apparently Philip selected this term from his Spanish lexicon and then set about disguising it as a French word by turning the [ɛn] in the first syllable into a nasal vowel and deleting the final [o]. (One notes that if he had chosen English *simple* rather than Spanish *sencillo* to fill the gap, his ploy would have almost certainly have gone unnoticed!)[8]

Borrowing in the above sense is clearly a communication strategy (see below) of quite a sophisticated kind. It involves not only the 'on line' consultation of a lexicon or of lexicons other than that of the language in which communication is taking place, but also the use of lexical knowledge relative to this latter language in order to 'camouflage' the alienness of the borrowed items. Opinions vary about whether such borrowing can actually lead to changes in the learner's internalized system. Thus Krashen (1983: 142) claims that borrowing never leads to genuine interlanguage development and that if borrowed forms are held on to 'fossilization seems to occur', whereas Corder (1983: 94) assumes that communicatively successful borrowings 'are eventually incorporated into the interlanguage grammar'. We saw in the earlier part of this chapter that cross-linguistic influence can lead to the fossilization of deviant meanings. Presumably, however, it is also possible for *non*-deviant forms and meanings of cross-lexical origin to become 'fossilized', and in this latter kind of case it is difficult to see how fossilization differs from progress.

[8] Cf. Philip's own comments (contained in one of the answers elicited by a general questionnaire about language and his language knowledge):

> With regard to French I often 'Frenchify' a Spanish or Latin word which I suspect might fit, and less regularly, a Latin word is called upon to do service in Spanish. (Singleton, 1987b: 331)

An interesting sidelight is shed on this question by recent research on 'code-copying' (Johanson, 1993; cf. discussion above of immigrant communities' adoption of L2 semantics and of code-switching; see also Backus, 1996; Boyd, 1993; Olshtain, 1989). Code-copying, as described by Johanson, is a process whereby individuals use elements from one language at their disposal when communicating in another language (even though the latter may be their L1), the 'copied' elements often becoming long-term or even permanent fixtures, eventually leading in many cases to adjustments in the language's resources for all of its users in a given location or social setting. Johanson cites a number of lexical examples from the Turkish spoken by (first-generation) Turkish speakers in Germany, including:

banof ('station') – cf. German *Bahnhof*
vaynak ('Christmas') – cf. German *Weihnachten*
doyç ('German') – cf. German *deutsch*

and with semantic specialization:

havuz ('home') – cf. German *Haus* ('house', 'home')
k'rank ('(reported) sick', 'unfit for work') – cf. German *krank* ('sick')
hay'm – ('hostel') – cf. German *Heim* ('home', 'institution' 'hall of residence', 'hostel')

In one sense this is 'fossilization', but in another sense it is the very opposite, leading as it does to language change. Indeed, taking a rather broader perspective, it exemplifies one of the most frequent mechanisms of diachronic lexical change (cf. Appel & Muysken, 1987): words are 'borrowed' by native speakers of a given language from an L2 to which they have access, are then taken up by the wider community, and are eventually naturalized within the language – totally losing any connotation of foreignness or deviancy.

The focus in the discussion so far has been on cross-linguistic components of performance – the learning and diachronic change outcomes referred to being essentially by-products of communication with a cross-lexical dimension. However, cross-linguistic issues also arise in relation to the deliberate learning of vocabulary. We have already seen this in connection with Cohen & Aphek's (1980) research on the use of mnemonic devices. A more recent study by Stoffer of vocabulary learning strategies (Stoffer, 1996) underlines the point. Stoffer used a self-report instrument of her own devising, the Vocabulary Learning Strategies Inventory (VOLSI) to assess the use of vocabulary-learning strategies by a large sample (N = 707) of American university students of various foreign languages – French,

German, Japanese, Russian and Spanish. Nine factors emerged from a factor analysis of the data:

(1) Strategies Involving Authentic Language Use
(2) Strategies Involving Creative Activities
(3) Strategies Used for Self-Motivation
(4) Strategies Used to Create Mental Linkages
(5) Memory Strategies
(6) Visual/Auditory Strategies
(7) Strategies Involving Physical Action
(8) Strategies Used to Overcome Anxiety
(9) Strategies Used to Organize Words.

This list is ordered in terms of proportional contribution to total scale variance. In terms of frequency, the overwhelmingly dominant category in overall terms was Factor 4 (Strategies Used to Create Mental Linkages), and highest scoring of the strategies included under this heading was the strategy of linking L2 words to L1 words. A further aspect of the data which is of interest in a cross-linguistic perspective is the language-particular variation which emerged: (a) the highest means for strategy use were reported by learners of languages which were lexically most distant from English (Japanese and Russian), and (b) whereas in respect of French, German and Spanish the most prominent factor was the set of mental linkage-creating strategies, for Russian the important factor was the memory-related one, and for Japanese, self-motivation. It is plausible to infer from such findings that (at least some categories of) L2 learners are quite adept at using their assessment of L1–L2 lexical distance as a basis for deciding how hard they need to work on vocabulary learning and for determining how far they will be able to exploit interlexical similarities (cf. the above references to the literature on psychotypology). Clearly, none of this would be possible if the lexicon of the L1 were unavailable for consultation and comparison during the processing of L2 items.

Whatever the strategies deployed, as was mentioned at the very beginning of this chapter, the amount of L2 vocabulary that is actually learned has a major impact on the capacity of the learner to perform various skills in the L2. Reading research, for example, has shown that L2 lexical proficiency is an absolutely critical factor in L2 reading. An oft-cited study in this connection is Koda's (1989) investigation of the progress of 24 students enrolled on a first-year Japanese programme at Ohio University. This showed that, of the various components of their knowledge of Japanese that were tested, 'vocabulary knowledge was the most highly correlated with reading comprehension' (Koda 1989: 537). What is particularly interesting about Koda's study in the present context, however, is the extent to which she found transferred vocabulary knowledge to have played a role in differentiating the good readers from the poor readers (see also Koda, 1997).

Koda divided her sample into those whose L1 experience had given them some knowledge of Chinese characters (known in Japanese as *Kanji*) – i.e., speakers of Chinese and Korean – and those coming from purely alphabetic L1 backgrounds – i.e., speakers of American English, Brazilian Portuguese and Peruvian Spanish. The *Kanji* writing system, in which individual characters represent whole words, is used in Japanese alongside a sound-based syllabary system (*Kana* – subdivided into *Hiragana* and *Katakana*, the latter being used exclusively for words borrowed from Western languages). When the results of the *Kanji* group and the non-*Kanji* group were compared, it was found that 'vocabulary knowledge was the single most significant factor distinguishing the two groups' (Koda 1989: 533). This difference remained constant even when the *Kanji* items in the vocabulary test (which accounted for 30% of the test items) were controlled for:

> Given the fact that neither group had any prior exposure to Japanese, these results seem to suggest that transferred vocabulary knowledge considerably facilitates the learning of Hiragana, or L2 specific vocabulary. Importantly, it is this knowledge – overall (i.e., Kanji and Hiragana) vocabulary – which directly influences L2 reading comprehension. (*ibid.*: 534)

Moreover, vocabulary knowledge was found to correlate with word-recognition speed, and the *Kanji* group performed consistently better in this area – including on the two *Hiragana* word-recognition tests – which seems to indicate 'that transferred vocabulary knowledge also facilitates the mastery of L2 word recognition skills' (*ibid.*). These findings clearly show that transferred vocabulary knowledge is drawn on both in the acquisition of further L2 lexical knowledge and in the development of L2 lexical-processing competencies – which, like the rest of the evidence reviewed in this subsection, offers no comfort whatsoever to the notion of complete and utter separation between the L1 lexion and the L2 lexicon.

With regard to productive skills, a particularly interesting piece of research is that conducted by Hill (1991). This particular investigation reveals that what may be transferred is a set of semantic preferences based on the L1 lexicon. Hill cites a number of studies which suggest that L1 semantic and lexico-semantic structure plays a role in shaping L2 development (e.g., Giacobbe & Cammarota,

1986; Graham & Belnap, 1986; Harley & King, 1989; Ijaz 1986; Ramsey, 1981; Strick, 1980; Tanaka & Abe, 1985). His own research looks at the oral production in English of 158 Kenyan learners of English with an L1 background in one of the following languages: Dholuo, Nandi or Olunyore. These three languages tend (like, e.g., Romance and Semitic languages) to have verbs of motion which express (according to Talmy's (1985) classification) Motion + Path (cf. French *entrer*, *sortir*, *descendre*, *monter*), as opposed to English, in which (as in, e.g., Chinese) verbs of motion are mostly of the Motion + Manner/Cause type (verbs such as *run*, *totter*, *sail*, *drift*). Hill found that in a task which involved the retelling of a narrative in English twice (7–10 days separating these two retellings), his subjects exhibited 'a persistent preference for particular verb categories in the field of motion, even after exposure to a TL [target language] model and despite the fact that actual verbs changed in a good many cases between the two retellings' (Hill, 1991: 31). As compared with native-speaker controls, the Kenyan subjects 'tended to use far more path-specifying verbs' (*ibid.*). Once again, the L1 factor manifests itself unmistakably. It is not entirely clear in this case at what precise level or in what manner the L1 lexical knowledge is intervening (is it influencing which L2 verbs are more securely acquired, or is it influencing which of the stored L2 verbs are most frequently selected for use?), but in any case the evidence bespeaks cross-lexical connectivity.

It has to be said, on the other hand, that evidence of cross-linguistic influence does not support the idea of full integration between the L1 lexicon and the L2 lexicon either. For instance, research conducted within the error-analysis paradigm suggests that in overall terms, productive errors with a cross-linguistic dimension are relatively thin on the ground. It will be recalled that the claim of the Contrastive Analysis Hypothesis that transfer was the 'chief source' of learner difficulty (James, 1971: 5–6, citing Lado, 1964) was originally put in doubt by the fact that many L2 errors, to quote Dušková's (1969: 19) comment on her data, 'seem to have little, if any, connection with the mother tongue'. Similar findings were reported in other studies conducted around the same time:

> A number of other studies yielded conclusions which suggested that no more than a third of learners' errors were attributable to language transfer (Lance, 1969; George, 1971; Brudhiprabha, 1972; all reported in Richards & Sampson, 1974, p. 5). (Singleton, 1981: 4f.)

A comparable order of percentages of cross-linguistically induced errors emerges from Singleton's (1990b) survey of some small-scale studies of transfer phenomena carried out at the University of Dublin. Even if one considers lexical errors as a case apart, the cross-linguistic factor is usually not overwhelming; thus, for example, Grauberg's above-cited (1971) study finds that transfer accounts for no more than a half of productive errors. In other words, there are *prima facie* indications that a considerable proportion of L2 productive processing – including lexical processing – does not call on L1 resources.

Research into communication strategies

Finally in this part of the chapter, let us briefly consider research into communication strategies (for more extensive surveys and discussion see, e.g., Bialystok, 1990; R. Ellis, 1994: 396ff.; Faerch & Kasper, 1983a; Faerch *et al.*, 1984: 154ff.; Kellerman, 1991; Palmberg, 1979; Poulisse, 1990, 1993; Tarone, 1977, 1980; Varadi, 1980). There are essentially two aspects of this research that bear on the integration/separation question. The first relates to the content of the previous subsection and has already been demonstrated by some of the data quoted: communication strategies deployed by L2 users very often make use of knowledge of languages other than that in which communication is taking place. Further examples of this phenomenon will be given below. The second aspect of this research which is relevant to lexical organization is the similarity which emerges between communication strategies used in L1 and those used in L2.

A difficulty that immediately arises in any discussion of communication strategies is that opinions vary widely on what they actually are. Two rather prominent dimensions of this particular difficulty are, on the one hand, a dispute about the extent to which communication strategies are separable from other aspects of language processing, and, on the other, a variety of opinions about how communication strategies are to be classified. In relation to the former controversy, probably the most widely held view is that communication strategies are responses to difficulty or problematicity of some kind encountered during communication. Thus, for example, Faerch *et al.*'s definition states that communication strategies are 'problem-solving devices that learners resort to in order to solve what they experience as problems in speech production and reception' (Faerch *et al.*, 1984: 154; see also, e.g., Corder, 1977; Faerch & Kasper, 1983b; Littlewood, 1984; H. Stern, 1983; Tarone, 1980). The implication of this kind of definition (made explicit in, e.g., Faerch & Kasper, 1983b) is that communication strategies fall by their nature into the category of potentially conscious language use. Bialystok (1990), however, takes a different line, arguing (1990: 146) that 'the communicative strategies used by second language learners are consistent with descriptions of language processing where no problem is perceived' and therefore that 'Strategic language use ... is not fundamentally different from nonstrategic language use'. Tarone's more recent pronouncements (Tarone & Yule, 1989; Yule & Tarone, 1990) also represent strategic communication as continuous with non-strategic communication. With regard to the classification of communication strategies, some researchers (e.g., Faerch & Kasper, 1984; Paribakht, 1985; Tarone, 1977; Varadi, 1980) have produced quite extensive hierarchized taxonomies, while others have attempted to reduce the number of strategy types to just two (e.g., Bialystok, 1990; Kellerman, 1991; Kellerman *et al.*, 1987; Poulisse, 1990) or three (Poulisse, 1993).

The detail of these particular debates does not concern us here. Whether or not perceived problematicity is seen as critical, and whether or not qualitative differences are postulated between strategic processing and other kinds of processing, the consensus is that strategic language use is a real phenomenon, and that it constitutes 'the means by which a system can perform beyond its formal limitations and communication can proceed from a limited linguistic system' (Bialystok, 1990: 147). Moreover, however the various manifestations of strategic language use are analysed, grouped and categorized, there seems to be little factual disagreement about the kinds of data that are likely to be generated when an L2 system is called on to 'perform beyond its formal limitations'.

One aspect of strategic L2 use that is ubiquitously mentioned in the communication strategies literature is the deployment in diverse ways of knowledge of languages other than that in which communication is taking place. Thus, for example, 'conscious transfer' – covering 'literal translation' and 'language switch' – is one of Tarone's (1977) categories; Faerch *et al.* (1984) have a category labelled 'L1 based strategies' which includes 'code-switching', 'Anglicizing' (where the L2 is English; the more general term is *foreignizing*) and 'literal translation'; Kellerman (1991: 150) sees resorting to 'another language (the L1 typically, but not inevitably)' as one of the 'two fundamental ways' in which his 'code strategy' operates (the other being the exploitation of L2 productive processes); and Poulisse (1993) refers to recourse to L1 as well as L2 items in her 'Substitution Strategy' and to the application of L1 as well as L2 morphological and phonological encoding procedures in her 'Substitution Plus' strategy.

A number of the examples cited in the previous subsection may well – as was noted – have resulted from the strategic tapping of lexical resources other than those of the language of communication. Some further instances of lexically focused, cross-linguistically fuelled strategies from various sources are given below.

Code-switching:

my ***knallert*** (Danish word for *moped*) (Faerch *et al.*, 1984: 156)
Je suis dans la ***wrong*** *maison* (Littlewood, 1984: 86)
Un bureau pour ***cosmetics*** *et* ***perfume*** (*ibid.*)

Foreignization:

pruke (Anglicized version of Dutch word *pruik* – 'flute') (Kellerman, 1991: 151)
[*seʀk*] (Gallicized form of Spanish *cerca* – 'near') (Singleton, 1987b: 342)

Literal translation:

I take myself in the neck (Danish *Jeg tager mig selv i nakken* – 'I pull myself together') (Faerch *et al.*,1984: 156)
bus stop place (Swedish *busshållplats* – 'bus stop') (Palmberg, 1979: 59)

Obviously, in order for strategies of the above kind to be applied, there must be the possibility of interaction between the mental lexicons associated with the languages involved.

To return to a more theoretical perspective, the one dimension of the current discussion about the nature of communication strategies that directly relates to the present discussion is the above-mentioned similarity between strategies exhibited by L2 users and those applied by L1 users. Kellerman (e.g., 1991, 1993) and Bialystok (e.g., 1990) have reacted to suggestions that strategic language use should be formally taught to L2 learners (e.g., Willems, 1987) by emphasizing that 'such behaviour is surprisingly commonplace amongst native speakers' (Kellerman, 1991: 153). Kellerman (*ibid.*), referring to Isaacs & Clark (1987), cites in this connection L1 situations 'where one member of a pair of speakers is an expert and the other a novice and the novice needs to have some term explained or to find out what something is called' and, referring to J. Carroll (1983), also points to selection by companies of 'trade names that are often highly descriptive of the products they designate'. He also summarizes (*ibid.*: 157–158) a whole range of research (Bongaerts *et al.*, 1987; Bongaerts & Poulisse, 1989; Davidson *et al.*, 1986; Kellerman, *et al.*, 1990) which indicates that referential strategies and the ways in which speakers structure definitions are substantially the same whether an L1 or an L2 is being used.

For Kellerman and Bialystok such evidence is deployed in the service of their objection to the notion that one should explicitly teach communication strategies in the L2 classroom ('Teach the learners more language and the strategies will take care of themselves' – Kellerman, 1991: 158). In the present context, however, the relevance of such evidence lies in what it says about processing overlap between the L1 lexicon and the L2 lexicon. Whatever the precise relationship between strategic language use and other varieties of language use, the former is clearly an aspect of language processing, and the very considerable portion of strategic language use which is lexically oriented has to be regarded as coming under the heading of lexical processing. If, then, it is the case that strategic language use is essentially common ground between L1 and L2 processing, this must constitute yet another argument in favour of the view that the L1 mental lexicon and the L2 mental lexicon are connected.

Concluding summary

This chapter has reviewed a range of research relating to the L2 mental lexicon and has discussed such research with particular reference to two important issues: (1) the question of whether the L2 mental lexicon is intrinsically more form-based than the L1 mental lexicon, and (2) the question of whether or not there is connectivity between the L1 lexicon and the L2 lexicon.

With regard to (1), it has offered arguments against accepting Meara's interpretation of the Birkbeck Vocabulary Project data as supporting the formal view of the L2 mental lexicon, and, in a survey of a variety of research areas which pertain to form and meaning in the mental lexicon, it has brought to light an abundance of evidence in support of the view that, while formal processing may play a particularly important part in the early stages of the learning of a new word – in both L2 and L1 – meaning rather than form poses the greater challenge in lexical acquisition – again in both L2 and L1 – and lexical units are increasingly processed *qua* meaning rather than *qua* form as their integration into the mental lexicon progresses.

With regard to (2), the chapter has referred to a wide spectrum of research which seems to rule out the notion that the L1 and the L2 lexicon are completely disconnected from each other, and also to findings which render the proposition of total integration equally difficult to sustain. It appears from the evidence reviewed that L1 and

L2 lexis are separately stored, but that the two systems are in communication with each other – whether via direct connections between individual L1 and L2 lexical nodes, or via a common conceptual store (or both). It also seems likely, on the basis of the current state of research, that the relationship between a given L2 word and a given L1 word in the mental lexicon will vary from individual to individual, depending on how the words have been acquired and how well they are known, and also on the degree to which formal and/or semantic similarity is perceived between the L2 word and the L1 word in question.

PART III

EVIDENCE FROM THE TRINITY COLLEGE DUBLIN MODERN LANGUAGES RESEARCH PROJECT

5 The Trinity College Dublin Modern Languages Research Project in broad outline[1]

This part of the book reports on some relevant findings from the Trinity College Dublin (henceforth TCD) Modern Languages Research Project (henceforth MLRP). As was indicated in the Foreword and Introduction, although this project did not focus specifically or exclusively on the lexicon, it nevertheless gave rise to data which shed light on some much-debated lexical issues. These data have already been discussed elsewhere in diverse presentations and publications, but this volume seems an appropriate place in which to bring the relevant findings together for consideration of a more integrated kind. On a more personal note, the project was the trigger which occasioned my own return to an interest in lexical research; on this ground alone, as far as I am concerned, it warrants acknowledgement as a factor in the genesis of this book.

The project was inaugurated in October 1988. It was based in the TCD Centre for Language and Communication Studies, but also had the active support of the TCD Departments of French, Germanic Studies, Italian and Spanish. Its general aim was to monitor the L2 development of university-level learners and to examine the possibility of connections between these learners' L2 development and their previous general educational and language-learning experience. After a pilot phase from October 1988 until September 1990, the project became fully operative in October 1990. Data collection ended in 1995. The account of the TCD MLRP given in this chapter outlines the project's subjects and methodology, sketches the approach taken to its computerization, and indicates the kinds of lexical issues that have been explored using project findings.

[1] For an overview of this project in its initial stages, see Singleton (1990a). Some parts of the present account are, by kind permission of the General Editor of the *CLCS Occasional Papers* series, based quite closely on sections of the above- mentioned earlier report.

Subjects

The subjects involved in the MLRP were drawn from the TCD Departments of French, Germanic Studies, Italian and Spanish. They were all full-time students enrolled on undergraduate degree courses offered by those departments. From 1990–91 until 1994–95 the entire yearly intake of students in the above departments was asked to supply us (via questionnaire) with information about their general education and their language-learning experience, and we also tracked the progress of all questionnaire respondents in terms of their annual university language-examination results. Only relatively small subsamples of subjects, however, were involved in our attempts to gather actual L2 data and introspective data which went beyond the generalities of the questionnaire. These were volunteers recruited from among the students of French and the students of German. Where more students volunteered than were needed, we operated a selection process based on questionnaire data, our objective being to make each subsample as varied as possible. The numbers involved were as follows:

From the 1990–91 intake: 10 students of French
18 students of German (of whom 9 were *ab initio* learners)
From the 1991–92 intake: 10 students of French
16 students of German (of whom 7 were *ab initio* learners)

Unfortunately, as in all projects of this kind, there was a certain attrition of volunteers as the years went by: some changed subjects, some went abroad, some withdrew from College, and some simply ceased turning up at elicitation sessions. Indeed, such was the fall-off in numbers after the 1992–93 round of data collection that meaningful quantitative analysis of data gathered beyond this point in respect of the volunteer samples of students of French and German was no longer possible, although more qualitative types of analysis remained an option.

Methodology

We collected four broad categories of data:

- background information about our subjects with particular reference to their educational and language-learning experience and achievements prior to entering university;

- information about the performance of our subjects in university language examinations as they progressed through their degree courses;
- samples of the L2 performance of our subjects;
- introspective data relative to our subjects' attitudes and motivation *vis-à-vis* their language studies and relative to particularities of their L2 performance.

The procedures employed to elicit such data will be discussed one by one. However, before this part of the discussion is embarked on, it is worth saying a little more about the extent of the data-gathering operation as it respectively applies to the various above-mentioned types of data. We actually began by envisaging the inclusion of all undergraduate students of French, German, Italian and Spanish in the entire data collection process in all of its dimensions. It very rapidly became clear, though, in the pilot phase of the project, that this all-embracing approach was impracticable.

The difficulties arose mainly in connection with the elicitation of samples of subjects' L2 performance. In order to ensure that such elicitation took in the whole sample, it was necessary to schedule elicitation sessions during – that is, at the beginning or end of – obligatory classes in the languages in question. This put extremely tight constraints on what could be attempted, since we were operating, more or less literally, on borrowed time. Another problem we encountered was that the fact that a class was in principle obligatory did not guarantee 100 per cent attendance. Accordingly, the aspiration we had to build a longitudinal dimension into the project began to look rather unrealistic, since every time we tried to elicit L2 data from a given L2 group it turned out to be differently composed. The clinching point in our decision to abandon our earlier plan, however, was that it rapidly became clear to us that our limited human resources were simply not adequate to the task of analysing the huge and varied mass of data that would result from 'blanket' elicitation of actual language data. We concluded that this last consideration would also very much apply in relation to the introspective data we wished to elicit.

The lessons learned during the pilot phase of the MLRP led us to organize the continuation of the project on two levels. At the first, more general, level, education and language-background data continued to be elicited, via questionnaire, from all first-year undergraduate students of French, German, Italian and Spanish, and the university language-examination results of all of these subjects continued to be monitored as they proceeded through their degree course. It seemed to us that some very broad correlations might be possible on the basis of these two sets of data which might bear on issues in L2 acquisition research and which might also be of interest to the participating departments for more immediate practical purposes. At the second level, L2 data and introspective data were elicited from a small subsample of students, whose progress was followed much more closely than that of the great mass of subjects, and whose ongoing co-operation was encouraged by the payment to them of a small sum of money each time they took part in an elicitation session. Because of the particular foreign-language expertise of the researchers who were permanently involved at this second level of the project, only students of French and German were recruited to participate at this level.

Turning now to the particular instruments and procedures we utilized to elicit our data, some of these have already been mentioned; the complete inventory is as follows: a general educational and language-background questionnaire, annual university language examinations, modified C-tests with associated introspection, word-association tests, story-tell and translation tasks with associated introspection, and open-ended interviews on motivation. Each of these will be dealt with in turn.

The MLRP questionnaire

A questionnaire was administered year by year throughout the duration of the project to all first-year undergraduate students in the four participating language departments. The questionnaire had an explanatory preamble and 20 sections. The explanatory preamble provided instructions on completing the questionnaire, asking subjects to read through the document carefully before beginning to fill it in, requesting the use of block capitals, advising subjects that they could use the margins for their answers if they found themselves short of space, supplying notes on particular questions that might pose problems, giving a contact address in case of difficulty. The information sought by the various sections focused on personal and current study details, general education and examination history, and language-learning.

The advantages and disadvantages of questionnaires as research instruments have been widely enough discussed not to require further treatment here. Our own reason for using questionnaires (rather than, say, open or guided interviews) in order to gather background information from our entire sample was largely practical: we simply did not have the time or personnel at our disposal to collect the required data in a more 'subject-friendly' manner.

University language examinations

As far as the university language examinations set by the various participating departments are concerned, a full description of the precise forms these assumed would take us disproportionately far afield in the present context, given the very limited role the results of the tests concerned have in the overall MLRP scheme of things. Suffice it to say that these examinations were highly eclectic in nature, including traditional integrative tasks such as translation and essay writing alongside discrete-point grammar tests and 'modern' procedures such as cloze. Because of the variety of test types and combinations of test types employed, and because the examination process was entirely beyond the control of the MLRP, there was no possibility of using examination results as a reliable guide to particular aspects of learner progress in a comparative perspective across the entire MLRP sample. These results could be seen only as very broad indications as to the general level of learner proficiency, and even as such they had to be treated on a department-by-department basis.

C-tests and associated introspective instruments

To come now to our own elicitation of data indicative of the state of our subjects' L2 competence, the instrument we used for this purpose during the pilot phase of the project was the C-test. This is a reduced redundancy procedure originally developed in Germany. It is fully described in a special issue of *Fremdsprache und Hochschule* (No. 13/14), the first three articles of which (Klein-Braley, 1985a; Raatz, 1985a; Raatz & Klein-Braley, 1985) provide an introduction to the rationale, design and operation of the test. Other key texts in this connection include: Grotjahn, 1987a; Klein-Braley, 1985b, 1997; Klein-Braley & Raatz, 1984. Essentially, the C-test sets the task of restoring to wholeness a short written text, every second word of which has had its second half deleted. To refine this account a little, the first sentence of the text is in fact left intact to provide a contextualizing lead-in; one-letter words are ignored (except elided forms such as French *l'*, *d'*, *s'*, etc., which are counted as belonging to the words to which they are attached); and where a word has an odd number of letters, one more letter is removed than is left standing.

Our initial decision to use the C-test (cf. Little & Singleton, 1992; Singleton & Singleton, 1997) was heavily influenced by the case made in its favour by its originators and advocates, Klein-Braley & Raatz (see references above and below). Because of the dense distribution of C-test deletions (as compared with the frequency of deletions in standard cloze tests), C-test data are researcher-friendly in terms of their encompassability and codability, and, moreover, such data are likely to include a representative sample of all word classes in the text. Also, the demonstrated fact that native speakers find C-tests relatively easy to complete seems to signify that the errors and difficulties of non-native C-test-takers will be particularly revealing about aspects of L2 development. Finally, the C-test appears to offer particular advantages with reference to lexical research; since subjects taking the C-test are unable to manipulate the ordering of the units constituting the C-test text, the knowledge that is probed by the test would appear to be essentially lexical in nature – knowledge of content words, grammatical words, word structure, collocability, colligability, grammatical class adherence of particular items, subcategorization frames, etc. (see discussion of Chapelle's critique below and see also above, Chapter 1).

Given that the C-test is a relatively recent arrival on the scene, that it has mostly been employed as a proficiency test, and that its capacity to yield information relevant to lexical competence has been the subject of some criticism (Chapelle, 1994), it is probably necessary to give rather careful consideration to the appropriateness of using the procedure as a means of investigating L2 acquisition and processing. Data elicitation via C-test is a far cry from the observation of spontaneous language production, and artificial, interventionist methods of gathering evidence about the normal development and use of language have not been without their critics. For example, Ellis & Beattie, while acknowledging that it is possible to learn much from experimental findings, argue that 'an over-concentration on isolated decoders processing text has caused psycholinguists to spend a lot of time and effort discovering things ... that a greater awareness of the conversational decoding would have made more obvious and less surprising' (A. Ellis & Beattie, 1986: 229). In not dissimilar vein, R. Carter (1987: 161), referring specifically to the word association test data collected under the auspices of the Birkbeck Vocabulary Project (see, e.g., Meara, 1984), points to a number of limitations of such data, including the possibility that working with single words may obscure or misrepresent 'the map drawn between words by speakers'.

Ellis & Beattie's and Carter's remarks are fairly representative of expressions of scepticism or pleas for caution in relation to experimental evidence in psycholinguistics. The main thrust of such scepticism or caution is typically that the nature of experimental procedures tends to be remote from that of normal language use, and that the language stimuli employed in such procedures tend to be divorced from normal discoursal context. This whole discussion links up, of course, to the general debate about the respective merits of qualitative versus quantitative research. Our own view coincides with that advanced by Larsen-Freeman & Long (1991), namely, that absolutes in this matter are not warranted, and that there is no reason why a given piece of research should not deploy a range of elicitation techniques and/or observational strategies, provided that the interpretation of the data so gathered is always sensitive to the conditions under which they were collected.

In a way the C-test represents in itself a kind of half-way house between an experimental and a naturalistic approach. It is experimental to the extent that it requires subjects to assemble in a particular place at a particular time in order to perform an imposed task of a kind that would not form a usual part of their language-using experience. On the other hand, the language units on which subjects have to work in a C-test are not presented *in vacuo*, but, on the contrary, are contextualized in authentic discourse, real text. It is even possible to argue that the C-test task bears some relation to 'real-life' linguistic tasks, given that there are occasionally circumstances beyond the groves of Academe in which one is presented with the problem of decoding/reconstituting a written signal that has been degraded by happenstance (inkstains, raindrops, tearing, fading, etc.).

There is a further point to be made about the 'naturalness' of the C-test which emerges from the discussion of modularity in Chapter 3. Whereas, for example, Fodor (1983) is inclined to the view that the processing of gapped written text is so unnatural that it must rely on mechanisms other than those involved in normal linguistic communication, the dominant view amongst psycholinguists appears to be that, in terms of subjects' exploitation of contextual cues, a degraded written stimulus is more likely than an undegraded written stimulus to provoke processing that resembles the processing of speech (see, e.g., Becker & Killion, 1977; Fischler & Bloom, 1980; Stanovich & West, 1983; A. Ellis & Beattie, 1986: 225–226; Harris & Coltheart, 1986: 170).

Empirical investigations of the validity of the C-test show correlations with other criteria relative to language proficiency (school marks, teachers' judgements, results of other kinds of language tests) that Grotjahn (1992b) qualifies as 'astonishingly high'.[2] Grotjahn cites in this connection a veritable litany of studies: Grotjahn (1987a, 1987b, 1992c); Jakschik (1992, 1993); Klein-Braley (1985b, 1985c); Klein-Braley & Raatz (1984, 1990); Raatz (1985b). The clear implication is that what language learners do when taking C-tests bears a close relationship to their language performance in other circumstances.

It is true that some researchers, notably Baur & Meder (1989), see the area of language proficiency tapped by the C-test as essentially that of the literacy skills as opposed to the interactive-communicative domain. Grotjahn is sympathetic to this view relating the above distinction to Cummins' (e.g., 1979, 1980) distinction between 'Cognitive/Academic Language Proficiency (CALP)' and 'Basic Interpersonal Communicative Skills (BICS)', and suggesting that the C-test is to be seen as a 'CALP-test' (Grotjahn, 1992b: 8). There are a number of possible responses to this suggestion. One is the psycholinguistic argument put earlier that the processing of degraded written stimuli such as C-tests appears in some respects to resemble the processing of speech more than does the processing of undegraded written text; degraded written stimuli, like ephemeral spoken stimuli, force subjects to rely heavily on contextual cues, to implement more 'top-down' strategies than are necessary in order to deal with intact written signals, which for their part are more amenable to a 'bottom-up' approach. A second response to Grotjahn's suggestion is that C-test results have actually been found to correlate quite well with the results of tests which expressly set out to be 'communicative' in nature (see, e.g., Wright, 1990). A third response is that, in any case, the CALP/BICS distinction is not at all clear; Cummins (1980) rejects a straightforward equation between CALP and literacy skills and BICS and oral/aural skills, but fails to provide definitions of CALP and BICS which amount to any kind of alternative operationalization of the concepts (cf. Harley, 1986: 31; Singleton, 1989: 112ff.). In fact, it seems highly unlikely that a hard-and-fast distinction between CALP and BICS is possible even in principle, which is presumably why Cummins himself has tended to move away from the CALP/BICS dichotomy and has reframed the distinction in terms of degrees of context embeddedness (see, e.g., Cummins, 1983, 1984).

There are good grounds, therefore, for treating with caution

[2] 'die ... erstaunlich hohen Korrelationen von C-tests mit verschiedenen Aussenkriterien (z.B. Schulnoten, Lehrerurteilen über den Sprachstand der Schüler, Ergebnisse in anderen Sprachtests) ...' (Grotjahn, 1992b: 7).

Grotjahn's statement that the C-test is a 'CALP test'. It is obvious that C-tests do not require subjects to call on skills that are specific to forms of communication which are interactive in the immediate, social sense (initiating conversations, turn-taking, interrupting, etc.); however, it is equally obvious that, on the one hand, communication is not limited to this kind of interaction and, on the other, interactive communication also draws on competencies deployed in non-interactive language use. Cummins' own acknowledgement that different kinds of language proficiency are continuous with each other should cause us to think very carefully indeed about a claim that a given test addresses only cognitive/academic proficiency.

A particular test form effect that has been noted by some researchers working on the C-test (e.g., A. Cohen *et al.*, 1984) has been a tendency for some C-test takers to concentrate on the local environment of the slot being filled, the formal particularities of the part of the word left standing, and to fail to take account of semantico-pragmatic context. However, our data from the piloting of the C-test in our project did not show significant signs of the effect in question (although individual instances of the phenomenon did crop up – for examples, see Little & Singleton, 1992). On the contrary, the majority of responses elicited by our pilot C-tests were related to the meaning of the larger context (see Singleton & Little, 1991).

Grotjahn (personal communication) suggested that one possible reason for this might be that our C-tests were a little longer than the 60–70-word texts that have customarily been used and that they thus provided a larger measure of semantico-pragmatic information and a better basis for the activation of normal context-reading processes. I personally am now inclined to some scepticism in relation to Grotjahn's suggestion and to see any divergences between our results and others' principally in terms of differences of learner proficiency level and consequent test difficulty. We did, though, take Grotjahn's communication to heart at the time of its receipt, which happened to coincide with the period when we were revising our C-test instruments for the post-pilot phase of the MLRP. We in fact decided to try to provide an even richer contextual framework by using C-test texts for the post-pilot phase of the project which ran to approximately 150 words. Also, to ensure equality of contextualization across texts, we in each case mutilated 50 words counting backwards from the end of the text (ignoring proper names, dates and numerals). This meant that the amount of unmutilated lead-in text was roughly equal in every case, which is, of course, not true if the lead-in is a grammatical unit of arbitrary length (the opening sentence). To further encourage semantico-pragmatic processing we saw to it that every text came equipped with a title.[3] By way of illustration, one of the C-tests from the post-pilot phase of the project, Modified French C-test 1, is given in full below, together with the unmutilated text on which it is based and an English translation of the same.

Le feu aux portes de Marseille

De violents incendies ont éclaté mardi 21 août dans les Bouches-du-Rhône et le Var où ils ont parcouru près de 9 000 hectares et détruit une quinzaine de maisons. Ils étaient contenus, mais pas maîtrisés mercredi matin. Le plus grave de ces incendies s'est déc____ au mil___ de l'aprè_____ dans l__ quartiers s__ de Marseille e_ s'est pro____ en quel____ heures ve__ la com____ de Cassis, o_ deux mi___ personnes o__ dû êt__ évacuées, do__ quatre ce___ par l_ mer.

Dep___ le dé___ de l'é__, personne n_ doutait q__ le mis____ et l_ sécheresse s_ conjugueraient u_ jour po__ mettre e_ danger l_ Provence. Il suff_____ d'une étin_____. 'J'ai v_ partir l_ feu a_ pied d__ muret', rac____ une habi_____ du quar____ de l_ Panouse. 'J'ai auss____ appelé l__ pompiers q__ sont arr____ un qu___ d'heure pl__ tard. To___ la col____ était e_ flammes.' I_ était 15h45, ma___.

Le feu aux portes de Marseille

De violents incendies ont éclaté mardi 21 août dans les Bouches-du-Rhône et le Var où ils ont parcouru près de 9 000 hectares et détruit une quinzaine de maisons. Ils étaient contenus, mais pas maîtrisés mercredi matin. Le plus grave de ces incendies s'est déclaré au milieu de l'après-midi dans les quartiers sud de Marseille et s'est propagé en quelques heures vers la commune de Cassis, où deux mille personnes ont dû être évacuées, dont quatre cents par la mer.

Depuis le début de l'été, personne ne doutait que le mistral et la sécheresse se conjugueraient un jour pour mettre en danger la Provence. Il suffisait d'une étincelle. 'J'ai vu partir le feu au pied d'un muret', raconte une habitante du quartier de la Panouse. 'J'ai aussitôt appelé les pompiers qui sont arrivés un quart d'heure plus tard. Toute la colline était en flammes.' Il était 15h45, mardi.

Fire at the Gates of Marseilles

Fierce fires broke out on Tuesday, August 21, in the Bouches-du-Rhône and Var areas, where they ran through nearly 9,000 hectares and destroyed some fifteen houses. The fires had been contained, though not fully brought under control, by Wednesday morning. The most serious of these fires erupted in the middle of the afternoon in the southern quarters of Marseilles

[3] On the potential of titles for facilitating comprehension, see, e.g., Dooling & Lachman (1971).

and spread in a few hours to the Cassis district, where two thousand people had to be evacuated, four hundred of them by sea.

Since the beginning of the summer, no one had doubted but that the strong offshore wind (the *mistral*) and the drought would one day combine to put Provence in danger. One spark was all that was required. 'I saw the fire start at the base of a small wall', tells a woman living in the Panouse quarter. 'I immediately called the fire-brigade, which arrived a quarter of an hour later. The whole hill was ablaze.' It was 3.45 on Tuesday afternoon.

A question that has been put to us (by, e.g., Granger, Meara – personal communications) is whether the C-test does not perhaps go *too* far in the direction of encouraging the use of contextual cues. The idea underlying this kind of question seems to be that whereas word-association tests, with their context-free stimuli, may be capable of tapping directly and 'purely' into the subject's internal lexical store, the C-test more or less forces the subject to exploit contextual cues in order to find solutions. This kind of concern resembles Fodor's (1983) claim that gapped-text tasks may provoke the activation of more context-sensitive 'back-up mechanisms'. However, it would be curious indeed if the C-test task, which at least in some respects resembles normal textual comprehension, were to activate more extraordinary, abnormal processing than the word-association task, which resembles absolutely nothing in ordinary communication. We have seen, moreover, that the processing of degraded written textual stimuli seems to utilize contextual cues in ways that are in some respects similar to the use of such cues in the ordinary processing of speech. No such evidence exists in relation to word-association tests, which are suspected by some lexicologists (e.g., Sinclair, 1993), in fact, of drawing on a different type of lexical knowledge from that which subserves normal linguistic communication. If it were the case, then, that C-test results from a given group of learners or a given learner type suggested a picture of the mental lexicon of the learners or learner type concerned that differed radically from that yielded by word-association test results, we should surely have to give more weight to the former than to the latter. It turns out that we do not actually need to make this kind of choice; when stimulus difficulty and learner level are taken into account, C-test findings and word-association test findings are actually convergent rather than contradictory (see below).

Chapelle (1994; cf. Singleton & Singleton, 1998) poses some very fundamental questions about the validity of the C-test as an avenue of insight into lexical competence. A first response to such concerns is simply to recall that the principal challenge of the C-test is to find appropriate lexis for particular environments. If this is not a lexical task, then it would be most interesting to learn what kind of a task it is! One can also note that the C-test-taker receives additional assistance from precisely the kinds of cues – the initial elements of the target forms – that are routinely exploited in word recognition and indeed in lexical search in productive mode. With regard to word recognition, experimental findings from word-monitoring tasks (see Marslen-Wilson & Tyler, 1980) have shown that, in normal speech, target words which took on average 369 milliseconds to say could be identified on average within 200 milliseconds – which must mean (among other things) that in a suitably constraining context recognition takes place on the basis of the initial segments of the words in question. With regard to lexical processing in language production, the evidence from 'tip-of-the-tongue' phenomena is that the beginning of a word acts as a constant guide to lexical search, being significantly less affected by lexical error than subsequent elements (see, e.g., R. Brown & McNeill, 1966).

Chapelle's critique has the following questions as its point of departure:

> if . . . the C-test is so clearly a vocabulary task, why did its developers originally present the method as a means for constructing tests of overall language proficiency calling on multiple aspects of linguistic knowledge . . .? Why is a 'contextualized' test best for vocabulary assessment when some other vocabulary tests present items with little or no context . . .? Why are the observed correlations with other language tests interpreted as evidence that C-tests are good vocabulary tests? (Chapelle, 1994: 158–159)

Despite the fact that Chapelle is sometimes cited as someone who espouses a 'broader conception' of lexical ability (see, e.g., Read, 1997: 318ff.), and despite the fact that she distances herself from the notion that 'vocabulary ability is isolated from other language abilities' (Chapelle, 1994: 164, fn. 2), it is difficult not to interpret the above questions as bespeaking a view of the lexicon which is distinctly narrower than that which emerges from the recent conclusions of linguistic and psycholinguistic research (see Chapter 1).

Chapelle goes on, in fact, to be quite explicit about what she thinks 'vocabulary ability' consists of. She talks about this 'ability' as having three components: '(1) the context of vocabulary use; (2) vocabulary knowledge and processes; and (3) the metacognitive strategies required for language use' (Chapelle, 1994: 164). Of these, (1) relates to the constraints on linguistic choices imposed by context, (2) relates specifically to lexical knowledge and processing, and (3) relates to the very broad phenomenon which seems to coincide with what other writers refer to as 'strategic competence'. Clearly, (1) and (3) are relevant not just to 'vocabulary ability' but to language ability generally. With regard to (2), which most closely approximates to the domain of mental lexicon research as it has hitherto been defined, and indeed to the domain addressed by the C-test-based research to which her article refers, she describes it as covering the following elements:

> (1) the number of content words a person knows within a particular context; (2) what a person knows about each content word (linguistic and pragmatic characteristics); (3) how morphemes are stored in the mental lexicon (organization); and (4) the vocabulary processes associated with lexical access. (Chapelle, 1994: 165)

One can immediately point to certain inconsistencies in Chapelle's treatment. Thus, on the one hand, she calls into question the value of contextualized instruments for investigating lexical competence, while, on the other, she sees such competence as partly comprised of knowledge with reference to 'a particular context'. How, one is entitled to ask, is one supposed to gauge capacity to use words in context without including contextualized elicitation somewhere within one's approach? A further inconsistency relates to Chapelle's specification of 'content words' in the first two parts of her definition and her lack of specificity in this regard in the remainder. How are we to interpret this? Is she really claiming that content words alone are the stuff of lexical knowledge (later comments in her article would appear to confirm that this is her position)? Is she hedging her bets? In any case, we reject the implication that there is a hard-and-fast distinction between 'content words' (or 'full words') and 'grammatical words' (or 'empty words'), which runs counter to what most lexicologists now seem to be saying on the matter. One thinks, for example, of Lapaire's compelling critique of this particular dichotomy (referred to in Chapter 1), which puts us on our guard against being duped by the words-as-containers-of-meaning metaphor.

More generally, one can take issue with the rather limited vision of lexical knowledge which Chapelle proposes in the above-quoted passage. As the discussion in Chapter 1 clearly demonstrates, this position is seriously at odds with the current conception of the lexicon in linguistics and applied linguistics. In contrast, our own claim that C-test data are essentially lexical data is strongly supported by recent theoretical reflections and empirical findings relative to the nature of the lexicon. What the test very obviously taps into is knowledge of the lexico-grammatical specificities of a given language, all of which fall within the ambit of lexicon as currently defined by informed opinion. That which it does not directly measure – phonetic/phonological proficiency and more abstract, language-independent principles of linguistic organization – falls for the most part outside that definition. Interestingly in this connection, Chapelle's own earlier research found that correlations between C-test results and the results of a test which was in a very narrow sense lexical (a multiple-choice vocabulary test) were higher than correlations beween C-test results and those of a number of other test types (Chapelle & Abraham, 1990).

As for the question of why the results of what we claim is an essentially lexical test should correlate so well with other measures of general language proficiency, the answer is simply that the lexicon is at the very heart of most aspects of language use. Thus, various studies have shown the critical importance of lexical knowledge across a wide range of L2 activities, notably reading (see, e.g., Koda, 1989; Laufer, 1992), written production (see, e.g., Laufer & Nation, 1953; Linnarud, 1986) and listening comprehension (see, e.g., P. Kelly, 1991).

There is one final point to be made in relation to Chapelle's critique before moving on. Chapelle calls into doubt the legitimacy of the inferences which we drew from the C-test data we elicited during the pilot phase of the MLRP – notably in respect of lexical organization and lexical processes. Whether or not one accepts her arguments on this point, the fact is that, as will be clear from the chapters that follow, virtually everything we inferred on these matters on the basis of C-test data alone was subsequently supported by a whole range of other data types – word-association data, data from story-tell and translation tasks, and introspective data.

The pattern of data elicitation via C-test which we established in 1990–91 was to administer two (modified) C-tests to our MLRP Level II subsamples in December and a further two in May. French C-tests were of course administered to the subsample of students of French, and the same four German C-tests were administered to both the *ab initio* and the advanced subsamples of students of German. Each student in each subsample re-encountered the same two pairs of C-tests every year as he/she advanced through his/her degree course, so that it is now possible to trace individual and collective longitudinal progress in respect of the same set of challenges. There was in principle an element of time pressure involved in the administration of these tests in the sense that subjects were given just 15 minutes to deal with each of the texts in a pair. In fact, however, no subject ever gave the impression of having been stretched by this condition.

The MLRP C-test was supplemented with an introspective instrument of a kind which we used with interesting results in a small study some years ago (see Singleton & Little, 1984b). The instrument in question, which was administered to the subjects immediately after they had completed the C-tests, listed the mutilated words in the two C-test texts, asking subjects to indicate those that had posed problems and to describe how they had resolved these problems. Subjects retained their C-test scripts during this part of the session, to which a period of up to 30 minutes was allotted (although most subjects completed this task well before the 30 minutes had actually elapsed). The deployment of this kind of instrument raises, of course, the question of the relationship between introspection and language processing.

On one view (see, e.g., Fodor, 1983) language processing proper takes place within an encapsulated language module totally inaccessible to conscious inspection. However, since modularists (see above, Chapter 3; see also Singleton, 1993a) seem dubious about the extent to which lexical processing *is* language processing proper and therefore falls within the language module, and since they appear dubious also about the extent to which L2 processing in general occurs intramodularly, the notion of encapsulation of the language module is not a final argument against the use of introspective data in L2 lexical processing research even for convinced modularists. The principal argument in favour of introspective methods is that they provide information about process which is not deducible from product. Interestingly, the most frequently cited critique of such methods (Seliger, 1983), while taking a highly sceptical line with regard to their usefulness in relation to L2 *learning*, does in fact acknowledge the possibility of their illuminating how learners *use* what they have learned. It is also noteworthy that the best-known book on introspection in L2 research (Faerch & Kasper, 1987a) is dominated by articles dealing with L2 processing/use rather than L2 learning, and that of these articles most have a strong lexical dimension. This is no accident; researchers consistently find that L2 lexical processing is something of which L2 users are relatively aware and on which they are able to offer very focused and detailed introspective commentary.[4]

The data elicited by the above-described MLRP instrument are self-evidently retrospective, and do not, therefore, provide 'on-line'

[4] This point has, for example, been made by Kellerman with reference to experience in the Nijmegen Project of eliciting retrospective data relative to communication strategies (Kellerman, 1993).

glimpses of processes in the way that 'think-aloud' data do (see below, discussion of think-aloud introspections collected in connection with translation task). However, the method employed to collect them does meet the general reliability criteria for the elicitation of retrospective reports discussed by Ericsson & Simon (1984), being characterized, notably, by immediacy, contextualization, directness, specificity, a lack of leading questions and a lack of forewarning. It is widely accepted that retrospective instruments administered under such conditions are especially suitable for the investigation of 'aspects of speech production attended to under task completion' (Faerch & Kasper, 1987b: 15). Into this last category must surely fall the seeking out of lexical solutions to C-test 'slots' that are immediately afterwards identified as particularly problematic. Some impression of the 'track record' of the retrospection in L2 research may be gained from, e.g., A. Cohen (1984), Haastrup (1987, 1991b), Poulisse (1990), Poulisse *et al.* (1987), Gillette (1987), Zimmermann (1989), Zimmermann & Schneider (1987).

Word-association tests[5]

As has already been indicated, although we are aware of the criticisms made of word-association tests and of the scepticism expressed relative to what their results actually reveal, our own view is that, sensitively and sensibly interpreted, word-association test data have the capacity to complement and corroborate findings which emerge from analyses of other types of lexical data. In any case, since word-association research has been so prominent in work on the mental lexicon, including work on the L2 mental lexicon (see, e.g., Meara, 1980, 1983b, 1984), a project focusing in part on lexical matters without a word-association test would probably have had to a face validity problem.

The piloting of the word-association test approach for our purposes was actually conducted within the framework of an M.Phil. dissertation project (Cunningham, 1990) outside the bounds of the MLRP. That study looked at the word-association test responses of two groups of primary-school-level learners of Irish as L2, one of which was based in an English-medium school and receiving input in Irish only during Irish lessons, and the other of which was based in an Irish-medium school and receiving input in Irish throughout the school day (except during English lessons). The results of the

[5] I am grateful to Louise Cunningham, Jennifer Ridley and Ema Ushioda for providing me with the raw material for these next three subsections.

investigation were in line with Söderman's (1989, 1993) finding that L2 learners who had received more input produced fewer 'clang' associates and more 'paradigmatic' associates than did learners with less experience of the target language.

The type of word-association test chosen for the MLRP was the 'continuous association' approach, which encourages subjects to produce as many associates as possible per stimulus word within a given time-span (see, e.g., Champagnol, 1974; Macnamara, 1967; Randall, 1980). According to Meara, this method has the advantage that 'stable response patterns can be found with as few as 15 subjects' (Meara, 1980: 238), whereas the standard single response test is deemed to yield stable results only when rather larger numbers of subjects are involved (see, e.g., Deese, 1965).

Three lists of 50 stimulus words were prepared – in English, French and German, respectively. The English stimuli were taken from the Kent–Rosanoff (1910; cf. Postman & Keppel, 1970) inventory of 100 frequently occurring, emotionally neutral English words. French translations of the English stimuli were obtained by consulting the stimuli used by Rosenzweig (1970), and German equivalents were obtained from the German list compiled by Russel (1970). All the main word classes were represented among the 50 stimulus words selected.

Word-association tests based on the above lists of stimuli were administered to the MLRP Level II subsample (1990–91 intake) for the first time in March 1991. The association test based on the English stimuli was administered to all subjects in the subsample, the test based on the French stimuli was administered to students of French, and the test based on the German stimuli was administered to students of German. In March 1992, this exercise was repeated with the Level II subsample drawn from the 1991–92 intake, and the tests were re-administered to Level II subsample subjects from the 1990–91 intake. In March 1993, the same tests were again used with the entire Level II subsample.

The administration of the tests proceeded as follows. At the outset of each data-elicitation session the objectives of the study were briefly outlined to subjects orally. The broad lines of the procedure were also explained orally. Answer books were provided for each test. These comprised two sheets of blank lines numbered 1–50. At the head of the first sheet there were in addition four spaces for use with examples. The stimulus words did not appear in the answer books but were presented visually using a slide projector. Four examples were presented at first, and subjects were given time to write their responses in the appropriate spaces in the answer book. Subjects were assured that all responses were valid – that there were no 'right' or 'wrong' answers. They were then asked to respond to the 50 stimulus items of the test proper, writing down on the relevant line of the answer book as many associates as came to them for each stimulus in 30 seconds. At the end of the 30 seconds (timed by chronometer), the experimenter announced the number of the following word, which was then projected. A short interval was allowed after 20 words to reduce the likelihood of the chaining or switching of responses. In all cases the English test was administered prior to the L2 test.

Story-tell and written-translation tasks and the elicitation of associated introspection

The story-tell and written translation tasks used in the MLRP are in broad terms familiar from the second language classroom and from second language testing. They appeared to us initially, therefore, to have the advantage over the C-test and the word-association test of not confronting subjects with the terrors of *terra incognita*! They also seemed to have the advantage of a higher degree of 'ecological validity'. These points will be returned to later.

The tasks were administered in a single session on each elicitation occasion in which they were involved, these sessions being organized as follows:

March 1991: Level II subsample drawn from 1990–91 intake.
March 1992: Level II subsample drawn from 1990–91 intake plus Level II subsample drawn from 1991–92 intake.
March 1993: as in March 1992.

The possibility for longitudinal study offered by this arrangement was particularly valuable for the purposes of the researcher (Ridley) who has to date made most use of the data yielded by these tasks. Ridley's investigation of reflection and strategies in L2 learning (Ridley, 1997 – see below, Chapter 8) distinguishes itself from other similar studies (notably Abraham & Vann, 1987; Haastrup & Phillipson, 1983) precisely by virtue of its longitudinal dimension.

For the story-tell task, the Level II subsample subjects were given a series of 23 cartoon pictures from which all written text had been expunged. Subjects were asked to describe orally what was happening in each picture in sequence, and to imagine that they were telling the story to a listener who could not see the pictures. They told the story aloud first in English and then in either French or German – depending on which L2 group they belonged to. Certain lexical items were key to the story, for example the words for 'cigarette lighter', 'petrol pump', 'explosion'. As had been expected, most subjects experienced problems when recounting the story in L2 because of not having the requisite L2 lexical knowledge at their disposal. All of the subjects' efforts were recorded on audio-tape and subsequently transcribed. No time-limit was placed on this task.

With regard to the written-translation task, each Level II sub-sample subject was asked to translate without aid of a dictionary an English text into either French or German – again, depending on his/her L2 group affiliation. Subjects were particularly urged to try to get the original message across, and were told that they should not omit content simply because they did not know the relevant lexical items. Twenty words (all nouns) in the text were underlined; subjects were requested to focus on these items in particular and to be sure not to circumvent them in the translation by omission or reconstruction of content. The 157–word source text used for the translation task was adapted from an in-flight magazine; it was chosen for its highly message-oriented character and for the lexical problems it was deemed likely to pose. Subjects were given 40 minutes to complete their translation, and most finished comfortably within this time.

An introspective dimension was attached to the translation task. In this case subjects were asked to 'think aloud' as they performed the task – to report the thoughts that occurred to them as they proceeded through the translation. These introspective utterances were recorded on audio-tape. All subjects seemed able to provide this kind of running commentary on their performance, at least in respect of the lexical aspects of the task (cf. comments above on C-test-related introspection). A certain amount has already been said regarding immediate retrospection as an L2 research technique. As far as the think-aloud approach is concerned (cf. Claparède, 1934; Duncker, 1926), this is sometimes referred to as 'self-revelation' as opposed to 'self-observation' (retrospection) and 'self-report' (general statements about behaviour) (Cohen, 1987b). Its advantage over retrospection is that it has the potential to provide a fuller picture of those parts of the process under investigation which are accessible to introspection, since the introspective comments are produced while the process is actually happening. According to Cohen (1987b: 84), 'the bulk of the forgetting occurs right after the mental event'; if this is true, then the information yielded by retrospection even a few minutes after the event in question may be seriously incomplete. On the other hand, explicitly asking subjects to think aloud must carry with it the risk that the process being reported on is actually distorted by such on-line introspection. (Spontaneous think-aloud data of the sort incidentally elicited by the story-tell task may perhaps be less subject to this danger). It also has to be conceded (cf. Cohen, 1987b: 86) that think-aloud reports are not constituted exclusively of on-line commentary; they frequently contain data which are more in the nature of retrospective observation. Obviously, therefore, think-aloud data need to be interpreted with care. With this proviso, this kind of data can be extremely valuable in throwing light on processes that would otherwise remain entirely obscure – as is demonstrated by a fairly wide array of L2 studies in which the think-aloud technique has been employed (see, e.g., Dechert, 1987; Feldmann & Stemmer, 1987; Gerloff, 1987; Haastrup, 1987, 1991b; Hosenfeld, 1979; Krings, 1986a, 1986b, 1987; Lörscher, 1986; Sanguineti de Serrano, 1984).

To return to the story-tell and translation tasks themselves, it was suggested earlier that one point in favour of these tasks might be their familiarity – given that such exercises frequently crop up in L2 teaching and testing. In fact, this putative advantage did not appear to be of any great weight in the present study; it turned out that the subjects involved had had little previous experience of either task type. On the other hand, the 'ecological validity' of the tasks in question does seem to hold up. As far as the story-tell task is concerned, it is not at all difficult to imagine circumstances where one might have to narrate a series of events in an L2 to a speaker of the language who for one reason or another was unable to see what was going on. With regard to the translation task, as Grellet has pointed out (e.g., Grellet, 1993), translation is one of the most likely 'real life' tasks that anyone who has learned an L2 is liable to be called upon to perform – whether in a professional or in a purely personal/social context.

This is, of course, not to deny that there is a high degree of unnaturalness about eliciting L2 and introspective data via the tasks described. However, it seems to us that there is sufficient connection between these tasks and 'real life' to justify the working supposition that there are resemblances between the ways in which subjects try to solve their lexical problems when engaged in the tasks concerned and their lexical problem-solving strategies in less-contrived situations. An earlier study of strategic competence conducted by one of the MLRP researchers (see Ridley, 1991a, 1991b) within the framework of an M.Phil. project had used a simple oral interview as a data-gathering approach. On the basis of this experience, the researcher in question had felt that data-elicitation techniques which deliberately provoked the use of compensatory strategies (cf., e.g., Poulisse, 1990; Kellerman, 1991) in a highly focused manner would be required if her study of such strategies was to be taken a stage further. Data from the earlier study (and from other sources) could, however, be utilized to explore the relationship between strategic performance in more- and less-spontaneous L2 production.

The types and quantities of compensatory strategies deployed by subjects in the story-tell and translation tasks were also related to strategies used in the C-test task, to general proficiency as reflected in overall C-test scores and in school and university examination results, and to such aspects of language-learning experience as extent of knowledge of other L2s and teaching methodologies encountered. In addition, four *ab initio* learners of German were investigated in particular detail via an especially close analysis of their story-tell and translation data. Since these last-mentioned data-gathering ventures did not form part of the MLRP proper, in the sense that the data they generated were not incorporated into the MLRP database, no further description of the relevant instruments and procedures will be given here (but see below, Chapter 8).

Interviews on motivation

The foundations for the motivational dimension of the MLRP were laid in an M.Phil. project on acculturation and fossilization (Ushioda, 1991, 1993) based broadly on Schumann's (e.g., 1978a, 1978b) perspective. The findings of the project concerned suggested that degree of acculturation did not provide a sufficient explanation for ultimate L2 attainment. The researcher who had undertaken the work in question decided, accordingly, to pursue the issue of affect and motivation in L2 learning in a more thoroughgoing but less theoretically constrained manner within the framework of the MLRP. A full report of this motivational study conducted within the framework of the MLRP is to be found in Ushioda's (1996a) doctoral thesis, and some aspects of the study are drawn on in her (1996b) book.

The tradition which has dominated L2 motivation research over the past three decades has been the social-psychological line of investigation. Schumann's work on 'social distance' fits into this tradition, which is also – and perhaps more typically – represented by the studies of 'integrative orientation' and 'instrumental orientation' carried out by R. Gardner and Lambert (see, e.g., R. Gardner & Lambert, 1972; R. Gardner, 1985). While the social-psychological dimension of motivation in L2 learning continues to be recognized as important, there are some signs of the beginnings of a critique of the social-psychological research tradition on the grounds of its narrowness (see, e.g., Crookes & Schmidt, 1991). The MLRP work on motivation is to be seen as part of the endeavour to broaden the research agenda in this domain.

Our view is that the aim of uncovering how L2 learners perceive their motivation is best served by a data-elicitation approach which is as free as possible from pre-determined categories and assumptions. Even the provision of a large and varied range of reasons from which the learner can identify those relevant to him/her is bound to be selective in focus and to reflect the researcher's own assumptions. For example, Clément & Kruideneier provide their subjects with a total of 37 possible reasons for learning the target language, but all of these have reference to a future timescale only (Clément & Kruideneier, 1983: 290–291). Our own approach is quite straightforwardly to let the learner do the talking, with as little directional prompting from the researcher as possible.

The adoption of a minimally structured interview technique may bring with it the danger that the quality and quantity of elicited data will co-vary with the analytical acuity and the articulateness of individual subjects, a point that is noted by Skehan in respect of self-report data on learning strategies (Skehan, 1989: 80). Unlike the case of strategy research, however, where the ability to report language-learning strategies and the ability to learn languages may both to some extent depend on the same analytical and decontextualizing capacities in respect of verbal material, in the case of motivation, research subjects are being asked simply to retail their own perceptions of why they have made a particular choice in their life rather than to analyse verbal processes. Moreover, since clarity or vagueness of goal definition is in itself central to the empirical investigation, any variation in levels of specificity will itself constitute a relevant finding and will be highly pertinent to the overall research purpose.

For logistical reasons, the motivation research conducted within the MLRP framework was restricted to students of French from the Level II subsample. These students were interviewed twice, on both occasions having been reassured that the information obtained was to be used for research purposes only and would not form any part of their academic record. The first set of interviews took place in December 1991, when the subjects from the 1990–91 intake were into their second year and those from the 1991–92 intake were just three months into their university studies. Follow-up interviews were then carried out with both groups some fifteen months later, in March 1993.

In the first of the above-mentioned interviews, the researcher began (after some warm-up pleasantries) by asking the subject to outline what he/she saw as the key factor(s) involved in his/her decision to study French at university and underlying his/her efforts to make progress in the language. The researcher's principal role thereafter was to encourage the subject to expand on points by occasional prompting and to try to ensure that the subject did not overlook any relevant information. In relation to the latter aspect, the researcher had prepared an extensive set of notes for her own reference purposes. These notes comprised over one hundred items grouped into broad categories according to potential sources of motivation. They were referred to by the researcher only in the final stages of the interview, at which point she used them to inform her final promptings. They had no role in structuring the interview, which was conducted in a totally informal, 'freewheeling' manner; nor were they used as an *a priori* basis for the subsequent coding of the data.

The follow-up interview followed much the same kind of pattern, but in this case there was slightly more intervention on the part of the researcher, with a view to focusing subjects' attention on their recent language-learning experience. Subjects were asked about any changes they were aware of in how they perceived their French studies; they were also asked about the importance of success/failure in their language-learning endeavours and about what they did to keep their morale up.

The data elicited by these interviews were analysed using the features identified and prioritized by the learners themselves. These features were subsequently grouped together when they were seen to relate to common or similar sources. From such groupings in turn emerged broad motivational categories which provided a conceptual framework for organizing the totality of perspectives offered.

The above account of the interviews relative to motivation is offered primarily in order to complete the description of the MLRP. Its relevance to the topic of this volume may appear limited. On the other hand, one cannot in advance rule out the possibility that particular kinds and/or degrees of motivation may be correlated with different patterns of L2 lexical development and/or use. Moreover, given the prominence of language-related categories in the inventory that has so far emerged from the MLRP motivation research, the observations made by the students in question present an intrinsic interest in terms of what they have to say about subjects' 'lexical awareness' – the degree of salience of lexis in subjects' apprehension of language, the extent of subjects' consciousness of cross-linguistic lexical links, the role of perceptions of lexis in determining subjects' attitudes towards a language, etc.

Computerization[6]

When the MLRP was initiated in October 1988, it was envisaged that data would be collected and pre-coded using SPSS as software. After consultation with the Computer Laboratory in TCD, however, it was decided that Oracle V.5, which had recently been installed on the College Digital Vax Mainframe for academic use, would be more flexible and more accessible to staff and students using or inputting data. The software was updated to Oracle V.6 in 1991. Initially the full range of Oracle software was not licensed for academic use – SQL Plus V.3.0, SQL Language V.6 SQL Forms V.2.3 became available to us in 1990, and SQL Calc V.1.2 in 1991. Thanks to the generosity of the Oracle Corporation, a new update took place in late 1993, from which point on we had at our disposal SQL Menu, SQL Report Writer and SQL Graph.

Oracle, a relational database which was originally designed for commercial use, has required some adaptation for academic use. The range of statistics SQL Plus supports is very limited – basically, Mean, Count, Maximum, Standard Deviation, Sum and Variance. SQL Calc supports a wider range of mathematical functions. On the other hand, Oracle is easily exported into a range of statistical packages, as for example SPSS V.6.0 and Paradox V.3, and this effectively overcomes the difficulty. As Oracle becomes more widely used academically, it is probable that more statistical functions will be included in later versions.

The use of SQL Forms for inputting data offered several advantages. Staff and students inputting data needed no previous computer experience, as only ten keystrokes are required to insert, save, alter and edit data. Our experience was that three one-hour sessions sufficed to provide adequate data-processing induction for a group of four or five postgraduate students with no previous computer literacy.

Querying the database at forms level was also easily learned, which was obviously a boon to the researchers using it. A design objective was to make the forms resemble as far as possible the physical pages of each data-elicitation instrument. The data were not pre-coded, but were entered exactly as filled in by the respondents, with inbuilt constraints for purposes of data integrity. Data could then be transformed and upgraded using SQL Plus, then rapidly proofread from the original elicitation instrument.

The data were initially processed using SQL Plus, and edited and

[6] I am grateful to Emer Singleton for providing me with the raw material for this section.

produced for analysis by individual users as required. This could be laborious when dealing with data drawn from several different elicitation instruments. The use of SQL Report Writer considerably enhanced the presentation of data. Tables and files are able to be exported to most standard word-processors using Kermit software, and the computer teaching networks in TCD allow export of files from the Vax into a range of Apples and IBMs, which was of particular benefit to M.Phil. and Ph.D. students.

L2 lexicon-related issues explored to date using MLRP findings

This final section of the chapter gives a brief overview of those L2 lexicon-related issues which have to date been explored within the framework of the MLRP via conference papers and published articles. These are (1) the utility of the C-test in L2 lexical acquisition/processing research, (2) form and meaning in the L2 mental lexicon, (3) lexical transfer, (4) age and L2 lexical acquisition and (5) lexical problem-solving strategies.

The utility of the C-test in L2 lexical acquisition/processing research

The aptness of the C-test as an elicitation instrument in the context of research into the L2 mental lexicon has already been treated at length above. This topic has also been dealt with in a number of papers emanating from the MLRP, constituting the prime focus of two of these (Little & Singleton, 1992; Singleton & Singleton, 1998). Both these latter papers offer general grounds for using C-tests in L2 lexical research – broadly along the lines followed by the relevant discussion above – and both provide illustrations from the MLRP data of the kinds of light that C-test-elicited material can throw on lexical issues.

Form and meaning in the L2 mental lexicon

From the pilot phase of the MLRP onwards, one of the recurring themes of the publications it has generated has been the respective roles of form and meaning in the L2 mental lexicon (Singleton, 1993–94b, 1994, 1996a; Singleton & Little, 1991, 1992). The general thrust of these papers has been the calling into question of the view that the L2 mental lexicon differs qualitatively from the L1 mental lexicon in being phonologically rather than semantically organized and driven (see above, Chapter 4). An alternative view is proposed, namely, that the relative importance of form and meaning in lexical acquisition and processing is a function of the degree of familiarity/unfamiliarity of the item(s) in question rather than of the status (L1 or L2) of the language concerned. This alternative perspective is argued with the help of a variety of MLRP data which suggest that familiar L2 words are processed semantico-pragmatically for the most part and that, at least among advanced L2 learners, even L2 lexical errors are explicable largely in semantico-pragmatic terms (see below, Chapter 6). On the other hand, it is claimed (Singleton, 1996a), principally on the basis of MLRP introspective data, that *within* the formal domain it is phonology rather than orthography that constitutes the main reference point in L2 lexical retrieval.

Lexical transfer

A further issue that has been addressed in publications emerging from the MLRP since its inception has been that of cross-linguistic influence as a factor in lexical operations. One dimension of this question that has been examined in MLRP-generated publications is the question of the implications of the presence of cross-linguistic influence in lexical processing for the nature of the relationship between the L1 and L2 lexicons. If, as has sometimes been claimed, the two were qualitatively different and entirely separate, then no influence ought to be discernible across the L1–L2 boundary. In fact, as it has been easy to show from a range of variously elicited MLRP data, such influence is all too obvious (Ridley & Singleton, 1995a, 1995b; Singleton, 1996b, 1997; Singleton & Little, 1991, 1992) (see above, Chapter 4; below, Chapter 7). Some attention has been devoted in this connection to the extent and particularities of lexical transfer in particular circumstances with particular languages and to the implications thereof for modelling the L2 lexicon.

Age and L2 lexical acquisition

The age factor in L2 acquisition is a matter of abiding interest among L2 researchers, and, given the particular constellation of data collected under the auspices of the MLRP, it would be strange if such an issue were to be ignored within this context. Nor has it been. So far just two papers on age and the L2 lexicon have come out of the project (Singleton, 1992b, 1993b, summarized in Singleton, 1995a), and the findings reported therein are consistent with what is suggested by the literature at large, namely that L2 lexical acquisition is affected by the age factor in broadly the same way that – according to the current 'consensus view' (see, e.g. Singleton, 1989, 1992c, 1995b) – other aspects of L2 acquisition are affected by this factor. In particular in this connection, one can point to the fact that the students participating in the MLRP had learnt their L2s largely on the basis of rather thin amounts of input from formal instructional settings and that – just as in other studies based on L2 learning in formal contexts – any long-term benefits of exposure to these languages before age 12 seemed to be largely masked in such circumstances.

Lexical problem-solving strategies

A final major area of interest of the MLRP *vis-à-vis* the L2 lexicon has been that of strategic compensation in L2 use for lack of lexical knowledge (see above, Chapter 4; below, Chapter 8). The coinages produced by MLRP subjects when coping with lexical difficulty have been discussed in papers dating from the pilot phase of the project (Singleton & Little, 1991, 1992; Singleton & Singleton 1989). More recently, attention has been focused on inter-learner variation in strategic behaviour and on the question of whether there is a relationship between the strategy styles of individuals and their general metacognitive approach to the task of L2 learning (see Ridley, 1993, 1994, 1997; Little & Ridley, 1992; Ridley & Singleton, 1995a, 1995b). The MLRP findings suggest that learners do in fact vary quite considerably in their strategy preferences and that such preferences do indeed connect with their global approach to language-learning.

Concluding summary

This chapter has provided a general outline of a number of aspects of the Trinity College Dublin Modern Languages Research Project; the remaining chapters of the book are largely based on data from the MLRP. An account has been given of the subjects, methodology and computerization of the project. In the methodology section, particular attention has been paid to the use of the C-test, since this is a relatively unfamiliar instrument and one whose validity as way of gaining insight into the nature of the L2 lexicon has recently been challenged. Finally, a brief overview has been presented of five L2 lexicon-related issues which have been addressed by papers and publications that have so far emanated from the project.

6 *Findings on form and meaning in the L2 mental lexicon*

A large part of Chapter 4 was devoted to the question of whether or not the L2 lexicon is qualitatively different from the L1 lexicon in exhibiting 'primarily phonological' (Laufer, 1989: 17) as opposed to semantic connections between its 'entries'. In this connection, a critique was mounted of Meara's interpretation of the Birkbeck Vocabulary Project data as supporting the form-driven view of the L2 mental lexicon.

Meara's work was in fact the starting-point for our own scrutiny of the mental lexicon within the context of the TCD MLRP. In fact, at the outset, we expected to be confirming Meara's position and to be able to interpret our data in the same way that Meara had interpreted his word-association test results. However, from the pilot phase of the project onwards we were obliged to conclude that our findings simply would not fit into that particular mould. This chapter presents some of the evidence on which that conclusion was based.

C-test results from the pilot phase of the project

The first two papers on the L2 mental lexicon to emerge from the project were presented at the Ninth World Congress of Applied Linguistics and published shortly thereafter (Little & Singleton, 1992; Singleton & Little, 1991). These brought to bear on the issue of form and meaning in the L2 lexicon the results of the French and German C-tests administered during the 1988–89 session during the pilot phase of the TCD MLRP. At that stage of the development of the project, an earlier version of the questionnaire referred to in Chapter 5 was already being administered to all first-year students of French, German, Italian and Spanish in the first term of the academic year. At that stage, too, the C-test was already being used to elicit L2 data, though in its 'classic' form. In the pilot period of the project, an attempt was made to administer two C-tests to all first-year students

Table 6.1. *Numbers of subjects involved in French and German C-test data collection (Singleton & Little, 1991: 77, Table 1)*

French C-test1	French C-test2	German C-test1	German C-test2
49	34	40	51

of the above languages, one in the second term of the year and one in the third.

Both papers report on the results of this exercise in respect of students of French and German. It should be noted that because of absenteeism relative to the C-test administrations during 1988–89 (which at that stage took place during normal classes), each set of C-test data gathered in that year had to be regarded as a distinct corpus. The numbers of subjects involved in taking C-tests during 1988–89 are as shown in Table 6.1.

The C-test has been described and defended as an instrument for investigating lexical knowledge in Chapter 5. It is a reduced-redundancy procedure requiring the testee, essentially, to restore to wholeness a text nearly 50 per cent of whose constituent words have had their second half deleted. It is clear that the kinds of terms in which researchers have discussed word-association test results are for the most part not particularly pertinent to C-test responses. However, among C-test responses, as among word-association test responses, one can distinguish those which relate to the meaning of the stimulus and those which do not. A strong indication that a C-test response is motivated by the meaning of its stimulus (the mutilated string of letters plus the surrounding text) is that it is actually correct – in other words, appropriate to context and well-formed. Self-evidently, such a response is most unlikely to have been arrived at without the semantics of the stimulus context having been taken into account. The fact that in the pilot C-test data a high proportion of the C-test responses – a clear majority as far as three of the four tests were concerned – were correct (see Table 6.2) was therefore taken as strong *prima facie* evidence of a substantial semantico-pragmatic factor in the motivation of these responses.

Moreover, an examination by Singleton & Little (1991) of the incorrect responses elicited by the tests in question revealed that the vast majority of these too could be related to some aspect of contextual meaning. Most frequently such responses were simply formally deviant versions of items in the original texts or acceptable substitutes. For example, one particular slot in one of the German

Table 6.2. *Mean percentage scores on the C-tests (based on Singleton & Little, 1991: 77, Table 2)*

French C-test 1	French C-test 2	German C-test 1	German C-test 2
77.7	63.3	57.4	45.1

C-tests is completed in the original text as *südschottischen* ('southern Scottish'), the original phrase in which it occurs being *der kleinen südschottischen Gemeinde* ('of the small southern Scottish community'), and the string immediately preceding the blank being *südscho.* A formally deviant version of *südschottischen* proposed as a solution by a number of subjects in this instance was **südschottlandischen*, which, for all its ill-formedness, captures precisely what is required in semantic terms. In other instances, the solution proposed might not precisely fit the context at 'local' level but could nevertheless be seen to be based on a piecing together of meaning-related cues in the text as a whole. For example, a slot in one of the French C-tests is introduced by the string *réu*, completed as *réussi* ('succeeded' {past participle}) in the original text, the phrase in which it features being *a réussi à parler à ses enfants* ('has succeeded in talking to her children'). The response offered by one subject in this instance was the addition of *-ni*, so as to form the word *réuni* ('brought together', '(re)united'). This fits neither the syntactic frame nor the meaning of the immediate context; yet it can be seen to pick up the general theme of the text, namely the attempt of the author Marie Cardinal to bridge the generation gap by opening her house to the young people of her neighbourhood.

In quantitative terms (see Table 6.3), Singleton & Little (1991) estimate the preponderance of semantico-pragmatically motivated incorrect responses over incorrect responses with no connection to contextual meaning to be more than 4 to 1. Obviously, some degree of impressionism enters into an analysis of this kind, but only to a very marginal extent, since the vast majority of the errors counted as semantically motivated were clearly related to acceptable responses – that is to say, like the *südschottlandischen* example rather than the *réuni* example.

A further matter considered by Singleton & Little (1991) in relation to the semantico-pragmatic motivation of C-test responses is the question of heterogeneity of response. Meara (1984) notes that his subjects' responses to L2 stimuli tended not only to be different from responses to the same stimuli elicited from native speakers, but

Table 6.3. Percentages of semantically motivated errors (relative to total numbers of incorrect responses) (Singleton & Little, 1991: 77, Table 4)

French C-test 1	French C-test 2	German C-test 1	German C-test 2
84.4	90.9	87.3	89.1

also to diverge more markedly from subject to subject than the native-speaker responses, a finding which he takes as indicating that the L2 mental lexicon is more 'loosely organized' than the L1 mental lexicon. Singleton & Little's reading of Meara's results in this connection is that they reflect simply a particular case of the general principle that difficult tasks elicit divergent solutions whereas simple tasks elicit convergent solutions. In support of this interpretation, they cite the fact that, in their own data, C-test slots which elicited more than five different solutions posed considerably more difficulty – as gauged by the mean percentage of correct responses they yielded – than slots eliciting no more than five solutions (see Table 6.4).

However, they consider the fact that heterogeneity of response *in itself* says nothing about the processes involved in the production of the responses in question, and in particular about the respective roles of semantic and non-semantic motivation, to be more important than the heterogeneity–difficulty connection. To take a concrete example. One of the German C-test slots has the stimulus *beri-*, the word in the original text being *berichten* ('report' {3rd person plural present}). This elicits 11 different solutions in all, including the non-response solution. Of the responses, 5 have no apparent link with the semantics of the stimulus context:

berinnen
berissen
berißte
beriechnet
beritten

The first 4 of these do not actually exist in German, and the fifth, *beritten* ('ridden over', 'broken in' (of a horse) {past participle}) connects with nothing in the text (which concerns the aftermath of the Lockerbie air disaster). On the other hand, the remaining 5 responses produced include the original word itself and 4 solutions which are derivationally and therefore semantically linked to it:

Table 6.4. *Mean percentages of correct responses associated with slots eliciting up to and more than 5 different solutions (Singleton & Little, 1991: 78, Table 6)*

	French C-test 1	French C-test 2	German C-test 1	German C-test 2
Up to 5	89.6	84.5	82.2	69.5
More than 5	55.6	35.5	39.5	29.3

berichten
berichte
berichtet
berichtete
bericht

This, for Singleton & Little, is an instructive illustration of the uselessness of the criterion of heterogeneity of response as an indicator of the nature of underlying processing, although, as they say, in fact, it is not typical; in *most* cases in their data, even where a wide variety of different responses has been elicited by a particular C-test slot, the majority of the solutions offered can be linked to the *semantics* of the stimulus.

The above suggestion that heterogeneity of response is likely to be associated with difficulty, as well as the notion, discussed in Chapter 4, that the exploitation of formal knowledge and formal clues is likely to be associated with items which are less familiar or more problematic in given contexts, both receive support from Little & Singleton's detailed breakdown of the responses to C-test slots which were correctly completed by a minority of subjects. Since C-test 1 elicited markedly more correct responses than C-test 2 in both French and German (see Table 6.5), the focus in relation to C-test 1 was on items that elicited correct responses from no more than 50% of subjects, whereas in relation to C-test 2 the focus was on items that elicited correct responses from no more than 25% of subjects. The general picture that emerges in all cases is that slots which subjects found difficult to complete in the contexts in question provoked a multiplicity of responses, many of which were based on formal cues alone.

C-test results from 1990 onwards

Similar results from later C-test administrations within the framework of the TCD MLRP are reported in a subsequent series of

Table 6.5. *Percentages of C test items that elicited correct responses from 0–25, 26–50, 51–75 and 76–100 per cent of subjects (Little & Singleton, 1992: 178, Table 3)*

	0–25	26–50	51–75	76–100
French C-test 1	2.6	15.8	18.4	63.2
French C-test 2	20.9	16.3	18.6	44.2
German C-test 1	19.4	16.7	19.4	44.4
German C-test 2	28.6	26.8	23.2	21.4

papers. Thus, Singleton & Little (1992) and Singleton (1993a) present the results from the first administrations of the (modified) French C-tests to the students of French recruited to the project proper from the 1990–91 intake. With regard to the role of semantics, the results show that on all the tests in question (1) a majority of the solutions proposed were correct and appropriate (thus context-related) (Table 6.6), (2) a majority of the unacceptable responses were also related to contextual meaning (Table 6.7), and (3), accordingly, the percentages of responses with no relation to the contextual meaning were very small (Table 6.8). Singleton & Little (1992) also point out that a majority of introspective comments associated with the C-test data (57.9% in the case of the post-pilot results they were dealing with) explicitly refer to the meaning of the context and/or to some other semantico-pragmatic aspect of arriving at a response.

These particular results were the subject of a discussion (see Singleton, 1993a) on the topic of modularity and the lexicon (see above, Chapter 3). Like the findings of the earlier MLRP studies, they provide a persuasive demonstration of context effects. They could therefore be interpreted as running counter to a Fodorian, modularist view of language processing. However, as Singleton (1993a: 259) points out, modularists could explain them away as (a) the outcome of the operation of an extramodular back-up system (triggered by the unnaturalness of the C-test task), (b) the 'mimicking' of 'cognitive penetration' through the 'dumb' excitation by occurring lexical forms of related lexical nodes, (c) 'postperceptual' processes or (d) processing performed by an extramodular Monitor of some kind associated with L2 knowledge accumulated via instruction beyond the 'Critical Period' for 'true' language acquisition.

This last explanation would be strengthened if it could be shown that context effects were associated with conscious problem-solving and that 'bottom-up'-type responses unrelated to context were

Table 6.6. *Percentages of acceptable solutions (based on Singleton & Little, 1992: 397, Table 1 and Singleton, 1993a: 258)*

Modified French C-test 1 (December 1990)	Modified French C-test 2 (December 1990)	Modified French C-test 3 (May 1991)	Modified French C-test 4 (May 1991)
81.2	75.0	86.2	75.6

Table 6.7. *Percentages of unacceptable responses which were semantically motivated (relative to total number of unacceptable responses in each case) (based on Singleton, 1993a: 258)*

Modified French C-test 1 (December 1990)	Modified French C-test 2 (December 1990)	Modified French C-test 3 (May 1991)	Modified French C-test 4 (May 1991)
73.7	88.9	96.8	86.7

Table 6.8. *Percentages of solutions which were unrelated to contextual meaning (relative to the total number of responses – acceptable and unacceptable – in each case) (based on Singleton, 1993a: 259)*

Modified French C-test 1 (December 1990)	Modified French C-test 2 (December 1990)	Modified French C-test 3 (May 1991)	Modified French C-test 4 (May 1991)
4.3	2.6	0.4	2.6

associated with unconscious processing. Our results show the contrary. 'Non-contextual' responses were, for example, more often than not elicited by C-test slots which also elicited introspective comments indicating problematicity and, therefore, by implication, conscious deliberation (see Tables 6.9 and 6.10).

Another kind of evidence that might be interpreted as helpful to the view that conscious L2 processes are extramodular, and therefore qualitatively different from unconscious processes, would be evidence that the respective products of conscious and unconscious processing were different in kind. In fact, it emerges from the MLRP data that in many cases where an identical solution has been offered a number of

Table 6.9. *Percentages of 'non-contextual' responses associated with the presence and the absence of commentary indicating consciousness of problematicity (relative to response totals) (based on Singleton, 1993a: 259)*

	Modified French C-test 1 (December 1990)	Modified French C-test 2 (December 1990)	Modified French C-test 3 (May 1991)	Modified French C-test 4 (May 1991)
Comment	24.6	8.1	2.5	9.6
No comment	1.4	1.8	0.0	0.8

Table 6.10. *Percentages of 'non-contextual' responses associated with the presence and the absence of commentary indicating consciousness of problematicity (relative to error totals) (based on Singleton, 1993a: 259)*

	Modified French C-test 1 (December 1990)	Modified French C-test 2 (December 1990)	Modified French C-test 3 (May 1991)	Modified French C-test 4 (May 1991)
Comment	42.9	14.7	8.0	21.4
No comment	13.3	9.6	0.0	6.3

times in response to a given slot, some instances have been commented on (and, thus, one assumes, produced with some degree of deliberation) while others have not (Singleton, 1993a: 260).

Proponents of the modularity hypothesis would, however, have no difficulty in accounting for the above results. They could place the entirety of late-acquired, instructed L2 knowledge outside the language module (where encapsulation is not an issue and consciousness may not signify) and/or explain away the findings in question in terms of the intervention of unconscious but 'postperceptual' central processes. The only possible conclusion (cf. Singleton, 1993a: 260) is that with regard to L2 lexical processing (at least as far as the late-acquired, instructed L2 lexicon is concerned), evidence which at first seems to run counter to the modular position is apparently always going to be amenable to a 'modularity-friendly' interpretation.

The findings of subsequent studies based on the post-pilot C-test results are of a piece with those reported above. Among published accounts of such later work one can cite a paper first presented in

1992 and published four years later (Singleton, 1996a), a paper presented in 1993 and published in 1994 (Singleton, 1994), and references to the MLRP findings in a general introduction to L2 lexical acquisition (Singleton, 1993–94b). These make reference to data from the 1991–92 intake of students of French as well as to data from the 1990–91 intake. The latter group is labelled French Group A and the former French Group B. As was made clear in Chapter 5, each C-test elicitation session involved a pair of C-tests; the pair used in the December session were different from the pair used in the May session, but the same pair were used each December with each group and each May with each group.

The results from these various C-test administrations coincide with earlier-reported results (see Tables 6.11 and 6.12, below) inasmuch as a large proportion of the C-test 'slots' were correctly and appropriately filled, this proportion never falling below 61% in respect of either group on any of the four tests. This finding is again interpreted as *prima facie* evidence that most responses took contextual meaning into account. Also as in earlier reported results, the majority of unacceptable responses were clearly related to the meaning of the context, the proportion of such responses never falling below 68% of the totality of unacceptable responses from either group on any test. It is inferred from these results that subjects arrived at their proposed solutions primarily on grounds of meaning, an inference confirmed – as previously – by their introspections.

That is not to say, however, that formal factors had no role in the process of filling the C-test 'slots'. One of the above-mentioned studies (Singleton, 1996a) homes in on the formal dimension by focusing on the minority of instances where reference was made by subjects in their introspective comments to formal aspects of the items considered and/or offered as possible solutions. Such comments were found to fall into three categories: (i) references to the length of words required, based on knowledge of specific conditions of the test, (2) references to the graphemic form of words considered/proposed, and (3) references to the way items considered/proposed sounded.

The occurrence of comments in the first category is explicable in terms of the fact that, as part of the test instructions they received, subjects were informed about the broad lines of the procedure for deletions in the preparation of the C-tests and were thus aware of the approximate length of the target items. Since such comments arise specifically from the requirements of the C-test and are taken to be of limited relevance to lexical processing in other circumstances, they are excluded from further consideration.

Comments in category (2) comprise references to the 'look' of a

Table 6.11. *Percentages of acceptable solutions (based on Singleton, 1993–94b: 10, Table 1; Singleton, 1994: 48, Table 10*

	December 1990		May 1991		December 1991		May 1992	
	Modified French C-test 1	Modified French C-test 2	Modified French C-test 3	Modified French C-test 4	Modified French C-test 1	Modified French C-test 2	Modified French C-test 3	Modified French C-test 4
French Group A	81.2	75.0	86.2	75.6	84.4	82.0	86.8	78.8
French Group B					70.2	61.0	75.8	62.5

Table 6.12. *Percentages of unacceptable responses which are clearly linked to the meaning of the context (relative to total numbers of unacceptable responses) (based on Singleton, 1993–94b: 11 Table 2; Singleton, 1994: 49, Table 2)*

	December 1990		May 1991		December 1991		May 1992	
	Modified French C-test 1	Modified French C-test 2	Modified French C-test 3	Modified French C-test 4	Modified French C-test 1	Modified French C-test 2	Modified French C-test 3	Modified French C-test 4
French Group A	73.7	88.9	96.8	86.7	81.0	77.8	97.8	68.0
French Group B					71.9	68.5	75.6	68.7

word and to whether or not it had previously been seen in its written form. For example:

I was not certain about the spelling
I think I've read this word before ...

Comments such as the above are seen as having obvious relevance to the normal processing of the written forms of an L2.

Comments in category (3) refer to how items 'sounded' and to whether or not they had been 'heard' before. For example:

. . . it sounds familiar to me
I heard 'le Mistrale' [*sic*] mentioned on the French news recently . . .

The expressions used in such comments suggest that, despite the fact that the test task was focused on written language, recourse was had in these instances to phonological memory codes. This interpretation is supported by further evidence relative to the data in question and also by introspective evidence from other studies focused on C-tests.

With regard to our own data, those administering the MLRP C-tests noted that, when taking the tests, subjects often lifted their heads and silently or near-silently mouthed words while appearing to listen to themselves. This is anecdotal, but it does correspond to a common experience of language-users confronting lexical uncertainty. Also, the internal evidence of subjects' reports of having 'heard' certain items sometimes reinforces the implication that it is a phonological coding that is being referred to – e.g., *Mistrale* (in the above-quoted comment), which is misspelt, but in such a way that its pronunciation is not misrepresented. As far as evidence from other studies is concerned, the 'think-aloud' data reported by Feldman & Stemmer (1987), for example, reveals that attention to sound via oral repetition is a strategy employed by C-test-takers for both assisting recall and checking provisional responses.

Table 6.13 details the proportions of references to graphemic form and to sound, relative to the total numbers of references to form (excluding references to word length – see above). The numbers involved are small (overall total of references to formal aspects of words other than length = 75), but it is striking that, despite the fact that the tasks involved are written tasks, a large proportion of the form-oriented comments refer to sound (44% overall). A further interesting finding emerges from an examination of the nature of the form-oriented comments. Such comments are either 'positive' in the sense of justifying a particular choice ('looks right', 'sounds familiar', etc.) or 'negative' in the sense of calling a particular choice into question ('not certain about the spelling', 'have never heard it used

Table 6.13. *Proportions of references to graphemic form and sound (relative to total numbers of references to lexical form elicited, excluding references to word length) (based on Singleton, 1996a: 83, Table 1)*

		December 1990		May 1991		December 1991		May 1992	
		Modified French C-test 1	Modified French C-test 2	Modified French C-test 3	Modified French C-test 4	Modified French C-test 1	Modified French C-test 2	Modified French C-test 3	Modified French C-test 4
French Group A	Graphemic form refs.	0.14	0.67	0.50	0.50	0.60	0.60	0.60	0.59
	Sound refs.	0.85	0.33	0.50	0.50				
French Group B	Graphemic form refs.					0.55	0.43	0.67	0.67
	Sound refs.					0.45	0.57	0.33	0.33

Table 6.14. *Distribution of form-oriented comments in terms of formal aspect to which they were applied and in terms of positive/negative content (Singleton, 1996a: 84, Table 2)*

	Positive	Negative
Graphemic form refs.	15	28
Sound refs.	21	11

before', etc.). It transpires that there is a tendency for references to sound to be 'positive' in the above sense and for references to graphemic form to be 'negative' (see Table 6.14). The association between comments referring to sounds of words and positivity, and between comments referring to graphemic form and negativity is significant ($\chi^2 = 5.69$; $p < 0.05$).

These results suggest that, where the subjects in question focused on the form of possible solutions, phonological factors tended to play a larger role than graphological factors in the process of deciding which items to opt for; and that the way items 'looked' tended to be considered only after such decisions had actually been taken. This, in turn, suggests that where L2 lexical problems occasion a focus on form, the representations referred to tend to be primarily phonological rather than graphological, even in the context of a written L2 task. It is interesting to compare this inference with Service's (1992) interpretation of the results of her study of predictors of foreign-language-learning success (cf. discussion in Chapter 4). She found that not only quality of pronunciation in a pseudo-word repetition task but also accuracy of spelling in a delayed copying task involving pseudo-words were specifically related to foreign language learning (whereas abolity to match syntactic–semantic pairs seemed to have a more general relationship with academic success). She attempts to explain these results by postulating that both the repetition task and the writing (copying) task engage phonological memory, accuracy in both depending on the quality of traces in the phonological store.

Analysis of the post-1990 C-test results is still under way. However, enough has already been completed to confirm the trends revealed by earlier MLRP studies, some of which have been reported above. Beyond a certain point, it is clearly not only tedious but also fruitless to multiply references to results that are consistently oriented in the same direction. However, it may be of interest to provide a brief glimpse of what is emerging from our comparison of C-test results obtained from complete beginners in an L2 and results from

Table 6.15. *Percentages of acceptable solutions*

	December 1990		May 1991	
	Modified German C-test 1	Modified German C-test 2	Modified German C-test 3	Modified German C-test 4
German Group A Beg.	59.8	40.2	49.2	44.7
German Group A Adv.	80.2	72.0	70.8	70.0
Difference	20.4	31.8	21.6	25.3

advanced learners. As was explained in Chapter 5, in the case of the samples of students of German from whom we elicited L2 data, we were able to observe *ab initio* learners of German as well as learners who had come into the university with school experience of the language. The percentages of correct responses elicited by the 1990–91 administration of our (modified) German C-tests to the *ab initio* group of students of German (German Group A Beg.) and to the group of advanced learners of German (German Group A Adv.) recruited from the 1990–91 intake are given in Table 6.15.

The difference between the beginners' and advanced learners' scores on each of the tests is significant (at the 0.005 level for a one-tailed test – t = 3.63, 4.69, 4.42 and 5.26 respectively), which is hardly surprising. On the basis of the arguments rehearsed above, this suggests, *prima facie*, that the lexical processing associated with the advanced group's test-taking was more semantico-pragmatically driven than that associated with the beginners' group's efforts. However, it is worth noting that, even in this very early phase of their experience of German, sizeable proportions (never less than 40%) of the beginners' responses are correct, and therefore in all likelihood arrived at semantico-pragmatically.

Word association test results

Meara's work with word-association tests in the context of the Birkbeck Vocabulary Project has already been referred to in the present chapter and was discussed at length in Chapter 4. The word-association dimension of our own project, which is the aspect of the MLRP that is most obviously and directly comparable to the

Table 6.16. *MLRP French word-association test results: percentages of clang responses (relative to total numbers of responses) (based on Singleton, 1993–94b; 13, Table 3; Singleton, 1994: 50, Table 3)*

French Group A (March 1991)	French Group A (March 1992)	French Group B (March 1992)
2.1	3.6	0.4

Birkbeck studies, yields the finding that among our advanced L2 learners the vast majority of word-association test responses were semantico-pragmatically related to the stimuli which elicited them.

For example, from the results of the 1991 and 1992 administrations of the MLRP French word-association tests, which have already been published (Singleton, 1993–94b, 1994), it emerges that only a tiny proportion of the associates produced by the subjects involved are clang responses (see Chapter 4), all of the others having semantico-pragmatic connections with the stimuli concerned (Table 6.16).

More recently, a very detailed study of MLRP French word-association test results was conducted by Maréchal (1995). Maréchal took eight of the MLRP sample of students of French from the 1990–91 intake (Group A) and eight from the 1991–92 intake (Group B) for whom word-association data were available in both French and English. The data in question were from the 1992 administration of the MLRP word association tests, which, as was reported in Chapter 5, were of the multiple-response type (cf. Randall, 1980), where subjects produce as many responses as they can within a limited time-span (30 seconds in this case). The 50 English stimuli were taken from the Kent–Rosanoff (1910) standard list of frequently occurring and emotionally neutral items, and the French stimuli were taken from Rosenzweig's (1970) translation of this list.

Maréchal's classification system for student responses includes the 'traditional' categories of paradigmatic (P), syntagmatic (S) and clang associations (C) (see above, Chapter 4), but also a category to cover those cases where it is difficult to decide whether a response is paradigmatically or syntagmatically related to the stimulus (P/S), a category to cover other semantic links such as part–whole relations (Se), a category to cover other relationships that are difficult to classify (O), a category to cover non-French or non-English responses to French and English stimuli respectively (U), and a category to cover illegible responses (I). It should perhaps be added that, following Van

Roey (1990), Maréchal defines paradigmatic relations more strictly than many other researchers using word-association tests – in terms of synonymy, hyponymy, incompatibility and antonymy.

Maréchal's figures in relation to the semantic/formal divide are very clear. They show an overwhelming majority of responses in both L1 (English) and L2 (French) as being based on meaning relations, while only a tiny proportion are in the clang category (Table 6.17). That is not to say that there is a complete resemblance between the L1 and the L2 data sets. Clearly, the L2 data show fewer semantic associations and more clang associations than the L1 data. Z-tests applied to these differences yielded a Z-value of 15.49 in the case of the semantic responses and 9.06 in the case of the clang responses, both values indicating a highly significant difference ($p < 0.01$).

Three comments are called for in relation to these differences. First, some of the L2 responses produced in the O and U categories are in fact interpretable as semantic. With regard to the O category, for example, one response to the stimulus *lisse* ('smooth') is *bibliothèque* ('library'); this becomes explicable if one postulates a confusion between *lisse* and *lise* (1st and 3rd person singular of present subjunctive of *lire* – 'to read'), in which case, one is dealing with a straightforwardly semantic associate (cf. discussion of similar kinds of confusions in Chapter 4). With regard to the U category, many of the responses here are simply English words (in many instances words with French cognates) with a clear semantic relationship to the stimulus; thus *terre* ('earth') elicited *planet* (cf. French *planète*), *soldat* ('soldier') elicited *bayonet* (cf. French *baïonnette*), etc.

Second, it is hardly surprising that a person's L1 should be a more abundant source of semantic associates than his/her L2, even if the L2 has been learnt to an advanced level. The difference between the general richness of the lexis available in L1 as opposed to that available in L2 can be gauged by the most cursory comparison of the numbers of L1 responses produced as opposed to the numbers of L2 responses produced. The relevant overall figures are given in Table 6.18.

Third, in relation to the clang responses produced, it is noteworthy that the larger percentages of such responses in the L2 are largely the result of the input of just 4 of the 16 subjects. On the L1 tests, the number of clang associates per subject was between 0 and 3. On the L2 tests, the same range emerged for 12 of the 16 learners:

It appears that only four students give a higher proportion of clang associates. These give, respectively 7, 10, 22 and 43 clang responses, which

Table 6.17. *Percentages of semantic and clang associates (based on Maréchal, 1995: 71 Table 6)*

	Semantic (P + S + P/S + Se)	Clang
English		
French Group A	94.7	0.2
French Group B	95.9	0.2
Average	95.4	0.2
French		
French Group A	82.5	3.9
French Group B	86.8	1.7
Average	84.4	3.0

Table 6.18. *Total numbers of associates produced (based on Maréchal, 1995: 70 Table 5)*

English	French	Total
4852	3183	8035

is equivalent to 4.2, 3.6, 16.2, and 13 percent of their responses. (Maréchal, 1995: 74)

Apparently, the more restricted range of L2 lexical knowledge and/or the less secure nature of such knowledge have different effects on different individuals in terms of word-association test behaviour – leading in a minority of cases to a higher level of reliance on formal links.

In general, Maréchal's findings provide support for the view that the organization of the mental lexicon of advanced L2 learners is, like that of the L1 mental lexicon, predominantly meaning-based. Differences between the L1 and L2 data sets can readily be accounted for in terms of different levels of lexical knowledge in the two languages and also, to an extent, in terms of interaction between the nature of L2 lexical knowledge and individual learner characteristics.

Concluding summary

All in all, the three categories of MLRP data presented here – pilot C-test data, post-1990 C-test data, and word-association test data – corroborate each other in indicating that for advanced L2 learners the lexical interconnections and operational procedures that were to the fore in dealing with the tests in question were semantico-pragmatic in nature. Our interpretation of this finding is simply that most of the words involved in these tests were well-integrated into the mental lexicons of the learners concerned, and that *well-integrated* in the context of lexical acquisition (whether in L2 or L1) means connected up to the relevant network(s) of internalized lexical meanings – these meanings then constituting the dominant drives and determiners of the processing of such items. On this view, the items that our subjects dealt with in terms of their formal shape were likely to have been those with which they were less familiar and which, accordingly, in Saussurean terms, counted few or no 'series of *signifiés*' among their 'associative families' (cf. Saussure, *Cours de linguistique générale*, Part 2, Chapter 5).

7 *Findings on the cross-linguistic factor in lexical processing and acquisition*

A great deal of evidence of cross-linguistic influence at work in lexical acquisition and processing has already been reviewed, notably in Chapter 4. The phenomenon of interlexical interaction, like the question of whether the L2 lexicon has a more formal basis than the L1 lexicon, has been a major topic of interest within the MLRP since its inception – and for similar reasons. That is to say, the former issue like the latter bears on the nature of the relationship between the L1 and the L2 mental lexicon. If the L2 mental lexicon were qualitatively different from the L1 mental lexicon, one would expect interaction between them to be minimal or non-existent. Reversing the terms of this argument, the fact that there are, as we have seen, so many indications that interlexical interaction is commonplace has to be taken as *prima facie* evidence of the similarity of the L1 and L2 lexica.

From our own previous work in other contexts (e.g., Ridley, 1991b; Singleton, 1981, 1983, 1987a, 1987b; Singleton & Little, 1984b), it was clear to us that lexical transfer – to use the traditional term – was a reality. However, we did not initially make the connection between this and the question of whether or not there was a basic qualitative difference between the L1 and the L2 mental lexicon. It was our examination of the hypothesis that the L2 mental lexicon was essentially form-driven which brought this connection into focus. From that point onwards, the cross-lexical data which emerged from the MLRP – some of which are presented in the present chapter – took on a new relevance.

It should be noted that much of the material on cross-linguistically based word coinage discussed in this chapter might well be treatable under the heading of compensatory strategies – the topic of Chapter 8 – since what seems to be in question very often is an attempt to deal with a lexical problem in a given L2 by deliberately dipping into the lexical resources of other available languages. The way in which this overlap is dealt with is as follows: in the present chapter, discussion revolves around the implications of transfer (strategic or not) for the notion of cross-lexical connectivity, while in Chapter 8, the focus is on broader processing issues as well as on compensatory strategies without a cross-linguistic dimension.

C-test data from the pilot phase of the project

Cross-lexical influence and its implications began to be explored in one of the very early publications to emerge from the MLRP – Singleton & Little's (1991) article, which was discussed at some length in Chapter 6 in relation to the respective roles of form and meaning in the L2 mental lexicon. The cross-lexical data discussed in this paper are lexical coinages which figure in the responses to the French and German C-tests of the pilot phase of the project. The scene is set for an examination of the specifically cross-linguistic dimension by a general consideration of instances where subjects had produced forms which did not actually exist in the languages in question. The percentages of such coinages or 'creations' in relation to total numbers of non-scoring slots and to total numbers of incorrect responses are shown in, respectively, Table 7.1 and Table 7.2.

Singleton & Little (1991: 73) point out that lexical creations are not peculiar to L2 performance but are also a feature of L1 performance. They note that – in both L2 and L1 – such coinages may result from an imperfect command of spelling conventions (cf. Ringbom, 1987: 73ff.). They also refer to the possibility that lexical creations may be the consequence of faulty encoding of input (cf. Singleton, 1987a: 336ff.), pointing out that such deficient encoding can occur in L1 as well as in L2 – as is indicated by L1 mispronunciations such as the following:

/ˈkwɒntɪtɪv/ (for *quantitative*)
/kɑsouˈdʒenɪk/ (for *carcinogenic*)
/ˈtʃɔːzɪbəl/ (for *chasuble*)

With regard to the connection between lexical creations and cross-linguistic influence, Singleton & Little suggest that cross-linguistic influence has an important role in lexical innovation, and that this role is not restricted to L2 coinages. If it were, they say, how could one explain the phenomenon of new lexical items being introduced into a particular language system by 'borrowing'? Referring to Appel & Muysken (1987), they advert to the fact that innovation of this kind is almost invariably a consequence of 'borrowing' by native

Table 7.1. *Percentages of lexical 'creations' (relative to total numbers of non-scoring slots) (Singleton & Little, 1991: 78, Table 7)*

French C-test 1	French C-test 2	German C-test 1	German C-test 2
15.2	22.5	7.2	12.4

Table 7.2. *Percentages of lexical 'creations' (relative to total numbers of incorrect responses, i.e., with non-responses left out of account) (Singleton & Little, 1991: 78, Table 8)*

French C-test 1	French C-test 2	German test 1	German C-test 2
20.8	35.9	10.6	18.3

speakers of the host language from other languages to which they have access.

They also argue that, whereas the relatively frequent occurrence of such coinages might seem at first sight to support Meara's view concerning the looseness and randomness of the L2 mental lexicon (see above, Chapter 6), closer inspection reveals that the production of such forms is simply a function of ignorance. Coinages are clearly associated with the lower-scoring slots of the tests; the mean slot-score for slots eliciting one or more creation was consistently more than 20% lower than that for slots eliciting no creations (see Table 7.3), the differences in question all attaining significance at the $p < 0.05$ level.

With specific regard to innovations which show L1 influence, the frequency of occurrence of such items relative to other kinds of innovations in these results is shown in Table 7.4.

Singleton & Little note that a general problem confronting researchers interested in cross-linguistic lexical phenomena is the so-called 'attribution problem'. A given L2 error may often be attributable either to cross-linguistic influence or to over-generalization of an L2 rule (or indeed to both). A further aspect of the problem – related to the interpenetration of lexis and other dimensions of language – is that it is not always entirely clear whether the putative cross-linguistic influence is operating at a lexical level or at some other level. Singleton & Little suggest that this problem presents itself less acutely in the case of lexical creations. L2 lexical creations which can be related to lexical items in other languages are typically not easy to account for without reference to these other languages,

Table 7.3. *Mean percentages of correct responses associated with slots eliciting at least one lexical 'creation' and eliciting no lexical 'creations' (Singleton & Little, 1991: 78, Table 9)*

	French C-test 1	French C-test 2	German C-test 1	German C-test 2
At least 1	65.9	48.7	48.3	29.5
No creations	92.5	77.0	72.4	64.5

Table 7.4. *Percentages of L1-related 'creations' (relative to total numbers of 'creations') (Singleton & Little, 1991: 78, Table 10)*

French C-test 1	French C-test 2	German C-test 1	German C-test 2
12.5	30.8	0	4.4

and, because such errors tend to be highly idiosyncratic in nature, they can much more plausibly be related to 'local' particularities of the lexicon than to broad grammatical or semantic principles. The following selection of French coinages cited by Singleton & Little (1991: 76) illustrates the point:

**transcribé* (required word: *transformé*; cf. English *transcribed*)
**asylum* (required word: *asile*; cf. English *asylum*)
**fanaticisme* (required word: *fanatisme*; cf. English *fanaticism*)
**permité* (required word: *permis*; cf. English *permitted*)

Such coinages figure in the German data too. For example, Singleton & Little (1991: 75) mention the form **Army*, which was elicited by a German C-test slot whose target word was *Armee* ('army'). Singleton & Little argue that *Army* 'unambiguously shows the influence of the English word' and that 'its production cannot easily be explained in terms other than lexical' (*ibid.*). On the other hand, English/German coinages turn out to be markedly less frequent than English/French coinages – indeed, ten times less frequent in the pilot C-test data, a finding which Singleton & Little ascribe to psychotypological factors (cf. discussion in Chapter 4). Their argument in this connection (Singleton & Little, 1991: 75–76) runs as follows. Whereas English is in terms of its basic grammatical structure a Germanic language, in terms of its lexicon – thanks to the fall-out from the Norman invasion of England in the eleventh century – it might plausibly regarded as a Romance language. It is certainly the case that English-speaking learners of French rapidly realize that there are considerable numbers of English words which – after a relatively straightforward 'conversion' process – can readily be deployed in French. With regard to German, on the other hand, apart from loanwords and a handful of cases where English and German share virtually identical descendants of Proto-Germanic forms (*arm–Arm*, *ring--Ring*, *house--Haus*, etc.), 'converting' English words into their German cognates is rather more complicated, requiring one, at the very least, to take into account and put into reverse the Great English Vowel Shift and then to re-run the Second German Sound Shift. As Singleton & Little comment, given all of this, it is hardly surprising that the MLRP subjects attempted more English-based coinages in French than in German.

C-test data from 1990 onwards

The data yielded by the (modified) C-tests administered in the post-pilot phase of the MLRP were equally rich in evidence of cross-linguistic influence (see, e.g., Singleton, 1993b, Singleton, 1996b, 1997, forthcoming[b]; Singleton & Little, 1992). Thus, for example, it was a straightforward matter to find in the post-1990 corpus further instances of innovative C-test responses bearing a resemblance to languages at learners' disposal other than the language of the C-tests in question. For example (again from the French data):

**miste*	required word: *mistral*; cf. English *mist*)
**degrées*	(required word: *degrés*; cf. English *degree*)
**volcanos*	(required word: *volcans*; cf. English *volcanoes*)
**excludait*	(required word: *excluait*; cf. English *excluded*)

The new element available from the post-1990 C-test data was the information supplied by the introspections associated with the post-pilot C-tests. These introspections offer clear evidence of cross-linguistic operations, as the following examples show:

I chose an English word beginning with 'col' that sounded right for the context and translated it into French (required word: *colline*; solution offered: *colonie*).

I keep thinking of chairman but I can't think of a French word for what I want to say (required word: *chargé*, no solution offered).

On occasion, evidence of cross-lexical consultation was provided even where the end product was actually correct:

Not sure of how to spell the word for degrees (required word: *degrés*; solution offered: *degrés*).

Thought it meant 'in charge' so I put chargé (required word: *chargé*; solution offered: *chargé*).

In some instances, subjects seemed to be drawing on their knowledge of another L2 rather than their L1 (English). Thus:

I've got the feeling I got mixed up with an Irish word (required word: *failles*; solution offered: *failles*)
I thought it was la force ... it's la esfuerza (f) in Spanish (required word: *fonds*; solution offered: *force*)

Our experience is that, if one is to arrive at a full picture of the extent and the nature of cross-lexical consultation that goes on in the course of completing a task such the C-test task, one needs to take account both of internal evidence from the linguistic product and of introspective evidence. For example, in a recent study of three years' worth of French C-test data from the MLRP sample recruited in 1990 (Singleton, 1996c), the results of an analysis of cross-lexical consultation based on product were compared with those based on an analysis of introspective evidence, and the conclusion was reached that the absence of either of the analyses would have led to important facts being lost from view.

The study proceeded as follows. To begin with, words whose formal characteristics indicated some element of cross-lexical processing were identified. Since correct solutions reveal nothing about their processing genesis, the items in question were of necessity deviant, and, moreover, deviant in such a way as to render implausible any explanation of their origins which made no reference to a cross-linguistic factor. Most of the words falling into this category were cross-linguistic coinages of the kind exemplified above. In other cases, the lexical forms in question were ones that existed in French but not in the sense in which they appeared to be applied. Thus, *scientistes* ('scientistic', 'adherent of scientism') was used in the sense of 'scientist' (French *scientifique*), and *revenues* ('returned', 'come back' – feminine plural form of past participle) was used in the sense of 'revenues' (French *revenus*). The numbers of items so identified were modest; they appeared in just under 1% of the totality of C-test slots available over the three years (including those which elicited no response), taking into account all subjects and all adminstrations of all the tests.

The next stage of the study involved identifying those comments which explicitly mentioned translation or reference to a language other than French, and/or which specified particular French words to which recourse had been had in the problem-solving process –

whether these were translation equivalents of the perceived target item or items from the same semantic field. In some cases, the introspections were associated with solutions that worked, in others, with unacceptable solutions, and in others still, with slots that had been left blank. Again, the examples given above are typical. In quantitative terms they were associated with about 2% of the totality of C-test slots available over the three years (including those which elicited no response), taking into account all subjects and all administrations of all the tests.

Such comments suggest that cross-lexical consultation was variously used by the MLRP participants in trying to cope with the lexical problems that the C-tests posed. In some cases, the English (or other non-French) words that were referred to seemed to be utilized as conceptual foci, as points of departure for attempts at finding French glosses or semantic associates (e.g., 'I was trying to think of a word for region . . .'). In other cases, the actual forms of the non-French items being pondered on appeared to contribute to the hypothesizing about the forms of the French words under consideration (e.g., 'Realised English trans. would be "revenue", therefore French same but unsure of accuracy of word'). There are also instances where reference to non-French lexis can be seen to have had what looks like a sort of *post hoc* monitoring role (e.g., 'faibles, faines, failles, not entirely sure. The last one [the one actually chosen] sounds Irish!'). None of this information concerning the diversity of function of cross-lexical consultation would have been available, of course, in the absence of the introspective commentaries.

The final step in the study was to explore the relationship between the two groups of data analysed. What is particularly striking in this connection is that there is practically no overlap between them. Specifically, in all but three cases, the solutions (or non-responses) associated with introspections indicating cross-lexical consultation do not fall into the category of items in which cross-linguistic influence is detectable from the nature of the product. The exceptions are the following:

thought of volcano as in English . . . (required word: *volcans*; solution offered: *volcano*)
can't think of another word for income . . . (required word: *revenus*; solution offered: *revenues*)
I couldn't think of the infinitive for the French verb 'to exclude' . . . (required word: *excluait*; solution offered: *excludait*)

In other words, in the vast majority of cases where introspections suggest reference to English and other languages in subjects' attempts to deal with the French lexical problems that confronted them, the cross-linguistic processing in question left no apparent trace in the actual product. The converse is, of course, also true. The great bulk of solutions whose nature was such as to indicate a cross-linguistic dimension to their production were for their part unaccompanied by introspective comments which mentioned cross-lexical activity – the above three instances constituting the only exceptions.

On the basis of the foregoing, it is difficult to disagree with those who claim that introspective evidence is able to provide perspectives on cross-linguistic processing – at least in problem-solving situations – which it would be impossible to derive from the linguistic product alone. On the other hand, the other inescapable conclusion is that the nature of a linguistic product can very often give clues to underlying processing which – because, perhaps, of an absence of consciousness of problematicity on the part of the producer – fails to give rise to introspective commentary. In the light of these points, and in the light of the enormity of our ignorance, we can perhaps draw a general lesson for L2 research – namely, that we cannot afford to ignore any avenue that holds the possibility of supplying information and insights about L2 processes. Purism in this matter is entirely out of place, whether it be of the variety which rejects 'error analysis' as too 'product-oriented' or of the variety which rejects introspective evidence as too 'soft'.

Before leaving this study, it may be worth adding a footnote concerning the apparently rather weak quantitative showing here of the cross-lexical factor, as compared with the kinds of proportions that were cited in Chapter 4. In interpreting the figures reported above, it needs to be borne in mind that most of the solutions offered were actually non-deviant and unaccompanied by any introspective commentary. Moreover, the base figures to which the quoted percentages relate include non-responses. If one relates the number of cross-lexically processed items identified on the basis of linguistic product evidence alone to the total number of errors produced, the percentage of the former goes up to around 3%, and if one relates the number of cross-lexically oriented introspections to the total number of introspections, the percentage of the former goes up to 20%. Furthermore, it needs to be remembered that the instances of cross-lexical consultation selected on the basis of linguistic product evidence alone were identified using extremely strict criteria which ruled out possible and probable cases of transfer and retained only what were deemed to be absolutely certain cases. Similarly, in the identification of introspective evidence of cross-lexical consultation, many introspections implied some degree of reference to the mental lexicon of English insofar as they talked about efforts to understand and/or exploit the context, but were excluded by the rigorous terms of the criteria adopted. Even a slightly laxer approach to what was to be accounted as evidence of cross-linguistic influence would undoubtedly have brought the percentages up to the kinds of levels familiar from the transfer literature.

Other data

Turning now to data arising from other MLRP activities and instruments, a particularly interesting demonstration of the cross-linguistic factor at work comes from one of the interviews conducted as part of Ushioda's study of learner motivation (Ushioda, 1996a). The learner in question in this instance is a female second-year student of French and English. What this subject's comments appear to betoken is a kind of informal contrastive analysis of the lexical characteristics of the L1 and the L2. The accuracy of the perceptions resulting from this analysis is less important in the present context than the fact that it took place and that, as the extract cited below shows, it yielded generalizations about differences between L1 and the L2 lexical structure which are very likely to have made an impact on L2 performance:

> I like the / there is a way of expressing things that / it's different to English and it's sometimes more precise because they have verbs for absolutely everything whereas English / you can use other verbs and connect them together when you're saying things / and especially Irish / the way Irish people speak English / but French there's / you can make a verb out of almost anything you want / I like that / I think it is more precise / the structure of French is more precise / I find that interesting (Ushioda, 1996a: 253)

With regard to evidence of cross-linguistic influence at work in the actual L2 production of the MLRP subjects during the performance of tasks other than the C-test task, this very much confirms the picture which emerges from the C-test data. By way of illustration, there follow some examples of evidence of cross-lexical consultation taken from the MLRP French word-association test data, translation-task data and story-telling task data (cf. Singleton, 1993b, 1996b, 1997):

Word-association test data:

**fathome*	(stimulus: *mer* ('sea'); cf. English *fathom*)
**diamondes*	(stimulus: *voleur* ('thief'); cf. English *diamond*)
**lionesse*	(stimulus: *lion* ('lion'); cf. English *lioness*)

Translation-task data:

**alcohol* (expression to be translated: *liquor*; cf. English *alcohol*)

**harnesses de siège* (expression to be translated: *seat belts*; cf. English *harness*)

**affairs personales* (expression to be translated: *personal belongings*; cf. English *affair, personal*)

Story-telling task data:

attendant (referring to a picture of a petrol-pump attendant – French *pompiste* – cf. English *attendant*; *attendant* in French means 'waiting')

mécanique (referring to a picture of a petrol-pump attendant – see above – cf. English *mechanic*; *mécanique* means 'mechanical', the French word for *mechanic* being *mécanicien*)

**réqueste* (referring to a picture of someone asking for a light; cf. English *request*; the word *réqueste* does not exist in French; there is a word *requête*, meaning 'petition', 'request', but the usual word for 'request' would be *demande* (noun), *demander* (verb))

As in the case of the data elicited during the C-test administrations, the introspective dimensions of the translation task and the story-telling task[1] yield some very persuasive indications of subjects engaging in cross-lexical consultation. In these latter instances, the introspective data in question are of the 'think-aloud' kind, so that what we have are apparently 'on line' glimpses of cross-lexical processing. The following examples are typical:

zones is probably the same but it seems silly to write it down so I'll put *endroits* (–) no I'm going to keep it in *zones* (-) *certaines zones* (–) *dans notre avion sont réservées pour les passageurs* (–) *qui ont envie de fumer*... (translation task)

des liqueurs for *liquor* I find *liquor* unusual in the English that's why I'm having problems translating it ... (translation task)

toilet requisites would be *des réquisites de toilette*, *toiletteries*, *choses de toilette aussi* does réquisites exist in French as well? (translation task)

some of [the nouns] sound really English rather than proper French (translation task)

[1] In the case of the story-telling task, the introspective comments were not specifically elicited but were offered spontaneously by a few subjects.

if you say you have a light you say *vous avez du feu* but I don't know what the word for *lighter* is (--) *ils cherchent du feu pour* (--) *les cigarettes ...* (story-telling task)

We have seen from the discussion of the C-test results that the cross-lexical phenomenon is not confined to the MLRP French data but is also discernible, though in smaller measure, in the German data. Other parts of the MLRP data bank also contain examples of L1 influence in lexical production in German – as can be seen from the following examples of English/German coinages taken from the German translation data:

**Perfumer* (expression to be translated: *perfumes*)
**Razoren* (expression to be translated: *razors*)
**Packete* (expression to be translated: *packet*)

The precise relative proportions of cross-lexically arrived-at lexical offerings in German as opposed to French in various parts of the data bank have not been calculated in global terms. However, as has already been mentioned, it generally seems to be the case that the cross-linguistic factor looms larger in the French than in the German data. A relevant recent study in this connection is that of Ridley & Singleton (1995b), in which advanced learners of French and of German recruited to the second level of the MLRP in 1990–91 were compared in respect of frequency of recourse to L1 lexical knowledge in the translation task. This study found that the learners of French borrowed from English nearly twice as often as the learners of German. While less dramatic than the earlier reported finding of Singleton & Little's (1991) study, the difference identified is still substantial, and is amenable to the same kind of psychotypological explanation (see above).

A further dimension of the lexical transfer question is that of the role of proficiency. A number of oft-cited studies (e.g., Dommergues & Lane, 1976; Seliger, 1978; B. Taylor, 1975; see also Galvin, 1988 – summarized in Singleton, 1990b: 13 ff.) have suggested that there may be a progressive diminution of cross-linguistic influence in general as L2 proficiency increases. Ridley & Singleton (1995b) examined this issue in a lexical perspective by comparing how two different proficiency-level groups of university students of German – *ab initio* and advanced – approached the same (problematic) lexical items in the source text. It was found that the beginners were more inclined than the advanced learners to draw on their L1 lexical knowledge or on their knowledge of languages other than German (Ln), whereas the advanced learners were more disposed than the

Table 7.5. *Percentages of strategic use of L1 and Ln lexical knowledge by the* ab initio *and advanced learners of German in the MLRP 1990–91 subsamples (relative to total number of strategies used) (based on Ridley & Singleton, 1995b: 131, Table 1).*

	Beginners		Advanced	
	1st attempt (March 1991)	2nd attempt (March 1992)	1st attempt (March 1991)	2nd attempt (March 1992)
Use of L1	10	7	6	5%
Use of Ln	3	2	0.5	0.5%

Table 7.6. *Percentages of strategic use of knowledge of TL morphological knowledge by the* ab initio *and advanced learners of German in the MLRP 1990–91 subsamples (relative to total number of strategies used) (based on Ridley & Singleton, 1995b: 131, Table 2).*

	Beginners		Advanced	
	1st attempt (March 1991)	2nd attempt (March 1992)	1st attempt (March 1991)	2nd attempt (March 1992)
	3	4	12	6

beginners to try to exploit their knowledge of target language (TL) morphology (see Tables 7.5 and 7.6).

Further evidence of a proficiency factor comes from an earlier MLRP-based study (Ridley & Singleton (1995a) of one particular *ab initio* learner. This learner, who stood low on the lexical proficiency scale in relation to her peers, was a lexical risk-taker, innovating freely where her fellow students tended to go for the safe option. With regard to transfer, those of her innovations which were L1-based or Ln-based outnumbered her TL-based innovations by nearly four to one in total.

Concluding summary

Once again, the three categories of MLRP data discussed in this chapter – pilot C-test data, post-pilot C-test data and post-pilot data elicited by other means – corroborate each other in terms of what they have to say about the central issue under discussion – in this case the question of the existence of connections between the L2 lexicon and the L1(/Ln) lexicon. The clear evidence is that such connections do indeed exist and that they are very frequently made use of in L2 performance. There is no comfort in these data, in other words, for a strong separatist view of the relationship of the L2 lexicon and the L1 lexicon. This, in turn, as has already been argued, constitutes an argument in favour of the likelihood of essential qualitative similarity between the L2 lexicon and the L1 lexicon. On the other hand, the cross-lexical factor does not emerge so overwhelmingly strongly as to suggest total integration of the two lexicons either; on the contrary, its quantitative showing seems rather weak in places, although such weakness may be to some extent an artefact of the definitions and analytical procedures employed.

Other cross-linguistic issues on which the MLRP data shed light include: the determination of perceptions of language distance, the evidence here being that lexical similarities may override language-family affiliation; the value of introspective data in cross-lexical research, the resounding message that comes from the foregoing being that such data provide detailed information which would not be available from any other source; and the proficiency factor in cross-lexical consultation, the results of two MLRP studies being consistent with the view that lower proficiency is associated with higher levels of L1/Ln-based solutions to L2 problems.

8 *Findings on communication strategies*

As has already been indicated, and as the discussion of communication strategies in Chapter 4 makes abundantly clear, some of the MLRP data discussed in the previous chapter in the context of cross-lexical consultation could just as well have been discussed under the heading of communication strategies. All instances of subjects' responding to perceived lexical gaps or difficulties in language *x* by 'borrowing' elements from language *y* can be regarded as strategic, and we have seen not a few examples of such behaviour in the foregoing pages. However, our focus in the last chapter was on the evidence that such strategies provided of connections between the lexicon of the language being used and the lexicons of other languages known to the individual in question. This was, moreover, precisely the way in which these data were used in the early papers to emerge from the MLRP.

Our interest in other issues raised by communication strategies dates from the time when Jennifer Ridley joined the project. Ridley's own connections with strategy research began with some work she conducted outside of the MLRP for an M.Phil. dissertation (see Ridley, 1991a, 1991b). The (very welcome) additional dimension she brought to the MLRP was for the most part based on a continuation of her earlier research – in this case within the framework of a doctoral project (Ridley, 1994), now published in revised form (Ridley, 1997).

The present chapter will essentially summarize and comment on Ridley's work, which draws on data elicited by translation tasks, story-tell data, interview data and data from a test of impulsivity/reflectivity. The chapter will begin with a brief overview of the relationship between Ridley's project and the broader framework of the MLRP – including, in particular, an account of how she obtained her data – and will then go on to discuss her results under the headings of the themes of publications which have emerged from this research (Ridley & Singleton, 1995a, 1995b; Ridley, 1997).

Communication strategy research within the MLRP

The two research questions principally addressed by the MLRP strategy research are the following.

1 Do learners tend to use their own preferred strategy styles in their performance of L2 production tasks?
2 Is there a discernible link between L2 strategy styles and learners' perceptions and beliefs about the larger and longer-term task of L2 learning?

Ridley's doctoral thesis (1994) attempted to deal with these questions mostly through a very detailed analysis of data supplied by four *ab initio* learners of German from the 1990–91 intake of students of German volunteering to participate in the MLRP. Related exploration of these same questions was also conducted in other fora (Ridley & Singleton, 1995a, 1995b).

An account has already been given of the story-tell and written-translation tasks that were administered to all Level II subjects in March 1991, March 1992 and March 1993. It will be recalled that for the story-tell task the Level II subsample subjects were given a series of 23 cartoon pictures and were asked to describe orally what was happening in each picture in sequence first in English and then in either French or German – depending on which L2 group they belonged to. Certain elements (e.g., cigarette lighter) which were key to the story occasioned problems in the L2 version and typically had to be dealt with strategically by subjects. In the translation task (henceforth: translation task 1), subjects were asked to attempt a written translation of an English text into either French or German – again, depending on their L2 group affiliation – and were requested not to omit content simply because they did not know the relevant lexical items – especially in respect of 20 (particularly challenging) words which were underlined in the text. In this case subjects were also asked to 'think aloud' as they worked on the task.

In addition to the above tasks performed by all Level II subjects, some further data elicitation was undertaken in relation to the four *ab initio* learners of German who were the subjects of Ridley's doctoral research. They were given a second translation task (henceforth: translation task 2), they were interviewed in both L2 and L1, and they were tested in respect of 'reflective intentional control'. Some further information about each of these further data-gathering enterprises is given below.

Translation task 2 (see Ridley, 1997: 120)

This task was based on a text, 263 words in length, which was a slightly modified passage from a contemporary novel. It contained lexis which subjects were expected to find difficult to translate and, in addition, the nature of the extract was such that it would be likely to demand of subjects a certain amount of reflection about sentence-level meaning. As in the previous translation task, subjects recorded their think-aloud comments as they performed the task.

The L2 interviews (see *ibid.*: 121)

Ridley's four subjects were interviewed three times in German during the period of her study. The interviewers, who were native speakers of German, in each case began by posing a few general conversational questions and then went on to produce two sets of pictures, which they used as foci for discussion which was rather more challenging in terms of lexical content. All interviews were recorded on audio-cassette and subsequently transcribed.

The L1 interviews (see *ibid.*: 122)

Ridley's subjects were also interviewed three times in English. The three English interviews, like the L2 interviews, were recorded on audio-cassette and later transcribed. They were semi-structured, being designed to elicit specific information (for example, information about how subjects approached the challenge of L2 learning) while at the same time allowing subjects to comment freely on the topics broached. Apart from these interviews, the researcher also engaged the subjects in informal conversation on a number of occasions, and she used any additional information gleaned during these conversations in her construction of profiles of subjects' beliefs about their language learning.

The 'impulsive/reflective' test (see *ibid.*: 115–116)

A test aimed at investigating subjects' degree of impulsiveness/reflectivity was designed, based on an adaptation of instruments used by Kagan *et al.* (1964). The instruments in question are, first, a 'Picture Discrimination test', where the degree of impulsivity or reflectivity displayed by subjects in approaching the task is gauged by timing task performance. The second instrument is a DAL ('Draw A

Line') test, which requires subjects to draw a straight line down a piece of paper as slowly as possible.

Strategic L2 lexical innovation: a case study

The first-published exploration of MLRP data in the perspective of the above research questions (Ridley & Singleton, 1995a) was a case study of one of Ridley's four *ab initio* subjects. This particular subject – designated as 'Subject C' – seemed particularly inclined to respond to lexical problems in German by creating and deploying items that would not have been recognized as German by native speakers of that language.

There were a number of indications that Subject C had a lower level of lexical proficiency in German than the other three members of the subsample in question. Thus, her mean C-test scores were lower than those of the others, and in the German word-association tests in which she participated she produced both fewer responses and a lower proportion of acceptable German lexical items in her responses than any other member of the group (see Table 8.1). With regard to lexical creativity, C produced more L2 lexical innovations than the other three subjects in the subsample across a range of tasks. This is illustrated by Table 8.2, which gives figures for instances of lexical innovation elicited from the four subjects in question by four C-tests, four translations, two picture story-tell tasks and three L2 interviews.

An important aspect of Ridley's work was her attempt to classify responses to lexical problems in terms of whether they were based on impulsive 'feel' or on reflection/deliberation. The translation tasks, with their think-aloud dimension, offered most help in this regard. Thus, for example, reflectivity could be inferred from an overt 'on-line' comment on the lexical problem-solving process and/or a long time-lapse before the solution, while 'feel'-based strategies could be inferred from rising intonation (indicating problematicity) combined with rapidity (solution delivered in less than two seconds) and an absence of commentary. A profile of C's strategy-style in respect of the translation tasks, incorporating these and other dimensions, is provided in Table 8.3. From this table one can see that C exhibited a relatively high degree of impulsivity both in terms of spontaneous abandonment and of 'feel'-based solutions. Other evidence supporting the notion that C was inclined to solve her L2 lexical problems impulsively comes from the low degree, relative to her three peers, to which she monitored the message she was formulating – as judged by the number of overt references in her think-aloud

Table 8.1. *Word-association test results for the four* ab initio *learners focused on in Ridley's doctoral study (based on Ridley & Singleton, 1995a: 41, Table 1)*

Subject	Total number of responses		Percentage of acceptable TL forms	
	March 1991	March 1992	March 1991	March 1992
A	192	Absent	77	Absent
B	151	168	75	86
C	**97**	**118**	**65**	**86**
D	125	178	95	94

Table 8.2. *Numbers of instances of lexical innovation elicited across a range of L2 tasks from the four* ab initio *learners focused on in Ridley's doctoral study (based on Ridley & Singleton, 1995a: 141, Table 2)*

Subject	C-tests	Translations	Story-tell	L2 Interviews	Total
A	14	23	6	9	52
B	17	13	3	1	34
C	**18**	**37**	**19**	**9**	**83**
D	14	26	2	3	45

Table 8.3. *C's lexical problem-solving profile in respect of the translation tasks (percentages relate to total number of lexical problems experienced by C) (based on Ridley & Singleton, 1995a: 142, Table 3)*

	Translation task 1		Translation task 2	
Strategy	March 1991	March 1992	March 1991	March 1992
Abandonment				
• spontaneous	32	10	24	21
• after reflection	3	14	28	4
Impulsive feel	16	25	20	37
Reflective approximation	26	36	8	21
Deliberate innovation				
• L1/Ln-based	16	14	0	8
• L2-based	6	0	4	0

Table 8.4. *Numbers of instances of overt references to semantic aspects of lexical problem-solving in the think-aloud protocols of the four* ab initio *learners focused on in Ridley's doctoral study (based on Ridley & Singleton, 1995a: 144, Table 6)*

	Translation task 1		Translation task 2		
Subject	March 1991	March 1992	March 1991	March 1992	Total
A	1	12	15	10	38
B	3	7	13	27	50
C	3	2	8	13	26
D	9	3	14	19	45
				Mean	39.75

protocol to the meanings of the solutions she was offering (see Table 8.4). One can also cite her language teacher's description of her as 'intuitive' and her performance on the impulsive/reflective test, which emerged as the least reflective of the four (Ridley & Singleton, 1995a: 145).

In relation to innovations, C was found to have produced high numbers of lexical coinages in both impulsive mode and in reflective mode, but to have been particularly innovative in her more impulsive attempts. Thus, for instance, an average of 82% of her impulsive solutions in her attempts at translation task 1 were innovations – as compared with 20% of A's, 0% of B's and 25% of D's – while an average of 46% of her reflective solutions in her attempts at this task were innovations – as compared with 20% of A's, 14% of B's and 41% of D's. In many instances she deployed a coinage in preference to known, and much 'safer', alternatives. One example is her attempt to find a translation equivalent for 'a range of goods' in translation task 1 (see Ridley & Singleton, 1995a: 144). Whereas most of the MLRP German group translated this expression using the approximation *viele* ('many'), C quite deliberately concocted a noun based on her knowledge of German, commenting: 'I know *verschieden* is "different". I'll make a noun *das Verschiedenes*'. A more 'impulsive' example – this time from the picture story-tell is her rendering – apparently without any kind of reflection – of the idea 'the petrol has leaked out' by the expression *die Petrole ist gelichen* (which would certainly have native speakers of German scratching their heads!) (*ibid.*).

Interestingly, when some follow-up work was done on C, investigating the pattern of her strategy use in another L2 – in fact in the foreign language she knew best (French) – very similar findings emerged as far as her innovative tendencies were concerned, even where she seemed to have the appropriate word in her lexical store (see Ridley & Singleton, 1995a: 144). For example, she ran into problems when she confronted the task of translating *headphones* into French. She actually had the appropriate French word – *casque* – at her disposal but for some reason decided to risk a diminutive form thereof – *casquettes* – which unfortunately does not work in that sense (*casquette* means 'cap').

Concerning the relationship between C's impulsive and innovating approach to L2 lexical problems and her general approach to L2 learning (and L2 vocabulary learning in particular), in the L1 interviews C indicated that her learning approach was also rather short on deliberation (Ridley & Singleton, 1995a: 145). She claimed that she did not 'sit down and learn words', believing that it was best to 'pick up' L2 words from situations of use. Such ideas seemed partly to be based on her experience of learning French and Spanish, which appeared to involve her in consciously exploiting the fact that large numbers of lexical items in these languages can be converted into their English equivalents (or near-equivalents) by relatively straightforward transliteration procedures, and that reversing such procedures, taking an English word as a starting-point, can very often yield an acceptable French or Spanish word (cf. discussion of English/French borrowing in Chapter 7). One might conclude from C's pronouncements that it is possible to acquire a taste for playing around with the forms of the L2 and for conversion/innovation; for example, she reported that she liked the sound of German and that she positively enjoyed making up words. One might also conclude that this taste for innovation can even eclipse the communicative imperative. Certainly C dismissed the notion that native speakers might not be able to understand her coinages as 'tough luck', and rather cavalierly commented that one 'can always point at something or get by' in oral communication and use a dictionary when writing.

Cross-linguistic strategies and individual learner contrasts

Further evidence of inter-subject variability with regard to strategic profile is provided by a subsequent investigation of the data (Ridley & Singleton, 1995b; see also Singleton, 1997) which, on the one hand, broadened its scope to take in the entire *ab initio* cohort of MLRP volunteers from the 1990–91 intake of students of German

(N = 10), but, on the other, narrowed its focus somewhat in the sense of paying particular attention to strategies based on English (L1) or on L2s other than German (Ln).

The papers reporting this study make the point that the ten subjects under scrutiny presented as highly homogeneous in the sense that at university entry they were all absolute beginners in relation to the German language, that they were all totally devoid of experience in any German-speaking country, and that they were all being taught German at university by the same teachers in the same classes (see, e.g., Ridley & Singleton 1995b: 132). They go on to note, however, that, despite such homogeneity, individual members of the group differed widely in their patterns of strategy use.

This strategic variability is illustrated by Table 8.5, which sets out some percentages referring to three types of strategies categorized as 'reflective' (see above): (1) intentional approximations (synonyms or paraphrases), (2) intentional L1/Ln-based coinages and (3) intentional L2-based coinages. The data in this instance come from two attempts at translation task 1 (in 1991 and 1992), and the percentages relate to total numbers of lexical problems experienced by each subject on each attempt. It should be noted, incidentally, that subjects 1, 2, 3 and 4 in Table 8.5 correspond to subjects A, B, C and D respectively in the earlier section of this chapter.

Two points emerge from the table. First, it is clear that some subjects – notably Subjects 1, 3, 4, 8 and 9 – made predominant use of a specific strategy type at both attempts. This suggests a relatively constant individual strategy style, at least relative to this type of task. Second, with particular reference to the role of cross-linguistic strategies, it appears that one member of the group, Subject 9, relied particularly heavily on L1 knowledge as a resource-expansion strategy.

Subject 9 is indeed an extremely interesting case as far as use of cross-linguistic strategies is concerned. Especially revealing is his third attempt at translation task 1 in 1993, by which time he was a seasoned learner of German and had spent some months working in Germany (see Ridley & Singleton, 1995b: 133). Although he experienced fewer lexical problems on this attempt, he nevertheless tried to deal with 30% of them in a cross-lexical fashion. For example, he guessed the items *Bukel* for *belt*, *Rack* for *rack*, and *Selektion* for *range*. When interviewed immediately after his third attempt, he revealed in respect of his use of *Selektion* that he had initially considered the safer approximation *viele* ('many') for his translation of *a range of goods* (the solution of the majority), but that in the end he had decided to go ahead with what he had felt to be a relatively secure guess.

Table 8.5. *Percentage use of three types of reflective strategies on two attempts (1991, 1992) at translation task 1 by the 10 MLRP* ab initio *volunteers from the 1990–91 intake of students of German (percentages relate to total numbers of lexical problems experienced by each subject on each attempt) (based on Ridley & Singleton, 1995b: 132 Table 3)*

	Intentional approximation		Intentional L1/Ln-based coinage		Intentional L2-based coinage	
Subject	1991	1992	1991	1992	1991	1992
1	52	60	19	13	0	7
2	17	38	3	5	0	5
3	26	36	16	14	6	0
4	53	50	5	18	16	5
5	11	31	8	4	8	0
7	19	50	12	0	8	0
8	37	45	17	15	3	0
9	20	33	44	33	10	22
10	38	71	21	0	6	14

This learner, unlike the rather impulsive, risk-taking subject focused on earlier, seems to be characterized by a careful, deliberative approach to the deployment of cross-lexically based communication strategies. It appears that his pattern of strategy use, like that of our risk-taker, can be related to his general approach to coping with the L2 lexicon (see Ridley & Singleton, 1995b: 135). When he was asked about his perspective on L2 learning, his replies indicated that his approach to lexical problem-solving in L2 production was linked to a consciously acquired strategy which he deployed in dealing receptively with both German and French – namely that of deliberately exploiting his knowledge of English. He explained his success in French at school in terms of his meticulous attention to the French words which he encountered and especially in terms of his exploration of their possible associations with formally similar English items. He commented that he was conscious of sometimes applying roughly the same approach in L2 production, stating that he frequently coined words deliberately both in French and German. He also showed an awareness of the 'false friends' problem, and said that he tried to minimize its impact by relying on native-speaker or teacher feedback to validate or invalidate his coinages.

Reflection and strategies in L2 learning

Turning now to the major publication which has resulted from the MLRP strategy research (Ridley, 1997), this very detailed study, mostly focused on the L2 production and the comments of the four *ab initio* learners of German referred to above in the section on strategic L2 lexical innovation, essentially reinforces the indications from the foregoing that individuals develop their own strategic styles, and that these can be related to individual differences in general beliefs and perceptions about L2 learning. Given the length and the scope of this work, it would not be appropriate to attempt to give a full account of its content in the present context. However, it is worth citing a few samples of the further evidence it contains in favour of the notion of individual strategic styles, and it will also be of interest to refer in detail to the final profile put together by Ridley of one of the learners concerned. The subjects will be labelled A, B, C and D, as in the earlier section.

Tables 8.6 and 8.7 display data concerning subjects' deployment in the story-tell task and the two English–German translation tasks of, respectively, approximations and innovations. C's use of lexical creativity as a preferred compensatory strategy, which has already been discussed, again emerges fairly clearly from Table 8.7. With regard to use of known approximations, this appears from Table 8.6 to have been the preferred strategy of subjects A and D.

A broader dimension of the subjects' strategic styles – already discussed – is the degree to which they reflect and deliberate on the problem-solving process. Tables 8.8, 8.9 and 8.10 bear on this question. Table 8.8 quantifies the evidence of overt monitoring in the story-tell task and the translation tasks (self-repair in the story-tell task, references to semantic or grammatical aspects of the translation process in the translation tasks), while Tables 8.9 and 8.10 present the results of the impulsive/reflective test. The Picture Discrimination test (see Table 8.10) turned out not to be particularly discriminating in relation to these subjects, the average difference-identification time clustering around the 14–16 seconds range across the whole group. The other measures referred to in this connection, on the other hand, confirmed impressions gained from other sources. Thus, C once again comes across, thanks to her low levels of overt monitoring (see Table 8.8), as markedly less reflective and more impulsive than her peers in her approach to L2 lexical problem-solving. Moreover, the relative speed with which she attacked the line-drawing task (see Table 8.9), suggests that her impulsiveness was not confined to the language domain but constituted a trait in her personality with a rather more

Table 8.6. *Percentage use of known approximations on two attempts (1991, 1992) at the story-tell task and the two translation tasks by the four* ab initio *volunteers focused on in Ridley's doctoral study (percentages relate to total numbers of lexical problems experienced by each subject on each attempt) (based on Ridley, 1997: 193, Table 28)*

	Story-tell		Translation 1		Translation 2	
Subject	1991	1992	1991	1992	1991	1992
A	66	46	52	60	65	45
B	14	33	17	38	53	73
C	5	9	26	36	8	21
D	57	50	53	50	52	45

Table 8.7. *Percentage use of lexical creativity on two attempts (1991, 1992) at the story-tell task and the two translation tasks by the four* ab initio *volunteers focused on in Ridley's doctoral study (percentages relate to total numbers of lexical problems experienced by each subject on each attempt (based on Ridley, 1997: 194, Table 29)*

	Story-tell		Translation 1		Translation 2	
Subject	1991	1992	1991	1992	1991	1992
A	21	14	23	26	10	13
B	0	16	3	4	5	11
C	47	10	35	32	20	29
D	14	10	5	26	13	9

Table 8.8. *Numbers of instances of overt grammatical and semantic monitoring on two attempts (1991, 1992) at the story-tell task and the two translation tasks by the four* ab initio *volunteers focused on in Ridley's doctoral study (based on Ridley, 1997: 194, Table 30)*

	Story-tell		Translation 1		Translation 2		
Subject	1991	1992	1991	1992	1991	1992	Total
A	13	16	4	16	33	36	118
B	5	5	3	10	25	48	96
C	4	3	4	2	30	29	72
D	1	0	20	12	54	40	127

Table 8.9. *Results of the DAL test (Kagan* et al., *1964): length of time taken to draw a straight line by the four* ab initio *volunteers focused on in Ridley's doctoral study (based on Ridley, 1997: 207, Table 35)*

Subject	Time taken (seconds)
A	97
B	93
C	34
D	127
Mean	87.75

Table 8.10. *Results of the Picture Discrimination test (Kagan* et al., *1964): number of differences spotted and time taken by the four* ab initio *volunteers focused on in Ridley's doctoral study (based on Ridley, 1997: 207, Table 35)*

	First pair of pictures		Second pair of pictures		Overall
Subject	Number of differences identified	Time taken (seconds)	Number of differences identified	Time taken (seconds)	Average time taken for the identification of one difference (seconds)
A	11	97	7	168	14.8
B	11	95	9	227	16.1
C	11	125	8	137	13.8
D	14	160	11	228	15.6

general application. At the other end of the scale, D emerges from the overall count of instances of overt monitoring as the most reflective L2 processor (see Table 8.8), and from the results of the line-drawing task (see Table 8.9) as the least impulsive generally. On the other hand, one notes that the restriction of analysis to reactions to the semantic aspects of problems in the translation tasks alone (see above, Table 8.4) yields a different result, with B in this case leading the field in terms of instances of overt monitoring. A, for his part, turns in a fairly consistently reflective performance throughout, and, in one particular domain, namely oral performance, produces noticeably more instances of overt monitoring than B, C or D.

Subject A will be the focus of the detailed profile with which this section will conclude. As we have seen even from the amount of evidence cited above, this subject 'frequently tries to find an approximation ... when faced with lexical problems' (Ridley, 1997: 210) and 'regularly overtly monitors his use of grammar and lexis' (*ibid.*: 211). He seems from the L1 interviews to have been aware of his approach and behaviour in these areas, as the following quotations (all taken from Ridley, 1997: 211) illustrate.

Some of A's comments on the strategy of approximation:

I changed the vocabulary altogether to try and get across the same meaning
trying to think of alternatives for what I couldn't get
if I can get it in a few seconds I wait but if I can't I try and change the way I'm saying the sentence (-) or else ask for help

Some of A's comments on monitoring:

I was trying to be accurate
I do try to be as close to the text as possible

Some of A's comments on contrasts between oral and written performance in the perspective of monitoring:

[*re speaking*] I would try to be accurate but I would consider getting my message across more important than taking time about exactly what I wanted to say
[*re writing*] you have more time to be accurate grammatically I'd do my best to be so anyway

A's awareness of his approach in respect of performing in German can be linked to what he had to say about his beliefs and priorities in relation to the learning of German. Thus, he seems to have been fairly alert to the stage he was at in his acquisition of specific aspects of German grammar, to have been aware of his attachment to prescriptive rules as anchors in the process of learning German, and to have been conscious of a desire for a certain autonomy in exploring the German grammatical system. The following brief extracts from his L1 interview protocols (cited in Ridley, 1997: 212) illustrate these points:

there are certain things I've got control over and there certain things that I don't (-) for example I'm not totally sure about the passive yet

even when I do break the rules to accommodate the people I'm with I still return to them [the rules] and I don't want to actually forget what the rules are

sometimes having them [the rules] handed on a plate is necessary but I prefer to be guided rather than have someone tell you exactly what's what and not giving you what you may have scope for

If this last quotation would gladden the hearts of those who in recent times have advocated the promotion of autonomy in L2 learning and teaching, A's account of how he got to grips with the morphosyntax and the lexicon of German would offer similar transports of delight to the most dyed-in-the-wool traditionalist!

In [the L1 interviews] and other conversations he stresses the importance of learning rules . . . and of learning vocabulary. He says he learns rules by rote, and especially in the early stages writes out 'lots of' mnemonics to help him remember them. Subject A is heard to say on several occasions that he 'loves words'. In short, he makes a deliberate effort to learn grammatical rules and lexis. (Ridley, 1997: 212)

However, the adoption of a rote-learning approach by A appears to have constituted a metacognitive decision which was tailored to the particular demands of studying a new language *ab initio* under pressure, rather than a general policy in respect of L2 learning:

Subject A pays conscious attention to learning grammatical rules and vocabulary in German – a practice which he knows is necessary in order to meet the heavy demands of the German programme. However, in relation to learning French at school-level, he says that whatever he learnt was picked up when on holiday in France, and that he did not have to bother with putting effort into rule learning. With regard to Irish, he considers himself at near native speaker level, having learnt it in a natural context at a very early stage of his life. (Ridley, 1997: 213)

From the evidence provided by her four subjects, Ridley feels able to conclude that individual L2 learners do indeed exhibit personal styles when it comes to the deployment of communication strategies in response to lexical problems and that the strategic styles in question are closely linked to the way in which individuals approach the overall task of learning a given L2 in a particular situation:

In a sense this study has taken a long route to say what is intuitively known, namely that individual learners have their own preferred ways of going about producing and learning a foreign language. In highlighting the notion of a L2 learning/performance strategy style for every learner, we have emphasised what is obvious to language teachers: that each learner group comprises a set of individuals who often have their own objectives and priorities. (Ridley, 1997: 231)

Concluding summary

This chapter has looked at that dimension of the MLRP which has focused on individual styles in the pattern of strategy deployment in response to L2 lexical problems. The evidence presented in the chapter can plausibly be interpreted as indicating that individuals are possessed of their own preferred strategic styles and that individual profiles in terms of use of communication strategies can be related to individuals' beliefs and perceptions about how to go about acquiring a given L2 in specific circumstances – including, of course, acquiring the lexicon of the language in question.

One notes interesting parallels between the above conclusion and the discussion in Chapter 4 (revolving around, e.g., Weinreich, 1953; De Groot, 1995) concerning individual differences in lexico-semantic organization. However, whatever may be the facts about lexico-semantic organization, the implication is that different individuals make different use of the organizational resources on offer. Thus, for example, while connectivity between the L1 and the L2 lexicon seems to be universally present, individuals vary in the extent to which they exploit such connectivity in solving their L2 lexical problems. Perhaps the general lesson here is that our universalist proclivities in psycholinguistics and in second language acquisition research – indeed in linguistics generally – need always to be balanced by a firm resolve always to keep a weather eye on the situation (in the broadest possible sense) of the individual and on its consequences for learning and processing (cf. the postmodernist perspective outlined in, e.g., Masny, 1996).

PART IV

CONCLUSION

A recapitulation, some inferences and some hopes for the future

The ground covered in this book

This book began with some cautionary comments about its own content. In Chapter 1 it was acknowledged that, although words and the concept of the word are of prime importance in our understanding of the nature of language, the word escapes easy definition. It was further noted that, while the current conception of the lexicon no longer fits the traditional image of a mere inventory of content words, precisely this broadening and complexifying of the way in which the lexicon is understood has led to a blurring of the traditional distinction between lexicon and other domains of language – to the point where the viability of a separate lexical construct has begun seriously to be questioned. The chapter concluded with the suggestion that until the precise status of the lexicon becomes clearer, it is appropriate to opt for a provisional *modus operandi* which 'plays safe' in relation to the lexical construct by treating as lexical those areas which are most self-evidently language-particular – forms and meanings of individual items, collocational patterns, 'local' colligation (e.g., complementation of verbs), etc.

In Chapter 2 we explored some aspects of the challenge posed by lexical acquisition – isolating lexical units in the speech stream, connecting lexical forms to appropriate meanings, and acquiring lexis from written input – deriving from this exploration the conclusion that it is possible to identify a number of respects in which the L2 lexical-acquisition challenge closely resembles the L1 lexical-acquisition challenge. The chapter went on to home in on L1 lexical acquisition, arguing that this process is continuous – from the very first vocal milestones onwards, and that the bulk of the work that needs to be done in the construction of the L1 lexicon is semantico-pragmatic in nature. Finally, we returned to the question of the relationship between L1 and L2 development, recognizing that L2 lexical development differs from L1 lexical development insofar as it lacks a pre-speech dimension and insofar as it takes place against the background of an already acquired lexicon, but also noting that L2 learners confront many of the same kinds of puzzles and difficulties as L1 learners in both the formal and the semantic domain.

Chapter 3 examined some well-known models of lexical processing – Morton's logogen model, Marslen-Wilson's cohort model and Forster's search model – and also considered Levelt's 'blueprint for the speaker', which assigns a central mediating role to the lexicon. In addition, it also looked at the modularity hypothesis and connectionism from a lexical point of view. Some themes to emerge from this discussion include: the notion of componentiality combined with connectivity, doubts about the suggestion that lexical processing is strictly linear, the necessity of giving a plausible account of context effects, the difficulty of separating linguistic knowledge from pragmatic knowledge, the dynamic nature of lexical knowledge, the requirement on lexical models to exhibit a capacity to account for multilingual processing, and the growing importance of the idea that lexical processing is based on varying patterns of activation (and possibly inhibition) of very complex networks.

In Chapter 4 we turned specifically to a review of research relating to the L2 mental lexicon, focusing on two important issues in particular: (1) the question of whether the L2 mental lexicon is intrinsically more form-based than the L1 mental lexicon, and (2) the question of whether or not the L1 lexicon and the L2 lexicon are connected. With regard to (1), Meara's interpretation of the Birkbeck Vocabulary Project data as favouring the formal view of the L2 mental lexicon was challenged, and a variety of research findings was adduced in support of the position that, while formal processing may play a particularly important part in the early stages of the learning of a new word – in both L2 and L1 – as the learning of the new item advances, it is on meaning rather than form that the principal acquisitional effort is of necessity concentrated – again in both L2 and L1. Concerning (2), the chapter cited a range of research against the proposition that the L1 lexicon and the L2 lexicon are completely disconnected from each other, but also findings against the notion of total integration. The evidence reviewed suggests that L1 and L2 lexis may be separately stored, but that the two systems are in communication, and that the relationship between a given L2 word and a given L1 word in the mental lexicon will vary from individual to individual and will depend on the degree to which resemblances are perceived between the L2 item and the L1 item in question.

Chapter 5 comprised a general overview of the Trinity College Dublin Modern Languages Research Project (TCD MLRP) –

referring to subjects, methodology and computerization. The methodology section concentrated particular attention on the use of the C-test, because of its unfamiliarity and also because its validity as a means of gathering lexical data has been called into question. The chapter ended with a summary of issues related to the L2 lexicon which have been addressed by papers and publications emanating from the project.

The final three chapters – Chapters 6–8 – reported on MLRP findings which shed light on, respectively, form and meaning in the L2 mental lexicon, cross-linguistic aspects of the mental lexicon, and communication strategies in response to L2 lexical problems. The data discussed in Chapter 6 indicated that the lexical interconnections and operational procedures that were to the fore in subjects' responses to the MLRP instruments were semantico-pragmatic in nature. Chapter 7 presented evidence which, while not suggestive of full integration between the L2 mental lexicon and the L1 mental lexicon, certainly made it very clear that our subjects were making frequent use of connections between the two lexicons, which in turn pointed to the likelihood of an essential similarity between the L2 lexicon and the L1 lexicon. Chapter 8 looked at patterns of strategy deployment in response to L2 lexical problems posed by the MLRP instruments, and interpreted the MLRP data as indicating the existence of individual preferred strategic styles which could be related to beliefs and perceptions about the optimal approach to acquiring a given L2 in specific circumstances.

Some implications of the foregoing discussion

The conclusions which flow from the discussion in the various chapters summarized above have implications both for research and for teaching. An obvious starting-point for an exploration of such implications is what was said at the outset concerning current views of what the lexicon actually is. On the one hand, we can observe that the trend both in linguistic research and in language teaching towards an increasing interest in lexical matters seems to be fully justified by the evidence of the importance of lexis in the functioning of language. On the other hand, since it is now clear that there is a question mark over the extent to which it is in fact possible to conceive of lexis as separate from other aspects of language, it no longer makes any sense to see lexical research simply in terms of a focus on individual content words nor to see the teaching of lexis in terms of instruction around individual forms and concepts.

With regard to research, this must at the very least mean that we need to look very closely and critically at methodologies which address lexis in a decontextualized and piecemeal manner. This is not to say that such instruments are of no value in lexical research, but it is to say that the data collected using *only* such instruments are incapable of providing anything other than very partial insights into the nature of the lexicon. More radically, given the doubts that have been expressed about the possibility of identifying a distinct lexical construct, researchers would do well to exercise caution with regard to what they claim about the extent to which their data and their analyses are addressing strictly lexical issues. Even 'playing safe' in what we opt to include under the lexical heading, may not, as Chapter 1 suggests, in the end guarantee the security of the borders of lexical research.

On the pedagogical front, too, we need to re-examine our assumptions. In the light of our discussion of the domain of the lexicon, it becomes clear that much of what has passed for 'vocabulary teaching' in both L2 and L1 classrooms addresses only the tip of the tip of the lexical iceberg – whether or not we see that iceberg as separable from the icecap of language in its entirety. This criticism is as applicable to certain 'modern' approaches such as the use of lexical 'grids' as it is to more traditional approaches such as the rote learning of word lists. Again, there is no attempt being made here to 'rubbish' the techniques in question, which undoubtedly have useful roles to play; what very definitely is being suggested, on the other hand, is that approaches which deal in isolated items have to be supplemented by approaches which give full value to the collocational, grammatical and other dimensions of the lexicon.

Moving on to acquisition and processing issues, the message of a great deal of the content of this volume has been that L2 lexical acquisition and processing has much in common with L1 acquisition and processing. Not only are similar challenges set in both cases, but many of the operations involved are apparently identical. In general terms this obviously offers support to the longstanding research tradition which has assumed that, in respect of the lexicon as in other respects, the way things work in L1 constitutes a kind of 'default position' for the way things work in L2 also. The general implication for teaching is obviously that it is not appropriate to see the instructional treatment of the L2 lexicon as belonging to a different order of reality from L1 lexical instruction.

At a more detailed level, we have seen that the respective roles of form and meaning in lexical acquisition and processing are similar in L1 and L2. On the question of form, we have noted that establishing accurate internal representations of formal attributes is especially important in the early stages of dealing with new items. This points to the desirability of a research programme which would compare the formal minutiae of first attempts at reproducing novel lexical material with micro as well as macro aspects of progress towards the internalization of such material. It also suggests that the notion of language aptitude – and lexical aptitude in particular – might be fruitfully re-examined from the point of view of capacity to replicate form. A possible pedagogical reading of findings in this area is that the natural tendency to rehearse new lexis should be reinforced in class by the devising and deployment of at least some activities which encourage the repetition of forms, and that – at a metacognitive level – teachers should attempt to inculcate in learners the practice of privately repeating over to themselves any new lexical forms they encounter, wherever such encounters occur.

As far as meaning is concerned, two points of detail are worthy of note in the present context: the first is the importance in both L1 and L2 of semantic associations between lexical items; the second is the role of image in lexical operations – again in both L1 and L2. Concerning semantic associations – to the cross-linguistic aspect of which we shall return a little later – these (1) clearly inform the apprehension of new lexical items – even in the early stages of this process, (2) are a significant organizing element in the mental lexicon, and (3) are a factor in lexical access. Given these facts, lexical research which ignores the role of semantic associations in analysing lexical acquisitional and processing data – by, for example, focusing exclusively on formal factors – must be considered reductionist, and, as far as teaching lexis is concerned, there is clearly support for a policy of exploiting semantic associations through the promotion of associative mnemonic strategies. In relation to the role of image, the success of visualization techniques in L1 and L2 lexical learning would seem to cry out for further investigation, but already suggests that lexical research needs to be more attentive to visualization and imageability across the board. Regarding lexically oriented pedagogy, there seems to be a good empirical basis for the classroom use of the keyword technique and other visualizing practices, and indeed for encouraging the practice of visualization in more or less all circumstances.

It might be worth recalling, as a footnote to the above thoughts on the roles of form and meaning in the mental lexicon, that one facet of lexical acquisition which has been widely referred to in both the L1 and the L2 literature, namely the use of incidental lexical acquisition, provides excellent evidence of the operation of both formal and semantic processes. It will, of course, not come as a great surprise to most people that research confirms the reality of incidental vocabulary acquisition. The popular assumption has always been that people 'pick up' words from their general experience of linguistic interaction in the absence of any specific instruction.

One aspect of the discussion of incidental lexical learning that requires some attention from researchers is what precisely they mean by 'incidental'. If it is the case – and it seems to be – that in some schools of thought the concept of incidental is so narrow that it excludes the notion of any attention at all being paid by readers or listeners to the forms or meanings of the constituent elements of discourse to which they are exposed, then a large portion of the relevant research is actually defined out of the picture as *ir*relevant. If confusion is not to reign endlessly in this debate, some tuning of terminological violins is clearly called for. The more important point, however, is that, whatever the labels used, there is a widespread consensus that, in situations where learning is not the overt objective, lexical acquisition is enhanced when an active approach is taken towards exploiting all available clues in dealing with unfamiliar items. More research on the questions of precisely what is usefully exploitable in such situations – and in what ways – would be welcome, but there can be no doubt that context-based lexical acquisition is a reality and that studies of lexical acquisition need to take account of this reality.

Incidental vocabulary acquisition might at first sight appear to offer no role to the teacher. However, on a broad definition of 'incidental' at least, this impression is mistaken. There would seem to be good grounds for thinking that teachers could make a valuable contribution in this matter by intervening at a metacognitive level. On the evidence, it would appear that training learners in utilizing contextual information, drawing on knowledge of related forms, etc. in encounters with new words, coupled with simple general advice such as 'Try to work out what the word means before going to the dictionary', could yield substantial benefits in terms of numbers of words acquired and the durability of lexical gains.

Having considered some of the implications of similarities between the L1 mental lexicon and the L2 mental lexicon, let us now turn our attention to the implications of the evidence that the two lexicons are connected and in communication with each other. The obvious major difference, of course, between a situation where just one language is present 'in the head' of an individual and a situation where one or more additional languages have been learned is that in the first case there is no lexical system other than that of the L1 to refer to, whereas in the latter case the L1 lexical knowledge is a constant background against which all further lexical knowledge is acquired.

It is apparent from much of the research discussed above that consultation of the L1 lexicon will inevitably be a feature of the learning and use of L2 lexis. As we have seen, both the formal and the semantic dimensions of lexical acquisition and processing are affected by such cross-lexical consultation. For example, the fact that a particular L2 word may in formal terms resemble an L1 word may not only have an influence on how the former is pronounced or written by learners but it is also likely to lead to attempts to link it to the L1 word in semantic terms (see comments on semantic associations above), and may even cause it to be stored as a variant or dependency of the L1 item. No L2 lexical researcher can afford to ignore such facts as these. That is to say, any attempt to investigate L2 lexical acquisition or processing in isolation from the L1 lexical resources to which they have continual access will be likely to be fatally flawed by distorting incompleteness.

Lexical cross-consultation is also something that L2 teachers and learners have to be aware of. Let it be said immediately that, contrary to the impression that in the past has been given in some quarters by treating cross-linguistic influence exclusively in terms of 'interference', the inevitability of cross-lexical interaction is by no means unqualifiedly bad news. On the contrary, where related languages are concerned, the cross-lexical factor can greatly enhance accessibility in receptive mode (thus rendering the L2 lexical input more comprehensible and thus more readily acquirable than would otherwise be the case), and, even in productive mode, a carefully managed use of borrowing strategies can be extremely effective in stretching limited L2 resources. One response to the cross-lexical dimension, therefore, would be to 'make friends with' it by adopting a 'language awareness' approach and exploring areas where strategic transfer between given languages will and will not work. Another would be simply to take comfort in the indications that as proficiency increases, L2 lexical dependency on L1 seems to diminish. In any case, any temptation to react to cross-lexical influence by attempting to implement a systematic policy of extirpation needs to be resisted, since it is doomed to failure and is likely simply to inhibit and demotivate learners.

Exploring the L2 mental lexicon: some hopes of things to come

A number of observations have already been offered concerning areas where a need for more research is indicated. There are many others, but it would patently be a fool's errand to seek to enumerate them exhaustively. (Is there, after all, *any* corner of the territory of second language acquisition research which has been so comprehensively reconnoitred that further expeditions could be deemed superfluous?) A more feasible exercise in the present context is to consider what kinds of research are likely to be most useful to us in illuminating the issues raised in this book. My personal view of how research in this area should proceed can be summed up (with apologies to Grice!) in three maxims: be collaborative; be qualitative as well as quantitative; be durative. Discussion in the remainder of this section is organized under the rubrics of these three maxims.

Be collaborative

One conclusion that seems very clear from earlier chapters of the book, and indeed from the earlier sections of the present chapter, is that research into the L2 mental lexicon has to take account of what is going on in a whole spectrum of other areas. Thus, for example, in order to keep abreast of the state of the debate concerning the nature of the relationship between the lexicon and other linguistic domains, such research has to keep a weather eye on developments in (at least) linguistic theory, computational linguistics and general psycholinguistics; in order to continue to be informed by as wide a range as possible of relevant methodologies, findings and ideas, it has to be attentive to work being carried out with reference to L1 lexical acquisition and processing; and in order not to miss any lessons that might usefully be learned from the implementation of lexically oriented programmes and projects in the pedagogical sphere, it needs to stay aware of what is happening in language teaching and language testing.

Alas, no one poor mortal can be expected to be truly expert across such a range of specialisms. Hence the plea for collaboration. What is clearly required is the establishment of research teams including representatives from each of the various areas mentioned. This is not necessarily an impossible dream; we have the model set for us by research projects proceeding under the banner of 'cognitive science', which routinely involve co-operation between theoretical linguists, computer scientists and psychologists. We also have the example of a small number of linguistics departments where theoretical linguists, applied linguists and psycholinguists sit down together in order to bring their respective perspectives and their collective experience and knowledge to bear on specific issues that are of interest to all of them. The key to making such collaboration a more typical feature of our landscape is probably to focus on topics which facilitate a symbiotic relationship between researchers – topics which are of interest and importance to all members of the team and about which each member can genuinely learn from the input of other members. Since the lexicon sits at the crossroads of so many research paths in linguistics, lexical issues would appear to be particularly promising in this connection.

Be qualitative as well as quantitative

Research methodology textbook writers have been telling us for years – and in very persuasive terms – that both quantitative and qualitative research have contributions to make, and that there are no real grounds for seeing the quantitative paradigm and the qualitative paradigm as mutually antipathetic or as opposing camps in an ideological war. Indeed, an oft-repeated cliché in this context is that the best research has both a quantitative and a qualitative dimension. Unfortunately, the situation on the ground in second language acquisition research – and in other areas of linguistics – is that there is still very much a conflictual feeling in the air in respect of methodological predilections. Thus, for example, recipients of the newsletter of a certain language-research association recently had the dubious pleasure of reading an individual contribution which denounced qualitative research in such fervid and vitriolic terms that one might have suspected the Holy Inquisition of having had a hand in the matter. On the other hand, participants in a recent international language-awareness conference were treated to the spectacle of an eminent speaker being criticized by a no less eminent member of the audience for posing a research question which actually required a quantitative answer. (When such bigotry is confined to debates between peers it can perhaps be laughed off as mere academic knockabout; when, however, it is brought to bear in less equal encounters, such as the reviewing of articles submitted to journals or the examination of theses, it is anything but funny.)

The formulation of the above maxim might be taken to suggest that the quantitative camp has more to learn or is more at fault than the qualitative camp. In overall terms this is certainly not true. Perhaps, especially given the quasi-religious character of some of the exchanges between the two camps, a more appropriate formulation to cover the situation at large would have been: be ecumenical. However, there is perhaps a sense in which the qualitative approach stands in particular need of advocacy in the domain of lexical research. Lexical units look as if they are easy to isolate and easy to count, and, probably for this reason, the lexicon has tended to attract more quantitative attention than some other aspects of language. This applies not only at the language-descriptive level (word-frequency counts, etc.), but also at the psycholinguistic level (quantification of 'vocabulary size', mathematical modelling of 'vocabulary growth', etc.). In fact, as we have seen, it is a good deal less straightforward to identify the boundaries of lexical units than might once have been imagined, and this alone ought to give pause to those who are inclined to take an exclusively quantitative line in the lexical sphere. More generally, quantitative purists would do well to consider the cautionary observations of statistically sophisticated linguists such as Van Hout (e.g., 1996), who points out that for some purposes quantitative analysis is simply a confusing superfluity, as well as to reflect on the fact that certain types of evidence (introspective commentaries, for example) lose much of their value if one treats them simply as constellations of countables. Clearly, what we need to do in investigating the L2 mental lexicon is to take the textbook-writers' cliché to heart and to move forward under both quantitative and qualitative power.

Be durative

One of the criticisms which has been levelled at the current state of L2 lexical acquisition and processing research by Meara (e.g., 1993a) is that there are too many studies in this area which can be characterized as 'one-off'. The impression one has, at least from Meara's account – based, after all, on more than a decade's experience of compiling bibliographies in the lexical domain – is that many researchers treat the L2 mental lexicon as an interesting side-issue to dabble in for a time, but not a very long time. There are at least two unfortunate consequences of such transitoriness. On the one hand, discussion that arises in particular studies is not followed through, so that questions raised remain unanswered, lines of argument sketched remain undeveloped, and proposals advanced remain unsubstantiated. On the other hand, the time-frames within which many researchers have their 'lexical phase' is often too short to allow for the possibility of meaningfully longitudinal research.

With regard to the first point, there are, as is abundantly clear from the content of this book, no fewer issues to be resolved, insights to be fleshed out and tracts of *terra incognita* to be mapped in this domain than in any other area of L2 research. Indeed, because of its longstanding Cinderella status, it is more densely populated by question marks than most other areas. Continuity of treatment and perseverance of reflection on the part of individual L2 lexical acquisition and processing researchers are thus absolute necessities, if the research they engage in is to have any hope of making significant advances. With regard to the point about longitudinal research, the case that can be made for such research in relation to L2 lexical acquisition is in most respects identical to that which has been made a thousand times in relation to other aspects of L2 acquisition. There is one respect, however, in which the case for longitudinal research in respect of lexical acquisition is even stronger. We have seen that the learning of new lexis – in both L1 and L2 – is potentially a lifelong process. Accordingly, there is scope here for some very long-term longitudinal studies indeed.

And why should L2 lexical acquisition and processing research not think in years and even decades rather than weeks and months? In relation both to longitudinal research and to general investigative follow-through, surely we ought by now to have reached a stage where L2 lexical research can begin to resist the temptation to flit from topic to topic under the impetus of changing intellectual fashions, and can at last show some serious commitment to answering specific questions, however long it takes.

References

Aaronson, D. & Rieber, R. (eds.) 1975. *Developmental psycholinguistics and communication disorders*. New York: New York Academy of Sciences.

Aarts, F. 1991. OALD, LDOCE and COBUILD: three dictionaries of English compared. In Granger (ed.), 1991.

Abraham, R. & Vann, R. 1987. Strategies of two language learners: a case study. In *Learner strategies in language learning*, A. Wenden & J. Rubin (eds.). Hemel Hempstead: Prentice Hall International.

Abunuwara, E. 1992. The structure of the tringual lexicon. *European Journal of Cognitive Psychology* 4: 311–322.

Aitchison, J. 1981. *Language change: progress or decay?* London: Fontana.

Aitchison, J. 1992. *Introducing language and mind*. Harmondsworth: Penguin.

Aitchison, J. 1994. *Words in the mind: an introduction to the mental lexicon*. 2nd edn. Oxford: Blackwell.

Allen, E. & Vallette, R. 1972. *Modern language classroom techniques: a handbook*. New York: Harcourt, Brace Jovanovich.

Allen, R. E. 1990. *The Concise Oxford Dictionary*. 8th edn. Oxford: Oxford University Press.

Allport, A. & Funnell, E. 1981. The components of the mental lexicon. *Philosophical Transactions of the Royal Society of London* B 295: 397–410.

Anderman, G. & Rogers, M. (eds.) 1996. *Words, words, words: the translator and the language learner*. Clevedon: Multilingual Matters.

Anderson, J. & Jordan, A. 1928. Learning and retention of Latin words and phrases. *Journal of Educational Psychology* 19: 485–496.

Anderson, J. A. & Rosenfeld, E. (eds.) 1988. Neurocomputing: foundations of research. Cambridge, MA. MIT Press.

Anderson, J. R. 1976. *Language, memory and thought*. Hillsdale, NJ: Erlbaum.

Anderson, J. R. 1983. *The architecture of cognition*. Cambridge, MA: Harvard University Press.

Anderson, R., Reynolds, R., Schallert, D. & Goetz, E. 1977. Frameworks for comprehending discourse. *American Educational Research Journal* 14: 367–381.

Anglin, J. 1970. *The growth of word meaning*. Cambridge, MA: MIT Press.

Anglin, J. 1977. *Word, object and conceptual development.* New York: Norton.

Appel, R. & Muysken, P. 1987. *Language contact and bilingualism.* London: Edward Arnold.

Ard, J. & Gass, S. 1987. Lexical constraints on syntactic acquisition. *Studies in Second Language Acquisition* 9: 235–255.

Arenberg, D. 1983. Memory and learning do decline late in life. In *Aging: a challenge to science and society. Volume 3: Behavioural sciences and conclusions*, J. Birren, H. Thomae & M. Marois (eds.). Oxford: Oxford University Press..

Arnaud, P. 1989. Vocabulary and grammar: a multitrait-multimethod investigation. In Nation & Carter (eds.). 1989.

Arnaud, P. 1992. Objective lexical and grammatical characteristics of L2 written compositions and the validity of separate component tests. In Arnaud & Béjoint (eds.), 1992.

Arnaud, P. & Béjoint, H. (eds.) 1992. *Vocabulary and applied linguistics.* Basingstoke: Macmillan.

Arnberg, L. & Arnberg, P. 1985. The relation between code differentiation and language mixing in bilingual three- to four-year-old children. *Bilingual Review* 12: 20–32.

Arthur, B., Weiner, R., Culver, M., Lee, J. & Thomas, D. 1980. The register of impersonal discourse to foreigners: verbal adjustments to foreign accent. In *Discourse Analysis in Second Language Research*, D. Larsen-Freeman (ed.). Rowley, MA: Newbury House.

Asch, S. & Nerlove, H. 1969. The development of double-function terms in children: an exploratory investigation. In *The psychology of language: thought and instruction*, J. Cecco (ed.). New York: Holt, Rinehart & Winston.

Atkinson, R. & Raugh, M. 1975. An application of the mnemonic keyword method to the acquisition of a Russian vocabulary. *Journal of Experimental Psychology: Human Learning and Memory* 104: 126–133.

Backus, A. 1996. *Two in one: bilingual speech of Turkish immigrants in the Netherlands.* Tilburg: Tilburg University Press.

Baddeley, A., Papagno, C. & Vallar, G. 1988. When long-term learning depends on short-term storage. *Journal of Memory and Language* 27: 586–595.

Baetens Beardsmore, H. 1982. *Bilingualism: basic principles.* Clevedon: Multilingual Matters.

Baker, L. 1974. The lexicon: some psycholinguistic evidence. *UCLA Working Papers in Phonetics* 26.

Balota, D., Ferraro, F. & Connor, L. 1991. On the early influence of meaning in word recognition: a review of the literature. In *The psychology of word meanings*, P. Schwanenflugel (ed.). Hillsdale, NJ: Erlbaum.

Bar-Adon, A. 1959. *Lesonam hameduberet sel hayeladim beyisrael* (*Children's Hebrew in Israel*). Ph.D. thesis. Hebrew University of Jerusalem.

Bar-Adon, A. & Leopold, W. (eds.) 1971. *Child language: a book of readings*. Englewood Cliffs, NJ: Prentice-Hall.
Barrett, M. 1978. Lexical development and overextension in child language. *Journal of Child Language* 5: 205–219.
Barrett, M. 1983. Scripts, prototypes and the early acquisition of word meaning. *Working Papers of the London Psycholinguistics Research Group* 5: 17–26.
Barrett, M. 1986. Early semantic representations and early semantic development. In Kuczaj & Barrett (eds.), 1986.
Bates, E., Benigni, L., Bretherton, I., Camaioni, L. & Volterra, V. 1979. *The emergence of symbols: cognition and communication in infancy.* New York: Academic Press.
Bates, E., Bretherton, I. & Snyder, L. 1988. *From first words to grammar: individual differences and dissociable mechanisms.* Cambridge: Cambridge University Press.
Bates, E., Camaioni, L. & Volterra, V. 1975. The acquisition of performatives prior to speech. *Merrill-Palmer Quarterly* 21: 205–226.
Bateson, M. 1975. Mother–infant exchanges: the epigenesis of conversational interaction. In Aaronson & Rieber (eds.), 1975.
Baur, R. & Meder, G. 1989. Die Rolle der Muttersprache bei der schulischen Sozialisation ausländischer Kinder. *Diskussion Deutsch* 20: 119–135.
Beauvillain, C. & Grainger, J. 1987. Accessing interlexical homographs: some limitations of a language-selective access. *Journal of Memory and Language* 26: 658–672.
Bechtel, W. & Abrahamsen, A. 1991. *Connectionism and the mind.* Cambridge, MA: Blackwell.
Becker, C. & Killion, T. 1977. Interaction of visual and cognitive effects in word recognition. *Journal of Experimental Psychology: Human Perception and Performance* 3: 389–401.
Benoussan, M. & Laufer, B. 1984. Lexical guessing in context in EFL reading comprehension. *Journal of Research in Reading* 7: 15–32.
Benson, F. 1979. Neurologic correlates of anomia. In *Studies in neurolinguistics*, H. Whitaker & H. A. Whitaker (eds.), Volume 4. New York: Academic Press.
Benveniste, E. 1966. *Problèmes de linguistique générale I.* Paris: Gallimard.
Berger, D., Drosdowski, G. & Käge, O. 1985. *Duden: richtiges und gutes Deutsch.* Mannheim: Dudenverlag.
Bever, T. 1981. Normal acquisition processes explain the critical period for language learning. In *Individual differences and universals in language learning aptitude*, K. Diller (ed.). Rowley, MA: Newbury House.
Bialystok, E. 1983. Inferencing: testing the 'Hypothesis-Testing' hypothesis. In *Classroom-oriented research in second-language acquisition*, H. Seliger & M. Long (eds.). Rowley, MA: Newbury House.
Bialystok, E. 1990. *Communication strategies: a psychological analysis of second-language use.* Oxford: Blackwell.
Bialystok, E. 1991a. Metalinguistic dimensions of bilingual language proficiency. In E. Bialystok (ed.), 1991b.

Bialystok, E. (ed.) 1991b. *Language processing in bilingual children.* Cambridge: Cambridge University Press.
Biemiller, A. 1970. The development of the use of graphic and contextual information as children learn to read. *Reading Research Quarterly* 6: 75–96.
Bierwisch, M. & Schreuder, R. 1992. From concepts to lexical items. *Cognition* 41: 23–60.
Bley-Vroman, R. 1989. What is the logical nature of foreign language learning? In *Linguistic perspectives on second language acquisition*, S. Gass & J. Schachter (eds.). Cambridge: Cambridge University Press.
Bley-Vroman, R. 1994. Updating the Fundamental Difference Hypothesis. Paper presented at the Fourth Annual Conference of the European Second Language Association (EUROSLA), Aix-en-Provence.
Bloom, L. 1973. *One word at a time: the use of single word utterances before syntax*. The Hague: Mouton.
Bloom, P. (ed.) 1993. *Language acquisition: core readings*. Hemel Hempstead: Harvester Wheatsheaf.
Bloomfield, L. 1933. *Language*. New York: Holt, Rinehart & Winston.
Blum, S. & Levenston, E. 1978. Universals in lexical simplification. *Language Learning* 28: 399–416.
Boden, M. 1979. *Piaget*. London: Fontana.
Bolinger, D. 1965. The atomization of meaning. *Language* 41: 555–573.
Bomba, P. & Siqueland, E. 1983. The nature and structure of infant form categories. *Journal of Experimental Child Psychology* 35: 295–328.
Bongaerts, T., Kellerman, E. & Bentlage, A. 1987. Perspective and proficiency in L2 referential communication. *Studies in Second Language Acquisition* 9: 171–200.
Bongaerts, T. & Poulisse, N. 1989. Communication strategies in L1 and L2: same or different? *Applied Linguistics* 10: 253–268.
Borland, H. 1984. *The acquisition of some features of English syntax by four groups of adolescent immigrants to Australia*. Ph.D. thesis. University of Edinburgh.
Bowerman, M. 1976. Semantic factors in the acquisition of rules for word use and sentence construction. In *Normal and deficient child language*, D. Morehead & A. Morehead (eds.). Baltimore, MD: University Park Press.
Bowerman, M. 1978. The acquisition of word meanings: an investigation of some current conflicts. In Waterson & Snow (eds.), 1978.
Boyd, S. 1993. Attrition or expansion? Changes in the lexicon of Finnish and American adult bilinguals in Sweden. In *Progression and regression in language: sociocultural, neuropsychological and linguistic perspectives*, K. Hyltenstam & A. Viberg (eds.). Cambridge: Cambridge University Press.
Brady, S. 1986. Short-term memory, phonological processing and reading ability. *Annals of Dyslexia* 36: 138–153.
Brady, S., Mann, V. & Schmidt, R. 1987. Errors in short-term memory for good and poor readers. *Memory and Cognition* 15: 444–453.

Brady, S., Poggie, E. & Merlott, M. 1986. *An investigation of speech perception abilities in children who suffer in reading skill.* Status Report on Speech Research SR-85. Haskins Laboratories.

Brady, S., Shankweiler, D. & Mann, V. 1983. Speech perception and memory coding in relation to reading ability. *Journal of Experimental Child Psychology* 33: 345–367.

Braine, M. 1971. The acquisition of language in infant and child. In Reed (ed.), 1971.

Brami-Mouling, M. 1977. Notes sur l'adaptation de l'expression verbale de l'enfant en fonction de l'âge de son interlocuteur. *Archives de Psychologie* 45: 225–234.

Brédart, S. 1980. Un problème de métalinguistique: l'explication des échecs de communication chez l'enfant de 8 à 12 ans. *Archives de Psychologie* 48: 303–321.

Brédart, S. & Rondal, J.-A. 1982. *L'analyse du langage chez l'enfant: les activités métalinguistiques.* Brussels: Pierre Mardaga.

Bresnan, J. & Kaplan, R. 1982. Introduction: grammars as mental representations of language. In *The mental representation of grammatical relations*, J. Bresnan (ed.). Cambridge, MA: MIT Press.

Bretherton, I. 1988. How to do things with one word: the ontogenesis of intentional message making in infancy. In Smith & Locke (eds.) 1988.

Britton, J. 1970. *Language and learning.* Harmondsworth: Penguin.

Broeder, P. & Plunkett, K. 1994. Connectionism and second language acquisition. In N. Ellis (ed.), 1994d.

Browman, C. 1978. Tip of the tongue and slip: implications for language processing. *UCLA Working Papers in Phonetics* 42.

Brown, C. 1993. Factors affecting the acquisition of vocabulary: frequency and saliency of words. In Huckin, Haynes & Coady (eds.), 1993.

Brown, C. & Payne, M. 1994. Five essential steps of processes in vocabulary learning. Paper presented at the TESOL Convention, Baltimore, MD.

Brown, R. 1958a. How shall a thing be called. *Psychological Review* 65: 14–21.

Brown, R. 1958b. *Words and things.* Glencoe, IL: Free Press.

Brown, R. 1973. *A first language.* London: Allen & Unwin.

Brown, R. & Berko, J. 1960. Word association and the acquisition of grammar. *Child Development* 31: 1–14.

Brown, R. & McNeill, D. 1966. The 'tip of the tongue' phenomenon. *Journal of Verbal Learning and Verbal Behavior* 5: 325–327.

Brown, T. & Perry, F. 1991. A comparison of three learning strategies for ESL vocabulary acquisition. *TESOL Quarterly* 25: 655–670.

Brudhiprabha, P. 1972. *Error analysis: a psycholinguistic study.* MA thesis. McGill University.

Bruner, J. 1974–75. From communication to language – a psychological perspective. *Cognition* 3: 255–287.

Bruner, J. 1975. The ontogenesis of speech acts. *Journal of Child Language* 2: 1–19.

Bruner, J. 1980. Afterword. In *The social foundations of language and thought*, D. Olson (ed.). New York: Norton.
Bruner, J. 1983. *Child's talk*. Cambridge: Cambridge University Press.
Bruner, J. & Olver, R. 1963. Development of equivalence transformations in children. In *Basic cognitive processes in children*, J. C. Wright & J. Kagan (eds.). *Monographs of the Society for Research in Child Development* 28 (no. 2), Serial No. 86.
Bruner, J., Olver, R. & Greenfield, P. 1966. *Studies in cognitive growth*. New York: Wiley.
Butterworth, G. 1979. What minds have in common is space: a perceptual mechanism for joint reference in infancy. Paper presented to the Developmental Section, British Psychological Society, Southampton.
Bybee, J. 1988. Morphology as lexical organization. In Hammond & Noonan (eds.), 1988.
Callanan, M. & Markman, E. 1982. Principles of organization in young children's natural language hierarchies. *Child Development* 53: 561–572.
Calvet, L.-J. 1996. *Histoire de l'écriture*. Paris: Plon.
Campbell, R. 1983. Writing non-words to dictation. *Brain and Language* 19: 153–178.
Campbell, R. 1986. Language acquisition and cognition. In Fletcher & Garman (eds.), 1986.
Caramazza, A. & Brones, I. 1979. Lexical access in bilinguals. *Bulletin of the Psychonomic Society* 13: 212–214.
Carey, S. 1978. The child as word-learner. In *Linguistic theory and psychological reality*, M. Halle, J. Bresnan & A. Miller (eds.). Cambridge, MA: MIT Press.
Carey, S. & Bartlett, E. 1978. Acquiring a new word. *Papers and Reports on Child Language Development* 15: 17–29.
Carnap, R. 1956. *Meaning and necessity.* 2nd edn. Chicago: Chicago University Press.
Carroll, J. 1983. Toward a functional theory of names and naming. *Linguistics* 21: 341–371.
Carroll, J. B. 1971. Development of native language skills beyond the early years. In C. Reed (ed.), 1971.
Carston, R. 1988. Language and cognition. In Newmeyer (ed.), 1988.
Carter, A. 1974. Unpublished doctoral dissertation. University of California. *The development of communication in the sensorimotor period: a case study.*
Carter, A. 1978a. The development of systematic vocalizations prior to words: a case study. In Waterson & Snow (eds.), 1978.
Carter, A. 1978b. From sensori-motor vocalization to words: a case study of the evolution of attention-directing communication in the second year. In *Action, gesture and symbol: the emergence of language*, A. Lock (ed.). New York: Academic Press.
Carter, A. 1979. Prespeech meaning relations: an outline of one infant's sensorimotor morpheme development. In *Language acquisition*,

P. Fletcher & M. Garman (eds.) 1st edn. Cambridge: Cambridge University Press.

Carter, R. 1987. *Vocabulary: applied linguistic perspectives*. London: Allen & Unwin.

Carter, R. & McCarthy P. (eds.) 1988. *Vocabulary and language teaching*. London: Longman.

Cassirer, E. 1944. *An essay on man*. New Haven & London: Yale University Press.

Castner, B. 1940. Language development. In *The first five years of life: a guide to the study of the preschool child*, A. Gesell (ed.). London: Methuen.

Celce-Murcia, M. 1978. The simultaneous acquisition of English and French in a two-year-old child. In *Second language acquisition: a book of readings*, E. Hatch (ed.). Rowley, MA: Newbury House.

Champagnol, R. 1974. Association verbale, structuration et rappel libre bilingues. *Psychologie française* 19: 83–100.

Channell, J. 1988. Psycholinguistic considerations in the study of L2 vocabulary acquisition. In R. Carter & McCarthy (eds.), 1988.

Chapelle, C. 1994. Are C-tests valid measures for L2 vocabulary research? *Second Language Research* 10: 157–187.

Chapelle, C. & Abraham, R. 1990. Cloze method: what difference does it make? *Language Testing* 7: 121–146.

Chen, H.-C. & Ho, C. 1986. Development of Stroop interference in Chinese–English bilinguals. *Journal of Experimental Psychology: Learning, Memory and Cognition* 12: 397–401.

Chen, H.-C. & Leung, Y.-S. 1989. Patterns of lexical processing in a non-native language. *Journal of Experimental Psychology: Learning, Memory and Cognition* 15: 316–325.

Chen, M. & Wang, W. 1975. Sound change: actuation and implementation, *Language* 51: 255–281.

Chertok, L. 1989. *Hypnose et suggestion*. Paris: Presses Universitaires de France.

Chomsky, N. 1957. *Syntactic structures*. The Hague: Mouton.

Chomsky, N. 1959. Review of B. F. Skinner *Verbal behavior. Language* 35: 26–58.

Chomsky, N. 1972. *Language and mind*. Enlarged edn. New York: Harcourt Brace Jovanovich.

Chomsky, N. 1979a. Discussion des commentaires de Putnam. In Piattelli-Palmarini (ed.), 1979.

Chomsky, N. 1979b. A propos des structures cognitives et de leur développement: une réponse à Piaget. In Piattelli-Palmarini (ed.), 1979.

Chomsky, N. 1980a. *Rules and reprentations*. Oxford: Blackwell.

Chomsky, N. 1980b. Rules and representations. *The Behavioral and Brain Sciences* 3: 1–15, 42–61.

Chomsky, N. 1981. Principles and parameters in syntactic theory. In *Explanations in linguistics*, N. Hornstein & D. Lightfoot (eds.). London: Longman.

Chomsky, N. 1986. *Knowledge of language: its nature, origin and use*. New York: Praeger.
Chomsky, N. 1988. *Language and problems of knowledge: the Nicaraguan lectures*. Cambridge MA: MIT Press.
Chomsky, N. 1989. Some notes on economy of derivation and representation. *MIT Working Papers in Linguistics* 10: 43–74.
Chomsky, N. 1995. Bare phrase structure. In *Government and Binding Theory and the Minimalist Programme*, G. Webelhuth (ed.). Oxford: Blackwell.
Cieslicka-Ratajczak, A. 1994. The mental lexicon in second language learning. *Studia Anglica Posnaniensia* 29: 105–117.
Claparède, E. 1934. Genèse de l'hypothèse. *Archives de Psychologie* 24: 1–155.
Clark, E. 1973. What's in a word? In *Cognitive development and the acquisition of language*, T. E. Moore (ed.). New York: Academic Press.
Clark, E. 1983. Meanings and concepts. In *Handbook of child psychology. Volume III: Cognitive development*, P. Mussen (ed.). New York: Wiley.
Clark, E. 1987. The principle of contrast: a constraint on language acquisition. In *Mechanisms of language acquisition*, B. MacWhinney (ed.). Hillsdale, NJ: Erlbaum.
Clark, E. 1993. *The lexicon in acquisition*. Cambridge: Cambridge University Press.
Clark, M. 1976. *Young fluent readers*. London: Heinemann.
Clarke, R. & Morton, J. 1983. Cross-modality facilitation in tachistoscopic word recognition. *Quarterly Journal of Experimental Psychology* 35A: 79–96.
Clément, R. & Kruideneier, B. 1983. Orientations in second language acquisition: I. The effects of ethnicity, milieu and target language on their emergence. *Language Learning* 33: 273–291.
Coady, J. & Huckin, T. (eds.) 1997. *Second language vocabulary acquisition: a rationale for pedagogy*. Cambridge: Cambridge University Press.
Cohen, A. 1984. On taking language tests: what the students report. In Mac Mathúna & Singleton (eds.), 1984.
Cohen, A. 1987a. Verbal and imagery mnemonics in second-language vocabulary learning. *Studies in Second Language Acquisition* 9: 43–62.
Cohen, A. 1987b. Using verbal reports in research on language learning. In Faerch & Kasper (eds.), 1987a.
Cohen, A. & Aphek, E. 1980. Retention of second-language vocabulary over time: investigating the role of mnemonic associations. *System* 8: 221–235.
Cohen, A., Segal, M. & Weiss Bar-Simon-Tov, R. 1984. The C-test in Hebrew. *Language Testing* 1: 221–225.
Cohen, R., Duval, C., Pincemin, J. & Sautelet, M. 1992. Compte rendu d'expérience. Evaluation et opinions. In *L'apprentissage précoce de la lecture*, R. Cohen (ed.). 5th edn. Paris: Presses Universitaires de France.
Coleman, L. & Kay, P. 1981. Prototype semantics: the English word 'lie'. *Language* 57: 26–44.

Coles, M. 1982. *Word perception, first language script and learners of English as a second language.* MA dissertation. University of London, Birkbeck College.
Cook, V. 1988. *Chomsky's Universal Grammar: an introduction.* Oxford: Blackwell.
Cook, V. 1991. -*Second language learning and language teaching.* London: Edward Arnold.
Cook, V. 1992. Evidence for multicompetence. *Language Learning* 42: 557–591.
Cook, V. 1993. Wholistic multicompetence – jeu d'esprit or paradigm shift. In Kettemann & Wieden (eds.), 1993.
Cook, V. 1995. Multicompetence and effects of age. In Singleton & Lengyel (eds.), 1995.
Cook, V. 1996. Minimalism and L2 lexical processing. Contribution to the symposium 'L2 lexical processing', organized by D. Singleton & K. de Bot, at the Eleventh AILA World Congress of Applied Linguistics, Jyväskylä. Abstract in Dufva *et al.* (eds.), 1996.
Cook, V. & Newson, M. 1996. *Chomsky's Universal Grammar: an introduction.* 2nd edn. Oxford: Blackwell.
Corder, S.P. 1977. Simple codes and the source of the second language learner's initial heuristic hypothesis. *Studies in Second Language Acquisition* 1: 1–10.
Corder, S.P. 1978. Language-learner language. In *Understanding second and foreign language learning: issues and approaches*, J. Richards (ed.). Rowley, MA: Newbury House.
Corder, S.P. 1983. A role for the mother tongue. In Gass & Selinker (eds.), 1983.
Corrigan, A. & Upshur, J. 1982. Test method and linguistic factors in foreign-language tests. *IRAL* 20: 313–321.
Cottrell, G. & Small, S. 1983. A connectionist scheme for modelling word sense disambiguation. *Cognition and Brain Theory* 6: 89–120.
Cowie, A. 1983. On specifying grammar. In *Lexicography: principles and practice*, R. Hartmann (ed.). London: Academic Press.
Cowie, A. 1988. Stable and creative aspects of vocabulary use. In Carter & McCarthy (eds.), 1988.
Cowie, A., Mackin, R. & McCaig, I. 1975/1983. *Oxford Dictionary of Current Idiomatic English.* 2 volumes. Oxford: Oxford University Press.
Cristoffanini, P., Kirsner, K. & Milech, D. 1986. Bilingual lexical representation: the status of Spanish–English cognates. *Quarterly Journal of Experimental Psychology* 38A: 367–393.
Cromer, R. 1991. *Language and thought in normal and handicapped children.* Oxford: Blackwell.
Crookes, G. & Schmidt, R. 1991. Motivation: reopening the research agenda. *Language Learning* 41: 469–512.
Cruse, D. 1986. *Lexical semantics.* Cambridge: Cambridge University Press.

Crystal, D. 1980. *A first dictionary of linguistics and phonetics.* London: André Deutsch.

Crystal, D. 1986. Prosodic development. In Fletcher & Garman (eds.), 1986.

Cummins, J. 1976. The influence of bilingualism on cognitive growth: a synthesis of research findings and explanatory hypotheses. *Working Papers on Bilingualism* 9: 1–43.

Cummins, J. 1979. Cognitive/academic language proficiency, linguistic interdependence, the optimum age question and some other matters. *Working Papers on Bilingualism* 19: 198–203.

Cummins, J. 1980. The cross-lingual dimensions of language proficiency: implications for bilingual education and the optimal age issues. *TESOL Quarterly* 14: 175–187.

Cummins, J. 1983. Language proficiency and academic achievement. In *Current issues in language testing research*, J. Oller (ed.). Rowley MA: Newbury House.

Cummins, J. 1984. *Bilingualism and special education: issues in assessment and pedagogy.* Clevedon: Multilingual Matters.

Cunha de Freitas, A. 1992. Conscious learning: efficient learning. Paper presented at the NCCLA International Conference on Language Awareness, Bangor (Wales).

Cunningham, L. 1990. *L2 vocabulary: a study of the word association responses of beginning learners of Irish.* M.Phil. dissertation. University of Dublin.

Cutler, A. 1994. Segmentation problems, rhythmic solutions. In Gleitman & Landau (eds.), 1994.

Cutler, A. & Fay, D. 1982. One mental lexicon, phonologically arranged: comments on Hurford's comments. *Linguistic Inquiry* 13: 107–113.

Dagut, M. 1977. Incongruencies in lexical 'gridding' – and application of contrastive semantic analysis to language teaching. *International Review of Applied Linguistics* 15: 221–229.

Dagut, M. & Laufer, B. 1985. Avoidance of phrasal verbs by English learners, speakers of Hebrew – case for contrastive analysis. *Studies in Second Language Acquisition* 7: 73–79.

Darwin, C. 1877. A biographical sketch of an infant. *Mind* 2: 285, 292–294. Reprinted in Bar-Adon & Leopold (eds.), 1971.

Davelaar, E. & Besner, D. 1988. Word identification: imageability, semantics, and the content–functor distinction. *Quarterly Journal of Experimental Psychology* 40A: 789–799.

Davidson, R., Kline, S. & Snow, C. 1986. Definitions and definite noun phrases: indicators of children's decontextualized language skills. *Journal of Research into Childhood Education* 1: 37–48.

Davis, C., Sánchez-Casas, R. & García-Albea, J. 1991. *Bilingual lexical representation as revealed using a masked priming procedure.* Unpublished manuscript. St Louis University, Madrid. Cited by De Groot, 1993, 1995.

De Bot, K. 1992. A bilingual production model: Levelt's '*Speaking*' model adapted. *Applied Linguistics* 13: 1–24.

De Bot, K. & Bongaerts, T. 1996. Variation in lexical production. Contribution to the symposium 'L2 lexical processing', organized by D. Singleton & K. de Bot, at the Eleventh AILA World Congress of Applied Linguistics, Jyväskylä. Abstract in Dufva *et al.* (eds.), 1996.

De Bot, K. & Schreuder, R. 1993. Word production and the bilingual lexicon. In Schreuder & Weltens (eds.), 1993.

De Boysson-Bardies, B., Sagart, L. & Bacri, N. 1981. Phonetic analysis of late babbling: a case study of a French child.–*Journal of Child Language* 8: 511–524.

De Boysson-Bardies, B., Sagart, L. & Durand, C. 1984. Discernible differences in the babbling of infants according to target language. *Journal of Child Language* 11: 1–15.

De Groot, A. 1992. Determinants of word translation. *Journal of Experimental Psychology: Learning, Memory and Cognition* 18: 1001–1018.

De Groot, A. 1993. Word-type effects in bilingual processing tasks: support for a mixed-representational system. In Schreuder & Weltens (eds.), 1993.

De Groot, A. 1995. Determinants of bilingual lexicosemantic organisation. *Computer Assisted Language Learning* 8: 151–180.

De Groot, A., Dannenburg, L. & Hell, J. 1994. Forward and backward word translation by bilinguals. *Journal of Memory and Language* 33: 600–629.

De Groot, A. & Nas, G. 1991. Lexical representation of cognates and noncognates in compound bilinguals. *Journal of Memory and Language* 30: 90–123.

De Houwer, A. 1990. *The acquisition of two languages from birth: a case study.* Cambridge: Cambridge University Press.

Dechert, H. 1987. Analysing language processing through verbal protocols. In Faerch & Kasper (eds.), 1987a.

Dechert, H. & Raupach, M. (eds.) 1989a. *Interlingual processes*. Tübingen: Narr.

Dechert, H. & Raupach, M. (eds.) 1989b. *Transfer in language production.* Norwood, NJ: Ablex.

Deese, J. 1965. *The structure of association in language and thought.* Baltimore MD: Johns Hopkins University Press.

Dell, G. 1986. A spreading-activation theory of retrieval in sentence production. *Cognition* 93: 383–321.

Diller, K. 1971. *Generative Grammar, structural linguistics and language teaching.* Rowley, MA: Newbury House.

Dollerup, C. Glahn, E. Rosenberg Hansen, C. 1989. Vocabularies in the reading process. In Nation & Carter (eds.), 1989.

Dommergues, J.-Y. & Lane, H. 1976. On two independent sources of error in learning the syntax of a second language. *Language Learning* 22: 17–27.

Donnenworth-Nolan, S., Tanenhaus, M. & Seidenberg, M. 1981. Multiple code activation in word recognition: evidence from rhyme monitoring.

Journal of Experimental Psychology: Learning, Memory and Cognition 7: 170–180.
Dooling, D. & Lachman, R. 1971. Effects of comprehension on retention of prose. *Journal of Experimental Psychology* 88: 216–222.
Döpke, S. 1992. *One parent one language: an interactional approach*. Amsterdam: John Benjamins.
Dore, J. 1974. A pragmatic description of early language development. *Journal of Psycholinguistic Research* 3: 343–350.
Dore, J. 1978. Conditions for the acquisition of speech acts. In *The social context of language*, I. Markova (ed.). New Jersey: John Wiley & Sons.
Dore, J., Franklin, M., Miller, R. & Ramer, A. 1976. Transitional phenomena in early child language. *Journal of Child Language* 3: 13–28.
Dosher, B. 1982. Effect of sentence size and network distance on retrieval speed. *Journal of Experimental Psychology: Learning, Memory and Cognition* 8: 173–207.
Dromi, E. 1987. *Early lexical development*. Cambridge: Cambridge University Press.
Drosdowski, G., Müller, W., Scholze-Stubenrecht, W. & Wermke, M. 1991. *Duden: Rechtschreibung der deutschen Sprache*. Mannheim: Dudenverlag.
Dufva, H., Fadjukoff, E., Kelloniemi, L., Luukka, M.-R., Multasuo, T., Nieminen, J. & Taalas, P. (eds.) 1996. *Programme, abstracts: AILA 96*. Jyväskylä: University of Jyväskylä.
Duncker, K. 1926. A qualitative, experimental and theoretical study of productive thinking: solving of comprehensible problems. *Pedagogical Seminary* 33: 642–708.
Dupuy, B. & Krashen, S. 1993. Incidental vocabulary acquisition in French as a second language. – *Applied Language Learning* 4: 55–63.
Duquette, L. 1993. *L'étude de l'apprentissage du vocabulaire en contexte par l'écoute d'un dialogue scénarisé an français langue seconde*. Quebec: Université Laval, Centre International de Recherche en Aménagement Linguistique.
Dušková, L. 1969. On sources of errors in foreign language learning. *IRAL* 7: 11–36.
Eilers, R., Bull, D., Oller, D. & Lewis, D. 1984. The discrimination of vowel duration by infants. *Journal of the Acoustical Society of America* 75: 1213–1218.
Eilers, R., Gavin, W. & Wilson, W. 1979. Linguistic experience and phonemic perception in infancy: a cross-linguistic study. *Child Development* 50: 14–18.
Eimas, P. 1985. The perception of speech in early infancy. *Scientific American* 252: 46–52.
Eimas, P., Siqueland, E., Jusczyk, P. & Vigorito, J. 1971. Speech perception in infants. *Science* 171: 303–306.
Elliot, A. 1981. *Child language*. Cambridge: Cambridge University Press.
Ellis, A. 1985. *The production of spoken words*. In *Progress in the*

psychology of language, A. Ellis (ed.). 2 volumes. Hillsdale, NJ: Lawrence Erlbaum.

Ellis, A. & Beattie, G. 1986. *The psychology of language and communication*. London: Weidenfeld & Nicolson.

Ellis, N. 1994a. Consciousness in second language learning: psychological perspectives on the role of conscious processes in vocabulary acquisition. In *Consciousness in second language learning*, J. Hulstijn & R. Schmidt (eds.) (*AILA Review* 11).

Ellis, N. 1994b. Introduction: implicit and explicit language learning – an overview. In Ellis (ed.), 1994d.

Ellis, N. 1994c. Vocabulary acquisition: the implicit ins and outs of explicit cognitive mediation. In Ellis (ed.), 1994d.

Ellis, N. ed. 1994d. *Implicit and explicit learning of languages*. London: Academic Press.

Ellis, N. 1995. The psychology of foreign language vocabulary acquisition: implications for CALL. *Computer Assisted Language Learning* 8: 103–128.

Ellis, N. & Beaton, A. 1993. Factors affecting the learning of foreign language vocabulary: imagery keyword mediators and phonological short-term memory. *Quarterly Journal of Experimental Psychology: Human Experimental Psychology* 46A: 533–558.

Ellis, N. & Beaton, A. 1995. Psycholinguistic determinants of foreign language vocabulary learning. In Harley (ed.), 1995a.

Ellis, N. & Schmidt, R. 1996. Rules or associations in second language morphological processes. Contribution to the symposium 'L2 lexical processing', organized by D. Singleton & K. de Bot, at the Eleventh AILA World Congress of Applied Linguistics. Jyväskylä. Abstract in Dufva *et al.* (eds.), 1996.

Ellis, R. 1985. *Understanding second language acquisition*. Oxford: Oxford University Press.

Ellis, R. 1994. *The study of second language acquisition*. Oxford: Oxford University Press.

Ellis, R. 1996. Modified input and language acquisition. Paper presented at the eighteenth Annual Conference of the American Association for Applied Linguistics, Chicago.

Ellis, R., Tanaka, Y. & Yamazaki, A. 1995. Classroom interaction, comprehension, and the acquisition of L2 word meanings. In Harley (ed.), 1995a.

Elman, J. 1990a. Finding structure in time. *Cognitive Science* 4: 179–211.

Elman, J. 1990b. Representation and structure in connectionist models. In *Cognitive models of speech processing*, G. Altmann (ed.). Cambridge, MA: MIT Press.

Elman, J. & McClelland, J. 1984. Speech perception as a cognitive process: the interactive activation model. In *Speech and language advances in basic research and practice*, Volume 10, N. Lass (ed.). New York: Academic Press.

Emmorey, K. & Fromkin, V. 1988. The mental lexicon. In Newmeyer (ed.), 1988.

Entwisle, D. 1966. *Word associations of young children*. Baltimore, MD: Johns Hopkins University Press.

Entwisle, D., Forsyth, D. & Muus, R. 1964. The syntagmatic-paradigmatic shift in children's word associations. *Journal of Verbal Learning and Verbal Behavior* 3: 19–29.

Ericsson, K. & Simon, H. 1984. *Protocol analysis: verbal reports as data*. Cambridge, MA: MIT Press.

Ervin, S. 1961. Changes with age in the verbal determinants of word association. *American Journal of Psychology* 74: 361–372.

Evans, C. 1978. *Psychology: a dictionary of the mind, brain and behaviour*. London: Arrow.

Faerch, C. & Kasper, G. (eds.) 1983a. *Strategies in interlanguage communication*. London: Longman.

Faerch, C. & Kasper, G. 1983b. Plans and strategies in foreign language communication. In Faerch & Kasper (eds.), 1983a.

Faerch, C. & Kasper, G. 1984. Two ways of defining communication strategies. *Language Learning* 34: 45–63.

Faerch, C. & Kasper, G. (eds.) 1987a. *Introspection in second language research*. Clevedon: Multilingual Matters.

Faerch, C. & Kasper, G. 1987b. From product to process – introspective methods in second language research. In Faerch & Kasper (eds.), 1987a.

Faerch, C., Haastrup, K. & Phillipson, R. 1984. *Learner language and language learning*. Clevedon: Multilingual Matters.

Fantini, A. 1974. *Language acquisition of a bilingual child: a sociolinguistic perspective (to age 5)*. Brattleboro, VT: The Experiment Press.

Fantini, A. 1985. *Language acquisition of a bilingual child: a sociolinguistic perspective (to age 10)*. Clevedon: Multilingual Matters.

Feitelson, D., Goldstein, Z., Iraqi, J. & Share, D. 1993. Effects of listening to story reading on aspects of literacy acquisition. *Language Learning* 44: 449–491.

Feldman, J. & Ballard, D. 1982. Connectionist models and their properties. *Cognitive Science* 6: 205–254.

Feldmann, U. & Stemmer, B. 1987. Thin___ aloud a__ retrospective da__ in C-te__ taking: diffe____ languages – diffe____ learners – sa__ approaches? In Faerch & Kasper (eds.), 1987a.

Ferguson, C. 1975. Towards a characterization of English foreigner talk. *Anthropological Linguistics* 17: 1–14.

Fillmore, C. 1968. The case for case. In *Universals in linguistic theory*, E. Bach & R. Harms (eds.). New York: Holt, Rinehart & Winston.

Firth, J. 1957. A synopsis of linguistic theory, 1930–1955. In *Studies in linguistic analysis*. Special volume of the Philological Society. Oxford: Blackwell.

Fischler, I. & Bloom, P. A. 1980. Rapid processing of the meaning of sentences. *Memory and Cognition* 8: 216–225.

Flavell, J. 1963. *The developmental psychology of Jean Piaget*. Princeton, NJ: Van Nostrand.

Fletcher, P. & Garman M. (eds.) 1986. *Language acquisition: studies in first language development*. 2nd edn. Cambridge: Cambridge University Press.

Fodor, J. 1975. *The language of thought*. Hassocks, Sussex: Harvester Press; New York: Thomas Y. Crowell.

Fodor, J. 1979. Fixation de croyances et acquisition de concepts. In Piattelli-Palmarini (ed.), 1979.

Fodor, J. 1981. *Representations*. Cambridge, MA: MIT Press.

Fodor, J. 1983. *The modularity of mind: an essay on faculty psychology*. Cambridge, MA: MIT Press.

Fodor, J. 1987a. *Psychosemantics*. Cambridge, MA: MIT Press.

Fodor, J. 1987b. Modules, frames, fridgeons, sleeping dogs and the music of the spheres. In Garfield (ed.), 1987b.

Fodor, J. 1989. Why should the mind be modular? In *Reflections on Chomsky*, A. George (ed.). Oxford: Blackwell.

Fodor, J., Garrett, M. & Parkes, C. 1980. Against definitions. *Cognition* 8: 263–367.

Fodor, J. & Pylshyn, L. 1988. Connectionist and cognitive architecture: a critical analysis. In *Connections and symbols*, S. Pinker & J. Mehler, (eds.). Cambridge, MA: MIT Press.

Forrester, M. 1996. *Psychology of language: a critical introduction*. London: Sage.

Forster, K. 1976. Accessing the mental lexicon. In *New approaches to language mechanisms*, R. Wales & E. Walker (eds.). Amsterdam: North-Holland.

Forster, K. 1979. Levels of processing and the structure of the language processor. In *Sentence processing*, W. Cooper & E. Walker (eds.). Hillsdale, NJ: Erlbaum.

Forster, K. 1981. Priming and the effects of sentence and lexical contexts on naming time: evidence for autonomous lexical processing. *Quarterly Journal of Experimental Psychology* 33A: 465–495.

Forster, K. 1989. Basic issues in lexical processing. In Marslen-Wilson (ed.), 1989b.

Foss, D. 1982. A discourse on semantic priming. *Cognitive Psychology* 14: 590–607.

Freed, B. 1981. Foreigner talk, baby talk, native talk. *International Journal of the Sociology of Language* 28: 19–39.

Fromkin, V. 1971. The non-anomalous nature of anomalous utterances. *Language* 47: 27–52.

Fromkin, V. 1985. Evidence in linguistics. In *Linguistics and linguistic evidence*, R. Robbins & V. Fromkin, (eds.). Newcastle upon Tyne: Grevatt & Grevatt.

Gaies, S. 1977. The nature of linguistic input in formal second language learning: linguistic and communicative strategies. In *On TESOL 77*, H. Brown, C. Yorio & R. Crymes (eds.). Washington DC: TESOL.

Gaies, S. 1979. Linguistic input in first and second language learning. In *Studies in first and second language acquisition*, F. Eckman & A. Hastings, (eds.). Rowley, MA: Newbury House.

Gairns, R. & Redman, S. 1986. *Working with words: a guide to teaching and learning vocabulary*. Cambridge: Cambridge University Press.

Galisson, R. 1991. *De la langue à la culture par les mots*. Paris: CLE international.

Galvin, S. 1988. *Language transfer: advanced and intermediate students of EFL*. M.Phil. dissertation. University of Dublin.

Gardner, H., Kirchner, M., Winner, E. & Perkins, D. 1975. Children's metaphoric productions and preferences. *Journal of Child Language* 2: 125–141.

Gardner, R. 1985. *Social psychology and second language learning: the role of attitudes and motivation*. London: Arnold.

Gardner, R. & Lambert, W. 1972. *Attitudes and motivation in second language learning*. Rowley, MA: Newbury House.

Garfield, J. 1987a. Introduction: carving the mind at its joints. In Garfield (ed.), 1987b.

Garfield, J. (ed.) 1987b. *Modularity in knowledge representation and natural-language understanding*. Cambridge, MA: MIT Press.

Garman, M. 1990. *Psycholinguistics*. Cambridge: Cambridge University Press.

Garnica, O. 1977. Some prosodic and paralinguistic features of speech to young children. In *Talking to children*, C. Snow and C. Ferguson (eds.). Cambridge: Cambridge University Press.

Gass, S. & Selinker, L. (eds.) 1983. *Language transfer in language learning*. Rowley, MA: Newbury House.

Gass, S. & Selinker, L. 1994. The lexicon. Chapter 10 of *Second language acquisition: an introductory course*, S. Gass & L. Selinker. Hillsdale, NJ: Erlbaum.

Gasser, M. 1990. Connectionism and universals of second language acquisition. *Studies in Second Language Acquisition* 12: 179–199.

Gathercole, S. & Baddeley, A. 1989. Evaluation of the role of phonological STM in the development of vocabulary in children: a longitudinal study, *Journal of Memory and Language* 28: 200–213.

Gathercole, S. & Baddeley, A. 1990. Phonological memory deficits in language-disordered children: is there a causal connection? *Journal of Memory and Language* 29: 336–360.

Gathercole, V. 1987. The contrastive hypothesis for the acquisition of word meaning: a reconsideration of the theory.–*Journal of Child Language* 14: 493–531.

Genesee, F., Tucker, R. & Lambert, W. 1975. Communication skills in bilingual children. *Child Development* 46: 1010–1014.

George, H. 1971. English for Asian learners: are we on the right road? *English Language Teaching* 25: 270–277.

Gerard, L. & Scarborough, D. 1989. Language-specific lexical access of homographs by bilinguals. *Journal of Experimental Psychology: Learning, Memory and Cognition* 15: 305–313.

Gerloff, P. 1987. Identifying the unit of analysis in translation: some uses of think-aloud protocol data. In Faerch & Kasper (eds.), 1987a.

Geschwind, N. & Galaburda, A. 1985. Cerebral lateralization: biological mechanisms, association and pathology: I. A hypothesis and a program for research. *Archives of Neurology* 42: 428–459.

Giacobbe, J. 1993–94. Construction des formes lexicales et activité cognitive dans l'acquisition du français langue seconde. In Singleton (ed.), 1993–94a.

Giacobbe, J. & Cammarota, M.-A. 1986. Learners' hypotheses for the acquisition of lexis. *Studies in Second Language Acquisition* 8: 327–342.

Gibson, E. & Levin, H. 1975. On the perception of words: an application of some basic concepts. In *The psychology of reading*, E. Gibson & H. Levin (eds.), Cambridge MA: MIT Press.

Gillette, B. 1987. Two successful language learners: an introspective approach. In Faerch & Kasper (eds.), 1987a.

Gillis, S. & Deschutter, G. 1984. Transitional phenomena revisited: insights into the nominal insight. In *Proceedings of the Interdisciplinary Symposium on Precursors of Speech*. Stockholm.

Gilmore, D. 1990. *Manhood in the making: cultural concepts of masculinity.* New Haven, CT: Yale University Press.

Gleitman, L. & Landau, B. (eds.) 1994. *The acquisition of the lexicon.* Cambridge, MA: MIT Press.

Goodluck, H. 1991. *Language acquisition: a linguistic introduction.* Oxford: Blackwell.

Goodman, K. 1967. Reading: a psycholinguistic guessing game. *Journal of the Reading Specialist* 6: 126–135.

Gough, P. 1972. One second of reading. In *Language by eye and by ear*, J. Kavanagh & I. Mattingly (eds.). Cambridge, MA: MIT Press.

Gough, P. & Cosky, M. 1977. One second of reading again. In *Cognitive Theory II*, N. Castellan, D. Pisani & G. Potts (eds.). Hillsdale, NJ: Erlbaum.

Graham, C. & Belnap, R. 1986. The acquisition of lexical boundaries in English by speakers of Spanish. *IRAL* 24: 273–281.

Grainger, J. 1994. Le lexique bilingue: approches de la psychologie expérimentale. *Revue de Phonétique Appliquée* 112/113: 221–238.

Grainger, J. & Beauvillain, C. 1987. Language blocking and lexical access in bilinguals. *Quarterly Journal of Experimental Psychology* 39A: 295–319.

Grainger, J. & Dijkstra,T. 1992. On the representation and use of language information in bilinguals. In R. Harris (ed.), 1992.

Granger, S. 1993. Cognates: an aid or a barrier to successful L2 vocabulary development? *ITL Review of Applied Linguistics* 99/100: 43–56.

Granger, S. (ed.) 1991. *Perspectives on the English lexicon: a tribute to Jacques van Roey*. Louvain-la-Neuve: Institut de Linguistique (*Cahiers de l'Institut de Linguistique de Louvain* 17).

Grauberg, W. 1971. An error analysis in German of first-year university students. In *Applications of linguistics: selected papers of the Second International Congress of Applied Linguistics*, G. Perren & J. Trim (eds.). Cambridge: Cambridge University Press.

Green, D. 1986. Control, activation and resource: a framework and a model for the control of speech in bilinguals. *Brain and Language* 27: 210–223.

Green, D. 1993. Towards a model of L2 comprehension and production. In Schreuder & Weltens (eds.), 1993.

Grellet, F. 1993. Vers une approche communicative de la traduction. Paper presented at the 1993 National Conference of the French Teachers' Association of Ireland, Dublin.

Grenfell, M. 1995. The first foreign language. In *Language education in the National Curriculum*, C. Brumfit (ed.). Oxford: Blackwell.

Griffiths, P. 1986. Early vocabulary. In Fletcher & Garman (eds.), 1986.

Grinstead, W. 1915. An experiment in the learning of foreign words. *American Psychologist* 9: 407–408.

Grosjean, F. 1982. *Life with two languages: an introduction to bilingualism*. Cambridge, MA: Harvard University Press.

Gross, M. 1990. Lexique – grammaire LADL. Paper presented at the Ninth World Congress of Applied Linguistics (AILA 1990), Halkidiki-Cassandra.

Gross, M. 1991. Lexique et syntaxe. *Travaux de Linguistique* 23: 107–132.

Grossberg, S. & Stone, G. 1986. Natural dynamics of word recognition and recall: attentional priming, learning and resonance. *Psychological Review* 93: 46–74.

Grotjahn, R. 1987a. How to construct and evaluate a C-test: a discussion of some problems and some statistical analyses. In *Taking their measure: the validity and validation of language tests*, R. Grotjahn, C. Klein-Braley & D. Stevenson (eds.). Bochum: Brockmeyer.

Grotjahn, R. 1987b. Ist der C-Test ein Lesetest? In *Lehren und Lernen von Fremdsprachen im Studium*, A. Addison & K. Vogel (eds.). Bochum: AKS.

Grotjahn, R. (ed.) 1992a. *Der C-Test. Theoretische Grundlagen und praktische Anwendungen. Volume 1*. Bochum: Brockmeyer.

Grotjahn, R. 1992b. Der C-Test. Einleitende Bemerkungen. In Grotjahn (ed.), 1992a.

Grotjahn, R. 1992c. Der C-Test im Französischen. Quantitative Analysen. In Grotjahn (ed.), 1992a.

Grotjahn, R. (ed.), 1993. *Der C-Test. Theoretische Grundlagen und praktische Anwendungen. Volume 2*. Bochum: Brockmeyer.

Gruendel, J. 1977. Referential overextension in early language development. *Child Development* 48: 1567–1576.

Guillaume, P. 1927. Les débuts de la phrase dans le langage de l'enfant. *Journal de Psychologie Normale et Pathologique* 24: 1–25.

Gunzi, S. unpublished. *Early language comprehension and production.*

Haastrup, K. 1987. Using thinking aloud and retrospection to uncover learners' lexical inferencing procedures. In Faerch & Kasper (eds.), 1987a.

Haastrup, K. 1991a. *Lexical inferencing procedures or talking about words.* Tübingen: Narr.

Haastrup, K. 1991b. Developing learners' procedural knowledge in comprehension. In Phillipson *et al.* (eds.), 1991.

Haastrup, K. & Phillipson, R. 1983. Achievement strategies in learner/native-speaker interaction. In Faerch & Kasper (eds.), 1983a.

Hallé, P., De Boysson-Bardies, B. & Vihman, M. 1991. Beginnings of prosodic organization: intonation and duration patterns of disyllables produced by Japanese and French infants. *Language and Speech* 34: 299–318.

Halliday, M. 1961. Categories of the theory of grammar. *Word* 17: 241–292.

Halliday, M. 1966. Lexis as a linguistic level. In *In memory of J. R. Firth*, C. Bazell, J. Catford, M. Halliday & R. Robins (eds.). London: Longman.

Halliday, M. 1975. *Learning how to mean: explorations in the development of language*. London: Edward Arnold.

Halliday, M., McIntosh, A. & Strevens, P. 1964. *The linguistic sciences and language teaching*. London: Longman.

Hamers, J. & Lambert, W. 1972. Bilingual interdependence in auditory perception. *Journal of Verbal Learning and Verbal Behavior* 11: 303–310.

Hammond, M. & Noonan, M. (eds.) 1988. *Theoretical morphology.* London: Academic Press.

Harley, B. 1986. *Age in second language acquisition.* Clevedon: Multilingual Matters.

Harley, B. (ed.) 1995a. *Lexical issues in language learning.* Ann Arbor/Amsterdam/Philadelphia: Language Learning/John Benjamins Publishing Company.

Harley, B. 1995b. Introduction: lexical issues in language learning. In Harley (ed.), 1995a.

Harley, B. & King, M. 1989. Verb lexis in the written composition of young L2 learners. *Studies in Second Language Acquisition* 11: 415–439.

Harris, J. 1990. *Early language development: implications for clinical and educational practice*. London: Routledge.

Harris, M. 1992. *Language experience and early language development: from input to uptake*. Hove & Hillsdale, NJ: Lawrence Erlbaum.

Harris, M., Barrett, M., Jones, D. & Brookes, S. 1988. Linguistic input and early word meaning. *Journal of Child Language* 15: 77–94.

Harris, M. & Coltheart, M. 1986. *Language processing in children and adults*. London: Routledge & Kegan Paul.

Harris, M., Jones, D., Brookes, S. & Grant, J. 1986. Relations between the non-verbal context of maternal speech and rate of language development. *British Journal of Developmental Psychology* 4: 261–268.

Harris, M., Jones, D. & Grant, J. 1983. The non-verbal context of mothers' speech to children. *First Language* 4: 21–30.

Harris, M., Yeeles, C. & Oakley, Y. 1991. The development of comprehension in the first year of life. Paper presented to the 1991 Child Language Seminar, Manchester.

Harris, R. (ed.) 1992. *Cognitive processing in bilinguals*. Amsterdam: North-Holland.

Hasan, R. 1987. The grammarian's dream: lexis as most delicate grammar. In *New developments in systemic linguistics*, M. Halliday & R. Fawcett (eds.). London: Pinter.

Hatch, E. 1983. *Psycholinguistics – a second language perspective*. Rowley, MA: Newbury House.

Hatch, E. & Brown, C. 1995. *Vocabulary, semantics and language education*. Cambridge: Cambridge University Press.

Hatch, E. & Farhady, H. 1982. *Research design and statistics for applied linguistics*. Rowley, MA: Newbury House.

Hatch, E., Shapira, R. & Gough, J. 1978. Foreigner talk discourse. *ITL Review for Applied Linguistics* 39/40: 39–60.

Haugen, E. 1953. *The Norwegian language in America*. Philadelphia: University of Pennsylvania Press.

Henning, G. 1973. Remembering foreign language vocabulary: acoustic and semantic parameters. *Language Learning* 23: 185–196.

Henzl, V. 1973. Linguistic register of foreign language instruction. *Language Learning* 23: 207–222.

Henzl, V. 1975. Speech of foreign language teachers: a sociolinguistic register analysis. Paper presented at the Fourth AILA World Congress of Applied Linguistics, Stuttgart.

Herbst, T. 1987. A proposal for a valency grammar of English. In *A spectrum of lexicography*, R. Ilson (ed.). Amsterdam: John Benjamins.

Hickey, T. & Williams, J. (eds.) 1996. *Language, education and society in a changing world*. Clevedon: IRAAL/Multilingual Matters.

Hill, D. 1991. Interlanguage lexis: an investigation of verb choice. *Edinburgh Working Papers in Applied Linguistics* 2: 24–36.

HMSO. 1967. *Children and their primary schools* (The Plowden Report). London: HMSO.

Hosenfeld, C. 1979. A learner in today's foreign language classroom. In *The learner in today's environment*, W. Born (ed.). Montpellier, VT: Capital City Press.

House, J. & Blum-Kulka, S. (eds.) 1986. *Interlingual and intercultural communication. Discourse and cognition in translation*. Tübingen: Narr.

Hsia, S. 1994a. The significance of segmental awareness in learning a second language. Unpublished manuscript. Hong Kong: City Polytechnic of Hong Kong.

Hsia, S. 1994b. ESL learners' knowledge of subcomponents in words: reporting on data from Hong Kong Chinese learners. Paper presented at the Colchester Round Table on Linguistic and Psychological Approaches to L2 Acquisition of Vocabulary, University of Essex.

Huckin, T. & Bloch, J. 1993. Strategies for inferring word meanings in context: a cognitive model. In Huckin, Haynes & Coady (eds.), 1993.

Huckin, T., Haynes, M. & Coady, J. (eds.) 1993. *Second language reading and vocabulary learning*. Norwood, NJ: Ablex.

Hudson, R. 1980. *Sociolinguistics*. Cambridge: Cambridge University Press.

Hulme, C., Maughan, S. & Brown, G. 1991. Memory for familiar and unfamiliar words: evidence for a long-term memory contribution to short-term memory span. *Journal of Memory and Language* 30: 685–701.

Hulstijn, J.1992. Retention of inferred and given word meanings: experiments in incidental vocabulary learning. In Arnaud & Béjoint (eds.), 1992.

Hulstijn, J. 1993–94. L'acquisition incidente du lexique en langue étrangère: ses avantages et ses limites. In Singleton (ed.), 1993–94a.

Hulstijn, J. 1997. Mnemonic methods in foreign language vocabulary learning. In Coady & Huckin (eds.), 1997.

Hulstijn, J. & Tangelder C. 1991. Intralingual interference: lexical errors as a result of formal and semantic similarities among English word-pairs. Paper presented at the First Annual Meeting of the European Second Language Association (EUROSLA), Salzburg.

Hulstijn, J. & Tangelder, C. 1993. Semantic and phonological interference in the mental lexicon of learners of English as a foreign language and native speakers of English. In *Actes: 1er Congrès International: Mémoire et Mémorisation dans l'Acquisition et l'Apprentissage des Langues / Proceedings: 1st International Congress: Memory and Memorization in Acquiring and Learning Languages*, J. Chapelle & M.-T. Claes (eds.). Louvain-la-Neuve: CLL.

Humphreys, G., Evett, L. & Taylor, D. 1982. Automatic phonological priming in visual word recognition. *Memory and Cognition* 10: 576–590.

Hussian, R. 1981. *Geriatric psychology: a behavioral perspective*. New York: Van Nostrand Reinhold.

Ijaz, I. 1986. Linguistic and cognitive determinants of lexical acquisition in a second language. *Language Learning* 36: 401–451.

Inhelder, B. 1979. Langage et connaissance dans le cadre constructiviste. In Piattelli-Palmarini (ed.), 1979.

Inhelder, B. & Piaget, J. 1964. *The early growth of logic in the child: classification and seriation*. London: Routledge & Kegan Paul.

Isaacs, E. & Clark, H. 1987. References in conversation between experts and novices. *Journal of Experimental Psychology: General* 116: 26–37.

Ittzés, K. 1991. Lexical guessing in isolation and context. *Journal of Reading* 34: 360–366.

Jackendoff, R. 1990. *Semantic structures*. Cambridge, MA: MIT Press.

Jackendoff, R. 1992. *Languages of the mind: essays on mental representation*. Cambridge, MA: MIT Press.

Jackson, H. 1988. *Words and their meaning*. London: Longman.

Jacobs, B. & Schumann, J. 1992. Language acquisition and the neurosciences: towards a more integrative perspective. *Applied Linguistics* 13: 282–301.

Jakobovits, L. 1969. Second language learning and transfer theory: a theoretical assessment. *Language Learning* 19: 55–86.

Jakschik, G. 1992. Zum Einsatz des C-Tests in den psychologischen Diensten der Arbeitsämter. Ein C-Test für Deutsch als Zweitsprache. In Grotjahn (ed.), 1992a.

Jakschik, G. 1993. Der C-Test für erwachsene Zweitsprachler als Einstufungsinstrument bei der Schulausbildung. In Grotjahn (ed.), 1993.

James, C. 1971. The exculpation of contrastive linguistics. In *Papers in contrastive linguistics*, G. Nickel (ed.). Cambridge: Cambridge University Press.

Jessner, U. 1996. Towards a dynamic view of multilingualism. In *Language choices: conditions, constraints, and consequences*, M. Pütz (ed.). Amsterdam: John Benjamins.

Jin, Y.-S. 1990. Effects of concreteness on cross-language priming in lexical decisions. *Perceptual and Motor Skills* 70: 1139–1154.

Johanson, L. 1993. Code-copying in immigrant Turkish. In *Immigrant languages in Europe*, G. Extra & L. Verhoeven (eds.). Clevedon: Multilingual Matters.

Kagan, J., Rosman, L., Day, D., Albert, J. & Phillips, W. 1964. Information processing in the child: significance of analytic and reflective attitudes. *Psychological Monographs. General and Applied* 78: 1–37.

Karmiloff-Smith, A. 1979. *A functional approach to child language: a study of determiners and reference*. Cambridge: Cambridge University Press.

Karmiloff-Smith, A. 1986. Some fundamental aspects of language development after age 5. In Fletcher & Garman (eds.), 1986.

Katz, J. & Fodor, J. 1963. The structure of a semantic theory. *Language* 39: 170–210.

Katz, J. & Postal, P. 1964. *An integrated theory of linguistic descriptions*. Cambridge, MA: MIT Press.

Kellerman, E. 1977. Towards a characterization of the strategy of transfer in second language learning. *Interlanguage Studies Bulletin* 2: 58–145.

Kellerman, E. 1978. Giving learners a break: native language intuitions as a source of predictions about transferability. *Working Papers on Bilingualism* 15: 309–315.

Kellerman, E. 1979. Transfer and non-transfer: where are we now? *Studies in Second Language Acquisition* 2: 37–57.

Kellerman, E. 1983. Now you see it, now you don't. In Gass & Selinker (eds.), 1983.

Kellerman, E. 1991. Compensatory strategies in second language research: a critique, a revision, and some (non-) implications for the classroom. In Phillipson *et al.* (eds.), 1991.

Kellerman, E. 1993. Responsibility in communication strategy research. Paper presented in the 'Language and linguistics' series of public lectures at the Centre for Language and Communication Studies, Trinity College, Dublin.

Kellerman, E., Ammerlaan, A., Bongaerts, T. & Poulisse, N. 1990. System and hierarchy in L2 compensatory strategies. In Scarcella, Andersen & Krashen (eds.), 1990.

Kellerman, E., Bongaerts, T. & Poulisse, N. 1987. Strategy and system in L2 referential communication. In *The social context of second language acquisition*, R. Ellis (ed.). Englewood Cliffs, NJ: Prentice-Hall.

Kellerman, E. & Sharwood Smith, M. (eds.) 1986. *Crosslinguistic influence in second language acquisition*. Oxford: Pergamon.

Kelly, M. & Martin, S. 1994. Domain-general abilities applied to domain-specific tasks: sensitivity to probabilities in perception, cognition, and language. In Gleitman & Landau (eds.), 1994.

Kelly, P. 1991. Lexical ignorance: the main obstacle to listening comprehension with advanced foreign language learners. *IRAL* 29: 135–149.

Kemler, D. & Smith, L. 1979. Accessing similarity and dimensional relations. *Journal of Experimental Psychology: General* 108: 133–150.

Kent, G., & Rosanoff, A. 1910. A study of association in insanity. *American Journal of Insanity* 67: 37–96.

Kerkman, J. 1984. Wordherkenning in twee talen. In *Het leesproces*, A. Thomassen, L. Noordman & P. Eling (eds.). Lisse: Swets & Zeitlinger.

Kettemann, B. & Wieden, W. (eds.) 1993. *Current issues in European second language acquisition*. Tübingen: Narr.

Kirsner, K., Lalor, E. & Hird, K. 1993. The bilingual lexicon: exercise, meaning and morphology. In Schreuder & Weltens (eds.) 1993.

Kirsner, K., Smith, M. C., Lockhart, R. & Jain, M. 1984. The bilingual lexicon: language-specific units in an integrated network. *Journal of Verbal Learning and Verbal Behavior* 23: 519–539.

Klein-Braley, C. 1985a. Reduced redundancy as an approach to language testing. – *Fremdsprachen und Hochschule: AKS Rundbrief* 13/14: 1–13..

Klein-Braley, C. 1985b. A cloze-up on the C-test: a study in the construct validation of authentic tests. *Language Testing* 2: 76–104.

Klein-Braley, C. 1985c. C-tests and construct validity. – *Fremdsprachen und Hochschule: AKS Rundbrief* 13/14: 55–65.

Klein-Braley, C. 1997. C-tests in the context of reduced redundancy testing: an appraisal. *Language Testing* 14: 47–84.

Klein-Braley, C. & Raatz, U. 1984. A survey of research on the C-test. *Language Testing* 1: 134–146.

Klein-Braley, C. & Raatz, U. 1990. Die objektive Erfassung des Sprachstands im mutter- und fremdsprachlichen Unterricht durch C-Tests. In *Deutsch als Fremdsprache in Europa*, A. Wolff & H. Rössler (eds.). Regensburg: Arbeitskreis Deutsch als Fremdsprache beim DAAD.

Koda, K. 1989. The effects of transferred vocabulary knowledge on the development of L2 reading proficiency. *Foreign Language Annals* 22: 529–540.

Koda, K. 1997. Orthographic knowledge in L2 lexical processing: a cross-linguistic perspective. In Coady & Huckin (eds.), 1997.

Kolers, P. 1963. Interlingual word associations. *Journal of Verbal Learning and Verbal Behavior* 2: 291–300.

Kolers, P. 1966. Reading and talking bilingually. *American Journal of Psychology* 79: 357–376.

Krashen, S. 1981. *Second language acquisition and second language learning*. Oxford: Pergamon.

Krashen, S. 1983. Newmark's 'ignorance hypothesis' and current second language acquisition theory. In Gass & Selinker (eds.), 1983.

Krashen, S. 1989. We acquire vocabulary and spelling by reading: additional evidence for the input hypothesis. *Modern Language Journal* 73: 440–464.

Krings, H. 1986a. Translation problems and translation strategies of advanced German learners of French. In House & Blum-Kulka (eds.), 1986.

Krings, H. 1986b. *Was in den Köpfen von Übersetzern vorgeht. Eine empirische Untersuchung zur Struktur des Übersetzungsprozesses an fortgeschrittenen Französischlernern*. Tübingen: Narr.

Krings, H. 1987. The use of introspective data in translation. In Faerch & Kasper (eds.), 1987a.

Krishnamurthy, R. 1987. The process of compilation. In Sinclair (ed.), 1987b.

Kroll, J. & Curley, J. 1988. Lexical memory in novice bilinguals: the role of concepts in retrieving second language words. In *Practical aspects of memory: current research and issues*, M. Gruneberg, P. Morris & N. Sykes (eds.). Chichester: John Wiley.

Kuczaj, S. & Barrett, M. (eds.) 1986. *The development of word meaning*. New York: Springer.

Kuhl, P. & Miller, J. 1975. Speech perception by the chinchilla: voice–voiceless distinction in alveolar plosive consonants. *Science* 190: 69–72.

Kuhl, P. & Miller, J. 1978. Speech perception by the chinchilla: identification functions for synthetic VOT stimuli. *Journal of the Acoustical Society of America* 63: 905–917.

Kuhl, P. & Miller, J. 1982. Discrimination of auditory target dimensions in the presence or absence of variation in a second dimension by infants. *Perception and Psychophysics* 31: 279–292.

Kuhl, P. & Padden, D. 1982. Enhanced discriminability at the phonetic boundaries for the voicing feature in macaques. *Perception and Psychophysics* 32: 542–550.

Kuhl, P. & Padden, D. 1983. Enhanced discriminability at the phonetic boundaries for the place feature in macaques. *Journal of the Acoustical Society of America* 73: 1003–1010.

Labov, W. 1973. The boundaries of words and their meanings. In *New ways of analyzing variation in English*, J. Fishman (ed.). Washington, DC: Georgetown University Press.

Lado, R. 1957. *Linguistics across cultures*. Ann Arbor: University of Michigan Press.

Lado, R. 1964. *Language teaching: a scientific approach*. New York: McGraw-Hill.

Lakoff, G. 1987. *Women, fire and dangerous things: what categories reveal about the mind*. Chicago: University of Chicago Press.

Lambert, W. 1990. Persistent issues in bilingualism. In *The development of second language proficiency*, B. Harley, P. Allan, J. Cummins & M. Swain (eds.). Cambridge: Cambridge University Press.

Lamiroy, B. 1991. Où en sont les rapports entre les études de lexique et la syntaxe? – *Travaux de Linguistique* 23: 133–139.

Lance, D. 1969. *A brief study of Spanish–English bilingualism*. Final report. Research Project Orr-Liberal Arts-15504. College Station, Texas A. and M. University.

Langer, S. 1960. *Philosophy in a new key*. 3rd edn. Cambridge, MA: Harvard University Press.

Lanza, E. 1990. *Language mixing in infant bilingualism: a sociolinguistic perspective*. Ph.D. thesis. Georgetown University.

Lapaire, J.-R. 1994. Le vide et le plein dans l'étude du langage. *Modèles Linguistiques* 15: 119–130.

Larsen-Freeman, D. & Long, M. 1991. *An introduction to second language acquisition research*. London: Longman.

Lasky, R., Syrdal-Lasky, A. & Klein, R. 1975. VOT discrimination by four to six and a half month old infants from Spanish environments. *Journal of Experimental Child Psychology* 20: 215–225.

Laufer, B. 1988. The concept of 'synforms' (similar lexical forms) in vocabulary acquisition. *Language and Education* 2: 113–132.

Laufer, B. 1989. A factor of difficulty in vocabulary learning: deceptive transparency In Nation & Carter (eds.), 1989.

Laufer, B. 1990a. Ease and difficulty in vocabulary learning: some teaching implications, *Foreign Language Annals* 23: 147–155.

Laufer, B. 1990b. 'Sequence' and 'order' in the development of L2 lexis: some evidence from lexical confusions. *Applied Linguistics* 11: 281–296.

Laufer, B. 1990c. Words you know: how they affect the words you learn. In *Further insights into contrastive linguistics*, J. Fisiak (ed.). Amsterdam: John Benjamins.

Laufer, B. 1991a. *Similar lexical forms in interlanguage*. Tübingen: Narr.

Laufer, B. 1991b. Why are some words more difficult than others? Some intralexical factors which affect the learning of words. *IRAL* 28: 293–307.

Laufer B. 1991c. The development of lexis in the production of advanced L2 learners. *The Modern Language Journal* 75: 440–448.

Laufer, B. 1992. How much lexis is necessary for reading comprehension? In Arnaud & Béjoint (eds.), 1992.

Laufer, B. 1993–94. Appropriation du vocabulaire: mots faciles, mots difficiles, mots impossibles. In Singleton (ed.), 1993–94a.
Laufer, B. 1997. What's in a word that makes it hard or easy: some intralexical factors that affect the learning of words. In Schmitt & McCarthy (eds.), 1997.
Laufer, B. & Benoussan, M. 1982. Meaning is in the eye of the beholder. *English Teaching Forum* 20: 10–14.
Laufer, B. & Nation, P. 1995. Vocabulary size and use: lexical richness in L2 written production. *Applied Linguistics* 16: 307–322.
Leech, G. 1981. *Semantics: the study of meaning*. 2nd edn. Harmondsworth: Penguin.
Lemmens, M. & Wekker, H. 1991. On the relationship between lexis and grammar in English learners' dictionaries. In Granger (ed.), 1991.
Leopold, W. 1939. *Speech development of a bilingual child: a linguist's record. Volume 1*. Evanston, IL: Northwestern University Press.
Leopold, W. 1947. *Speech development of a bilingual child: sound learning in the first two years. Volume 2*. Evanston, IL: Northwestern University Press.
Levelt, W. 1989. *Speaking: from intention to articulation*. Cambridge, MA: MIT Press.
Levelt, W. 1993a. Accessing words in speech production. In Levelt (ed.), 1993b.
Levelt, W. (ed.) 1993b. *Lexical access in speech production*. Oxford: Blackwell.
Levenston, E. 1979. Second language acquisition: issues and problems. *Interlanguage Studies Bulletin* 4: 147–160.
Levine, D. 1990. *Introduction to cognitive and neural modeling*. Hillsdale, NJ: Lawrence Erlbaum.
Lewis, M. 1993. *The lexical approach: the state of ELT and a way forward*. Hove: Language Teaching Publications.
Lewis, M. 1997. *Implementing the lexical approach*. Hove: Language Teaching Publications.
Lewis, M. M. 1936. *Infant speech: a study of the beginnings of language*. New York: Harcourt Brace.
Lewis, M. M. 1959. *How children learn to speak*. New York: Basic Books.
Linebarger, M. 1989. Neuropsychological evidence for linguistic modularity. In *Linguistic structures in language processing*, G. Carlson & M. Tanenhaus (eds.). Dordrecht: Kluwer.
Linnarud, M. 1983. On lexis: the Swedish learner and the native speaker compared In *Cross language analysis and second language acquisition* 2, K. Sajavaara (ed.). Jyväskylä: University of Jyväskylä.
Linnarud, M. 1986. *Lexis in composition*. Lund: Lund Studies in English.
Little, D. 1994. Words and their properties: arguments for a lexical approach to pedagogical grammar. In *Perspectives on pedagogical grammar*, T. Odlin (ed.). Cambridge: Cambridge University Press.
Little, D., Devitt, S. & Singleton, D. 1989. *Learning foreign languages from authentic texts: theory and practice*. Dublin: Authentik.

Little, D. & Ridley, J. 1992. Language awareness, language processing and L2 learning: an empirical study of some university-level learners of German. Paper presented at the NCCLA Conference on Language Awareness, Bangor (Wales).

Little, D. & Singleton, D. 1992. The C-test as an elicitation instrument in second language research. In Grotjahn (ed.), 1992a.

Littlewood, W. 1984. *Foreign and second language learning: language acquisition research and its implications for the classroom*. Cambridge: Cambridge University Press.

Lock, A. 1980. *The guided reinvention of language*. London: Academic Press.

Locke, J. 1983. *Phonological acquisition and change*. New York: Academic Press.

Locke, J. 1988. The sound shape of early lexical representations. In M. D. Smith & Locke (eds.), 1988.

Lorimer, F. 1928. *The growth of reason: a study of the role of verbal activity in the growth of the structure of the human mind*. London: Kegan Paul, Trench & Trubner.

Lörscher, W. 1986. Linguistic aspects of translational processes: towards an analysis of translational processes. In House & Blum-Kulka (eds.), 1986.

Lyons, J. 1963. *Structural semantics: an analysis of part of the vocabulary of Plato*. Oxford: Blackwell (*Publications of the Philological Society* 20).

Lyons, J. 1968. *Introduction to theoretical linguistics*. Cambridge: Cambridge University Press.

Lyons, J. 1973. Structuralism and linguistics. In *Structuralism: an introduction*, D. Robey (ed.). Oxford: Clarendon Press.

Lyons, J. 1977. *Semantics*. 2 volumes. Cambridge: Cambridge University Press.

Lyons, J. 1981. *Language, meaning and context*. London: Fontana.

Lyons, J. 1995. *Linguistic semantics: an introduction*. Cambridge: Cambridge University Press.

Mac Mathúna, L. & Singleton, D. (eds.) 1984. *Language across cultures. Proceedings of a symposium held at St Patrick's College, Drumcondra, Dublin, 8–9 July, 1983*. Dublin: Irish Association for Applied Linguistics.

MacKain, K. 1982. Assessing the role of experience on infants' speech discrimination. *Journal of Child Language* 9: 527–542.

MacKain, K. 1988. Filling the gap between speech and language. In M. Smith & Locke (eds.), 1988.

Maclaran, R. 1976. The variable (ʌ): a relic form with social correlates. *Belfast Working Papers in Language and Linguistics* 1: 45–68.

Maclaran, R. 1983. *On the interaction of semantics and pragmatics*. Dublin: Trinity College, Centre for Language and Communication Studies (*CLCS Occasional Paper* 8).

Maclaran, R. & Singleton, D. 1984a. Native speaker clarifications and the notion of simplicity. Paper presented at the Seventh World Congress of Applied Linguistics (AILA 1984). Brussels. Abstract in *AILA Brussels 84: Proceedings. Volume 3*, J. den Haese & J. Nivette (eds.). Brussels: ITO/VUB.

Maclaran, R. & Singleton, D. 1984b. Foreigner register. In Singleton & Little (eds.), 1984a.

Macnamara, J. 1967. The linguistic independence of bilinguals. *Journal of Verbal Learning and Verbal Behavior* 2: 250–262.

Macnamara, J. & Kushnir, S. 1971. Linguistic independence of bilinguals: the input switch. *Journal of Verbal Learning and Verbal Behavior* 10: 480–487.

MacWhinney, B. & Leinbach, J. 1991. Implementations are not conceptualizations: revising the verb learning model. *Cognition* 48: 21–69.

Mägiste, E. 1984. Stroop tasks and dichotic translation: the development of interference patterns in bilinguals. *Journal of Experimental Psychology: Learning, Memory and Cognition* 10: 304–315.

Malakoff, M. 1992. Translation ability: a natural bilingual and metalinguistic skill. In R. Harris (ed.), 1992.

Malakoff, M. & Hakuta, K. 1991. Translation skill and metalinguistic awareness in bilinguals. In E. Bialystok (ed.), 1991b.

Mandler, J. 1988. How to build a baby: on the development of an accessible representational system. *Cognitive Development* 3: 113–136.

Mandler, J. & Bauer, P. 1988. The cradle of categorization: is the basic level basic? *Cognitive Development* 3: 237–264.

Mandler, J., Bauer, P. & McDonough, L. 1991. Separating the sheep from the goats: differentiating global categories. *Cognitive Psychology* 23: 263–299.

Marcus, S. & Frauenfelder, U. 1985. Word recognition – uniqueness or deviation? A theoretical note. *Language and Cognitive Processes* 1: 163–169.

Maréchal, C. 1995. *The bilingual lexicon: study of French and English word association responses of advanced learners of French*. M. Phil. dissertation. University of Dublin.

Markman, E. 1985. Why superordinate category terms can be mass nouns. *Cognition* 19: 311–353.

Markman, E. 1989. *Categorization and naming in children*. Cambridge, MA: MIT/Bradford Books.

Markman, E. 1993. Constraints children place on word meanings. In P. Bloom (ed.), 1993.

Markman, E. & Hutchinson, J. 1984. Children's sensitivity to constraints on word meaning: taxonomic vs. thematic relations. *Cognitive Psychology* 16: 1–27.

Markman, E. & Wachtel, G. 1988. Children's use of mutual exclusivity to constrain the meanings of words. *Cognitive Psychology* 20: 121–157.

Marslen-Wilson, W. 1973. *Speech shadowing and speech perception*. Ph.D. thesis. MIT.

Marslen-Wilson, W. 1975. Sentence perception as an interactive parallel process. *Science* 189: 226–228.

Marslen-Wilson, W. 1978. Sequential decision processes during spoken word-recognition. Paper presented at the Psychonomic Society meeting, San Antonio, Texas. (Summarized in Harris & Coltheart 1986: 161ff.)

Marslen-Wilson, W. 1980. Speech understanding as psychological process. In *Spoken language generation and understanding*, J. Simon (ed.). Boston: Reidel.

Marslen-Wilson, W. 1984. Function and process in spoken word recognition. In *Attention and performance. Volume X: Control of language processes*, H. Bouma & D. Bouwhuis (eds.). Hillsdale, NJ: Erlbaum.

Marslen-Wilson, W. 1987. Functional parallelism in spoken word recognition. *Cognition* 25: 71–102.

Marslen-Wilson, W. 1989a. Access and integration: projecting sound onto meaning. In Marslen-Wilson (ed.), 1989b.

Marslen-Wilson, W. (ed.) 1989b. *Lexical representation and process*. Cambridge, MA: MIT Press.

Marslen-Wilson, W. 1990. Activation, competition and frequency in lexical access. In *Cognitive models of speech processing: psycholinguistics and computational perspectives*, G. Altmann (ed.). Cambridge, MA: MIT Press.

Marslen-Wilson, W. 1993. Issues of process and representation in lexical access. In *Cognitive models of speech processing*, G. Altmann & R. Shillcock (eds.). Hillsdale, NJ: Erlbaum.

Marslen-Wilson, W. & Tyler, L. 1980. The temporal structure of spoken language understanding. *Cognition* 8: 1–71.

Marslen-Wilson, W. & Tyler, L. 1981. Central processes in speech understanding, *Philosophical Transactions of the Royal Society* B 295: 317–22.

Marslen-Wilson, W. & Tyler, L. 1987. Against modularity. In Garfield (ed.), 1987b.

Marslen-Wilson, W. & Welsh, A. 1978. Processing interactions and lexical access during word-recognition in continuous speech. *Cognitive Psychology* 10: 29–63.

Martinet, A. 1949. La double articulation linguistique. *Travaux du Cercle Linguistique de Copenhague* 5: 30–37.

Martinet, A. 1957. Arbitraire linguistique et double articulation. *Cahiers Ferdinand de Saussure* 15: 105–116.

Martohardjono, G. & Flynn, S. 1995. Is there an age factor for Universal Grammar? In Singleton & Lengyel (eds.), 1995.

Masny, D. 1996. *Examining assumptions in second language research: a postmodern view*. Dublin: Trinity College, Centre for Language and Communication Studies (*CLCS Occasional Paper* 45).

Matthei, E. & Roeper, T. 1983. *Understanding and producing speech*. London: Fontana.

McClelland, J. & Rumelhart, D. 1981. An interactive activation model of context effects in letter perception: Part 1. An account of basic findings. *Psychological Review* 88: 375–407.

McClelland, J., Rumelhart, D. & Hinton, G. 1986. The appeal of parallel distributed processing. In Rumelhart *et al.* (eds.), 1986.

McClelland, J., Rumelhart, D. & the PDP Research Group (eds.) 1986. *Parallel distributed processing: explorations in the microstructure of cognition. Volume 2: Psychological and biological models*. Cambridge, MA: MIT Press.

McDonough, S. 1981. *Psychology in foreign language teaching*. London: George Allen & Unwin.

McNeill, D. 1966. A study of word association. *Journal of Verbal Learning and Verbal Behavior* 5: 548–557.

McNeill, D. 1968. Development of the semantic system. Unpublished.

McNeill, D. 1970. *The acquisition of language*. New York: Harper & Row.

McShane, J. 1979. The development of naming. *Linguistics* 13: 155–161.

McShane, J. 1980. *Learning to talk*. Cambridge: Cambridge University Press.

McShane, J. 1991. *Cognitive development: an information processing account*. Oxford: Blackwell.

McShane, J. & Dockrell, J. 1983. Lexical and grammatical development. In *Speech production. Volume 2*, B. Butterworth (ed.). London: Academic Press.

Meara, P. 1978. Learners' word associations in French. *Interlanguage Studies Bulletin* 3: 192–211.

Meara, P. 1980. Vocabulary acquisition: a neglected aspect of language learning. *Language Teaching and Linguistics Abstracts* 13: 221–246.

Meara, P. 1983a. *Vocabulary in a second language*. London: CILT.

Meara, P. 1983b. Word associations in a foreign language: a report on the Birkbeck Vocabulary Project 2. *Nottingham Linguistic Circular* 2: 29–37.

Meara, P. 1984. The study of lexis in interlanguage. In *Interlanguage*, A. Davies, C. Criper & A. P. R. Howatt (eds.). Edinburgh: Edinburgh University Press.

Meara, P. 1987. *Vocabulary in a second language. Volume 2*. London: CILT.

Meara, P. 1992. Vocabulary in a second language: Volume 3. *Reading in a Foreign Language* 9: 761–837.

Meara, P. 1993a. The bilingual lexicon and the teaching of vocabulary. In Schreuder & Weltens (eds.), 1993.

Meara, P. 1993b. Assumptions about vocabulary acquisition and where they come from. Paper presented at the Tenth World Congress of Applied Linguisics (AILA 1993), Amsterdam.

Meara, P. 1996a. The classical research in L2 vocabulary acquisition. In *Words, words, words: the translator and the language learner*, G. Anderman & M. Rogers (eds.). Clevedon: Multilingual Matters.

Meara, P. 1996b. Emergent properties of simple bilingual lexicons. Contribution to the symposium 'L2 lexical processing', organized by

D. Singleton & K. de Bot, at the Eleventh AILA World Congress of Applied Linguistics, Jyväskylä. Abstract in Dufva *et al.* (eds.), 1996.

Meara, P. & Ingle, S. 1986. The formal representation of words in an L2 speaker's lexicon. *Second Language Research* 2: 160–171.

Meisel, J. 1977. Linguistic simplification: a study of immigrant workers' speech and foreigner talk. In *The notions of simplification, interlanguages and pidgins and their relation to second language pedagogy: sctes du 5ème Colloque de Linguistique Appliquée de Neuchâtel*, S. P. Corder & E. Roulet (eds.). Neuchâtel/Geneva: Faculté des Lettres / Librairie Droz.

Merriman, W. 1986a. How children learn the reference of concrete nouns: a critique of current hypotheses. In Kuczaj & Barrett (eds.), 1986.

Merriman, W. 1986b. Some reasons for the occurrence and eventual corrections of children's naming errors. *Child Development* 57: 942–951.

Mervis, C. 1987. Child-basic object categories and early lexical development. In *Concepts and conceptual development: ecological and intellectual factors in categorization*, U. Neisser (ed.). Cambridge: Cambridge University Press.

Mervis, C. & Crisafi, M. 1982. Order of acquisition of subordinate-, basic-, and superordinate-level categories. *Child Development* 53: 258–266.

Meyer, R. 1910. Bedeutungssysteme. *Zeitschrift für vergleichende Sprachforschung auf dem Gebiete der indogermanischen Sprachen* 4: 352–368.

Meyer, D. & Schvaneveldt, R. 1971. Facilitation in recognizing pairs of words: evidence of a dependence between retrieval operations. *Journal of Experimental Psychology* 90: 227–234.

Milroy, J. 1978. Lexical alternation and diffusion in vernacular speech. *Belfast Working Papers in Language and Linguistics* 3: 101–114.

Minsky, M. 1975. A framework for representing knowledge. In *The psychology of computer vision*, P. Winston (ed.). New York: McGraw-Hill.

Mohanty, A. 1994. *Bilingualism in a multilingual society.* Mysore: Central Institute of Indian Languages.

Mondria, J. & Wit-de Boer, M. 1991. The effects of contextual richness on the guessability and the retention of words in a foreign language. *Applied Linguistics* 12: 249–267.

Moore, T. & Carling, C. 1982. *Understanding language: towards a post-Chomskyan linguistics*. Basingstoke: Macmillan.

Morais, J., Cary, L., Alegria, F. & Bertelson, P. 1979. Does awareness of speech as a sequence of phones arise spontaneously? *Cognition* 7: 323–331.

Moreau, M.-L. & Richelle, M. 1981. *L'acquisition du langage*. Brussels: Madaga.

Morse, P. 1972. The discrimination of speech and nonspeech stimuli in early infancy. *Journal of Experimental Child Psychology* 14: 477–490.

Morse, P. & Snowdon, C. 1975. An investigation of categorical speech

discrimination by rhesus monkeys. *Perception and Psychophysics* 17: 9–16.
Morton, J. 1961. *Reading, context and the perception of words*. Ph.D. thesis. University of Reading.
Morton, J. 1964a. A preliminary functional model for language behaviour. *International Audiology* 3: 216–215. Reprinted in Oldfield & Marshall, eds.
Morton, J. 1964b. The effects of context on the visual duration threshold for words. *British Journal of Psychology* 55: 165–180.
Morton, J. 1968. Considerations of grammar and computation in language behavior. In *Studies in language and language behavior*, J. Catford (ed.). Ann Arbor: University of Michigan Press.
Morton, J. 1969. Interaction of information in word recognition. *Psychological Review* 76: 165–178.
Morton, J. 1970. A functional model of human memory. In *Models of human memory*, D. Norman (ed.). New York: Academic Press.
Morton, J. 1978. Facilitation in word recognition: experiments causing a change in the logogen model. In *Proceedings of the conference on the processing of visible language*, P. Kolers, M. Wrolstad & H. Bouma (eds.). New York: Plenum.
Morton, J. 1979. Word recognition. In *Psycholinguistics series 2: structures and processes*, J. Morton & J. Marshall (eds.). London: Elek.
Morton, J. & Patterson, K. 1980. A new attempt at an interpretation, or, an attempt at a new interpretation. In *Deep dyslexia*, M. Coltheart, K. Patterson & J. Marshall (eds.), London: Routledge & Kegan Paul.
Moscovitch, M. 1977. The development of lateralization of language functions and its relation to cognitive and linguistic development: a review and some theoretical speculations. In Segalowitz & Gruber (eds.), 1977.
Nagy, W. 1997. On the role of context in first- and second-language vocabulary learning. In Schmitt & McCarthy (eds.), 1997.
Nagy, W. & Herman, P. 1985. Incidental vs. instructional approaches to increasing reading vocabulary. *Educational Perspectives* 23: 16–21.
Nation, P. 1982. Beginning to learn foreign vocabulary: a review of the research, *RELC Journal* 13: 14–36.
Nation, P. 1990. *Teaching and learning vocabulary*. Boston, MA: Heinle & Heinle.
Nation, P. 1993. Vocabulary size, growth and use. In Schreuder & Weltens (eds.), 1993.
Nation, P. & Carter, R. (eds.) 1989. *Vocabulary acquisition*. Amsterdam: Free University Press (*AILA Review / Revue de l'AILA* 6).
Nation, P. & Coady, J. 1988. Vocabulary and reading. In Carter & McCarthy (eds.), 1985.
Nelson, E. and Rosenbaum, E. 1968. Sociolinguistic dimensions of youth culture. Paper presented at the meeting of the American Educational Research Association, Chicago.
Nelson, K. 1973a. Some evidence for the cognitive primacy of categorization and its functional basis. *Merrill-Palmer Quarterly* 19: 21–39.

Nelson, K. 1973b. *Structure and strategy in learning to talk. Monographs of the Society for Research in Child Development* 38 (nos. 1–2), Serial No. 149.

Nelson, K. 1974. Concept, word and sentence. *Psychological Review* 8: 267–285.

Nelson, K. 1977. The syntagmatic–paradigmatic shift revisited: a review of research and theory. *Psychological Bulletin* 84: 93–116.

Nelson, K. 1981. Acquisition of words by first-language learners. In Winitz (ed.), 1981.

Nelson, K. 1982. The syntagmatics and paradigmatics of conceptual development. In *Language. Volume II: Language, thought and culture*, S. Kuczaj (ed.). Hillsdale, NJ: Lawrence Erlbaum.

Nelson, K. 1988. Constraints on word learning? *Cognitive Development* 3: 221–246.

Nelson, K. & Bonvillian, J. 1978. Early language development: conceptual growth and related processes between 2 and $4\frac{1}{2}$ years. In *Children's language. – Volume 1*, K. Nelson (ed.). New York: Gardner.

Nelson, K. & Lucariello, J. 1985. The development of meaning in first words. In *Children's single word speech*, M. Barrett (ed.). Chichester: Wiley.

Newcombe, F. & Marshall, J. 1985. Sound-by-sound reading and writing. In *Surface dyslexia*, M. Coltheart, K. Patterson & J. Marshall (eds.). London: Erlbaum.

Newmeyer, F. (ed.) 1988. *Linguistics: the Cambridge survey. Volume III. Language: psychological and biological aspects*. Cambridge: Cambridge University Press.

Ninio, A. & Bruner, J. 1978. The achievement and antecedents of labelling. *Journal of Child Language* 5: 1–15.

Nortier, J. & Schatz, H. 1992. From one-word switch to loan: a comparison between five language pairs. *Multilingua* 11: 173–194.

Obler, L. & Albert, M. 1978. A monitor system for bilingual language processing. In *Aspects of bilingualism*, M. Paradis (ed.). Columbia, SC: Hornbeam Press.

Odlin, T. 1989. *Language transfer: cross-linguistic influence in language learning*. Cambridge: Cambridge University Press.

Ogden, C. & Richards, I. 1936. *The meaning of meaning*. 4th edn. London: Routledge & Kegan Paul.

O'Gorman, E. 1996. An investigation of the mental lexicon of second language learners. *Teanga: The Irish Yearbook of Applied Linguistics* 16: 15–31.

Oldfield, R. & Marshall, J. (eds.) 1968. *Language: selected readings*. Harmondsworth: Penguin.

Oller, D., Wieman, L., Doyle, W. & Ross, C. 1976. Infant babbling and speech. *Journal of Child Language* 3: 1–11.

Olshtain, E. 1989. Is second language attrition the reversal of second language acquisition? *Studies in Second Language Acquisition* 11: 151–165.

Orne, M. & Hammer, A. 1974. Hypnosis. In *Macropaedia* Volume 9. Encyclopaedia Britannica.
Padron, Y. & Waxman, H. 1988. The effect of ESL students' perceptions of their cognitive strategies on reading achievement. *TESOL Quarterly* 22: 146–150.
Palmberg, R. 1979. Investigating communication strategies. In *Perception and production of English: papers on interlanguage*, R. Palmberg (ed.). Åbo: Åbo Akademi, Department of English.
Palmer, F. 1971. *Grammar.* Harmondsworth: Penguin.
Papagno, C., Valentine, T. & Baddeley, A. 1991. Phonological short-term memory and foreign-language vocabulary learning, *Journal of Memory and Language* 30: 331–347.
Paradis, M. 1981. Neurolinguistic organization of a bilingual's two languages. In *The Seventh LACUS Forum*, J. Copeland & P. Davis (eds.). Columbia, SC: Hornbeam Press.
Paradis, M. 1995. Neuropsychological models of bilingualism. Paper presented at the University of Nijmegen workshop 'Bilingual processing: models, methods and metaphors', Groesbeek (The Netherlands).
Paribakht, T. 1985. Strategic competence and language proficiency. *Applied Linguistics* 6: 132–146.
Paribakht, T. & Wesche, M. 1993. Second language vocabulary acquisition through reading: can instruction make a difference? Paper presented at the Centre de Recherche en Enseignement et Apprentissage Symposium on Vocabulary Research / Colloque sur la recherche en vocabulaire, Ontario.
Paribakht, T. & Wesche, M. 1996. Incidental and instructed L2 vocabulary acquisition through reading: a comparative introspective study. Contribution to the symposium 'Incidental L2 vocabulary acquisition: theoretical, methodological and pedagogical issues', organized by T. Paribakht & M. Wesche, at the Eleventh AILA World Congress of Applied Linguistics, Jyväskylä. Abstract in Dufva *et al.* (eds.), 1996.
Paribakht, T. & Wesche, M. 1997. Vocabulary enhancement activities and reading for meaning in second language vocabulary acquisition. In Coady & Huckin (eds.), 1997.
Peal, E. & Lambert, W. 1962. The relation of bilingualism to intelligence. *Psychological Monographs: General and Applied* 76: 1–23.
Peters, A. 1983. *The units of language acquisition.* Cambridge: Cambridge University Press.
Phillips, T. 1981. *Difficulties in foreign language vocabulary learning and a study of some of the factors thought to be influential.* MA dissertation. University of London, Birkbeck College.
Phillipson, R., Kellerman, E., Selinker, L. Sharwood Smith, M. & Swain, M. (eds.) 1991. *Foreign/second language pedagogy research: a commemorative volume for Claus Faerch.* Clevedon: Multilingual Matters.

Piaget, J. 1952. *The origins of intelligence in children*. New York: Norton.
Piaget, J. 1979. La psychogenèse des connaissances et sa signification épistémologique. In Piattelli-Palmarini (ed.), 1979.
Piaget, J. & Inhelder, B. 1969. *The psychology of the child*. London: Routledge & Kegan Paul.
Piattelli-Palmarini, M. (ed.) 1979. *Théories du langage, théories de l'apprentissage. Le débat entre Jean Piaget et Noam Chomsky*. Paris: Editions du Seuil. English language version: *Language and learning: the debate between Chomsky and Piaget*. Cambridge, MA: Harvard University Press, 1980.
Picoche, J. 1977. *Précis de lexicologie française: l'étude et l'enseignement du vocabulaire*. Paris: Nathan.
Pinker, S. 1994. How could a child use verb syntax to learn verb semantics? In Gleitman & Landau (eds.), 1994.
Pinker, S. & Prince, A. 1988. On language and connectionism: analysis of a parallel distributed processing model of language acquisition. *Cognition* 28: 73–193.
Plaut, D. & Shallice, T. 1994. *Connectionist modelling in cognitive neuropsychology*. Hillsdale, NJ: Lawrence Erlbaum.
Poplack, S., Sankoff, D. & Miller, C. 1988. The social correlates and linguistic processes of lexical borrowing and assimilation. *Linguistics* 26: 47–104.
Postman, L. & Keppel, G. (eds.) 1970. *Norms in word association*. New York: Academic Press.
Potter, M., So, K.-F., Von Eckardt, B. & Feldman, L. 1984. Lexical and conceptual representation in beginning and proficient learners. *Journal of Verbal Learning and Verbal Behavior* 23: 23–28.
Poulisse, N. 1990. *The use of compensatory strategies by Dutch learners of English*. Dordrecht: Foris.
Poulisse, N. 1993. A theoretical account of lexical compensation strategies. In Schreuder & Weltens (eds.), 1993.
Poulisse, N., Bongaerts, T. & Kellerman, E. 1987. The use of retrospective verbal reports in the analysis of compensatory strategies. In Faerch & Kasper (eds.), 1987a.
Premack, D. & Premack, A. 1983. *The mind of an ape*. New York: Norton.
Preston, M. & Lambert, W. 1969. Interlingual interference in a bilingual version of the Stroop color-word task. *Journal of Verbal Learning and Verbal Behavior* 8: 295–301.
Pulman, S. 1983. *Word, meaning and belief*. London: Croom Helm.
Quay, S. 1995. The bilingual lexicon: implications for studies of language choice. *Journal of Child Language* 22: 369–387.
Quine, W. 1960. *Word and object*. Cambridge, MA: MIT Press.
Quine, W. 1975. The nature of knowledge. In *Mind and knowledge*, S. Guttenplan (ed.). Oxford: Oxford University Press.
Raatz, U. 1985a. Tests of reduced redundancy – the C-test, a practical example. *Fremdsprachen und Hochschule: AKS Rundbrief* 13/14: 14–19.

Raatz, U. 1985b. The factorial validity of C-tests. *Fremdsprachen und Hochschule: AKS Rundbrief* 13/14: 42–54.

Raatz, U. & Klein-Braley, C. 1985. How to develop a C-test. *Fremdsprachen und Hochschule: AKS Rundbrief* 13/14: 20–22.

Radford, A. 1981. *Transformational syntax*. Cambridge: Cambridge University Press.

Ramsey, R. 1981. A technique for interlingual lexico-semantic comparison: the lexigram. *TESOL Quarterly* 15: 15–24.

Randall, M. 1980. Word association behaviour in learners of English as a second language. *Polyglot* 2: B4–D1.

Read, J. 1997. Vocabulary and testing. In Schmidt & McCarthy (eds.), 1997.

Reed, C. (ed.) 1971. *The learning of language*. New York: Appleton-Century-Crofts.

Regier, T. 1996. *The human semantic potential: spatial language and constrained connectionism*. Cambridge, MA: MIT Press.

Reich, P. 1976. The early acquisition of word meaning. *Journal of Child Language* 3: 117–123.

Rescorla, L. 1980. Overextension in early child language development. *Journal of Child Language* 7: 321–335.

Rey, A. & Rey-Debove, J. 1979. *Le petit Robert: dictionnaire alphabétique et analogique de la langue française*. Nouvelle édition. Paris: Le Robert.

Rheingold, H., Gewitz, J. & Ross, H. 1959. Social conditioning of vocalizations in the infant. *Journal of Comparative Physiology and Psychology* 52: 68–73.

Ricciardelli, L. 1992. Bilingualism and cognitive development in relation to Threshold Theory. *Journal of Psycholinguistic Research* 21: 56–67.

Ricciuti, H. 1965. Object grouping and selective ordering behavior in infants 12–24 months old. *Merrill-Palmer Quarterly* 11: 129–148.

Richards, J. & Sampson, G. P. 1974. The study of learner English. In *Error analysis: perspectives in second language acquisition*, J. Richards (ed.). London: Longman.

Ridley, J. 1991a. *Strategic competence in second language performance: a study of four advanced learners*. Dublin: Trinity College, Centre for Language and Communication Studies (*CLCS Occasional Paper* 28).

Ridley, J. 1991b. Transfer in L2 production: a case study. *Teanga: The Irish Yearbook of Applied Linguistics* 11: 40–47.

Ridley, J. 1993. Problem-solving strategies in *ab initio* learning. *Teanga: The Irish Yearbook of Applied Linguistics* 13: 84–90.

Ridley, J. 1994. *Reflection and strategy use: a study of four university-level 'ab initio' learners of German*. Ph.D. thesis. University of Dublin.

Ridley, J. 1997. *Reflection and strategies in foreign language learning*. Frankfurt am Main: Peter Lang.

Ridley, J. & Singleton, D. 1995a. Strategic L2 lexical innovation: case study of a university-level *ab initio* learner of German. *Second Language Research* 11: 137–148.

Ridley, J. & Singleton, D. 1995b. Contrastivity and individual learner contrasts. *Fremdsprachen Lehren und Lernen* 24: 123–137.

Ringbom, H. 1987. *The role of the first language in foreign language learning*. Clevedon: Multilingual Matters.
Ringbom, H. 1987. *The role of the first language in foreign language learning*. Clevedon: Multilingual Matters.
Ringbom, H. 1991. Crosslinguistic lexical influence and foreign language learning. In Phillipson *et al.* (eds.), 1991.

Robins, R. 1967. *A short history of linguistics*. London: Longman.

Robinson, P. 1989. Procedural vocabulary and language learning. *Journal of Pragmatics* 13: 523–546.

Rodgers, T. 1969. On measuring vocabulary difficulty: an analysis of item variables in learning Russian–English vocabulary pairs. *IRAL* 7: 327–343.

Romaine, S. 1982. *Socio-historical linguistics: its status and methodology*. Cambridge: Cambridge University Press.

Romaine, S. 1989. *Bilingualism*. Oxford: Blackwell.

Rosch, E. 1978. Principles of categorization. In *Cognition and categorization*, E. Rosch & B. Lloyd (eds.). Hillsdale, NJ: Lawrence Erlbaum.

Rosch, E., Mervis, C., Gray, W., Johnson, D. & Boyes-Braem, P. 1976. Basic objects in natural categories. *Cognitive Psychology* 8: 382–439.

Rosenzweig, M. 1970. International Kent-Rosanoff word association norms, emphasizing those of French male and female students and French workmen. In Postman & Keppel (eds.), 1970.

Rumelhart, D., Hinton, G. & McClelland, J. 1986. A general framework for parallel distributed processing. In Rumelhart *et al.* (eds.) 1986.

Rumelhart, D. & McClelland, J. 1982. An interactive activation model of context effects in letter perception: Part 2. The contextual enhancement effect and some tests and extensions of the model. *Psychological Review* 89: 60–94.

Rumelhart, D. & McClelland, J. 1986. On learning the past tenses of English verbs. In McClelland *et al.* (eds.), 1986.

Rumelhart, D., McClelland, J. & the PDP Research Group (eds.) 1986. *Parallel distributed processing: explorations in the microstructure of cognition. Volume 1: Foundations*. Cambridge, MA: MIT Press.

Rumelhart, D. & Norman, D. 1982. Simulating a skilled typist: a study of skilled cognitive motor performance. *Cognitive Science* 6: 1–36.

Russel, W. 1970. The complete German language norms, for responses to 100 words from the Kent-Rosanoff Association Test. In Postman & Keppel (eds.), 1970.

Ryle, G. 1949. *The concept of mind*. New York: Barnes & Noble.

Saeed, J. 1997. *Semantics*. Oxford: Blackwell.

Sampson, G. 1980. *Schools of linguistics: competition and evolution*. London: Hutchinson.

Sánchez-Casas, R., Davis, C. & García-Albea, J. 1992. Bilingual lexical processing: exploring the cognate/non-cognate distinction. *European Journal of Cognitive Psychology* 4: 293–310.

Sandoz, C. 1992. Syntaxe et formation des mots: un type d'emploi de noms

verbaux en latin. *TRANEL* 18 (Institut de Linguistique, Université de Neuchâtel): 245–252.
Sanguineti de Serrano, N. 1984. Patterns of reading in L1 and L2. In Singleton & Little (eds.), 1984a.
Sapir, E. 1921. *Language*. New York: Harcourt Brace & World.
Särkkä, H. 1992. *Englantilais–suomalais–englantilainen yleiskielen käyttösanakirja / English–Finnish–English General Dictionary.* Helsinki: Kustannusosakeyhtiö Otava.
Saunders, G. 1988. *Bilingual children: from birth to teens*. Clevedon: Multilingual Matterse
Saussure F. de 1973. *Cours de linguistique générale*. Critical Edition prepared by Tullio de Mauro. Paris: Payot.
Savage-Rumbaugh, S. & Lewin, R. 1994. *Kanzi: the ape at the brink of the human mind*. New York: Wiley.
Sawers, R. 1982. *Harrap's Concise German and English Dictionary.* London: Harrap.
Scaife, M. & Bruner, J. 1975. The capacity for joint visual attention in the infant. *Nature* 253: 265–266.
Scarborough, D., Cortese, C. & Scarborough, H. 1977. Frequency and repetition effects in lexical memory. *Journal of Experimental Psychology: Human Perception and Performance* 3: 1–17.
Scarborough, D., Gerard, L. & Cortese, C. 1984. Independence of lexical access in bilingual word recognition. *Journal of Verbal Learning and Verbal Behavior* 23: 84–99.
Scarcella, R., Andersen, E. & Krashen, S. (eds.) 1990. *Developing communicative competence in a second language*. New York: Newbury House.
Schanen, F. 1995. Bilan et perspectives de la didactique d'une langue étrangère: le cas de l'allemand. In *La linguistique appliquée aujourd'hui: problèmes et méthodes*. Amsterdam: De Werelt.
Schank, R. & Abelson, R. 1977. *Scripts, plans, goals and understanding*. Hillsdale, NJ: Lawrence Erlbaum.
Schank, R. & Kass, A. 1988. Knowledge representation in people and machines. In *Meaning and mental representations*, U. Eco, M. Santambrogio & P. Violi (eds.). Bloomington, IN: Indiana University Press.
Schmidt, R. 1988. The potential of parallel distributed processing for SLA theory and research. *Hawai'i Working Papers in ESL* 7: 55–56.
Schmitt, N. & McCarthy, M. (eds.) 1997. *Vocabulary: description, acquisition and pedagogy.* Cambridge: Cambridge University Press.
Scholfield, P. & Vougiouklis, P. 1992. The role of awareness when guessing the meaning of an unknown word. Paper presented at the NCCLA International Conference on Language Awareness, Bangor (Wales).
Schouten-van Parreren, C. 1985. *Woorden leren in het vreemde-taalonderwijs*. Appeldorn: Van Walraven.
Schouten-van Parreren, C. 1989. Vocabulary learning through reading: which conditions should be met when presenting words in texts? In Nation & Carter, (eds.), 1989.

Schouten-van Parreren, C. 1992. Individual differences in vocabulary acquisition: a qualitative experiment in the first phase of secondary education. In Arnaud & Béjoint (eds.), 1992.

Schreuder, R. & Weltens, B. (eds.) 1993. *The bilingual lexicon*. Amsterdam: Benjamins.

Schumann, J. 1978a. *The pidinization process: a model for second language acquisition*. Rowley, MA: Newbury House.

Schumann, J. 1978b. The Acculturation Model for second language acquisition. In *Second language acquisition and foreign language teaching*, R. Gingras (ed.). Arlington VA: Center for Applied Linguistics.

Schwartz, G. and Merten, D. 1967. The language of adolescence: an anthropological approach to the youth culture. *The American Journal of Anthropology* 72: 453–468.

Segalowitz, S. & Gruber, F. (eds.) 1977. *Language development and neurological theory*. New York: Academic Press.

Seibert, L. 1930. An experiment on the relative efficacy of studying French in associated pairs vs. studying French words in context. *Journal of Educational Psychology* 21: 297–314.

Seidenberg, M. 1995. Language and connectionism: the developing interface. In COGNITION *on Cognition*, J. Mehler & S. Franck (eds.). Cambridge, MA: MIT Press.

Seidenberg, M. & Tanenhaus M. 1979. Orthographic effects on rhyme monitoring. *Journal of Experimental Psychology: Human Learning and Memory* 5: 546–554.

Seidenberg, M., Tanenhaus, M., Leiman, J. & Bienkowski, M. 1982. Automatic access of the meanings of ambiguous words in context: some limitations of knowledge-based processing. *Cognitive Psychology* 14: 489–537.

Seliger, H. 1978. On the evolution of error type in high and low interactors. *Indian Journal of Applied Linguistics* 4: 22–30.

Seliger, H. 1983. The language learner as a linguist: of metaphors and realities. *Applied Linguistics* 4: 179–191.

Service, E. 1989. *Phonological coding in working memory and foreign-language learning*. Helsinki: University of Helsinki, Department of Psychology. *General Psychology Monographs* No. B9, 1989.

Service, E. 1992. Phonology, working memory and foreign-language learning. *Quarterly Journal of Experimental Psychology* 45A: 21–50.

Service, E. 1993. Phonological and semantic aspects of memory for foreign language. In *Actes: 1er Congrès International: Mémoire et Mémorisation dans l'Acquisition et l'Apprentissage des Langues / Proceedings: 1st International Congress: Memory and Memorization in Acquiring and Learning Languages*, J. Chapelle & M.-T. Claes (eds.). Louvain-la-Neuve: CLL.

Service, E. 1993–94. Contribution des codes mémoriels à l'apprentissage lexical. In Singleton (ed.), 1993–94a.

Service, E. & Craik, F. 1993. Differences between young and older adults in

learning a foreign language. *Journal of Memory and Language* 32: 608–623.
Service, E. & Kohonen, V. 1995. Is the relation between phonological memory and foreign language learning accounted for by vocabulary acquisition? *Applied Psycholinguistics* 16: 155–172.
Seymour, P. 1973. A model for reading, naming and comparison. *British Journal of Psychology* 64: 35–49.
Shannon, B. 1991. Faulty language selection in polyglots. *Language and Cognitive Processes* 6: 339–350.
Sinclair, J. 1987a. Grammar in the dictionary. In Sinclair (ed.), 1987b.
Sinclair, J. (ed.), 1987b. *Looking up: an account of the COBUILD Project in lexical computing and the development of the Collins COBUILD English language dictionary*. London: Collins.
Sinclair, J. 1991. *Corpus, concordance, collocation*. Oxford: Oxford University Press.
Sinclair, J. 1993. Mens et corpora: implications of corpus studies for psycholinguistics. Paper presented in the 'Language and linguistics' series of public lectures at the Centre for Language and Communication Studies, Trinity College, Dublin.
Sinclair, J. & Jones, S. 1974. English lexical collocations. *Cahiers de Lexicologie* 24: 15–61.
Singleton, D. 1981. *Language transfer: a review of some recent research*. Dublin: Trinity College, Centre for Language and Communication Studies (*CLCS Occasional Paper* 1).
Singleton, D. 1982. Applied linguistics: what exactly have we been applying? *Studies*, Autumn 1982: 280–295.
Singleton, D. 1983. Alien intrusions in learner French: a case study. *Teanga: Journal of the Irish Association for Applied Linguistics* 3: 87–128.
Singleton, D. 1987a. The fall and rise of language transfer. In *The advanced language learner*, J. Coleman & R. Towell (eds.). London: CILT.
Singleton, D. 1987b. Mother and other tongue influence on learner French. *Studies in Second Language Acquisition* 9: 327–346.
Singleton, D. 1989. *Language acquisition: the age factor*. Clevedon: Multilingual Matters.
Singleton, D. 1990a. *The TCD Modern Languages Research Project: objectives, instruments and preliminary results*. Dublin: Trinity College, Centre for Language and Communication Studies (*CLCS Occasional Paper* 26), and Alexandria, VA: *ERIC Reports* ED 333 723.
Singleton, D. 1990b. *The cross-linguistic factor in second language learning: a report on some small-scale studies recently conducted at the CLCS*. Dublin: Trinity College, Centre for Language and Communication Studies (*CLCS Occasional Paper* 24).
Singleton, D. 1992a. *French: some historical background*. Dublin: Authentik.
Singleton, D. 1992b. Age and the L2 mental lexicon. Paper presented at the Fourteenth Annual Meeting of the American Association for Applied Linguistics, Seattle.

Singleton, D. 1992c. Second language acquisition: the when and the how. *AILA Review* 9: 46–54.

Singleton, D. 1993a. Modularity and lexical processing: an L2 perspective. In *Current issues in European second language research*, B. Kettemann & W. Wieden (eds.). Tübingen: Narr.

Singleton, D. 1993b. Exploring the L2 mental lexicon: CLI and the age factor. Paper presented at the Third Annual Conference of the European Second Language Association, Sofia.

Singleton, D. (ed.) 1993–94a. *L'acquisition du lexique d'une langue étrangère*. Paris: ENCRAGES (Issue 3 of *Acquisition et Interaction en Langue Etrangère*).

Singleton, D. 1993–94b. Introduction: le rôle de la forme et du sens dans le lexique mental en L2. In Singleton (ed.), 1993–94a.

Singleton, D. 1994. Learning L2 lexis: a matter of form? In *The dynamics of language processes: essays in honor of Hans W. Dechert*, G. Bartelt (ed.). Tübingen: Narr.

Singleton, D. 1995a. Introduction. A critical look at the critical period hypothesis. In Singleton & Lengyel (eds.), 1995.

Singleton, D. 1995b. Second languages in the primary school: the age factor dimension. *Teanga: The Irish Yearbook of Applied Linguistics* 15: 155–166.

Singleton, D. 1996a. Formal aspects of the L2 mental lexicon: some evidence from university-level learners of French. In *Approaches to second language acquisition*, K. Sajavaara & C. Fairfeather (eds.). Jyväskylä: University of Jyväskylä (*Jyväskylä Cross Language Studies Series*, No. 17.)

Singleton, D. 1996b. Crosslinguistic lexical operations and the L2 mental lexicon'. In Hickey & Williams (eds.), 1996.

Singleton, D. 1996c. Cross-lexical consultation: out of the horse's mouth. *Revista Canaria de Estudios Ingleses* 32/33: 9–18.

Singleton, D. 1997. Cross-linguistic aspects of the mental lexicon. In *Language history and language modelling*, R. Hickey & S. Puppel (eds.). Berlin: Walter de Gruyter & Company.

Singleton, D. 1998. *Lexical processing and the 'language module'*. Dublin: Trinity College, Centre for Language and Communication Studies (*CLCS Occasional Paper*).

Singleton, D. & Lengyel, Z. (eds.) 1995. *The age factor in second language acquisition: a critical look at the Critical Period Hypothesis*. Clevedon: Multilingual Matters.

Singleton, D. & Little, D. (eds.) 1984a. *Language learning in formal and informal contexts*. Dublin: Irish Association for Applied Linguistics.

Singleton, D. & Little, D. 1984b. A first encounter with Dutch: perceived language distance and language transfer as factors in comprehension. In Mac Mathúna & Singleton (eds.), 1984.

Singleton, D. & Little, D. 1991. The second language lexicon: some evidence from university-level learners of French and German. *Second Language Research* 7: 61–82.

Singleton, D. & Little, D. 1992. Le lexique mental de l'apprenant d'une langue étrangère: quelques aperçus apportés par le TCD Modern Languages Research Project. In *Acquisition et enseignement/apprentissage des langues*, R. Bouchard, J. Billiez, J.-M. Colletta, V. de Nuchèze & A. Millet (eds.). Grenoble: LIDILEM.

Singleton, D. & Singleton, E. 1989. Lexical creativity: some examples and some possible implications for the mental lexicon. Paper presented at the Annual Meeting of the Association for French Language Studies, Portsmouth.

Singleton, D. & Singleton, E. 1998. The C-test and L2 acquisition/processing research. In *University language testing and the C-test*, J. A. Coleman (ed.). Portsmouth: University of Portsmouth (*Occasional Papers in Linguistics*), 150–178.

Skehan, P. 1989. *Individual differences in second-language learning*. London: Edward Arnold.

Skinner, B. 1957. *Verbal behavior.* New York: Appleton-Century-Crofts.

Skuttnabb-Kangas, T. 1976. Bilingualism, semilingualism and school achievement. *Linguistische Berichte* 45: 55–64.

Smedts, W. 1988. De beheersing van de nederlandse woordvorming tussen 7 en 17. In *First language acquisition*, F. Van Besien (ed.). Antwerp: Association Belge de Linguistique Appliquée / Universitaire Instelling Antwerpen (*ABLA Papers* No. 12).

Smith, B. 1988. The emergent lexicon from a phonetic perspective. In Smith & Locke (eds.), 1988.

Smith, M. 1926. An investigation of the development of the sentence and the extent of vocabulary in young children. *University of Iowa Studies in Child Welfare* 3: 92.

Smith, M. D. & Locke, J. (eds.) 1988. *The emergent lexicon: the child's development of a linguistic vocabulary.* London: Academic Press.

Smith, N. & Wilson, D. 1979. *Modern linguistics: the results of Chomsky's revolution*. Harmondsworth: Penguin.

Smith, P. 1986 The development of reading: the acquisition of a cognitive skill. In Fletcher & Garman (eds.), 1986.

Snow, C. 1986. Conversations with children. In Fletcher & Garman (eds.), 1986.

Snowling, M. 1981. Phoneme deficits in developmental dyslexia. *Psychological Research* 43: 219–234.

Soares, C. & Grosjean, F. 1984. Bilinguals in a monolingual and a bilingual speech mode: the effect on lexical access. *Memory and Cognition* 12: 380–386.

Söderman, T. 1989. Word associations of foreign language learners and native speakers – a shift in response type and its relevance for a theory of lexical development. *Scandinavian Working Papers on Bilingualism* 8: 114–121.

Söderman, T. 1993. Word associations of foreign language learners and native speakers: the phenomenon of a shift in response type and its relevance for lexical development. In *Near-native proficiency in*

English, H. Ringbom (ed.). Åbo: Åbo Akademi, English Department Publications.
Sonaiya, R. 1991. Vocabulary acquisition as a process of continuous lexical disambiguation. *IRAL* 29: 273–284.
Soudek, L. I. 1982. The mental lexicon in second language learning. Paper presented at the Thirteenth International Congress of Linguistics, Tokyo.
Spring, D. & Dale, P. 1977. Discrimination of linguistic stress in early infancy. *Journal of Speech and Hearing Research* 20: 224–231.
Stanovich, K. 1980. Toward an interactive-compensatory model of individual differences in the development of reading fluency. *Reading Research Quarterly* 16: 32–71.
Stanovich, K. & West, R. 1983. On priming by a sentenced context. *Journal of Experimental Psychology: General* 112: 1–36.
Stanovich, K., West, R. & Freeman, D. 1981. A longitudinal study of sentence context effects in second grade children: tests of an interactive-compensatory model. *Journal of Experimental Child Psychology* 32: 185–199.
Stark, R. 1980. Stages of speech development in the first year of life. In *Child phonology. Volume 1: Production*, G. Komshian, J. Kavanagh & C. Ferguson (eds.). New York: Academic Press.
Stark, R. 1986. Prespeech segmental feature development. In Fletcher & Garman (eds.), 1986.
Starkey, D. 1981. The origins of concept formation: object sorting and object preference in early infancy. *Child Development* 52: 489–497.
Stemberger, J. & MacWhinney, B. 1988. Are inflected forms stored in the lexicon? In Hammond & Noonan (eds.), 1988.
Stern, D., Jaffe, J., Beebe, B. & Bennett, S. 1975. Vocalizing in unison and in alternation: two modes of communication within the mother–infant dyad. In Aaronson & Rieber (eds.), 1975.
Stern, H. 1983. *Fundamental concepts of language teaching*. Oxford: Oxford University Press.
Stevick, E. 1996. *Memory, meaning and method: a view of language teaching*. Boston, MA: Heinle & Heinle.
Stock, R. 1976. *Some factors affecting the acquisition of foreign language lexicon in the classroom*. Ph.D. thesis. University of Illinois.
Stoffer, I. 1996. Vocabulary learning strategies as related to individual difference variables. Paper presented at the Thirtieth TESOL Convention. Chicago.
Streeter, L. 1976. Language perception of 2–month old infants show effects of both innate mechanisms and experience. *Nature* 259: 39–41.
Strick, G. 1980. A hypothesis for semantic development in a second language. *Language Learning* 30: 155–176.
Stubbs, M. 1986. *Educational linguistics*. Oxford: Blackwell.
Sugarman, S. 1981. The cognitive basis of classification in very young children: an analysis of object ordering trends. *Child Development* 52: 1172–1178.

Swan, M. 1997. The influence of the mother tongue on second language vocabulary acquisition and use. In Schmitt & McCarthy (eds.), 1997.

Swinney, D. 1979. Lexical access during sentence comprehension: (re)consideration of context effects. *Journal of Verbal Learning and Verbal Behavior* 18: 645–660.

Taeschner, T. 1983. *The sun is feminine: a study on language acquisition in bilingual children*. Berlin: Springer.

Taine, H. 1877. Acquisition of language by children. *Mind* 2: 252–259. Reprinted in Bar-Adon & Leopold (eds.), 1971.

Talmy, L. 1985. Lexicalization patterns: semantic structure in lexical forms. In *Language typology and syntactic description. Volume III: Grammatical categories and the lexicon*, T. Shopen (ed.). Cambridge: Cambridge University Press.

Tanaka, S. & Abe, H. 1985. Conditions on interlingual semantic transfer. In *On TESOL 84: a Brave New World for TESOL*, P. Larson, E. Judd & D. Messerschmidt (eds.). Washington, DC: TESOL.

Tanenhaus, M., Dell, G. & Carlson, G. 1987. Context effects in lexical processing: a connectionist approach to modularity. In Garfield (ed.), 1987b.

Tanenhaus, M. & Donnenworth-Nolan, S. 1984. Syntactic context and lexical access, *Quarterly Journal of Experimental Psychology* 36A: 649–661.

Tanenhaus, M., Leiman, J. & Seidenberg, M. 1979. Evidence for multiple stages in the processing of ambiguous words in syntactic contexts. *Journal of Verbal Learning and Verbal Behavior* 18: 427–440.

Tarone, E. 1977. Conscious communication strategies in interlanguage. In *On TESOL 77*, H. Brown, C. Yorio & R. Crymes (eds.). Washington, DC: TESOL.

Tarone, E. 1980. Communication strategies, foreigner talk, and repair in interlanguage. *Language Learning* 30: 417–431.

Tarone, E. & Yule, G. 1989. *Focus on the language learner*. Oxford: Oxford University Press.

Taylor, B. 1975. The use of overgeneralization and transfer learning strategies by elementary and intermediate students of EFL. *Language Learning* 25: 72–107.

Taylor, H., Lean, D. & Schwartz, S. 1989. Pseudoword repetion ability in learning disabled children. *Applied Psycholinguistics* 10: 203–219.

Taylor, I. 1976. Similarity between French and English words: a factor to be considered in bilingual language behavior? *Journal of Psycholinguistic Research* 5: 85–94.

Tiedemann, D. 1787. Observations on the development of mental faculties of children. Translated by C. Murchison & S. Langer in their article: Tiedemann's observations on the development of the mental faculties of children. *Pedagogical Seminary* 34: 205–230. Reprinted in abridged form in Bar-Adon & Leopold (eds.), 1971.

Todd, G., Gibson, A. & Palmer, B. 1968. Social reinforcement of infant babbling. *Child Development* 39: 591–596.

Tomlinson, B. 1996. Helping L2 readers to see. In Hickey & Williams (eds.), 1996.

Towell, R. & Hawkins, R. 1994. *Approaches to second language acquisition*. Clevedon: Multilingual Matters.

Tréville, M.-C. 1993a. *Rôle des congénères interlinguaux dans le développement du vocabulaire réceptif*. Québec: Centre International de Recherche en Aménagement Linguistique.

Tréville, M.-C. 1993b. Une expérience d'accès à la lecture en L2 et de développement du vocabulaire à partir des mots communs à L1 et à L2. Paper presented at the Centre de Recherche en Enseignement et Apprentissage Symposium on Vocabulary Research / Colloque sur la recherche en vocabulaire, Ontario.

Tréville, M.-C. & Duquette, L. 1996. *Enseigner le vocabulaire en classe de langue*. Vanves: Hachette.

Trier, J. 1931. *Der deutsche Wortschatz im Sinnbezirk des Verstandes*. Heidelberg: Carl Winter.

Tuacharoen, P. 1979. An account of speech development of a Thai child: from babbling to speech. In *Studies in Thai and Mon-Khmer phonetics and phonology: in honor of Eugenie J. A. Henderson*, T. Thongkum, V. Panupong, P. Kullavanijaya & M. Tingsabadh (eds.). Bangkok: Chulalongkorn University Press.

Tyler, L. & Wessels, J. 1983. Quantifying contextual contributions to word recognition processes. *Perception and Psychophysics* 34: 405–420.

Tzelgov, J., Henik, A. & Leiser, D. 1990. Controlling Stroop interference: evidence from a bilingual task. *Journal of Experimental Psychology: Learning, Memory and Cognition* 16: 760–771.

Tzeng, O. & Wang, W. S.-Y. 1983. The first two R's. *American Scientist* 71: 238–243.

Ullmann, S. 1962. *Semantics: an introduction to the science of meaning*. Oxford: Blackwell.

Ushioda, E. 1991. *Acculturation theory and language fossilization: a comparative case study*. M.Phil. dissertatation. University of Dublin.

Ushioda, E. 1993. *Acculturation theory and language fossilization: a comparative case study*. Dublin: Trinity College, Centre for Language and Communication Studies (*CLCS Occasional Paper* 37).

Ushioda, E. 1996a. *Language learners' motivational thinking: a qualitative study*. Ph. D. thesis. University of Dublin.

Ushioda, E. 1996b. *Learner autonomy 5: the role of motivation*. Dublin: Authentik.

Valentine, C. 1942. *The psychology of early childhood*. London: Methuen.

Van Hout, R. 1996. Statistical odds in language research. Keynote paper presented at the Sixth Annual Conference of the European Second Language Association (EUROSLA 6). Nijmegen.

Van Roey, J. 1990. *French–English contrastive lexicology – an introduction*. Louvain-la-Neuve: Peeters.

Van Vlack, S. 1992. Linguistics M.Phil. assignment on language acquisition/processing. University of Dublin.

Varadi, T. 1980. Strategies of target language learner communication message adjustment. *IRAL* 18: 59–71.
Verhallen, M. & Schoonen, R. 1993. Lexical knowledge of monolingual and bilingual children. *Applied Linguistics* 14: 344–363.
Vihman, M. & Miller, R. 1988. Words and babble at the threshold of language acquisition. In Smith & Locke (eds.), 1988.
Volterra, V., Bates, E., Benigni, L., Bretherton, I. & Camaioni, L. 1979. First words in language and action: a qualitative look. In Bates *et al.* (ed.), 1979.
Volterra, V. & Taeschner, T. 1978. The acquisition and development of language by bilingual children. *Journal of Child Language* 5: 311–326.
Von Frisch, K. 1967. *The dance and orientation of bees*. Cambridge, MA: Harvard University Press.
Vygotsky, L. 1962. *Thought and language*. Cambridge, MA: MIT Press.
Wade, C. & Tavris, C. 1996. *Psychology*. 4th edn. New York: HarperCollins.
Wallace, F. & Atkins, J. 1960. The meaning of kinship terms. *American Anthropologist* 62: 58–80.
Wallace, M. 1982. *Teaching vocabulary*. London: Heinemann.
Wang, W. 1969. Competing changes as a cause of residue. *Language* 45: 9–25.
Waterson, N. & Snow, C. (eds.) 1978. *The development of communication*. New York: Wiley & Sons.
Waxman, S. 1994. The development of an appreciation of specific linkages between linguistic and conceptual organization. In Gleitman & Landau (eds.), 1994.
Weinreich, U. 1953. *Languages in contact*. New York: Linguistic Circle of New York.
Weir, C. 1988. *Communicative language testing with special reference to English as a foreign language*. Exeter: University of Exeter (*Exeter Linguistic Studies* 11).
Weir, R. 1966. Some questions on the child's learning of phonology. In *The genesis of language*, F. Smith & G. Miller (eds.). Cambridge: Cambridge University Press.
Weisberg, P. 1963. Social and nonsocial conditioning of infant vocalization. *Child Development* 34: 377–388.
Werker, J. & Tees, R. 1984. Cross-language speech perception: evidence for perceptual reorganization during the first year of life. *Infant Behavior and Development* 7: 49–63.
West, R. & Stanovich, K. 1978. Automatic contextual facilitation in readers of three ages. *Child Development* 51: 1215–1221.
Whalen, D., Levitt, A. & Wang, Q. 1991. Intonational differences between the reduplicative babbling of French- and English-learning infants. *Journal of Child Language* 18: 501–516.
Whitaker, H. A. 1978. Bilingualism: a neurolinguistics perspective. In *Second language acquisition research: issues and implications*, W. Ritchie (ed.). New York: Academic Press.

Wilkins, D. 1972. *Linguistics in language teaching*. London: Edward Arnold.
Wilkins, D. 1976. *Notional syllabuses. A taxonomy and its relevance to foreign language curriculum development*. Oxford: Oxford University Press.
Wilkins, D. 1994. Lexical structures and second language acquisition. Paper presented at the EUROSLA/BAAL Joint Workshop 'Linguistic and psychological approaches to L2 acquisition of vocabulary', University of Essex.
Willems, G. 1987. Communication strategies and their significance in foreign language teaching. *System* 15: 351–364.
Willis, D. 1990. *The lexical syllabus*. London: Collins.
Wingfield, A. & Byrnes, D. 1981. *The psychology of human memory*. New York: Academic Press.
Winitz, H. ed.1981. *Native language and foreign language acquisition*. New York: The New York Academy of Sciences.
Winnick, W. & Daniel, S.1970. Two kinds of response priming in tachistoscopic recognition. *Journal of Experimental Psychology* 84: 74–81.
Witelson, S. 1977. Early hemispheric specialization and interhemispheric plasticity: an empirical and theoretical review. In Segalowitz & Gruber (eds.), 1977.
Woodrow, H. & Lowell, F. 1916. *Children's association frequency tables. Psychological Monographs* 22 (No. 97).
Woodworth, R. 1938. *Experimental psychology*. New York: Holt.
Woutersen, M. 1996a. Proficiency and the bilingual lexicon. Paper presented at the Eighteenth Annual Conference of the American Association for Applied Linguistics. Chicago.
Woutersen, M. 1996b. Modelling the bilingual lexicon: the pros and cons of repetition priming. Contribution to the symposium 'L2 lexical processing', organized by D. Singleton & K. de Bot, at the Eleventh AILA World Congress of Applied Linguistics, Jyväskylä. Abstract in Dufva *et al.* (eds.), 1996.
Woutersen, M. 1997. *Bilingual word perception*. Nijmegen: Katholieke Universiteit Nijmegen.
Woutersen, M., Cox, A., Weltens, B. & de Bot, K. 1994. Lexical aspects of standard dialect bilingualism. *Applied Linguistics* 15: 447–473.
Wright, F. 1990. What makes a test communicative? – *Teanga: Journal of the Irish Association for Applied Linguistics* 10: 53–62.
Yongqi Gu, P. 1996. False friends: error patterns of vocabulary recognition. Paper presented at the Eleventh World Congress of Applied Linguistics, Jyväskylä.
Younger, B. & Cohen, L. 1983. Infant perception of correlations among attributes. *Child Development* 54: 858–867.
Yule, G. & Tarone, E. 1990. Eliciting the performance of strategic competence. In Scarcella, Andersen & Krashen (eds.), 1990.
Zimmermann, R. 1989. A partial model of lexical search in L1–L2 translations. In Dechert & Raupach (eds.), 1989a.

Zimmermann, R. & Schneider, K. 1987. The collective learner tested: retrospective evidence for a model of lexical search. In Faerch & Kasper (eds.), 1987a.

Zurer Pearson, B., Fernández, S. & Oller, D. 1995. Cross-language synonyms in the lexicons of bilingual infants: one language or two? *Journal of Child Language* 22: 345–368.

Index

Aarts, 16, 280
Abe, 185, 323
Abelson, 35, 317
Abraham, 206, 210, 280, 286
Abrahamsen, 123, 282
abstraction in lexical development, 76–77, 78, 79, 82
Abunuwara, 178, 280
accessing L1 and L2 lexicons separately, 170–172
acculturation, 213
activation metaphor, 175
adult second language acquisition, 79
age and L2 lexical acquisition, 79, 167, 217, 218–219, 225, 227
agnosia, 114
Aitchison, 4, 26, 35, 65, 85, 98, 99, 117, 121, 126, 127, 141, 147, 280
Albert, M., 175, 312
Allen, E., 142, 280
Allen, R. E., 15, 21, 280
Allport, 19, 280
Anderman, 5, 280, 309
Anderson, J., 164, 280
Anderson, J. A., 121 (fn.), 280
Anderson, J. R., 102, 106, 125, 280
Anderson, R., 36, 280
Anglin, 73, 75, 76, 77, 78, 281
anomia, 98
anthropological linguistics, 34
aphasia, 19, 114
Aphek, 154, 164, 182, 287
Appel, 182, 239, 281
Ard, 135, 281
Arenberg, 42, 281
Arnaud, 19, 281, 300, 304, 318
Arnberg, L., 174, 281
Arnberg, P., 174, 281
Arthur, 48, 281
Articulator, 106, 107, 108
Asch, 77, 281
assimilative encoding, 165, 180–181
Atkins, 34, 325
Atkinson, 156, 281
atomistic teaching strategies, 50–51
attribution problem, 240–241
audio-lingual methodology, 3, 51
Audition component, 107
auditory processing, 86, 87, 88, 89, 90–91, 102, 107, 116, 117, 118–121, 150, 163
aural processing *see* auditory processing
authentic texts in the classroom, 52

babbling, 53, 61–67, 74, 80
  shift/drift, 62–64
baby talk, 67
'backlash interference', 163–164
  see also code-copying
Backus, 163, 182, 281
Baddeley, 69, 80, 148, 150, 281, 295, 313
Baetens-Beardsmore, 166, 281
Baker, 98, 281
Ballard, 125, 293
Balota, 153, 281
Bar-Adon, 143, 281, 282, 289, 323
Barrett, 65, 66, 68, 71, 282, 298, 303, 310, 312
Bartlett, 74, 285
Basic Interpersonal Communicative Skills (BICS), 200–201
basic level of categorization, 71, 73–74
basic triangle, 29–30
Bates, 56, 65, 66, 69, 282, 325
Bateson, 62, 282
Bauer, 73, 307
Baur, 200, 282
Beaton, 142, 149, 151, 156, 292
Beattie, 9, 119, 120, 198, 199, 292

Beauvillain, 168, 171, 282, 296
Bechtel, 123, 282
Becker, 199, 282
behaviourism, 62
Belnap, 185, 296
Benoussan, 142, 143, 164, 282, 305
Benson, 98, 282
Benveniste, 26, 282
Berger, 28, 282
Berko, 76, 135, 284
Besner, 142, 289
Bever, 110, 282
Bialystok, 159, 169, 186, 187, 188, 189, 282, 307
Biemiller, 47, 283
Bierwisch, 84, 109, 283
bilingualism, 130, 146, 152, 165, 166, 168–178
  compound, 172–174, 176–178
  co-ordinative, 172–174, 176–178
  subordinative, 172–174, 176–178
biological endowment, 20, 42–43, 45, 54, 56–58, 62, 69, 79, 125
Birkbeck Vocabulary Project, 131–136, 165, 189, 198, 220, 233, 234, 270
Bley-Vroman, 79, 167, 283
Bloom, L., 65, 72, 283
Bloom, P. A., 115, 120, 199, 283, 293
Bloomfield, 13, 31, 283
'blueprint for the speaker', 84, 106–111, 126, 128, 129
Blum, 143, 283
Boden, 57, 283
Bolinger, 34, 283
Bomba, 55, 57, 283
Bongaerts, 175, 177, 188, 283, 290, 302, 314
Bonin, 124 (fn.)
Bonvillian, 74, 312
Borland, 147, 283
borrowing, 25–26, 28, 174–175, 181, 239–242, 257, 275
Bowerman, 70, 71, 283
Boyd, 163, 182, 283
Brady, 157, 283, 284
brain metaphor, 121, 127
Braine, 143, 284
Brami-Mouling, 9, 284
Brédart, 9, 284
Bresnan, 122, 284, 285
Bretherton, 65, 66, 67, 282, 284, 325
Britton, 41, 44, 47, 284
Broeder, 121, 284
Brones, 168, 285
Browman, 98, 284
Brown, C., 3, 36, 133, 145–146, 150, 159, 162, 284, 299, 300
Brown, R., 19, 56, 60, 62, 73, 74, 76, 77, 98, 135 147, 204, 284
Brown, T., 155, 284
Brugmann, 26
Bruner, 43, 55, 56, 58, 59, 74, 77, 284, 285, 312, 317
Brunerian approach, 43, 55, 56, 58, 59, 70
Budhiprabha, 185, 281
Butterworth, G., 56, 285
Bybee, 167, 285
Byrnes, 4, 326

Callanan, 78, 285
Calvet, 12 (fn.), 27 (fn.), 285
Cammarota, 165, 184, 296
Campbell, 56, 74, 89, 285
Caramazza, 168, 285
Carey, 45, 74, 285
Carling, 11, 310
Carnap, 32, 285
Carroll, J., 188, 285
Carroll, J. B., 42, 285
Carston, 112, 118, 119, 285
Carter, A., 65, 66, 285–286
Carter, R., 3, 10, 13, 15, 16, 23, 76, 77, 131, 281, 286, 288, 290, 304, 311, 317
Cassirer, 43, 286
Castner, 68, 69, 286
Celce-Murcia, 141, 286
Champagnol, 209, 286
Channell, 131, 286
Chapelle, C., 198, 203–206, 286
Chapelle, J., 300, 318
Chen, H.-C., 178, 286
Chen, M., 27, 286
Chertok, 115, 286
child-directed speech, 43–45, 67
Chomsky, 18, 23, 24, 42, 57, 61, 62, 104, 105, 112, 286, 287
Chomskyan models/ideas, 4, 18, 34, 37, 42,57, 58, 62, 104–105, 112–113, 123, 124, 128
Cieslicka-Ratajczak, 19, 287
clang responses, 133, 134, 135, 136, 209, 234, 235–236
Clarapède, 211, 287
Clark, E., 70, 71, 72, 175, 287

Clark, H., 188, 300
Clark, M., 46, 287
Clarke, 88, 287
Clément, 214, 287
cloze, 115, 116, 117, 120, 166, 197, 198
Coady, 5, 157, 159, 284, 287, 300, 303, 311, 313
COBUILD, 22, 24
code-copying, 166, 174, 182
code-switching, 166, 169, 174–175, 182, 187, 188
cognates, 164–166, 168, 172–174, 177, 235, 241–242
Cognitive/Academic Language Proficiency (CALP), 200–201
cognitive hypothesis, 61
Cohen, A., 154, 155–156, 164, 182, 201, 208, 211, 212, 287
Cohen, L., 55, 326
Cohen, R., 47, 287
cohort model, 84, 91–99, 126, 127, 128, 129, 270
Coleman, L., 35, 287
Coles, 141, 288
collaborative research, 276–277
colligation, 15, 24, 32, 37, 38, 198, 269
collocation, 7, 15, 20–25, 32, 37, 38, 52, 198, 269, 272
Coltheart, 44, 45, 88, 93, 120, 199, 298, 308, 311, 312
communication strategies, 7, 71, 168, 179, 181, 186–189, 212–213, 219, 238–239, 248–249, 250–265, 271, 275
  abandonment, 254, 255
  approximation, 258, 259, 260, 261, 263
  borrowing, 25–26, 28, 174–175, 181, 239–242, 257, 275
  code-switching, 187, 188
  coinages, 179, 180, 219, 238–245, 246–249, 254–257, 258, 259, 260, 261
  foreignization, 187, 188
  translation, 187, 188
communicative language teaching, 3, 243–244
compensatory strategies *see* communication strategies
complementarity, 32–33
complexification of form–meaning relationships, 75, 78–79
componential analysis, 34–36
comprehension *see* reception
computational linguistics, 3, 16, 276
computer metaphor, 84, 121, 127
computerization of data, 216–217, 219, 271
concept development, 4, 42–43, 44, 47, 48, 53, 55–61, 70–79, 80–81
Conceptualizer, 106, 107, 109, 110
concrete versus abstract relations, 77–78
concrete versus abstract words, 155, 172–174
connectionism, 7, 83, 121–127, 128, 129, 270
connectivity between different components of the mental lexicon *see* interaction between different components of the mental lexicon
connotation, 52, 117, 143, 144
conscious language use, 186–187, 225–227, 252, 254, 255, 256, 257, 258, 259, 260–264
conscious learning, 152–154
consolidation of first language lexis, 68, 75–79
content words, 11, 14, 198, 205, 269, 271
context, 33–35, 37, 38, 45, 47, 52, 65–67, 69–70, 72, 73, 74–75, 84–88, 93–97, 104, 105, 106, 114–121, 128, 129, 131, 157–163, 167, 170–172, 173, 176, 179, 181, 197, 198,199, 200, 201, 203, 204, 205, 208, 221, 222, 223, 224, 225, 226, 227, 228, 229, 232, 242, 246, 264, 270, 272, 274
Contrastive Analysis Hypothesis, 185
Contrastive Hypothesis, 72
converseness, 32,33
cooing, 61, 80
Cook, 4, 18, 37 (fn.), 42, 58, 122, 124, 168–169, 177, 288
Corder, 181, 186, 288, 310
core vocabulary, 20
Corrigan, 20, 288
Cortese, 102, 317
Cosky, 101, 296
Cottrell, 125, 288
Cowie, 16, 24, 288
Craik, 148, 149, 150, 318–319
creativity
  in language use, 23–24, 94
  in the lexicon, 109, 179, 180, 219, 238–245, 246–249, 254–257, 258, 259, 260, 261
Crisafi, 73, 310

Cristoffanini, 168, 173, 288
Cromer, 59, 60, 61, 288
Crookes, 213, 288
cross-linguistic influence, 7, 48–50, 80–81, 82, 131, 141, 142, 143–144, 154, 163–167, 168–169, 170–175, 176, 177, 178–186, 187–188, 189–190, 215, 217, 218, 235, 238–250, 251, 255, 257–259, 265, 271, 273, 274–275, 178–186
Cruse, 10, 11, 109, 288
Crystal, 10 (fn.), 53, 63, 289
C-test, 196, 197–208, 210, 211, 213, 217, 219, 220–233, 236, 239–246, 247, 248, 254, 255, 271
cultural overlap, 48, 80
Cummins, 169 (fn.), 200–201, 289, 304
Cunha de Freitas, 161, 289
Cunningham, 135, 208, 289
Curley, 178, 303
Cutler, 43, 98, 289

Dagut, 144, 289
Dale, 64, 322
Daniel, 88, 326
Darwin, 52, 289
Davelaar, 142, 289
Davidson, 188, 289
Davis, C., 173, 289, 316
De Bot, 84, 109, 175, 177, 288, 289, 290, 292, 309–310, 326
De Boysson-Bardies, 63, 290, 298
De Groot, 172–174, 178, 265, 289, 290
De Houwer, 176, 290
Dechert, 163, 212, 290, 326
declarative knowledge, 106–107, 109, 128
Deese, 209, 290
Dell, 125, 126 (fn.), 290, 323
denotation, 32, 45, 52, 103–105, 117
DeSchutter, 66, 296
dictionaries, 15–16, 21–22, 24, 160, 257
dictionary metaphor, 84, 99
differences between the L1 and L2 lexicon *see* similarities between the L1 and the L2 lexicon
Dijkstra, 170, 296
Diller, 42, 282, 290
direct models of the mental lexicon, 84–99, 128
Dockrell, 71, 307
Dollerup, 47, 290
Dommergues, 248, 290
Donnenworth-Nolan, 90, 119, 290–291, 323
Dooling, 202 (fn.), 291
Döpke, 176, 291
Dore, 65, 66, 291
Dosher, 125, 291
double articulation, 25, 37
Draw A Line (DAL) test, 253–254, 260, 262
Dromi, 65, 66, 72, 73, 291
Drosdowski, 28, 282, 291
Duncker, 211, 291
Dupuy, 159, 160, 291
Duquette, 3, 162, 291, 324
Dušková, 185, 291

Eilers, 54, 64, 291
Eimas, 53, 54, 291
Elliot, 71, 291
Ellis, A., 9, 19, 119, 120, 198, 199, 291
Ellis, N., 142, 148, 149, 151, 152–154, 156, 177, 284, 292
Ellis, R., 50, 127, 155, 162–163, 186, 292, 302
Elman, 124, 127, 292–293
Emmorey, 90, 91, 98, 99, 103, 104, 112, 167, 293
empty words, 11, 205
see also grammatical words
encyclopedic knowledge, 103–105, 106, 108, 112, 128
Entwisle, 76, 135, 293
Ericsson, 208, 293
error analysis, 179–181, 185., 218, 245
Ervin, 76, 135, 293
essay-writing, 144–145, 197
etymology, 15, 16
Evans, 148, 151, 293
Evett, 90, 300
explicit learning, 152–154

Faerch, 186, 187, 188, 207, 208, 287, 290, 293, 296, 298, 303, 314
Fantini, 176, 293
Farhady, 147, 299
Fay, 98, 289
'feel'-based language use *see* impulsive language use
Feitelson, 162, 293
Feldman, J., 125, 293
Feldman, U., 212, 230, 293
Ferguson, 48, 293, 295, 322
Fillmore, 58, 293

first language attrition, 163–164
first language lexical acquisition, 4, 5, 7, 41–47, 52–79, 110, 141, 142–143, 145, 146, 147, 149, 150, 151, 156, 163–164, 167, 269, 276
 beyond the childhood years, 41–42, 75, 110, 143, 146, 147, 279
 in a formal setting, 46–47, 52
 in infancy/childhood, 42–47, 52–79, 141, 142, 143,147, 150, 269
 stages of, 4, 52–79
first language lexical processing 4, 5, 7, 83–129, 151, 152, 167, 173, 174, 178, 186, 188–189, 220, 235, 238, 239, 269, 276
 see also cross-linguistic influence
first words, 4, 53, 56, 62, 65–67, 68–74, 75, 81
Firth, 22, 54, 293
Firthian linguistics, 22–23
Fischler, 115, 120, 199, 293
fixed expressions, 23–24
Flavell, 57, 294
fluent restoration, 95, 118
fluidity of lexical meaning *see* vagueness of lexical meaning
Flynn, 20, 54, 308
Fodor, 34, 43, 56, 112–121, 122, 124, 128, 129, 199, 203, 207, 294, 301
Fodorian view of language and mind, 112–121, 122, 123, 128–129, 225
foreigner talk/register, 48
form and meaning, respective roles of, 7, 130–167, 173–174, 177–178, 179, 189, 217–218, 220–237, 238, 239, 270, 271, 272–274. 275
form words, 11
 see also grammatical words
Formulator, 106, 107, 109, 110
Forrester, 121, 294
Forster, 84, 91, 99–106, 108, 126, 128, 270, 294
Foss, 118, 119, 294
fossilization, 165–166, 181, 182, 213
frame, 36
Frauenfelder, 97, 307
Freed, 48, 294
frequency, 43, 47, 67, 91, 101, 102, 278
Fromkin, 90, 91, 98, 99, 103, 104, 112, 131, 167, 293, 294
full words, 11, 205
 see also content words
function words, 11
Funnell, 19, 280

Gaies, 50, 294–295
Gairns, 3, 295
Galaburda, 64, 296
Galisson, 3, 295
Gall, Franz Josef, 111
Galvin, 248, 295
gang effects, 167–168
Gardner, H., 71, 295
Gardner, R., 213, 295
Garfield, 111, 294, 295, 308, 323
Garman, 4, 19, 84, 88, 90, 91, 97, 100, 105, 106, 122, 123, 285–286, 289, 294, 295, 297, 301, 321, 322
Garnica, 43, 295
Gass, 84, 127, 131, 135, 281, 283, 288, 295, 301, 303
Gasser, 127, 295
Gathercole, S., 69, 150, 295
Gathercole, V., 72, 295
general knowledge *see* encyclopedic knowledge
generalization in lexical development *see* abstraction in lexical development
Genesee, 169, 295
George, H., 185, 295
Gerard, 171, 173, 295, 317
Gerloff, 212, 296
Geschwind, 64, 296
Giacobbe, 165, 180, 184, 296
Gibson, A., 323
Gibson, E., 140, 296
Gillette, 208, 296
Gillis, 66, 296
Gilmore, 34, 296
global amnesia, 152, 153
Goodluck, 54, 55, 62, 296
Goodman, 47, 296
Gough, J., 299
Gough, P., 89, 101, 296
Graham, 185, 296
Grainger, 168, 170–172, 282, 296
grammar, 3–4, 7, 9–10, 11, 13–14, 15–20, 21, 25, 38, 99, 100, 105, 106, 107, 108, 110, 112, 116, 128, 140, 142, 143, 146–147, 149, 166, 167, 168, 170, 174, 179, 197, 198, 201, 205, 222, 232, 241, 249, 260, 261, 263, 264, 269, 272
Grammatical Encoder, 107, 108

grammatical words, 11, 13, 14, 198, 205
Grammont, 26
Granger, 164, 203, 296–297, 305
grapheme–phoneme correspondence/
conversion, 89, 91, 102, 184
graphemic form *see* orthography
Grauberg, 179, 180, 186, 297
Green, 126 (fn.), 127, 169, 175, 297
Grellet, 212, 297
Grenfell, 51, 297
Griffiths, 61, 73, 297
Grinstead, 157, 297
Grosjean, 170, 297, 321
Gross, 3, 16–18, 297
Grossberg, 125, 297
Grotjahn, 197, 200–201, 297, 301, 306
Gruendel, 71, 297
Guillaume, 70, 298
Gunzi, 61, 69, 298

Haastrup, 157, 208, 210, 212, 293, 298
Hakuta, 169, 307
Hallé, 63, 298
Halliday, 22, 144, 298, 299
Hallidayan linguistics, 22–23
Hamers, 169, 298
Hammer, 115, 313
Harley, 5, 131, 185, 200, 292, 298, 304
Harris, J., 57, 298
Harris, M., 42, 43, 44, 45, 60, 61, 66, 68, 69, 70, 72, 74, 75, 78, 88, 93, 120, 199, 298–299, 308
Hasan, 22, 48, 299
Hatch, 3, 36, 131, 133, 145–146, 147, 150, 159, 286, 299
Haugen, 163, 166, 299
Hawkins, 109, 110, 324
Haynes, 5, 157, 284, 300
Henning, 154, 299
Henzl, 50, 299
Herbst, 16, 299
Herman, 157, 311
heterogeneity of response, 222–224
hierarchical classification in lexical development, 76, 77–78
Hill, 184–185, 299
Hinton, 123, 306, 316
Ho, 178, 286
homographs, 168
Hosenfeld, 212, 299
Hsia, 46, 299
Huckin, 5, 157, 284, 287, 300, 303, 313
Hudson, 26, 300
Hulme, 141, 151–152, 300
Hulstijn, 136–139, 155, 159 (fn.), 160, 292, 300
Humphreys, 90, 300
Hussian, 42, 300
Hutchinson, 45, 307
hypnosis, 115
hyponymy, 32, 34, 36, 78, 143, 235

idiom/idiomaticity, 24, 50, 144, 158
idiom principle, 24
idiosyncratic information, 3–4, 15, 18
Ijaz, 185, 300
imageability, 142, 151, 155–157, 273
imitation, 51, 58–59, 67, 69
immersion, 52
implicit learning, 152–154
impulsive language use, 254, 255, 256, 257, 259, 260, 262
impulsivity versus reflectivity, 251, 252, 253–254, 256, 257, 259, 260–264
incidental vocabulary acquisition, 157, 159–162, 273–274
incompatibility, 32, 235
indirect models of the mental lexicon, 84, 99–106, 128
individual approaches to language learning *see* learning stragegies
inductive processes, 20, 42
informational encapsulation, 113–121, 122, 129, 227
Ingle, 147, 310
Inhelder, 57, 58, 59, 300, 314
innate aspects of lexical development *see* biological endowment
innovations *see* communication strategies (coinages) *and* creativity in the lexicon
input, 4, 43–52, 54, 69–70, 73, 79, 81, 86, 88, 90, 91, 92, 94, 102, 162, 163, 180, 209, 219, 275
see also reception
instructed L2 lexical acquisition, 50–52
integration between the L1 and the L2 lexicon *see* separation between the L1 and the L2 lexicon
intelligence and vocabulary learning, 152, 153
interaction between different components of the mental lexicon, 4, 5, 83, 86–91, 100, 101, 109–110, 111, 128, 270

interactive activation *see* spreading activation
internal stability/coherence, 13–14
interview data, 196, 213, 246, 251, 252, 253, 254, 255, 257, 258, 263–264
intonation, 9, 63–64, 67, 254
intralexical difficulties, 136, 140–147
introspection, 195, 196, 197, 206, 207–208, 211–212, 213–215, 218, 225, 226, 227, 228, 230–232, 242–246, 247–248, 250, 252, 253, 254, 256, 257, 258, 259, 260, 263, 278
  retrospection, 207–208, 211, 212, 258
  self-observation, 211
  self-report, 211, 213–215, 257, 259, 263
  self-revelation, 211
  think-aloud, 208, 211–212, 230, 247, 252, 253, 254, 256
Isaacs, 188, 300
isolating lexical units in the speech signal, 43–45, 48, 51, 80, 81, 269
Ittzés, 157–158, 300

Jackendoff, 34, 35, 300–301
Jackson, 10, 301
Jacobs, 113, 301
Jakobovits, 163, 301
Jakschik, 200, 301
James, 163, 185, 301
Jessner, 169, 301
Jin, 173, 301
Johanson, 163, 182, 301
joint attention, 44–45, 56, 60
Jones, S., 22, 319
Jordan, 164, 280

Kagan, 253, 285, 301
Kaplan, 122, 284
Karmiloff-Smith, 75, 78, 79, 301
Kasper, 186, 187, 207, 208, 287, 290, 293, 296, 298, 303, 314
Kass, 35, 317
Katz, 34, 43, 301
Kay, 35, 287
Kellerman, 49, 144, 163, 164, 180, 181, 186, 187, 188, 189, 207, 212, 283, 301–302, 313, 314
Kelly, M., 43, 302
Kelly, P., 5, 130, 206, 302
Kemler, 58, 302
Kent, 133, 209, 234, 302
Kent-Rosanoff list, 133, 209, 234
Keppel, 209, 314, 316
Kerkman, 173, 302
keyword technique, 51, 155, 273
Killion, 199, 282
King, 185, 298
Kirchner, 295
Kirsner, 169, 173, 174, 288, 302
Klein-Braley, 197, 198, 200, 297, 302, 315
Koda, 5, 130, 183–184, 206, 303
Kohonen, 148, 149, 319
Kolers, 170, 173, 303, 311
Kram, 90
Krashen, 50, 159, 160, 181, 291, 302, 303, 317, 326
Krings, 212, 303
Krishnamurthy, 22, 303
Kroll, 178, 303
Kruideneier, 214, 287
Kuhl, 54, 64, 303
Kushnir, 170, 307

Labov, 35, 303–304
Lachman, 202 (fn.), 291
Lado, 81, 185, 304
Lakoff, 35, 304
Lambert, 169, 171, 213, 295, 298, 304, 313, 314
Lamiroy, 17–18, 304
Lance, 185, 304
Lane, 248, 290
Langer, 43, 304, 323
language disorders, 19, 98, 114, 150, 152, 153
language examination data, 195, 196, 197, 213
language faculty *see* modularity
language loss, 170
language teaching, 3, 20, 47, 50–52, 156, 189, 212, 213, 264, 271, 272, 273, 274, 275, 276
language testing, 19–20, 166, 168–169, 195, 196, 197–206, 210, 213, 276
Lanza, 176, 304
Lapaire, 11, 205, 304
Larsen-Freeman, 199, 281, 304
Lasky, 54, 304
Laufer, 5, 20, 130, 131, 136, 140–147, 154, 164, 206, 220, 282, 289, 304–305

learnability, 20, 131, 136–147, 149
learner autonomy, 263–264
learning strategies, 50–52, 142, 143, 145, 149, 151, 154–157, 161–162, 164, 182–183, 214, 252, 257, 259, 260, 263–265, 271, 272, 273
Leech, 34, 35, 305
Leinbach, 127, 307
lemma, 106, 107–108
Lemmens, 16, 305
Leopold, 61, 64, 282, 289, 305, 323
Leung, 178, 286
Levelt, 84, 106–111, 126, 128, 129, 270, 305
Levenston, 140, 143, 283, 305
Levin, 140, 296
Levine, 121 (fn.), 305
Lewin, 56, 317
Lewis, M., 3, 20, 305
Lewis, M. M., 65, 72, 305
lexeme, 10, 11, 13, 48, 107
lexical awareness, 8–9, 215
lexical change, 25–26, 182, 239–240, 241–242
lexical confusions, 132, 133, 136–140, 142, 146–147
lexical creations *see* communication strategies (coinages) and creativity in the lexicon
lexical creativity *see* creativity in the lexicon
lexical decision, 85, 90, 101, 102, 116, 173, 177
lexical diffusion, 26–27
lexical fields, 31, 32, 52, 72
lexical grids, 272
lexical guessing, 131, 157–159, 160
lexical hypothesis, 108
lexical-redundancy rules, 109
lexical subsystems *see* lexical fields
lexical words, 10
see also content words
lexicography, 15–16, 21–22
lexicon, definition of, 7, 14–38, 269, 271, 272, 276
library metaphor, 84, 99–100
Lightfoot, 286
Linebarger, 113, 305
Linnarud, 5, 130, 144, 206, 305
listening *see* auditory processing
literacy and the lexicon, 9, 41, 49–52, 79, 81, 157
Little, 20, 49, 52, 198, 201, 207, 217, 218, 219, 220–225, 226, 238–242, 305–306, 307, 317, 320–321
Littlewood, 186, 188, 306
loanwords *see* borrowing
'local' information *see* idiosyncratic information
Lock, 66, 285, 306
Locke, 62, 63, 64, 284, 306, 321, 325
logogen model, 84–91, 92, 93–94, 126, 128, 129, 270
'London School' *see* Firthian lingustics
Long 199, 282, 304
long-term research, 276, 278–279
Lorimer, 65, 306
Lörscher, 212, 306
Lowell, 77, 326
Lucariello, 68, 312
Lyons, 10, 12, 14, 30, 31–34, 35, 45, 48, 72, 306

Mac Mathúna, 287, 306, 320
MacKain, 54, 55, 64, 306
Mackin, 24, 288
Maclaran, 27, 48, 104, 306–307
Macnamara, 170, 209, 307
MacWhinney, 127, 167, 287, 307, 322
Mägiste, 178, 307
Malakoff, 169, 307
Mandler, 73, 307
Marcus, 97, 307
Maréchal, 133, 136, 234–236, 307
marginalization of lexical issues, 3
Markman, 45, 78, 285, 307
Marshall, 84, 90, 311, 312
Marslen-Wilson, 84, 91–99, 118, 119, 126, 127, 128, 129, 204, 270, 294, 307–308
Martin, 43, 302
Martinet, 25, 308
Martohardjono, 20, 54, 308
Masny, 265, 308
master file, 100–103, 105–106
mathematical modelling, 278
Matthei, 97, 99, 102, 103, 308
McCaig, 24, 288
McCarthy, 3, 286, 288, 305, 311, 315, 317, 323
McClelland, 123, 124, 125, 127, 292–293, 308–309, 316
McDonough, S., 148, 306

McNeill, 19, 76, 98, 135, 147, 204, 284, 309
McShane, 43, 55, 66, 71, 72, 74, 75, 78, 125, 142, 309
meaning *see* semantics; form and meaning, respective roles of
Meara, 4, 5, 77, 131–136, 140, 147, 157, 159 (fn.), 164, 165, 177, 198, 203, 208, 209, 220, 222, 233, 240, 270, 278, 309–310
Meder, 200, 282
Meisel, 48, 310
memory, 4, 23 (fn.), 69, 72, 80, 89, 99, 114, 123, 131, 141, 148–157, 159–160, 165, 167, 175, 178, 180, 183, 230, 232, 239
Merriman, 72, 310
Merten, 41, 318
Mervis, 45, 73, 310, 316
metaphorical meaning, 34, 71, 77, 143, 144
Meyer, D, 102, 310
Meyer, R., 30, 310
Milech, 173, 288
Miller, C., 174, 314
Miller, J., 54, 64, 303
Miller, R., 65, 67, 70, 71, 291, 325
Milroy, 27, 310
minimal free form, 13–14
minimalism, 18
Minsky, 36, 310
mixed representational system, 172–174
models of lexical acquisition/processing, 7, 64, 72, 172, 175, 176, 218, 83–129, 270
modularity, 7, 83, 111–121, 122, 128–129, 167, 207, 225–227, 270
Mohanty, 169, 310
Mondria, 5, 160, 161, 310
Moore, T., 11, 310
Morais, 46, 310
Moreau, 55, 63, 65, 67, 310
morphological complexity, 140, 142, 143
morphology *see* grammar
morphosyntax *see* grammar
Morse, 54, 64, 310
Morton, 84–91, 126, 128, 129, 270, 287, 311
Moscovitch, 64, 311
motivation, 195, 196, 213–215, 246
multicompetence, 168–169
multilingualism *see* bilingualism
multiple meaning *see* polysemy
Muysken, 182, 239, 281

Nagy, 157, 159, 311
naming insight, 66–67, 74
Nas, 173, 290
Nation, 3, 5, 51, 130, 159, 206, 281, 290, 304, 305, 311, 317
nativism *see* biological endowment
naturalistic second language lexical development, 48–50, 51, 52, 79, 264
Nelson, E., 41, 311
Nelson, K., 56, 58, 60, 66, 68, 69, 71, 74, 75, 135, 159, 311–312
neogrammarians, 26
Nerlove, 77, 281
Newcombe, 90, 312
Newson, 4, 18, 42, 58, 122, 124, 288
Ninio, 56, 60, 74, 312
non-words, 69, 89, 92, 93, 101–102, 140, 141, 149, 150, 152, 157, 158
Norman, 125, 311, 316
Nortier, 174, 312

Obler, 175, 312
Odlin, 163, 305, 312
Ogden, 29, 312
O'Gorman, 134, 312
Oldfield, 84, 311, 312
Oller, D., 63, 291, 312, 327
Olshtain, 163–164, 182, 312
Olver, 77, 285
one-word utterance stage, 62, 63, 152
oral interaction and lexical acquisition, 157, 162–163
Orne, 115, 313
orthography, 7, 11, 12, 14, 15, 27–29, 38, 46, 89–91, 99, 100, 101, 102, 132, 133, 140, 157, 172, 184, 218, 228, 230–232, 239
  alphabetic, 12, 28, 46, 184
  logographic, 27–28, 46, 184
  syllabic, 28, 46, 184
ostensive definition/ostension, 44, 45, 47, 48, 50, 60, 79
Ostmann, 26
output, 4, 86, 87, 89, 90, 102, 112
  see also production
over-extension, 70–72, 73, 76, 81

Padden, 54, 303
Padron, 156, 313

Palmberg, 186, 188, 313
Palmer, F., 10, 20, 313
Papagno, 80, 148, 151, 164, 281, 313
paradigmatic associations, 76, 78, 135–136, 209, 234, 235
Paradis, 175, 312, 313
parallel distributed processing *see* connectionism
parallel processing versus serial processing, 122–123
Paribakht, 161, 187, 313
parts of speech, 140, 142
Patterson, 84, 311, 312
Payne, 150, 284
Peal, 169, 313
pedagogical grammar, 20
perceived language distance *see* psychotypology
perception *see* reception
peripheral access files, 99–103, 105–106
Perry, 155, 284
Peters, 24, 313
Phillips, T., 141, 142, 313
Phillipson, 210, 293, 298, 301, 313, 315
philology, 18
phoneme *see* phonetics/phonology
phonetics/phonology, 7, 9, 11, 12–13, 14, 15, 25–27, 38, 43–44, 45, 53–55, 62–64, 69, 80, 89–91, 92, 93, 94, 95, 96, 97, 98, 99, 100, 101, 102, 106, 107, 108, 110, 112, 118, 119, 128, 131–136, 140, 141, 147, 148–151, 154, 157, 167, 168, 170, 180, 181, 187, 206, 217–218, 220, 228, 230–232
phonological working memory, 69, 80, 89, 141, 148–151, 157
Piaget, 57, 58, 59, 300, 314
Piattelli-Palmarini, 59, 286, 300, 314
Picoche, 10, 314
pictogen, 90
Picture Discrimination test, 253, 260, 262
Pinker, 43, 124, 294, 314
Plaut, 124 (fn.), 127, 314
Plowden Report, 47
Plunkett, 121, 284
polar antonymy, 32, 33, 235
polyglottism *see* bilingualism
polysemy, 30, 45, 104, 143–144
Poplack, 174, 314
positional mobility, 13–14
Postal, 34, 43, 301
Postman, 209, 314, 316
Potter, 176, 178, 314
Poulisse, 186, 187, 188, 208, 212, 283, 302, 314
pragmatics, 64, 65, 66, 81, 93, 94, 96, 103–105, 106, 107, 110, 112, 117, 118, 128, 143, 158, 160, 163, 164, 167, 201, 202, 205, 218, 221, 222, 225, 233, 234, 237, 269, 270, 271
  see also context
Premack, A., 56, 314
Premack, D., 56, 314
Preston, 171, 314
primary level of articulation, 25, 37
priming, 85–86, 87–88, 102–103, 118–119, 152–153, 169, 171, 173, 177
Prince, 124, 314
problem solving, 113, 114, 186, 212, 217, 219, 226, 243, 245, 248, 254–265
procedural knowledge, 106–107, 109
production, 11, 23, 24, 53, 55, 61, 62, 63, 64, 65, 66, 66, 67, 68, 69, 71, 72, 73, 74, 75, 77, 80, 81, 86, 87, 88, 95, 98, 100, 106, 108, 109–110, 120, 122, 123, 143, 153, 161,179–181, 184–186, 204, 206, 208, 240, 246, 259, 260, 263, 264, 275
  see also output
proficiency, 20, 41, 117, 132, 134, 135, 136, 141, 142, 154, 156, 157, 166, 176–178, 198, 199, 200, 201, 206, 213, 248–249, 250, 254, 275
pronounceability, 140–141, 149, 151
prototypes, 35–36, 55, 57
pseudo-words *see* non-words
psychotypology, 164, 180, 183, 241–242, 248, 250
Pulman, 35, 314
Pylshyn, 124, 294

qualitative versus quantitative research, 199, 276, 277–278
Quay, 176, 314
questionnaire data, 194, 196–197
Quine, 45, 57, 314

Raatz, 197, 198, 200, 302, 314–315
Radford, 3, 18, 109, 315
Ramsey, 185, 315
Randall, 209, 234, 315
Raugh, 156, 281

Raupach, 163, 290, 326
Read, 204, 315
reading, 46–47, 49–50, 51–52, 70, 87, 88, 89, 101, 102, 109, 119–121, 125, 156–157, 158, 159, 160, 161, 183–184, 206, 230
  see also visual processing
recency, 99, 102
reception, 23, 46–47, 48, 49, 50, 51–52, 61, 69, 70, 84, 85, 86, 87, 88, 89, 90–91, 92, 93, 94, 95, 96, 97, 98, 99, 100, 101, 102, 106, 107, 109, 112, 116, 117, 118–121, 125, 127, 140, 150, 153, 154, 156–157, 158, 159, 160, 161, 162–163, 166, 172, 183–184, 202 (fn.), 203, 204, 206, 275
  see also input
recognition *see* reception
Redman, 3, 295
Reed, 284, 285, 315
reference/referentiality, 29–30, 32, 45, 56, 60, 64, 65–67, 68, 71,74–75, 82, 188–189
referent, 29, 30, 44, 45, 56, 72, 88, 90
reflective language use *see* conscious language use
Regier, 124 (fn.), 127, 315
rehearsal, 148, 151, 160, 163, 273
Reich, 73, 315
repeition *see* imitation
Rescorla, 71, 315
restructuring of first language lexis *see* consolidation of first language lexis
re-valuation of lexical issues, 3–4, 5, 6
Rey, 22, 315
Rey-Debove, 22, 315
Rheingold, 62, 315
rhyme monitoring, 96–97
Ricciardelli, 169, 315
Ricciuti, 58, 315
Richards, I., 29, 312
Richards, J., 185, 288, 315
Richelle, 55, 63, 65, 67, 310
Ridley, 208 (fn.), 210, 212, 218, 219, 238, 248–249, 251–265, 306, 315
Ringbom, 163, 164, 180, 239, 316, 321–322
Robins, 26, 298, 316
Robinson, 20, 316
Rodgers, 140, 141, 142, 316
Roeper, 97, 99, 102, 103, 308
Rogers, 5, 280, 309
Romaine, 26, 164, 166, 316
Rondal, 9, 284
Rosanoff, 133, 209, 234, 302
Rosch, 35, 73, 316
Rosenbaum, 41, 311
Rosenfeld, 121 (fn.), 280
Rosenzweig, 209, 234, 316
rote-learning, 51, 264, 272
Rumelhart, 121, 123, 124, 125, 126, 306, 316
Russel, 209, 316
Ryle, 106, 316

Saeed, 10, 34, 316
Sampson, G., 23 (fn.), 316
Sánchez-Casas, 173, 289, 316
Sandoz, 18, 316–317
Sanguineti de Serrano, 212, 317
Sankoff, 174, 314
Sapir, 9, 317
Särkkä, 22, 317
Saunders, 176, 317
Saussure, 30, 237, 317
Saussurean linguistics, 26, 30, 31, 32
Savage-Rumbaugh, 56, 317
Sawers, 22, 317
Scaife, 56, 317
Scarborough, D., 102, 171, 173, 295, 317
Scarborough, H., 102, 317
Schanen, 20, 317
Schank, 35, 317
Schatz, 174, 312
schema-theoretic models, 36
Schmidt, 127, 177, 213, 283, 288, 292, 317
Schmitt, 3, 305, 311, 315, 317, 323
Schneider, 208, 327
Scholfield, 158, 317
Schoonen, 146, 325
Schouten-van Parreren, 157, 159–160, 317–318
Schreuder, 5, 84, 109, 175, 283, 290, 297, 302, 309, 311, 314, 318
Schumann, 113, 213, 301, 318
Schvaneveldt, 102, 310
Schwartz, G., 41, 318
scripts, 35–36
search model, 84, 99–106, 126, 128, 270
second language lexical research, deficiencies of, 4–5
secondary level of articulation, 25, 37

segmental awareness, 46
Seibert, 157, 318
Seidenberg, 90, 119, 124, 290–291, 318, 323
Seliger, 207, 248, 282, 318
Selinker, 84, 127, 288, 295, 301, 303, 313
Semantic Feature Theory, 71, 72, 301
semantic field *see* lexical field theory
semantics, 7, 11, 13, 14, 15, 20–23, 25, 29–37, 42–45, 47, 48–52, 53, 54, 55–61, 64–67, 68–79, 80–82, 86–87, 91, 93–94, 95, 96, 99, 100, 101, 103–105, 106, 107, 108, 109, 110, 112, 116, 117, 118, 127, 130–167, 168, 170, 173, 174, 175–176, 177–178, 179, 180, 181, 182, 184–185, 188–189, 190, 201, 202, 217–218, 220–237, 238, 239, 243, 244, 253, 256, 260, 261, 262, 269, 270, 271, 272, 273, 274, 275
sense-relations, 32–37, 38, 143–145, 235
sensori-motor stage, 57, 58
separation between the L1 and the L2 lexicon, 5, 7, 83, 130, 167–189, 190, 218, 238–250, 251, 265, 270, 271, 273, 274–275
serial processing versus parallel processing, 122–123
Service, 115, 148, 149, 150, 157, 164, 232, 318–319
Seymour, 90, 319
Shallice, 124 (fn.), 127, 314
Shannon, 174, 319
shared reference *see* joint attention
Sharwood Smith, 163, 302, 313
shift in word association response type, 76, 78, 81, 135–136
sign (with socially shared meaning), 59
similarities between the L1 and the L2 lexicon, 5, 7, 41, 79–82, 83, 111, 130–190, 217–218, 220–237, 238, 250, 269–270, 271, 272, 273, 274
Simon, H., 208, 293
Sinclair, 16, 22, 24, 36, 203, 319
Singleton, D., 4, 5, 6, 25, 26, 48, 49, 51, 52, 62, 110, 111, 112, 113, 131, 158, 163, 165, 175, 179, 180, 181 (fn.), 185–186, 188, 193 (fn.), 198, 200, 201, 203, 207, 217, 218, 219, 220–234, 238–249, 251, 252, 254–259, 287, 288, 290, 292, 300, 305, 306, 307, 308, 309–310, 315, 317, 318, 319–321, 326
Singleton, E., 198, 203, 216, 217, 219, 321
Siqueland, 55, 58, 283, 291
situational knowledge *see* context
Skehan, 214, 321
Skinner, 62, 321
Skuttnabb-Kangas, 169 (fn.), 321
slips of the tongue, 19
Small, 125, 288
Smedts, 41, 143, 321
Smith, B., 61, 321
Smith, L., 58, 302
Smith, M., 68, 321
Smith, N., 57, 105, 112, 167, 321
Smith, P., 46, 321
Snow, 43, 44, 285, 289, 295, 321, 325
Snowdon, 54, 80, 310
Snowling, 157, 321
Soares, 170, 321
Söderman, 135–136, 209, 321–322
Sonaiya, 145, 322
Soudek, 131, 322
sound *see* phonetics/phonology
'special teaching', 60, 158
specificity of meaning in lexical acquisition, 143, 145
speech/speaking, 4, 8–9, 12, 13, 24, 25, 43–44, 45, 48, 50, 51, 53–55, 59–60, 62, 63, 64, 65, 67, 74, 79, 80, 81, 82, 84, 86, 88, 95, 97, 98, 100, 106–111, 119, 120, 121, 123, 128, 148, 152, 153, 163, 175, 176, 180, 186, 188–189, 199, 200, 208, 212, 263, 269, 275
Speech Comprehension System, 107
speech perception *see* auditory processing
speech shadowing, 95, 118
speech sound discrimination, 53–55
spelling *see* orthography
spreading activation, 125–126, 127, 129
Spring, 64, 322
Stanovich, 47, 199, 322, 325
Stark, 63, 64, 322
Starkey, 58, 322
Stemberger, 167, 322
Stemmer, 212, 230, 293
Stern, D., 62, 322
Stern, H., 186, 322
Stevick, 124, 125, 322
Stock, 141, 142, 322

Stoffer, 182, 322
Stone, 125, 297
story-tell data, 196, 206, 210–213, 246, 247, 248, 251, 252, 254, 255, 256, 260, 261
strategic competence, 205, 212
strategic styles, 219, 252, 254–265, 271
Streeter, 54, 322
Strick, 185, 322
Stroop test, 171, 178
structuralism, 30
structuralist semantics, 30–35, 72
Stubbs, 8, 322
stylistic information/knowledge, 99, 106, 143, 144
subcategorization, 15, 198
Sugarman, 58, 322
superordinateness, 32, 76, 78, 143
Swan, 163, 323
Swinney, 116, 117, 119, 120, 323
symbol (non-codified signifier), 59
symbolic function, 58–59
symbolic paradigm/symbolism, 123–125, 129
synonymy, 11, 22, 29, 32, 33, 34, 36, 72, 143, 144–145, 177, 235, 258
see also translation equivalents
syntagmatic associations, 76, 78, 134, 135–136, 234
syntagmatic–paradigmatic shift, 76, 78, 81, 135–136
syntax *see* grammar
synthetic teaching strategies, 50–51

Taeschner, 175–176, 323, 325
Taine, 52, 323
Talmy, 185, 323
Tanaka, S., 185, 323
Tanaka, Y., 162, 292
Tanenhaus, 90, 119, 122, 290–291, 305, 318, 323
Tangelder, 136–139, 300
TARCE (Test d'Aptitude à la Récognition des Congénères Ecrits), 166
Tarone, 186, 187, 323, 326
Tavris, 121 (fn.), 325
Taylor, B., 248, 323
Taylor, D., 90, 300
Taylor, H., 157, 323
Taylor, I., 173, 323
teacher talk, 50
teenage slang, 41
Tees, 54
theoretical linguistics, 4, 18, 20, 34, 104–105, 276
Tiedemann, 52, 323
'tip of the tongue' states/errors, 98, 147, 204
Todd, 62, 323
Tomlinson, 156, 324
Towell, 109, 110, 319, 324
transfer *see* cross-linguistic influence
translation data, 133, 145–146, 162, 168, 173–174, 178, 196, 197, 206, 210–213, 246, 247, 248–249, 251, 252, 253, 254, 255, 256, 257, 258–259, 260, 261
translation equivalents, 51, 176, 179, 243
Tréville, 3, 166, 324
Trier, 31, 72, 324
Trinity College Dublin Modern Languages Research Project, 6, 7, 131, 193–265, 270–271
Tuacharoen, 64, 324
two-word utterance stage, 62
Tyler, 84, 93, 94, 98, 118, 119, 204, 308, 324
types and tokens, 10
Tzelgov, 178, 324
Tzeng, 46, 324
Ullmann, 10, 12, 30, 31, 324
unconscious learning, 152–154
under-extension, 70, 71, 72–73, 81
Universal Grammar, 37, 58, 79, 124, 125
universals, 37, 43, 56, 58, 73
see also Universal Grammar
Upshur, 20, 288
Ushioda, 9 (fn.), 208 (fn.), 213, 246, 324

vagueness of lexical meaning, 70, 71, 81
Valentine, C., 61, 324
Vallar, 281
Vallette, 142, 280
Van Hout, 278, 324
Van Roey, 234–235, 324
Van Vlack, 167, 324
Vann, 210, 280
Varadi, 186, 187, 325
'Vbl', 109
Verhallen, 146, 325
Vihman, 65, 67, 70, 71, 298, 325
visual processing, 86, 87, 88, 89, 90–91, 116, 117, 120, 150
see also reading

visualization, 51, 142, 151, 155–157, 183, 273
'vocabulary explosion', 68, 74–75, 142
Vocabulary Learning Strategies Inventory (VOLSI), 182–183
vocabulary size, 3, 46–47, 60, 68–70, 152, 154, 278
voice onset time (VOT), 53
Volterra, 66, 175–176, 282, 325
Von Frisch, 56–57, 325
Vougiouklis, 158, 317
Vygotsky, 58, 61, 325

Wade, 121 (fn.), 325
Wallace, F., 34, 325
Wallace, M., 3, 325
Wang, W., 27, 286, 325
Wang, W. S-Y., 46, 324
Waxman, H., 156, 313
Waxman, S., 73–74, 325
Weinreich, 163, 166, 172, 173, 176, 265, 325
Weir, C., 115 (fn.) , 325
Weir, R., 63, 325
Weisberg, 62, 325
Wekker, 16, 305
Welsh, 84, 92, 94, 95, 96, 118, 308
Weltens, 5, 290, 297, 302, 309, 311, 314, 318, 326
Werker, 54, 325
Wesche, 161, 313
Wessels, 93, 98, 324
West, 47, 199, 322, 325
Whalen, 63, 325
Whitaker, H., 170, 282
Wilkins, 9, 20, 50, 326
Willems, 188, 326
Willis, 3, 326
Wilson, D., 57, 105, 112, 167, 321
Wingfield, 4, 326
Winnick, 88, 326
Wit-de Boer, 5, 160, 161, 310
Witelson, 64, 326
Woodrow, 77, 326
Woodworth, 76, 326
word association, 19, 76, 78, 81, 131–136, 151, 154–155, 164, 165, 167, 173, 177, 178, 196, 198, 203, 206, 208–210, 221, 222–223, 233–237, 246, 254, 255, 259, 273
  continuous association, 209, 234
word, definition of, 7, 10–14, 38, 269
word expression, 10, 48
word form, 10, 11
word-formation rules, 41–42, 109
word length, 140, 141, 228, 230
word monitoring, 95–96
words and language, 7, 8–10, 38, 269, 271
Woutersen, 173, 176–178, 326
Wright, F., 200, 326
writing, 1, 12, 21, 27–29, 46–47, 49, 51, 86, 88, 90, 91, 100, 102, 119, 120, 141, 144–145, 157, 165, 171, 179,184, 197, 199, 200, 203, 206, 209–210, 211, 230, 232, 247, 252, 257, 263, 269, 275
  see also orthography

Xiao Hong, 27 (fn.)

Yamazaki, 162, 292
Yongqi Gu, 133, 326
Younger, 55, 326
Yule, 187, 323, 326

Zimmerman, 208, 326–327
Zurer Pearson, 176, 327